Too Politically Sensitive

—■—

Michale Callahan

with

Jake Aurelian

ISBN: 978-0-615-28103-2
Library of Congress #: 2009923655

Cover photos by Christopher Kemp. Cover design by Jill Brinkoetter.

Land of Lincoln Press

This book is dedicated to the Innocence Project and all of those who unselfishly dedicate themselves to seek the truth and fight for justice in an adversarial system.

ACKNOWLEDGMENTS

———————————■———————————

The United States of America, land of the free, our most cherished right, freedom of speech, one of the first amendments provided by our forefathers to protect us from government malfeasance and tyranny. This country became a melting pot of immigrants, from every nation, religious background and race, believing in the ideals created in our Constitution. For over two hundred years, men and women shed their blood at home and abroad and sacrificed their lives defending those ideals.

This true story starts with a murder in a small town and the wrongful conviction of two men, but quickly escalates into a conspiracy of deceit, hypocrisy, misconduct and cover-up by one of the most corrupt states in the United States. This story is about standing up and speaking out to expose that misconduct. This story is about a government that wants to muzzle its employees, even if it means covering up its criminal acts. What type of government wants to silence its employees or any citizen?

The jury in my First Amendment civil rights case told me I needed to tell this story, but when I took on the project to write this book, many people said I was crazy to attempt to write such a complex book with so many different tentacles. First, pointing out the tragedy of what happened to Dyke and Karen Rhoads and the egregious railroading of the two men accused of their brutal murders. Then how I spoke out and stood up to the misconduct of the powerful and corrupt state of Illinois, exposing its deceit and hypocrisy while enduring continuous attacks on my family.

When I spoke out against the state's malfeasance, it was my First Amendment right to do so. That isn't true any longer. In 2006, the United States Supreme

Court, pushed by the George W. Bush administration, shredded the freedom of speech protections for those American citizens who work as government employees. But when I retired from the Illinois State Police, I became a full citizen once again, with the right to speak out, and with no restrictions, so here I am exercising that right to expose all those who have violated their oath to protect us and our Constitution.

After almost three years of research, writing, re-writing and revising, and a superlative editing job from my editor, the "book," as we all so affectionately refer to it, is ready. Despite the fact that my First Amendment fight is now before the United States Supreme Court, closure will come soon enough, with either success or denial, but I can no longer wait on those I have so little faith in anymore.

This book is written from my personal experiences and the interactions and interviews of several people who either lived this with me or shared their personal experiences with me. I am sure there will be those, many whom have been hired by the state and others with their own self interests, who will try and refute or attack the credibility of the words written in this book. With multi-million dollar lawsuits filed against a corrupt state that refuses to admit its wrongs, just like our former and criminally charged governors, their integrity is their own worst enemy. John Adams once said that facts are stubborn things, and to support the facts I utilized thousands of documents and the very testimony of those who were exposed to back up this tragic and deceitful story.

The sources in *Too Politically Sensitive* are voluminous and encompass several thousand police documents from several local, county, state and federal law enforcement agencies, including investigative reports, investigative files, memorandums, e-mails, directives, notes, letters, policies, internal investigation files, FOIA information, intelligence reports and intelligence data. Thousands of pages of court transcripts, depositions, court orders, motions, complaints, affidavits, appeals and court opinions, from both federal and state courts, were also utilized.

Special thanks to Bill Clutter, Director of Investigations for the Downstate Illinois Innocence Project, who provided me with the tremendous amount of work and documents he had compiled on this case for over twenty years. His efforts in this case and many others throughout Illinois have helped to exonerate many of the wrongfully convicted men and women imprisoned in Illinois—one of the leading states for wrongful convictions in the United States. Without Bill's dedication, and the unselfish work of attorneys Michael Metnick, from Springfield, Richard Kling and Susanna Ortiz, from Chicago's Kent Law School, Larry Marshall and Karen Daniels for the Center on Wrongful Convictions, Blum Law Clinic at Northwestern University, and David Protess, of the Medill School of Journalism at Northwestern University, there would be no story to tell, and two wrongfully convicted men would likely still be imprisoned, or even worse.

Also invaluable to the book was the media and their accounts of this tragic story, both historically and within recent years. Many of the journalists mentioned in this book questioned the state's version of the truth long before I became involved, men and women like Eric Zorn and Hal Dardick of the *Chicago Tribune*, Jim Dey of the Champaign *News-Gazette*, Gary Henry of the *Paris Beacon News*, Dusty Rhodes of *The Illinois Times*, Terry Bibo of the *Peoria Journal Star*, Sarah Antonacci of the *Springfield Journal Register* and producers Doug Longhini and Ira Sutow from CBS's *48 Hours*.

It was the collective efforts of all of these people that questioned the State of Illinois, asking questions and wanting the truth.

For a comprehensive list of the sources used in *Too Politically Sensitive*, see our web site at www.toopoliticallysensitive.com.

Of course none of this could have been accomplished without the real heroes in this endeavor, my family, the ones who stood by me and were willing to risk everything we have so that I could fight this battle.

First and foremost, my beautiful wife, Lily, whose love never wavered in the most difficult and stressful of times. She has been everything to me, and it was her strength, persistence and encouragement that was the driving force for me to never give up and quit. Her support was always there in the toughest of times, even when the state and others attacked us with their vicious and unscrupulous lies, trying to discredit us in any pathetic way they could.

To my son, Tanner, who I am so very proud of for his accomplishments as a young man, and for his understanding when I wasn't always there for him. And I can't forget my promise to mention his good friend, who I always affectionately refer to as Snidely Whiplash.

To my mother, Roseann Callahan, who I have never told I love her enough, and who came through for me once again, both emotionally and financially, supporting my fight to the United States Supreme Court and the writing of this book.

To my attorney, John Baker, who was as sickened as I was by the conduct of the state when I first told him my story, and then he, too, saw their deceit and hypocrisy. John fought beside me and has continued to stand by me through all the ups and downs, when many others would have abandoned this fight long ago. Together we took on the mighty State of Illinois and we exposed its misconduct, and together we have continued to fight for freedom of speech. He has become the brother I never had.

There are many good men and women in the Illinois State Police who also supported, encouraged and stood by me, and for the sake of saving a forest, I cannot mention everyone. But special mention must be given to those in the state police who came forward, with nothing to gain but future ostracism from a deceitful and vindictive department, who stood up under the most difficult of circumstances and told the truth. Men and women like Edie Casella, Ruby Gordon-Phillips, John Strohl, Greg Dixon, Brian Henn, Dave McLearin, Russ Perkins and Ron Haring.

When finally faced with the daunting task of sitting down and trying to make this complex story into a book, I had the good fortune to meet Jake Aurelian. Jake taught media and English at the college level, has authored over 500 pop culture articles and was looking at expanding into writing novels. The night we met through a mutual friend, I sat and told him my unbelievable story. I doubt he ever imagined that night that we would begin a journey like this. But he listened, he went home and he Googled my name; a few days later he called and we began our adventure. Countless nights and weekends were spent researching and organizing an almost impossible story to tell in just one book. We spent hours writing and re-writing, organizing and re-organizing, revising and re-revising, and Jake sat there weekend after weekend listening to me ramble on, sometimes more emotionally than I wanted, but he, too, came to understand and feel the pain and betrayal in all the tragic events intertwined in this story. His faith in a government of the people, by the people and for the people, now as suspect as mine.

Jake would like to give a heartfelt thank you to his family for their encouragement and for believing in his goals, and above all, both of us would like to thank them for trusting us and supporting the "book."

Also a special thanks to Taylor Pensoneau, noted author on Illinois history, for his friendship and his expertise in steering us in all the right directions.

And of course, the biggest acknowledgement goes to the memory of Dyke and Karen Rhoads, and to all of their family members.

"Karen and Dyke ended their lives and started a nightmare for the rest of us for the rest of our lives," noted Andrea Trapp, Dyke Rhoads' sister.

This true story is every citizen's worst nightmare, when the cover-up of any crime is more important than the injustice done to its victims.

Since when is murder...

TOO POLITICALLY SENSITIVE

CHARACTER APPENDIX

With the Illinois Attorney General's Office
Bertocchi, Joel, assistant attorney general under James Ryan
Madigan, Lisa, current Illinois Attorney General
Mandeltort, Ellen, deputy attorney general, Criminal Division
McNaught, Karen, assistant attorney general, Civil Division
Ryan, James, former Illinois Attorney General
Spence, Robert, assistant attorney general under James Ryan
Walsh, William, former chief of investigations for Attorney General Madigan

With the Illinois Appellate Prosecutor's Office
Parkinson, Ed, special prosecutor
Rands, David, special prosecutor
Vujovich, Michael, special prosecutor

With the Illinois Governor's Office
Bettenhausen, Matt, deputy governor under George Ryan administration
Blagojevich, Rod, governor of the State of Illinois, 2002–2009
Londrigan, Thomas, chief legal counsel under Rod Blagojevich administration
Ryan, George, former governor of Illinois, 1998–2002
Ottenhoff, Abby, spokesperson for Governor Blagojevich
Thompson, James, former governor of Illinois and part of the law firm of Winston and
  Strawn

With the Illinois State Police
Adams, Lance, area commander, Division of Internal Investigations

Bernardini, Michael, master sergeant, Zone 5

Bond-Yokely, Suzanne, head of EEO office

Britt, Michael, sergeant

Brown, Doug, first deputy director

Brueggemann, Charles, deputy director of the Division of Operations, Rod Blagojevich administration

Callahan, Michale, lieutenant, District 10 and Zone 5

Carper, Diane, lieutenant colonel, Division of Operations, Springfield

Casella, Edie, major, Zone 5

Dillon, Lance, special agent, Zone 5

Dixon, Greg, sergeant, Zone 5

Eack, Kevin, legal counsel, Springfield

Eckerty, Jack, sergeant, former case agent on the Rhoads murder investigation

Fay, James, deputy director, Division of Administration

Fermon, Steve, captain, Zone 5

Gryz, Joseph, major, Zone 1

Hackett, Terry, trooper, Dist. 10

Halloran, Ben, sergeant, Zone 5

Haring, Ron, retired master sergeant. contractual employee

Harney, Tim, intelligence analyst, Springfield

Henn, Brian, master sergeant, Zone 5

Hill, Dwain, master sergeant, Tech Services, Springfield

Hill, Jill R., lieutenant, Division of Forensics; captain, Zone 5

Hill, Kent, Financial Crimes Unit, Springfield

Jensen, Keith, head legal counsel

Johnson, Robert, retired commander

Karpawicz, Richard, assistant deputy director of Division of Internal Investigations.

Kaupas, Ken, captain, special assignment, assigned to renewed Rhoads investigation

Kent, Dan, deputy director of Division of Operations, George Ryan administration

Knight, Gary, crime scene tech, original Rhoads investigation

Koehler, Craig, lieutenant, Zone 6

Kroncke, Bill, Zone 5

Kuba, Dennis, retired investigator

Marlow, Jeff, special agent, Zone 5, assigned to renewed Rhoads investigation

Martin, Tommy, Division of Forensics

McCormick, Matt, special agent, Zone 5, assigned to renewed Rhoads investigation

McDevitt, Dan, retired commander

McGrew, Charles, retired master sergeant, supervisor over original Rhoads investigation

McLearin, Dave, master sergeant, Zone 5

Metcalf, Ken, former area commander

Murphy, Mark, polygraph examiner

Nelson, Harold "Skip," deputy director, Division of Internal Investigations

Nolen, Sam, former director under George Ryan administration

Outlaw, Freddie, sergeant, Division of Internal Investigation

Parker, Andre, assistant deputy director, Division of Operations, George Ryan administration

Perkins, Russ, master sergeant, lieutenant, Zone 5

Phillips-Gordon, Ruby, secretary, Dist. 10 and Zone 5

Reed, Dan, master sergeant, District 10 and Zone 5

Reed, Tracy, secretary, Springfield and Zone 5

Rokusek, Rick, lieutenant colonel, Zone 1

Rollings, Gary, lieutenant, District 10

Shanks, Lou, VMEG agent, contractual employee with Financial Crimes Unit

Sheridan, Bill, lieutenant, Division of Internal Investigations

Snyder, Tony, sergeant, Zone 5

Snyders, Mike, assistant deputy director, Division of Operations, Rod Blagojevich administration

Steidl, Rory, master sergeant, Dist. 10

Strohl, John, captain, Dist. 10

Talley, Val, master sergeant, Zone 5

Trent, Larry, director under Rod Blagojevich administration

Voges, Sue, sergeant, Zone 5

Woods, Rich, lieutenant colonel, Division of Operations

Journalists

Bibo, Terry, *Peoria Journal Star*

Dardick, Hal, *Chicago Tribune*

Dey, Jim, *Champaign News-Gazette*

Henry, Gary, *Paris Beacon News*

Kass, John, *Chicago Tribune*

Rhodes, Dusty, *Illinois Times*

Mills, Steve, *Chicago Tribune*

Zorn, Eric, *Chicago Tribune*

Judges

Alito, Samuel, Justice, United States Supreme Court

Andrews, H. Dean, Edgar County Circuit judge

Baker, Harold, United States District Court, Central District

Breyer, Stephen, Justice, United States Supreme Court

Ginsburg, Ruth Bader, Justice, United States Supreme Court

Glenn, James R., Edgar County Circuit judge

Kennedy, Anthony, Justice, United States Supreme Court

Komada, Paul, Illinois Appellate Court
McCuskey, Michael, United States District Court, Central District
Pallmeyer, Rebecca, United States District Court, Northern District
Resch, Tracy, Illinois Supreme Court
Ripple, Kenneth Francis, United States 7th Circuit Court of Appeals
Roberts, John, Chief Justice, United States Supreme Court
Robinson, James, K., judge presiding over Steidl and Whitlock's original trials
Scalia, Antonin, Justice, United States Supreme Court
Souter, David, Justice, United States Supreme Court
Stevens, John, Paul, Justice, United States Supreme Court
Thomas, Clarence, Justice, United States Supreme Court

Lawyers
Baker, John, civil attorney for Mike Callahan
Christoff, Mark, defense attorney
Daniels, Karen, civil attorney for Randy Steidl
Gagliardo, Joseph, civil attorney for Steve Fermon
Johnston, Iain, civil attorney for Charles Brueggemann and ISP command
Kling, Richard, civil attorney for Herb Whitlock, post conviction
Leahy, Mary, Springfield attorney
Leid, Michael, civil attorney for Diane Carper
Metnick, Michael, attorney for Randy Steidl, post conviction
Muller, John, Randy Steidl's defense attorney in 1987
Ortiz, Susanna, civil attorney for Herb Whitlock, post conviction
Rotskoff, Peter, civil attorney for Randy Steidl, post conviction
Tulin, Ron, defense attorney for Herb Whitlock in 1987
Weiner, Lawrence, civil attorney for Steve Fermon

Local, County and other State of Illinois Law Enforcement Personnel
Boren, Tom, chief of police, Paris Police Department (2000)
Cash, Gary, Paris Police Department
Fryman, Kenneth, Illinois Secretary of State Police
Heltsley, Mike, Edgar County Sheriff's deputy (1987)
Hopper, Roger, Paris Police Department
McDaniel, Dick, former Edgar County Sheriff's deputy and Illinois Securities Commission
Parrish, James, Paris Police Department, lead detective in original Rhoads investigation
Ray, Gene, chief of police, Paris Police Department (1986)
Stark, Phillip, Edgar County Sheriff's deputy, potential suspect
Todd, Ted, Edgar County Sheriff's deputy
Wesley, Troy, Illinois Secretary of State (FBI Task Force)
Wheat, Gary, Paris Police Department

Paris, Illinois, Investigation
Acklen, Stan, witness
Armstrong, Elaine, witness
Baden, Michael, MD, forensic pathologist
Board, Debbie, witness
Board, Jr., Herb "Duke," potential suspect
Board, Sr., Herb, witness
Board, Jerry, potential suspect
Board, Sonya, witness
Brasher, Terry, witness
Brlach-Cooper, Paula, witness
Burba, Mark "Smoke," potential suspect
Busby, Marilyn, witness
Busby, Tim, witness
Campbell, Ollie, witness
Cash, Penny, witness
Clutter, Bill, private investigator, director of the Illinois Downstate Innocence Project
Comstock, Donnie, witness
Cunningham, Clifford "Bud," witness
Dunlap, Michael, witness
Edwards, Marcia, witness
Elledge, Maxine, witness
Farris, Chris, witness
Foley, James, witness
Furry, Barb, witness
Gones, Scott "Cricket," witness
Harris, Frank E., witness
Herrington, Betty, witness
Herrington, Darrell, witness
Johnson, Beverly, witness
Jones, Bryan, witness
Klein, Nanette, witness
Knuth, Mark A., witness
Land, Nancy, witness
Lewis, Tammy, witness
Light, Ben, witness
Lynch, Beecher, witness
Lynch, Carroll, witness
Magers, Margaret Lynn, witness, juror
Marietta, Robert, witness

McClaskey, Charles, witness
McFatridge, Michael, prosecutor in Rhoads case and Edgar County State's Attorney
Morgan, Bob, potential suspect
Murphy, John E. MD, pathologist who performed autopsies in 1986
Myers, Paula, witness
Newlin, Sean, witness
Newman, Terry, witness
Perisho, Julie, witness
Peterson, Dale, potential suspect
Pitts, Monica, witness
Quinn, Tonya Lee, witness
Reinbolt, Debbie, convicted accomplice, witness
Rhoads, Carolyn, Dyke Rhoads' mother
Rhoads, Dyke, victim
Rhoads, Karen, victim
Rhoads, Tony, Dyke Rhoads' brother
Richey, Terry, witness
Robinson, Carol, witness
Sheperd, William, witness
Sinclair, Phillip, witness
Slater-Wallace, Carol, witness
Spessard, Marge, Karen Rhoads' mother
Steidl, Debbie (Hopper), witness
Steidl, Randy, convicted for the murder of Dyke and Karen Rhoads in 1987
Tate, Carla, witness
Tate, James, witness
Tate, Terri Ann, witness
Taylor, Loren, witness
Temples, Larry, witness
Trapp, Andrea, Dyke Rhoads' sister
Trover, Ed, witness
Trover, Eva Jean, witness
Uselman, Dennis, witness
Wakefield, Della, witness
Wells, Lester, witness
Wheeler, Lisa, witness
Whitlock, Herbert, convicted for the murder of Karen Rhoads in 1987
Wilhoit, Connie, witness
Wilhoit, Mike, witness
Wright, Herschel, potential suspect
Wright, Randy, witness
Wright, Sherm, witness

Young, Mercer, witness

With the U.S. Attorney's Office
Bass, Tim, Central District, Urbana office
Collins, Patrick, assistant U.S. attorney, Northern District
Cox, Rick, Central District, Urbana office
Fitzgerald, Patrick, U.S. attorney, Northern District
Giulianni, Rudy, former U.S. attorney over the Pizza Connection Case

United States Federal Law Enforcement Personnel
Cousins, Herb, FBI, former special agent in charge, Springfield office
Grant, Robert, FBI, special agent in charge, Chicago office
Jensen, Eric, ATE, field agent, Indianapolis office
Shay, Robert, FBI, Champaign office
Swigman, Ron, DEA, analyst
Temples, Ken, FBI, Danville office
Williams, Nate, FBI, Champaign office

Others of Mention
Badalamenti, Gaetano, former head of the Sicilian mafia
Bush, George W., the former President of the United States of America
Callahan, Lily, wife of Michale Callahan
Callahan, Tanner, son of Michale Callahan
Ceballos, Richard, plaintiff in *Garcetti v. Ceballos*, infamous U.S. Supreme Court ruling
Cellini, William, Illinois "Combine" powerbroker
Cruz, Rolando, wrongfully convicted in the Jeanine Nicarico case
Fitzgerald, Peter, former United States Senator from Illinois
Galbo, Joe, former owner of Joe's Pizza, Georgetown, Illinois
Garcetti, Gil, district attorney in Los Angeles, defendant in infamous U.S. Supreme Court ruling, *Garcetti v. Ceballos*
Gilbert, Ronald, Diablo biker missing since 1984, suspected murder victim
Golden, Larry, professor of political studies and legal studies, co-founder of the Downstate Innocence Project
Griffin, Jennifer, ex-girlfriend of Bud Cunningham
Gutierrez, Jessie, witness
Gutierez, Teresa, witness
Harper, Joel, murder victim
Harper, Julie Rae, wrongfully convicted for the murder of her son Joel
Hernandez, Alejandro, wrongfully convicted for the murder of Jeanine Nicarico
LaBaume, Richard, potential witness to unsolved homicide of Connie Wilhoit
Landsaw, Gary, Diablo biker missing since 1984, suspected murder victim

Levine, Stuart, convicted in the pay-to-play politics under the George Ryan
    administration
Mascari, Michael, former associate to the Sons of Silence motorcycle gang
McNay, Betty, murder victim, unsolved murder
Nicarico, Jeanine, murder victim
Nicholson, Bradley, narcotics trafficker.
Picco-Fyans, Leslie Jack, Steve Fermon's brother-in-law
Picco, Sr., John, assassinated Springfield businessman associated to organized crime
    figures
Picco, Jr., John, son of John Picco, Sr., who watched his father gunned down in the streets
    of Springfield
Protess, David, Northwestern University journalism professor
Rezko, Tony, convicted in the pay-to-play politics under the Rod Blagojevich
    administration.
Smith, Kelsey, convicted for murdering her one-year-old daughter
Smith, Madyson Nicole, murdered by her mother, Kelsey Smith
Stine, Michael "Gunner," potential suspect in murder of Connie Wilhoit
Snook, Steven, narcotics trafficker
Vitale, Eno, son of Joe Vitale, owner of Joe's Pizza, Paris, Illinois
Vitale, Joe, former owner of Joe's Pizza, convicted Mafioso in the infamous Pizza
    Connection Case
Zito, Frank, organized crime figure from Springfield, Illinois

Author's Note

———————————————■———————————————

Since when is the murder of anyone "too politically sensitive?" In a state as rich in political corruption as Illinois, it's more of a reality than a question. This tragic and complex story begins with the 1986 murder of a young, newlywed couple, Dyke and Karen Rhoads, which sent shockwaves through the small town of Paris, Illinois—a sinister town with a history of unsolved homicides, ruthless motorcycle gangs and, yes, even the Sicilian Mafia.

After two local barflies are railroaded into prison for their murders, life resumed back to normal, except for the victims' families who still had too many questions left unanswered, along with the two men who adamantly maintained their innocence.

When the Illinois State Police was asked to review the case fourteen years later, they assured the victims' families and the convicted men that their "foremost interest . . . in this and any case is to seek the truth and ensure justice is served."

I was the Illinois State Police Investigations Commander assigned to review the brutal double homicide. My ideals and faith in my department were destroyed when the search for the truth was stymied by a politically compromised state police command that deemed the case "too politically sensitive." Every citizen's worst nightmare is when murder or any crime is ignored for the state's own selfish interests.

The story continues with my fight against the biggest adversary I would ever face, my own corrupted command. What ensued was a conspiracy of lies, cover-ups and hypocrisy at the highest levels of state government under two of Illinois' most corrupt governors. After facing retaliation by the state police hierarchy for speaking out against their misconduct, their crimes covered up by the state's top politicians, using our First Amendment protections, I made the life-altering decision to fight back and expose the state's conspiracy in order to protect every American citizen from the fear of being wrongfully imprisoned or ignored by the uncaring and corrupt government of a state where image, money and politics are more important than a search for truth and justice. My vindication was the truth that was exposed, and a jury that saw the corruption of a powerful state willing to keep innocent men in prison and ignore the real killers for the sake of politics. However, my vindication was short lived when the United States Supreme Court, under the George W. Bush administration, shredded first amendment protections for government employees speaking out on misconduct like you will read in this book. This true story serves as a warning and foreboding example of just what can happen when government employees are silenced to protect the state's scandalous acts.

This book does not solve the murder of Dyke and Karen Rhoads. I never got that chance. The purpose is to show the mockery done to their name and to those of us who place our trust in the men and women who take an oath to seek truth, justice and protect our Constitution.

The suspects identified in this case are just that, only suspects—no one is accused of murder, no one has been charged with murder, nor has anyone ever been proven guilty beyond a reasonable doubt for the brutal murders of Dyke and Karen Rhoads, including the two men wrongfully convicted.

This book is about everyone's worst fear—a deceitful and hypocritical government willing to cover up scandal and its misconduct, all for the sake of the politicians that take an oath to protect us. And when you're done reading this book, ask yourself this important question: just who will police the police when they refuse to police themselves, especially now when the people who would speak out have been silenced.

Chapter 1

Murder and Mayhem

—————————■—————————

Paris, Illinois: July 6, 1986.

The community profile on Paris, Illinois, claims it's "A town whose values might have been painted by Norman Rockwell." From outward appearances, Paris looks like an innocent little rural town where everyone knows one another, life is carefree and simple and the community is rustic, friendly and peaceful. The surrounding area depicts a sleepy farming community with countryside scattered with grazing cattle, crisscrossing train tracks and endless, rural fields. The Paris downtown square surrounds a majestic and architecturally beautiful courthouse that one would think inspires truth and justice. The community profile also boasts that, "Paris appeals to young couples just starting out in life, ready to raise a new generation." Unfortunately, that wouldn't happen for Dyke and Karen Rhoads.

At approximately 4:00 a.m., Terry Newman was awakened by a loud noise he described as "glass breaking." When Newman looked out his bedroom window, he saw his neighbor's house in flames. Frantically, he dressed himself and ran outside to the south side of the burning home. Finding the side door locked, Newman pounded his fists against the door in an attempt to awaken the residents. Frustrated, he ran to the front door. Once again finding the door locked, he continued pounding—screaming at the top of his lungs in a vain attempt to alert the young newlywed couple that lived there. In the confusion, Newman looked over and saw a neighbor woman who was also frantically attempting to awaken the couple. After her efforts failed, she gave up and called the fire department. Unknown to them, the couple was already dead, lying in pools of their blood, brutally stabbed to death before the fire was started.

The call to the firehouse was around 4:39 a.m. and the firemen who responded to the blaze at 433 E. Court Street had no idea what they were walking into. Arriving at the scene, they found the northeast portion of the home completely engulfed in flames. The back door to the kitchen was open but they couldn't gain entry because of the intensity of the fire. Two firemen finally managed to enter the residence and made their way up the stairs to the young couple's bedroom. Crawling on hands and knees because of the heavy smoke, the firefighters entered the bedroom and discovered the gruesome murder scene. The young newlyweds were lying on the bedroom floor—their naked bodies bloody and butchered from a total of over 50 stab wounds.

While fighting the fire, firemen removed the bodies in body bags and the crime scene was disturbed forever. Illinois State Police (ISP) Crime Scene Technician Gary Knight stated the obvious when he testified, "the removal of the bodies . . . takes away from our ability to reconstruct the crime scene." It was quickly determined that the gasoline fueled fire was arson with the obvious intent of destroying evidence of the gruesome murders.

The neighbors milling around outside the residence, most of Paris and even the victims' families were under the impression the young newlyweds had died from the fire. That afternoon the family members were officially informed the couple was murdered. Following the notification to the family, the press was briefed and newspaper accounts exclaimed, "The murders continue to send shockwaves through the Paris community today as many residents reported being terrified since the couple was slain." Other news accounts stated that the town was in "utter shock" and "local residents are arming themselves in the wake of the murders."

The newlywed couple found murdered in their bedroom that early July morning was Dyke and Karen Rhoads. Married only a little over three months, Dyke and Karen were in the infancy of their marriage when their lives were brutally taken from them.

Both grew up and spent most of their lives in the Paris area. After both graduated from nearby Eastern Illinois University, the couple eventually married and began their life together in Paris. Family members described their relationship as true "kindred spirits" and wedding photos depicted a very attractive young couple obviously very much in love. Just like many struggling young couples first starting out, they rented the two story house on Court Street.

Dyke Allen Rhoads was six feet and 175 pounds on a lean, athletic body. With brown eyes to match his dark brown, clean cut hair, he was a strikingly handsome young man. During high school, he excelled in athletics, and after graduating from college, he began working for Chem-Lawn, a lawn care business based in nearby Terre Haute, Indiana. Prior to the murder, witnesses reported Dyke was somewhat depressed because Chem-Lawn was closing their office. According to family, Dyke was going to start a new job at Edgar Electric in the near future. Those interviewed depicted Dyke as happily married and very much in love with and jealously protective of Karen. Some witnesses claimed Dyke could be quick tempered, but no one identified any enemies nor was he ever in trouble with the law. Tony Rhoads, describing his brother before he was married, said, "Dyke had been an occasional pot smoker, but Karen was adamantly against drugs." Dyke's friends also knew Karen was very much against drugs. And once they married, Dyke distanced himself from that crowd. Not one person interviewed during the entire investigation pinpointed one time Dyke Rhoads ever used pot or any other drug after his marriage to Karen. Not one person interviewed said they ever saw Dyke deal any type of narcotic. In late August of 1986, the attorney for the Rhoads family publicly stated, "I want to particularly commend the state's attorney for taking pains to clear any rumors of alcohol or drug involvement with the victims." And the toxicology reports confirmed this; there were no traces of any type of drug in either Dyke or Karen. Yet, the eventual motive for the double murder would end up being a "drug deal gone bad" between Dyke Rhoads and two local barflies.

Karen Rhoads, formerly Karen Spessard, was considered very attractive, if not beautiful. She was athletically built with blue-eyes and light brown hair. Karen had grown up in nearby Ridge Farm just north of Paris. She was described by family and friends as a very religious and moral young woman. Witnesses interviewed said Karen was well aware of Dyke's past and it was also well documented that she told him she would not marry him unless he quit smoking even the "occasional" joint. Except for some workplace concerns and associates, no family, friends or witnesses identified any enemies Karen may have had.

The autopsies were conducted by Dr. John E. Murphy in Springfield, Illinois. Dyke Rhoads, just three days shy of his 28th birthday, suffered 28 stab wounds. According to Murphy, the cause of death was "Internal and external hemorrhage due to multiple stab wounds (28) of the neck, trunk and left arm." The most significant wound was six inches in depth and "passed through his heart and lung." The majority of the other 27 wounds were 1-to-1 ½ inches in depth and described as "superficial" by Murphy. Fourteen of those stab wounds were to his back, and Dyke was likely the first to die before the killer or killers turned their attention on Karen. In 1995, noted pathologist Dr. Michael Baden stated:

It is my opinion, to a reasonable degree of medical certainty that the stabbing of Dyke Rhoads occurred while he was face down on the bed. Supporting this opinion is the fact that the majority of his wounds were to the back; the absence of any defense wounds; the large presence of blood splatter on the top mattress of the bed and the blood splatter over the night stand.

The autopsy report revealed 25-year-old Karen Rhoads "suffered twenty-six stab wounds" and "two of the wounds, one in her right side and one in the middle of her chest, penetrated her heart." Wounds to her left hand, wrist and arm were indicative of defense wounds while attempting to fend off her attacker. The presence of the defense wounds meant that, unlike Dyke, Karen fought for her life. Dr. Murphy's autopsy report indicated Karen's death was caused by "Internal and external hemorrhage due to multiple stab wounds (26), of the head, neck, chest, abdomen, back, arms, left hand and left leg." Murphy identified the two "significant wounds," both of which measured six inches in depth, as the fatal blows. Like her husband, the majority of the other stab wounds were 1-to-1 ½ inches in depth. Additionally, the report read, "No spermatozoa were present on examination."

Karen and Dyke died before the onset of the fire since no soot was found in their lungs. It seemed obvious the killers knew what they were doing when they dealt the strategic death blows. With most of the wounds less than two inches in depth, one could speculate that one or both were tortured. The killers calculatingly plunged a knife into Karen and Dyke—an inch to two inches at a time—until they decided to deal the well-placed death blows. A brutal and terrible way to die. State's Attorney Michael McFatridge opted for a different opinion, publicly stating, "There are no signs of torture, mutilation, or sexual molestation; and both deaths are the result of hemorrhage due to multiple stab wounds." With 54 stab wounds to their bodies, Dyke and Karen Rhoads were obviously mutilated.

The Paris Police Department, in conjunction with the Illinois State Police (ISP) and the Edgar County State's Attorneys' Office, investigated the homicide. At the onset of the investigation, State's Attorney McFatridge complimented the Paris Police Department "which immediately determined the gravity of the situation and called in assistance of the State," and he was also thankful for " . . . the prompt response of the Illinois State Police Division of Criminal Investigation and their detectives as well as technicians." For the next 11 months, with the assistance from the Paris Police Department, Illinois State Police agents "spearheaded" the investigation.

James Parrish was the lead detective assigned to investigate the Rhoads double homicide from the Paris Police Department. Parrish was a typical small-town detective, but he also had a reputation for a quick temper. The lead investigator for the State Police admitted, "Parrish had a tendency to get a little heavy-handed during the investigation." An FBI report referenced that Parrish was suspended twice from the Paris Police Department for "brutality"—one time for beating a female with a nightstick. The family members were promised by the Paris Police Department "that Parrish would never work the streets again." According to the report, the family became upset when they learned Parrish had been promoted to detective in order "to keep him off the streets."

Police Chief Gene Ray of the Paris Police Department also played a significant role in his department's alleged investigative activities. But these two small-town cops were more involved in covering up lies, cutting deals and squirreling away evidence than they were in solving this shocking crime.

Sergeant Jack Eckerty was the Illinois State Police investigator assigned as the case agent to the Rhoads investigation. Eckerty was considered a seasoned investigator and was assigned to the Division of Criminal Investigation office out of Champaign, Illinois. Eckerty was no stranger to Paris, and it was well known that he and State's Attorney Mike McFatridge had shared many a bar stool together in the local Paris pubs. Paris is hidden away on the eastern border of Illinois and Indiana. During the 1980s, Paris was considered Eckerty and other officers' "secret drinking hole." It was a small town out of the mainstream where the officers could sneak away, sit on a bar stool or carouse with the local women and not worry about getting caught. Eckerty never had a problem sitting on a bar stool, but he didn't fare so well with the local women and got his ass kicked when he got caught carousing with the State's Attorney's secretary. Caught-in-the-act, the secretary's irate husband probably would have killed Eckerty if he hadn't managed to pull his gun. Battery charges were filed against the distraught husband. Eckerty's marriage survived the scandal, but the secretary's ended in a nasty divorce. Years later, the attorney for the angry husband explained how he called his client after the bitter divorce one day. The ex-husband was well into a bottle of Jack Daniels, and he could hear him shooting his gun off in the background. The distraught man told him he was target shooting and when he finished his bottle of whiskey, he was, "fixin' to go into town, find Eckerty on a bar stool and shoot 'em." The attorney said he made it to Paris in record time or there likely would have been another homicide in the little town.

Edgar County State's Attorney Mike McFatridge also took a significant role in the investigation as well as prosecuting the case. McFatridge was well known as a big partier and it wasn't just alcohol. Over the years, several witnesses and police reports surfaced with rumors of McFatridge's alleged cocaine use; but these claims were never proven. In an affidavit provided by Special Agent Ken Temples of the FBI, he stated, " . . . that poor guy, McFatridge, had all kinds of rumors going on about him."

There were other State Police and Paris officers who sporadically assisted in the Rhoads murder investigation, but it was Eckerty, Parrish and McFatridge who were responsible for the outcome of the investigation.

During the first two-and-a-half months, the investigation was getting no-where and nothing was developing. By late August, one newspaper account quoted McFatridge as saying, "More than 1,000 man-hours of investigative work have been completed and 100 individual interviews conducted." To make things worse for investigators, the crime scene produced no physical evidence leading to any suspects. Potential suspects were identified, but the case file indicated they were cleared as quickly as their names surfaced. No murder weapons were found—although a drawer full of knives was found scattered onto the kitchen floor. Two freshly washed knives that fit the victim's wounds were found in the kitchen sink, but investigators didn't bother to submit them to the lab for testing.

The investigators could not come up with a motive for the brutal and obvi-ously pre-meditated murders. In a statement to the press, McFatridge advised, "Burglary does not appear to be the motive. The murders do not appear to be random killings, but were likely directed at the couple." Yet Dyke and Karen were well liked with no known enemies. Not one person interviewed provided a motive for why the young couple had been murdered, other than Karen Rhoads' boss.

Karen worked as a secretary and a laboratory technician in quality control at Morgan Manufacturing, a company that produced dog food. Bob Morgan, Kar-en's boss, was a true American success story—he literally came into Paris poor and in debt yet would go on to become a powerful multi-millionaire. When he was interviewed, Morgan described Karen as a "very excellent employee." and "to his knowledge, Karen has never had any problems with any employee at the company." Through "small talk with Karen," he learned that Dyke was excessively jealous. Morgan told officials "that his contact with Karen was no more than an employee-boss situation."

Morgan also gave his motive why he believed the couple was murdered: "it was his opinion that it was at least two or more suspects with the intention of rape, and that it was an impulse killing." Years later, in a second interview with private investigator Bill Clutter, Morgan repeated his theory. He said Karen was very attractive, and she was probably outside when a couple of motorcycle gang members drove by Karen's home and saw her out mowing the grass in her shorts. Then he speculated the bikers probably went to a local bar, got drunk and decided to go back later that night and rape Karen. But Karen Rhoads was not sexually molested.

Despite his statement that "his contact with Karen was no more than an employee-boss situation," Morgan made rounds at the local bars offering a generous $25,000 reward for information about the murders.

However, several people interviewed indicated Karen was not happy with her job and was concerned with things she "had seen" at work.

Marge Spessard, Karen's mother, was one of the people who said her daughter was upset about things she had seen at Morgan Manufacturing. Just before she was murdered, Karen told her mother that Bob Morgan would not be happy with her if he knew what it was she had seen. Karen never told her mother what it was she had seen that disturbed her so much. According to reports, Karen also told her mother she was having problems with a co-worker named "Smoke" Burba. Karen said she wanted to quit her job and the only reason she remained at Morgan Manufacturing was because "Bob promised her a big bonus in the fall." This was confirmed in a letter from Karen to an ex-boyfriend named Tim Busby.

Years later, Marge Spessard repeated many of these same workplace concerns Karen related just prior to her murder. But Karen's mother gave even more specific information that was never documented and ignored by the original investigators and prosecutor. According to Marge, shortly before her death, Karen met her mother for coffee. Marge remembered how Karen pulled out some packets of coffee creamer she had taken from work. Marge said Karen interjected and said they shouldn't use the creamers "because they were probably full of dope." Could that be what Karen saw at work that troubled her enough to make her want to quit her job?

ISP Sergeant Tony Snyders reflected on some of the rumors about Morgan and Smoke Burba:

> There were rumors flying from day one on this . . . reference to Bob Morgan and Smoke Burba. Snyders stated that during his years with the State Police, there has never been any evidence of Morgan being involved with drug distribution. He said that Morgan moved into town with a small business and made lots of money in a short amount of time. He said people spread rumors about Morgan, but there has never been any evidence that he has been involved with anything illegal.

In an FBI interview years later, Bob Morgan also acknowledged the rumors. The FBI report indicated, "Morgan related an incident when Parrish was a Paris police officer and drove by Morgan, he rolled down his car window and told Morgan, 'You know what, I know damn well you're into drugs, it's just that you're too good at it.'"

Besides Karen's mother, there were other witnesses who came forward with information about Karen's concerns with her workplace.

Timothy A. Busby, Karen's ex-boyfriend, at one time himself a suspect, advised investigators he spoke with Karen shortly before her death. Karen told Busby she "observed Bob Morgan . . . and an employee named 'Smoke' Burba put a machine gun and bags of money into the trunk of Morgan's car." Karen told Busby that after placing the guns and cash into the car, Morgan and Burba left for Chicago "on business." According to the report, Karen told Busby she was suspicious because of the enormous cash flow that was going through the dog food business, especially since the "products were not paid for by cash. They were an accounts only business."

In another report, Jane and Lon Gardner, Karen's sister and brother-in-law, related the same story about the incident with the machine gun and money. Years later, another FBI report concerning this incident was more detailed when federal agents interviewed another one of Karen's sister and brother-in-law, James and Terri Ann Tate. James Tate recalled a conversation with Karen one week before her murder:

> . . . Tate recalled that a portion of the conversation concerned an incident between Karen Rhoads and Robert Morgan. James Tate described this part of the conversation as either verbatim or very similar:
>
> James Tate: "How's your job?"
>
> Karen Rhoads: "I'm thinking of quitting."
>
> James Tate: "I thought you had a good job?"
>
> Karen Rhoads: "I thought so too until recently."

The report continued that Karen was at work one evening when a mysterious phone call came in, and "a male caller asked for Morgan." Karen advised the caller Morgan had just left the office but she glanced out the window and observed him still in the parking lot. The report continued, "The caller told Karen Rhoads that 'This is a very important call. And I really need to talk to him. Could you run and tell him 'Chicago' is calling.'" Karen ran down the stairs to get Morgan and she:

. . . observed Morgan standing next to a car with the car trunk open. Karen Rhoads saw that Morgan was carrying what appeared to be a machine gun and Karen Rhoads looked into the open car trunk and observed a number of other machine guns. Tate recalled that Karen Rhoads quoted Morgan telling her, "Why are you here?" and "You shouldn't have seen this." Tate further advised that Morgan swore at Karen Rhoads which was not typical for Morgan.

After this incident, Karen told her brother-in-law, "I'm going to turn in my two week notice." James Tate informed the FBI he told the Paris Police Department about this incident right after the murders, but once again the investigators never documented any interview with James Tate.

Tim Busby's mother, Marilyn, was also interviewed. She told investigators that Karen was "like a daughter" and the two continued their close relationship after Tim and Karen's relationship ended. According to Marilyn, she had lunch with Karen at a Danville, Illinois, country club. Marilyn indicated "on this date, Karen stated that an employee at the Morgan Manufacturing Company named 'Smoke' Burba was giving her a lot of trouble. Karen made the statement that it was getting 'real bad' and that she was going to have to make application for a new job."

Smoke Burba, his wife Marsha and his brother Gerald all worked for Bob Morgan. Smoke's wife was an over-the-road truck driver and Smoke, depicted as a tough and intimidating man, was considered Bob Morgan's right-hand-man. Despite his name frequently coming up in the first two months of the investigation, Smoke was never even interviewed by investigators. In fact, investigators didn't even bother to document Smoke's real name, which was "Mark."

According to a witness, Paula Myers: "Guy Griffin, who worked for Morgan, stated to her that Karen Rhoads announced to Bob Morgan on the Friday before she was murdered that she was quitting." In future years, Guy Griffin also confided to Dyke's younger sister that Dyke and Karen's death wasn't over a bag of cannabis, but over something Karen had stumbled on at work that she saw being put into the bumper of a car.

These were not the only witnesses who reflected Karen's workplace concerns. But for whatever reason, investigators didn't bother to investigate her concerns or the suspicious activities she had seen. Despite this, Jack Eckerty would admit years later that, "Bob Morgan was always a suspect in my mind and still is to this day." Eckerty would also testify years later that Bob Morgan was considered a suspect in the original investigation. A news article reflected Eckerty's testimony:

Eckerty noted that Morgan's name came up because he was Karen Rhoads' employer. . . . Eckerty said since Morgan was Karen Rhoads' employer, he was looked at as a suspect. He also testified that he saw Morgan at the crime scene the morning following the double homicide. He noted that he was aware that Karen Rhoads has made statements about noticing cash and machine guns at her workplace which concerned her. "Is that why you looked at Morgan as a suspect because he showed up at the crime scene and there were statements made about cash and guns?" [Eckerty was asked.] "Yes," said Eckerty.

Yet Bob Morgan was interviewed only once by police during the original investigation. While Eckerty acknowledged Bob Morgan was a suspect, he also admitted that when the first alleged eyewitness came forward, "Mike McFatridge steered us away from all the other suspects."

There might have been a reason why McFatridge "steered" the investigators from all the other suspects. Two weeks before the couple's murder, two local barflies named Gordon "Randy" Steidl and Herbert Whitlock went to the FBI and made allegations against State's Attorney Mike McFatridge. Some of the allegations involved the State's Attorney involvement in narcotics trafficking and protecting a local businessman—Karen Rhoads' boss. Those same two barflies would, ironically, be arrested and convicted for the murders of Dyke and Karen Rhoads.

Throughout the initial investigation, no one could imagine why anyone would kill the young newlywed couple. For the first two-and-a-half months, the case file reflected the haphazard and fruitless investigation. At the August 1986 Coroner's Inquest, one detective admitted that investigators could not even "determine the sequence of death." Frustrated by the lack of success of the investigation, the townspeople began spreading rumors throughout the small town. These rampant rumors were filled with speculation as to why Dyke and Karen were killed. There were unconfirmed rumors of clandestine drug trips to Florida, prowlers and Peeping Toms in the Rhoads neighborhood and, of course, the motorcycle gang rape of Karen Rhoads. Investigators were seemingly all over the place, basically taking down information yet disregarding many of the leads generated from the information.

Amidst the gossip and innuendo, many credible witnesses who possessed pertinent information were ignored by investigators. Leads and information which led to other suspects besides the two local barflies was ignored by investigators.

The investigation floundered until September of 1986, when the first of the breaks came, and the first alleged eyewitness, the town drunk, Darrell Herrington, stumbled into police hands. The second break came five months later, when the second alleged eyewitness, a schizophrenic, alcoholic, drug addict named Debbie Reinbolt came forward with an equally bizarre story.

Both eyewitnessess had a medical history of mental illness severe enough they had received electroshock therapy. One said he drank for 12 hours that day, from noon until midnight, and by his own admission was "pretty drunk!"; the other stated she drank 18 beers, smoked three joints and popped a bunch of co-deine pills the night of the murders. These two alleged eyewitnesses, along with some manipulation, lying, creative report writing, withholding of evidence and a little intimidation by police and prosecutor, made the State's case.

Chapter 2

Integrity, Service & Pride

———————■———————

I grew-up in the mid-1950s and 1960s, a time without elaborate video games, high definition televisions, the Internet, cell phones or iPods. Our entertainment consisted of reading super-hero comic books, playing sandlot baseball and playing games like "cops and robbers." Our heroes back then weren't overpaid, steroid-injected athletes or multi-millionaire rappers with the rap sheets to match. During those simpler days, we looked up to role models like baseball players, the neighborhood cop-on-the-beat and, until George W. Bush, even the President. Until *Serpico*, the words "cop" and "corruption" never went together. No . . . things were much simpler during my childhood, and the people I grew up admiring and respecting were worthy of that admiration.

Although I loved baseball, I didn't have the slightest chance of ever becoming a big league ball player. So in 1980, I walked through the Illinois State Police Academy doors full of elation. Like other idealistic young police officers, I was actually naive enough to think I could make a difference in the world.

For the majority of my career with the Illinois State Police, I was steadfast in my belief no one was beyond reproach, no one was above the law and we would always do the right thing. Like many of the countless other men and women in the Illinois State Police, I spent my career doing real police work. I loved the challenge of being a cop, I loved the camaraderie I had with my fellow officers, I loved the day-to-day challenges, and I like to think that in some small way, maybe, I made a little difference. I certainly met a lot of challenges during my career and took on my fair share of adversaries. I loved my job, and I loved my department. No one was prouder than I was when I became an Illinois State Police officer.

"Integrity, Service and Pride" is the motto of the Illinois State Police. I can't begin to count how many times I heard that motto ring out so proudly by so many. I can still remember my lungs filling deeply with air and shouting those words with the utmost of pride.

I spent my early days with the Illinois State Police as a trooper in the Chicago area. After spending three-and-a-half years proving myself on the road, my dream came true, and I became a Special Agent in the Illinois State Police Division of Criminal Investigation.

The bulk of my duties in the early years consisted of working undercover narcotics. I bought drugs from Colombians, "gang-bangers," motorcycle gang members and even "wise guys." I went undercover portraying everything from a mob fence to a mob hitman. On one occasion, I even bought bombs from two "nutcases" who thought they were terrorists, but these guys were nothing in comparison to the terrorists who attacked our country on September 11, 2001.

My job was to be a good guy playing a bad guy. It was like an actor playing a role. Yet, it was a deadly, real-life game of cat-and-mouse. I had to learn to read people fast, think quickly on my feet and react to dangerous situations at a moment's notice, and I learned to play off people's greed.

Whenever I worked undercover, there was always a tremendous rush of excitement afterwards, whether it was a single deal or the culmination of a long, drawn-out investigation. I was certainly no stranger to the dark side of human nature, and, like most cops, I was no stranger to risking my life. Every day provided new experiences and new challenges. I loved my job and I loved the excitement.

Sometimes it was hard to fit in as a bad guy and win the trust of an adversary. One assignment involved a two-year sting where my partner and I ran a resale shop in Waukegan. We spent an immense amount of time gaining the trust of the gang-bangers who ran the streets of both North Chicago and Waukegan. It wasn't just the gang-bangers who were initially suspicious of us, throughout the operation we also drew the attention of the local cops.

Only the Waukegan Chief of Police and my command knew about the sting. For two years, we ran that resale shop with no one wise to the fact we were cops. We went to great lengths to maintain our cover, so we never carried our badges or guns on us, in the car or in the shop. The only thing that could link us to our real identities were the police radios hidden underneath the driver's seats of our cars. My partner had the ingenious idea of placing T-shirts and fast food bags smeared with catsup and mustard around the radios to deter anyone from searching under the seats. His idea may have saved my life.

It was a hot summer day, and I had arranged for one of the local gang-bangers to set up a deal for me to purchase an ounce of cocaine. After he showed up at the shop, we jumped into my car and took off to purchase the coke. There was no way to know at the time but I was about to receive one of the biggest scares of my life.

We drove through a maze of side streets until the gang-banger had me turn down an alleyway. It was a dead end. No sooner had I pulled into the alleyway than a red Firebird with four other gang-bangers pulled in behind me and blocked in my car. I had never seen these guys before and the man who sat next to me was my only insurance. Everyone got out of the cars and I was immediately surrounded by the four men. One gang-banger stood on my left, while another stood on my right and I almost shit when the banger on the right pulled out a semi-automatic pistol. When I asked what was going on, the one who seemed to be their leader told me to relax. He explained they didn't know me and wanted to make sure I wasn't a cop. They were going to search my car and if I was cool, we'd do the deal. So while two gang-bangers stood on each side of me, the other two searched my car.

I was sure they could hear my heart pounding inside my chest. I certainly could! Several times I thought about running down that alley and weighed my options. Would the one guy really shoot me if I ran? Was he a good enough shot to hit me if I did? What do I do if they find my radios? Running was not an option though, because my legs were useless. Not only were they shaking like jelly, they felt like two lead weights. So, I stood there, trying to act cool and calm while they searched my car. Sure enough, my fears were realized when one of the gang-bangers went to search under my front seat where my police radios were hidden. Then I saw and heard his disgust as he pulled out a white T-shirt full of ketchup and mustard that had gotten all over his hands.

"Man! You're a pig! Look at this shit!" he said. Obviously deterred from searching anymore, he looked at me and said, "You need to clean this shit up!"

It had worked, and the search ended. Everything was cool and they sold me the ounce of coke, got in their car and left. I got away with it this time, but my heart continued pounding long after they left.

Prior to my marriage, in my early years as an agent, my personal life mirrored my undercover persona. I was single, carefree, and the dangers of my work didn't bother me in the least. I didn't have a family to worry about, and I didn't think I would ever settle down. By age 32, I came to the conclusion there was no such thing as true love and consigned myself to being a bachelor the rest of my life. Then BAM!—as fate would have it, I met *her*.

I remember the first time I saw her—at a crowded Chicago health club. She was working out in the aerobics room to Miami Sound Machine's "Bad Boy." In those days, I figured I was pretty hot, and considered myself somewhat of a ladies' man. I looked over and pointed her out to a friend standing next to me and jokingly told him, "You see that girl over there? I'm going to marry that girl." Knowing me, he just rolled his eyes and snickered.

It was two days later when I actually met Lily. When our eyes met, she gave me a smile that lit up the room and me, too. I knew she was interested by the way she was checking me out. Not one to let a moment like that escape, I walked up to her and gave her that age-old line, "Don't I know you from somewhere?"

Lily gave me an innocent little smile and said, "I don't know. Have we met before?"

Sensing her interest, my confidence grew, and I replied, "You do look familiar. Where have we met?"

Overlooking my pathetic response, she looked at me angelically and sweetly replied, "Yeah, I think I do know you."

I was sure now—she was hooked, "So where have we met?" I confidently asked.

Her innocent smile left and was replaced with a devilish grin as she shot-back, "You know. I think you were in one of my wet dreams."

Her sarcasm floored me, and I just stood there with my mouth wide open. I couldn't believe what had just come out of that sweet little mouth. This girl had just kicked my ass, and we both knew it. With an even bigger smirk on her face, she added, "You know, you can close your mouth any time you want!"

So, not only was Lily beautiful, but she had the brains and the feistiness which made me realize right on the spot she was the one for me, and like they say, the rest is history.

Two years later, at 34, I was happily married, but my professional life didn't change much. Now, my life took on a dual role—undercover agent by day, happily married man by night. As time went on, Lily started expressing concern over the type of work I was doing, "You need to grow up and quit playing cops and robbers," she said. She wanted to start a family in the future and she was right. Maybe it was time to focus on looking at my—and our—future.

Right after our marriage, I became involved in another long-term, undercover sting involving street gangs in the Chicago suburbs of Schaumburg and Hoffman Estates. I promised my wife it would be my last big hurrah working undercover. One night, I picked up two gang-bangers from Schaumburg and we proceeded to the Robert Taylor Homes on the south side of Chicago to purchase some fully automatic weapons. I wasn't alone—I had a small army of State Police and Hoffman Estates and Schaumburg police backing me up.

I had dealt with these gang-bangers many times—buying drugs, stolen cars and proceeds from local burglaries. That night, a deal had been arranged for me to purchase two fully automatic weapons from the uncle of my front seat passenger. I had a couple thousand dollars in my pocket, and the two gang-bangers knew it.

When we arrived at the Robert Taylor Homes, a series of multi-level high-rises in the projects of Chicago, I parked my Camaro in front of the uncle's building. The deal was supposed to go down at my car, but seconds after arriving, my car was surrounded by several gang members. My heart raced as the gang-banger directly outside my window opened up his coat and arrogantly displayed a nine millimeter in his waistband. Fearing the worst, I pulled my gun and shoved it into the rib cage of my front seat passenger. If I was going down, I was going to take somebody with me, and my gun became my bartering tool for my safety.

For what seemed like forever, numerous phone calls went back and forth between me, the gang-banger sitting next to me and the uncle inside the Robert Taylor Homes. Their intentions were to lure me into the Robert Taylor Homes for the gun purchase, and the uncle tried enticing me by displaying one of the machine guns from his second story window. With my gun stuck in the ribs of the gang member sitting next to me, the phone calls continued back and forth as they kept trying to lure me outside my car and into the projects, but I kept remembering my Master Sergeant's stern warning, "No matter what you do, don't go into the Robert Taylor Homes! I better not see your ass get out of your car!"

As the bartering broke down, I remember being torn between obeying my Master Sergeant's common sense orders, yet not wanting to disappoint the small army of police who secretly surrounded us. They, too, had spent long hours on this case, and no undercover cop wants to go home empty-handed. That night, however, common sense prevailed, and I left without the guns. I felt bad; I had let everyone down.

Months later, after we arrested the two gang-bangers who had sat in my car that night, they confessed their plan was to actually lure me into the projects, kill me, and steal my car and money. After all those years working undercover, I was once again reminded of the most important thing—every undercover cop wants a successful deal, but what is too often forgotten is that sometimes just going home safely at night is the success.

Despite the failure that night, we still won in the end. On March 27, 1991, the *Daily Herald* stated, "Authorities wrapped up the largest anti-gang sting operation in the history of the Northwest suburbs . . . arresting 25 people and recovering more than $600,000 worth of stolen property." Additionally, the article read, "'The key was exceptional undercover work by some of the top professionals in the law enforcement community in Illinois,' Schaumburg Police Captain Cliff Johnson said of Callahan and the other state police special agents . . .'"

Over the next five years, I was promoted to Sergeant and then Master Sergeant in the Illinois State Police, and Lily and I were blessed with our son, Tanner Michael Callahan. Even with a family and being a command officer, I still couldn't get away from my roots and I was placed in charge of a narcotics task force.

Like all cops, I had the same sense of invulnerability we all get, but my sense of invulnerability was soon to be shattered. Working undercover is not expected of a master sergeant, but I had a tentative young cop working a drug sting in a sleazy little biker bar located on the Fox River. He lacked experience and some confidence, so I decided to go undercover with him. After spending several months inside the bar gaining the suspects' confidence, we ended up arresting the owner of the bar and his girlfriend. End of case, or so I thought.

It was a perfect July day and almost seven months to the day after we arrested the bar owner and his girlfriend. My wife Lily, my three-year-old son Tanner and I were at a local carnival. It was about 5:00 in the afternoon, and our plans were to enjoy some rides, have dinner and watch an evening fireworks display. I was standing in line with my son, getting ready to take him on his favorite ride, "The Berry-Go-Round"—a ride made up of giant, spinning red strawberries. Lily had left to go purchase more ride tickets. Enjoying the peaceful afternoon, I was standing there holding my son's tiny little hand. Then, amidst the carnival music and commotion, I started to hear a voice that gradually became louder as it approached.

"Hey Narc!" the words bit into me. The voice was low and gradually intensified. "Hey, you fucking narc!"

With the noise of the carnival atmosphere, it took a few seconds for me to realize that the comments were directed at me.

"Hey, you fucking narc!" the words echoed through the fairground. The peace of that afternoon was suddenly ruined as I glanced to my right.

"Hey, you fucking narc!" the man continued screaming. Suddenly, all of the outside carnival noises vanished, and I was oblivious to everything else.

There he was—the bar owner and his girlfriend along with a small group of bikers. The man was angrily pacing back and forth, just 30 feet away, yelling in a pitched voice, "Hi, Narc! . . . Hey, Narc! . . . Hey, you fucking Narc! . . . I'm talking to you, Narc!"

He was spitting venom from his mouth. At first, I was embarrassed but when I saw the drug-induced anger in his eyes, any embarrassment was replaced with concern and fear for my young son's safety! When I looked directly at him, he turned to the others and said, "That's him! That's the Narc!"

He continued shouting profanities, becoming angrier and slowly creeping closer. I turned away in an attempt to ignore the verbal abuse. I think my refusal to acknowledge him only incensed him further.

Tensions heightened. My heart pounding, my main concern was my son. I was standing between my son and the angry mob and I held Tanner close to my side hoping to hide him from their sight. Tanner was oblivious to the verbal on-slaught and developing hostilities—he was too young and too innocent to even understand.

I was helpless to confront the jerk with my son by my side. Perhaps he sensed my vulnerability because my helplessness only gave him the courage to approach even closer and become more threatening. As the group advanced, I turned slightly, still trying to shield my son from their view.

I directed my attention at the man, telling him, "Get the fuck away from me!"

My words only seemed to anger him more, and he replied, "Fuck you!"

I will never forget the helplessness I felt at that moment, and the guilt for unwittingly placing my family in danger.

Still, I tried to ignore them. When it was our turn to get on the ride, still shielding Tanner, I dashed to the far side of the ride. My hopes were that the coke-crazed group would tire and just go on their way. Instead, the group walked around the ride and stood before the large, red strawberry Tanner and I had just entered. Pressing up against the fence that surrounded the ride from the midway, the man continued his abusive, verbal attack until his drug-crazed girlfriend spied my son.

Her words cut through my heart—"Hey, look! He's got a kid! That's his son!" I had my arms around Tanner and drew him even closer to shield his face from their view. No sooner had those words left her mouth, than my wife approached the ride. Unknowingly, Lily came up to the fence and began lovingly waving and yelling to Tanner.

My hope was the bikers wouldn't connect Lily's actions or words to us. I gave Lily a concerned look and nodded slightly toward the group that stood about 10 feet away from her. She immediately recognized something was wrong, but it was too late.

I heard the girlfriend yell, "There's his wife! That's his wife! Come on, let's get her!"

My heart sank as the ride began to slowly move forward in its circular pattern as the situation escalated with the two biker girls moving towards Lily. I rose from the giant strawberry, extending out as far as I could from the ride. I had my badge in hand, and demanded the operator to "Stop the ride immediately!" When the ride stopped, I grabbed my son and hurriedly climbed out of the Berry-Go-Round.

Running to my wife's side, I handed Tanner over to her and turned to put myself between my family and the advancing group.

The drug-crazed man turned to the others and threateningly said, "That's his family! Get a good look at them and don't forget what they look like!"

I told Lily to get out of the area. My heart was racing with a mixture of both fear and anger. This man had just violated the sanctity I was enjoying with my family and now he was threatening them. I confronted him face-to-face. The coke-crazed asshole didn't care—he just kept yelling, "Get a good look at his family! Don't forget what they look like!"

His obvious intention was seemingly to intimidate me by threatening my family, but how did I know if his intentions were more serious and not just idle threats. Fortunately, the local police showed up in force and the man was quickly arrested.

I had been threatened many times before during my career. You put people in prison, they don't consider you their friend. Most took responsibility for their own actions, but this was different. Never before was my family brought into the middle of my professional life.

An Assistant State's Attorney later told the press, " . . . all police officers are subject to disrespect and 'disgusting' comments. They accept that responsibility. They accept that burden, but they do not accept that their family will be subject to them . . . "

Jessie and Teresa Gutierrez were two witnesses who came forward on my family's behalf. Teresa Gutierrez stated in a police interview:

> . . . [Lily] stopped and looked very scared, yet confused. . . . (the man and his friends) seemed to be instigating an altercation and [they] closely watched [Callahan] and his family. My husband feared for [Callahan's] wife and child's safety because there were four of them. . . . It was obvious to me that [the man] did not care that there were children in the area and did not care that he made others feel threatened by his attitude and anger expressed towards [Callahan], his wife and his little boy.

The *Northwest Herald*, covering the trial, stated, "Witnesses described [the bar owner] as 'animalistic,' pointing, screaming and spewing obscenities at Callahan from across the children's section of the carnival. . . . Callahan said that the defendant pointed his finger at him and said, 'That's his family. Don't forget what they look like.'"

Mrs. Gutierrez also testified that the defendants hired "a private eye to find them and harass them on four different occasions to try and deter them from testifying." Bravely, she still took the stand and testified two-and-a-half years later telling the jury how she would never forget the terrified look on my wife's face that day.

In two separate jury trials, the bar owner was found guilty. One for unlawful delivery of crack cocaine and, in the second trial, for the harassment against my family. He was eventually sentenced to the Illinois Department of Corrections. Whether he intended to harm my family or not, the damage was done, and I would live with a certain amount of paranoia for my family's safety for the rest of my life. For the first time in my career, I felt vulnerable to the dangers of my job.

Because of the publicity surrounding the case, there were other unforeseen repercussions. Parents stopped letting their children come to our house and play with my son. Likewise, I shared similar concerns when Tanner left the protection of our home. Neighborhood friends, while still friendly, seemed nervous around us. People seemed to unintentionally distance themselves. This type of ostracizing is not uncommon in a policeman's life. I had seen it happen to others in my field and I didn't want my son or wife to be ostracized or live in fear because of my career. So, I requested a transfer downstate.

Despite all the negatives in all this, there were a few positives, and a phone call from one of my former commanders reminded me why I wanted to become a cop in the first place. The call was from retired ISP Captain Dan McDevitt. He and another former commander, Colonel Bob Johnson, had heard what happened to my family.

Concerned, Dan was calling to ask how my family was doing, and give us their support, and he simply asked, "Mike, what do you need us to do? Tell me and it willl get done." And if I had needed something, there was no doubt, it would have gotten done.

That was the Illinois State Police Command I knew most of my career. It didn't matter in those days if you were a colonel or a trooper—we always had each other's backs. The command in those days was much different than the arrogant, egotistical, and politically compromised command that would eventually take over the Illinois State Police by the end of my career; men and women whose rank and power were more important to them than the citizens they were supposed to be serving and protecting.

After taking a loss on our house, in July 1998, Lily, Tanner and I ended up in downstate Illinois. My transfer was to District 10, which encompassed nine counties in East Central Illinois; one of those counties was Edgar County, home to Paris.

When I arrived downstate, I was assigned to supervise another narcotics task force in investigations. My rank was still master sergeant, and I answered to the newly appointed investigations commander, Steve Fermon.

At 6'3" and 300-plus pounds, Fermon was a big and imposing man who liked to exude a charismatic facade emulating a stereotypical "Good Ole Boy," but he was quick to turn crimson red if ever challenged; it was always his way or no way. It was well known in the state police that it was not wise to cross Steve Fermon. He had a reputation for both ruthlessness and vindictiveness.

Initially, Fermon embraced my family and invited us to his house on several occasions, but it wasn't long before I'd start seeing the real Steve Fermon. One weekend we had some friends visiting from Chicago, and we invited Fermon and his wife to go out with us for dinner and drinks. It was a beautiful summer night and after dinner, we decided to go to a local campus bar that had a rooftop beer garden.

The bar was packed, but we managed to get a table on the rooftop and I went to get the first round of drinks. While I was at the bar, the owner of the bar sat down in my seat.

Fermon turned to the man and said, "Hey, that's my buddy's seat!"

The owner replied, "That's cool. When he gets back, I'll get up."

That wasn't good enough for Fermon, who told the owner, "Get the fuck out of that seat!" Without even giving the man a chance to reply, Fermon grabbed and threw him across the bar. The owner went flying through the air and struck a waitress carrying drinks. Beer went flying everywhere and both fell to the floor. The scene was chaotic.

The first thing I saw was a group of bouncers going after Fermon. I was unsure of what had happened at this point, but I put myself between the bouncers and Fermon. One of the bouncers maintained a cool head and explained Fermon had just thrown the owner across the bar for no reason. Behind me, Fermon was pacing back and forth, challenging and taunting the bouncers. I turned to him and said he should leave, after all, he was still up for promotion, and didn't need trouble like this.

I turned to the bouncer and apologized telling him we would all leave quietly, but it wasn't over—Fermon stood in the alley behind the bar, still taunting the bar owner and anyone else who wanted a piece of him to come over so he could "kick their fucking ass." I was beginning to see the real Steve Fermon. Then things started happening at work which made matters worse.

I encountered a different work ethic and culture than I was used to in the Chicago area. Downstate, ISP management seemed much more lax and maybe even a little sloppy in some cases. Accountability and supervision in some instances was almost non-existent. What I found most disturbing was that investigative reports and case management lacked the detail and professionalism demanded by the northern command. When I began auditing the case files, I discovered numerous instances of evidence, monies and case files missing—all of which had been ignored by previous supervisors.

I prepared a memo and reported these findings to Fermon, but he told me to hide the mismanagement of the cases by closing them or by showing the missing evidence was destroyed. At one point, he even ordered me to do it, but when I requested the illegal order be put in writing, he dropped the matter. He wasn't that stupid. But, after refusing his orders, Fermon started keeping me at arm's length, and our relationship was over before it even began.

Not long after his promotion to lieutenant, Fermon was whisked away to Springfield. George Ryan had just taken office as Illinois Governor, and things changed dramatically in the upper command of the Illinois State Police. Within a few months of his promotion to lieutenant, Fermon was appointed to a newly created position as the Statewide Investigations Officer, and he became a very powerful man among the politically compromised command anointed under the Ryan Administration.

When Fermon left District 10, his best friend, Master Sergeant Danny Reed, became the acting Investigations Commander.

In late 1999, John Strohl was named the new Captain of District 10. Shortly after that, the investigation commander's position Fermon had vacated was posted for promotion, and with encouragement from a lot of the people in the district, I put in for that promotion. The day after I put in for the promotion, I received a very angry call from Fermon.

I remember answering the phone and was instantly met with, "What the fuck do you think you're doing?" It was obvious he was upset that I had put in for the lieutenant's position, and Fermon repeated: "What the fuck do you think you're doing?"

I asked him, "What, you don't think I'm capable of being a lieutenant?"

He angrily replied, "No, you're more than capable! But you're ruining all of my plans!" Fermon hung up without explaining exactly what his plans were that I was ruining.

I assumed Fermon's plans involved keeping Danny Reed in control of District 10, and by having Reed in charge, Fermon would still maintain control of all the investigations in the area. I couldn't help but wonder—why was controlling District 10 investigations so important to Steve Fermon? But by putting my name in for the promotion, I had obviously disrupted his plans because he knew I wasn't a person he could control.

With Fermon's power and influence in Springfield, I didn't give myself much of a chance to get the promotion. It was no secret he was lobbying for Reed to become the new investigations commander. Later I learned just how upset Fermon was that I had put in for the lieutenant's position.

Prior to Fermon going to Springfield, Sergeant Greg Dixon was his staff officer. Later, Greg confided that Fermon was so upset with me that he started crying like a baby and pounded his fists furiously into the dashboard of Greg's car. It was very apparent I had not made a friend in Fermon. Whatever plans I ruined, they must've been big.

Then one day, Master Sergeant Dave McLearin, who ran one of the narcotic task forces in District 10, called to tell me he had just received a visit from Fermon. Dave said Fermon began questioning him and asked Dave, "What do you think about that cat Callahan?"

Dave said he felt Fermon was looking for him to badmouth me, but he replied, "He's okay. I don't have any problems with him."

Dave warned that Fermon started ranting about how upset he was with me and threatened, "I know how to fuck people, I'm from Springfield and I know how to do it without leaving a paper trail."

It was a Friday evening in March when Captain John Strohl called and informed me he had picked who he felt was the best man for the investigation commanders job . . . me.

As time went on, John Strohl and I became close friends and he confided in me that after picking me as his new lieutenant, he had received a very angry phone call from Fermon who "mother-fucked me up and down."

Fermon asked Strohl, "I thought we had a deal?"

John Strohl, however, is a man of strong convictions who sticks by his decisions and does what he thinks is right. John said he told Fermon, "I'm sorry Steve, but I picked who I thought was the best man." It was obvious I had pissed off a very powerful man in the ISP and from that day forward, I knew I would have to walk on egg shells because any mistake I made would be closely scrutinized by Fermon as a way to do me in.

CHAPTER 3
THE RHOADS CASE REVISITED

———————■———————

That April of 2000, there I was standing in front of the mirror trying to adjust my tie for what seemed to be about the tenth time. I wanted it to be perfect. I could probably count on both hands and two feet how many times in my career I had worn a tie. For the past 16 years I had mostly worn jeans and a t-shirt and I was used to looking at myself in the mirror and seeing long hair and a rough beard. That's the look you want when you're a baby-faced white guy trying to fit in as a bad ass undercover cop. Now as I looked in the mirror, I couldn't get over how short my hair was and how clean cut I looked. Damn, I looked like an FBI agent or something.

Finally, satisfied with my efforts, I grabbed my sports coat and walked downstairs. I grabbed my keys and quickly kissed my wife goodbye.

"What about breakfast?" Lily asked.

"No," I told her, "I don't want any breakfast." Especially her breakfast. Blueberries and oatmeal were not my idea of a breakfast. Besides, I was too excited, I couldn't wait to get to work. A quick stop at the local gas station and a large cup of coffee would be fine for me. I had a brand new command and a lot of work to do.

Life was good, and I couldn't be happier. I had just received my fourth promotion in the Illinois State Police. In 20 years, I had gone from a road trooper to Special Agent to Sergeant then Master Sergeant and now Lieutenant. I had been promoted much higher than I ever imagined when I first walked through the Academy doors of the State Police some 20 years earlier. I had spent the bulk of my career working narcotics. That was for the younger guys now. Those days were behind me, that was my past and this was my new future. I had paid my dues working in the streets and suburbs of Chicago and then my family had packed our bags and moved to Champaign, Illinois. Now, I was a newly promoted lieutenant over all of investigations in a nine county area. Now, I was the mentor and not the one being mentored.

I remember the day well. It was the beginning of spring and an unusually nice day for that time of year in east central Illinois. I pulled into a parking spot at the expansive state building which housed not only the state police investigations office but several other state agencies. I was the new guy on the block and as I walked down the hall to our small set of offices, I received the inquisitive stares I had expected. When I walked in to our office, I was greeted by a friendly and smiling Ruby Gordon-Phillips, who was the investigative office's secretary for more than 20 years. Truth be known, she probably ran the place, and we were just figure heads. I know she saved my ass on more than one occasion. Ruby was more like a mother to everyone in the office. If you had a question, professional or personal, she had an answer or a sympathetic ear.

I liked my new surroundings. Prior to this, my offices were in damp basements, cold warehouses or farmhouses out in the middle of nowhere. I loved working narcotics, but this was a nice change. I wasn't getting any younger. Working narcotics meant long hours and it's definitely a young man's game. I was ready for this change. I had a great Captain to work for, and I was surrounded by a great group of guys. I had all the faith in the world in them and knew we were going to make a formidable team. This was going to be a great job.

That same day, I received an assignment I was expecting from the Director of the State Police to review a 14-year-old double homicide. I walked into my office and saw the voluminous case file Ruby had placed in the middle of my desk. I was just getting my feet wet and getting to know the guys. Why this assignment now? I looked at this assignment as more of a nuisance than anything else.

Earlier in the year, rumblings from a private investigator named Bill Clutter and an impending episode of CBS's *48 Hours* had manifested deep concern within the Illinois State Police. The rumblings were that two innocent men were wrongfully convicted in that 14-year-old double homicide. The reason I received the assignment was summed up in an e-mail from Staff Officer James Wolf to my Lieutenant Colonel, Diane Carper:

> I think Lieutenant Callahan should take the lead on this and work
> with Lieutenant Rollings who is more familiar with the case to de-
> termine if Clutter's information warrants additional investigation.
> I also think having the Investigations Commander review the case

file etc., gives us additional credibility if this should get to a Mike Wallace type. Bottom line, we do not want anyone to be embarrassed or put in the hot seat for not investigating this or contacting individuals who state they have information about the incident.

The Patrol Commander, Lt. Rollings, had already advised that I could just "rubberstamp" the review of the investigation. There was no need to question the case file that sat before me, they had put the "right guys in jail." The Illinois State Police doesn't make mistakes like that and we would never put innocent men in prison, and to think otherwise was ludicrous. I knew the television show *48 Hours* was going to air a story on the homicide sometime in mid-May. That didn't give me long to review the case and make an assessment. I was told that Clutter, who was also the director of the Downstate Innocence Project, was making "waves" in the Director's office. Clutter made claims he had "new information" that proved the innocence of the two men imprisoned for the murders of Dyke and Karen Rhoads. Since their convictions both men had adamantly maintained their innocence. One of my tasks was to liaison with Clutter and look at all his "new information." The district's Patrol Commander, who had a limited history of involvement in the original Rhoads investigation, advised me he had already refuted Clutter's new information. Why would I question a fellow officer's assessment? Still, I set up a meeting with Clutter in the not-so-distant future.

After grabbing a cup of coffee, I settled into my seat and picked up the case file on my desk. Before I turned the first page, my phone rang. The man on the other end of the phone was a former ISP command officer named Charlie McGrew. I had met McGrew before and knew he was a supervisor in the investigations office I was now overseeing. In fact, he was the former supervisor over the homicide investigation sitting in front of me. I always prided myself in being a good judge of character. Working undercover, it's something you learn quickly in order to be successful or sometimes just stay safe. I really didn't care for McGrew from the minute I met him. Still, he was State Police, so maybe I was being too judgmental. After all, I was from Chicago and there was a big difference from being a cop in a big city and being a cop down in "God's Country." Charlie was an old timer and a "good ol' boy" who didn't mince words or beat around the bush. His call was all business and he got straight to his point.

"Is it true you're looking at the Rhoads case?" he asked.

I looked at the voluminous case file sitting on my desk. "Man, does news travel fast in this part of the state," I thought. "How did he know I was assigned to review the Rhoads case?" With *48 Hours* airing a show on the Rhoads murders in the near future, this case was no big secret, but my review of the case had not been made public.

I was candid with McGrew and told him I was assigned to review the Rhoads case file. I could tell by the tone of McGrew's voice he wasn't pleased, and he replied, "Don't make us old guys look bad, you hear." At first, his remark didn't cause me any concern, but still I was somewhat dumbfounded. How could I make them look bad? They had solved the crime and helped convict two men for the grisly murders. Besides, we're the Illinois State Police. How could we ever look bad? We don't make mistakes like that and we don't help convict innocent people. Still, there was no mistaking the deep concern in McGrew's voice and it was enough to set off a red flag.

McGrew was nervous and unmistakably upset I was reviewing the Rhoads case. And he repeated himself, "Don't make us old guys look bad, you hear." From the tone of his voice, his words weren't just a simple request. I became suspicious . . . why was McGrew so worried? I tried to rationalize away his obvious concern, but the suspicion wouldn't go away. Why would anyone be worried about "looking bad," when they had solved the case?

I got an uneasy feeling talking to McGrew so I pacified and assured him my job was not to "armchair quarterback" their investigation or to "make anyone look bad." That was true and at the time, it was not my intention to make anyone "look bad." Unless they deserved it and never, in my career, had it crossed my mind that any ISP officer would deserve to "look bad," especially in a murder investigation.

It was a perplexing phone call and I was relieved when it ended. Why so much concern over this 14-year-old homicide? Two men had been arrested for the gruesome murders, prosecuted and convicted in a court of law by two separate juries. One man was sentenced to life in prison, and the other given the death penalty. It doesn't get any more final than that. After I hung up the phone, I went into Ruby's office. She knew Charlie McGrew and had worked for him in the past.

"What's up with Charlie McGrew?" I asked her.

Ruby looked at me knowingly like she sometimes did. "Be careful, don't trust him," she said. She didn't have to tell me anymore. The strange phone call had made me suspicious enough. It was the tone and concern in McGrew's voice that triggered one of the first red flags and I decided I better give my undivided attention to the case file sitting on my desk.

As I started looking at the investigative case file, it wasn't long before I learned why McGrew was so worried. As I read, there were so many contradictions, I got a note pad and began applying them to the sections of reports I had questions about. There were red flags all over this case file and I went through a pad of notes in no time at all. Then the second phone call came into my office. The man on the other end of the phone identified himself as retired ISP Sergeant Jack Eckerty. I had never met Jack

Eckerty, and before this day, had not even heard of him. Yet by this time, I was very familiar with Jack Eckerty's report writing skills. And they were the worst I had ever seen. It was his reports that I had just stopped reading, interrupted by his phone call.

Eckerty was also quick to get to the point. Like McGrew, he heard I was reviewing the Rhoads case. I had never encountered this much concern over a case in my life. Especially one ending with a successful investigation and prosecution. When I told Eckerty I was reviewing the Rhoads case, obviously concerned, he nervously cut me off. His haunting words were not the words I ever expected to hear from the mouth of an Illinois State Police officer. "I want you to know, I'm a good cop," he said. "Please don't ruin my reputation. I'm not a dirty cop."

A little taken aback, this was almost like hearing a confession. Yet the nervousness and tone in Eckerty's voice left little doubt how concerned he was about the review. He repeated himself, "Please don't ruin my reputation." Like McGrew's phone call, I became uncomfortable. These were not the words I expected to hear from a man who had helped solve a heinous crime. They had received accolades for solving the murder, and now, 14 years later, this man was concerned because someone was reviewing his work. Why? If he did the right thing, why would he be so concerned? And why would he be worried about looking like a "dirty cop"?

If I wasn't suspicious from McGrew's call, Eckerty's call put me on full alert. This whole thing was starting to stink—the case file I was reviewing, the suspicious phone calls. Things were just not adding up. After I hung up the phone with Eckerty, I wasn't going to "rubberstamp" anything.

Not long after Eckerty's call, Sergeant Tony Snyder called my office.

"Lieutenant Callahan," he said, "Sergeant Snyder, sir. I hear you're reviewing the Rhoads case." Before I could even reply, he continued, "I want you to know Jack Eckerty was a good cop. Please don't ruin his reputation."

This wasn't just perplexing, it was becoming mind-boggling. Suddenly, everyone in the world seemed to know I was reviewing this crime, and there was an awful lot of nervous concern by the men who had allegedly helped solve it. I couldn't help but wonder what I had gotten myself into?

I called Ruby into my office. "Ruby," I said, "I think I'm going to need some more notepads."

Private investigator Bill Clutter had requested the Illinois State Police Director for a review of the Rhoads homicide based on new information he had obtained. The Director responded to Clutter's request:

> Lieutenant Callahan, District Ten Investigations Commander,
> will be contacting you to make arrangements to meet and discuss

additional information you indicated you are interested in sharing with the Illinois State Police. You will be informed of the results of this inquiry when a complete and thorough review of all documentation is complete. *Please be assured, the foremost interest of the Illinois State Police in this and any case is to seek the truth and ensure justice is served.* [emphasis added]

Clutter was not only a seasoned private investigator who had investigated over 20 capital murder cases, but is also Director of Investigations for the Downstate Innocence Project for Illinois. Illinois has one of the highest numbers of wrongfully convicted people in the United States. Over the years Clutter was instrumental in helping to free several wrongly convicted people, such as Joe Burrows, Rolando Cruz, Alejandro Hernandez, Verneal Jimerson, Dennis Williams and Julie Rea-Harper.

Now Clutter was focused on freeing the two local barflies who he believed were wrongfully convicted for the murders of Dyke and Karen Rhoads. Gordon "Randy" Steidl and Herb Whitlock were convicted in 1987 by two separate juries. Steidl spent 12 of the last 13 years on Death Row for the murder of both Dyke and Karen. His death sentence was eventually commuted to a life sentence. The jury was uncertain and deadlocked in Whitlock's trial so they decided to convict him of only one murder. So Whitlock was sentenced to life for the murder of Karen.

Clutter's March 2000 letter to the Director discussed several areas of concern. In May of 1999, an ISP sergeant wrote a report Clutter eventually obtained. In that report, Sonya Board and Debbie Board provided information that their ex-husband, Herbert "Duke" Board, Jr., told them he was involved in the murders of Dyke and Karen Rhoads and an innocent man named Steidl was convicted for the murders. Clutter's letter also indicated that Steidl and Whitlock had gone to the FBI on two prior occasions—the first time was in the spring of 1986 just a few weeks prior to the Rhoads murders. During this meeting Steidl and Whitlock provided information concerning political corruption and narcotics trafficking in Paris, specifically naming State's Attorney Mike McFatridge and his involvement. Clutter's letter continued, "Mr. Steidl was questioned by law enforcement at the Paris Police Department three days after the murders, on July 9, 1986, after reports were received from tavern sources." The "tavern sources" told investigators about "suspicious" remarks from Steidl that "there is something big coming down next weekend." Yet, Steidl was not referring to the murders of Dyke and Karen Rhoads as initially suspected, but to his recent meeting with the FBI. Clutter's letter continued that Steidl was initially interviewed and cleared by investigators and "was no longer the target of investigation" until the first eyewitness, Darrell Herrington, emerged.

The second meeting between Steidl and the FBI took place during Steidl's trial. At that meeting, Steidl told the FBI he believed Bob Morgan paid Darrell Herrington to be an eyewitness against him. Clutter indicated he found information supporting Steidl's claim.

If not for the *48 Hours* telecast questioning the wrongful convictions of Steidl and Whitlock, it's likely the ISP would have ignored Clutter. This was evidenced by an April 5, 2000, e-mail from Lt. Gary Rollings, who had sporadically worked on the Rhoads homicide. His e-mail read:

> I have talked to Sgt. Britt and received his report regarding his in-terview of Sonja Board. I also spoke with Detective Roger Hopper, Paris PD, who did the follow up on Sonja Board's information. He indicated that Sonja Board told him that when she was married to Herbert "Duke" Board, he would at times become angry and state that he had killed people before and indicated he had stabbed the Rhoads. Detective Hopper indicated that this was done apparently to intimidate Sonja Board. Detective Hopper stated that much of the details of the murder that Duke Board supposedly related to Sonja were not accurate. One in particular was that Duke claimed to have cut off Dyke Rhoads' penis and placed it in Karen Rhoads' mouth. That is a complete fabrication as it did not occur. Mr. Clutter would be aware of that . . . Also, Clutter attacked the credibility of both eyewitnesses and as in all eye-witness accounts there certainly are discrepancies. I think it is important to note one of the eyewitnesses, Debbie Reinbolt, testified that she was present in the bedroom when Randy Steidl and Herbert Whitlock stabbed the Rhoads and that she (Reinbolt) held Karen Rhoads down while Dyke Rhoads was being stabbed. Reinbolt plead guilty to conceal-ing a homicidal death and accepted a 5 year prison sentence.

Rollings' e-mail questioned and attacked Sonya's inaccurate account of Duke's confession to killing the Rhoads. Rollings' inference was to dismiss her credibility because of the inaccurate version that Duke had cut off Dyke's penis and stuffed it in Karen's mouth. But Rollings failed to mention another double homicide that had occurred close to Paris where a married couple named Dardeen was found murdered. The husband's penis was cut off and placed in his dead wife's mouth. Was Sonya's account fabrication or maybe Duke had confused the events of two separate homicides?

Rollings also rationalized that Debbie Reinbolt admitted to helping kill Dyke and Karen and she pleaded guilty and was sentenced to five years in prison. Therefore, Reinbolt had to have been truthful . . . because what person would confess to a crime like this unless they were guilty? But prisons are full of mentally ill, unstable drug addicts and alcoholics who have been manipulated into falsely confessing to crimes they didn't commit, people who are easily taken advantage of by the system.

Clutter reached out to the ISP because he believed in our integrity from prior cases he had sought help on. Years earlier, he had turned to the Illinois State Police *"to seek the truth and ensure justice was served"* in the wrongful convictions of two other men. In 1985, Rolando Cruz and Alejandro Hernandez were found guilty of the brutal rape and murder of 10-year-old Jeanine Nicarico. The command of the Illinois State Police in those days did not turn a blind eye to Clutter and his concerns. Based partly on the steadfastness of the Illinois State Police investigators, all charges were dropped against Cruz and Hernandez. Two separate juries had convicted the two men, but neither jury was told the truth. The ISP investigators and command officers, despite the politics, still stood up for the truth. Eventually, three DuPage County prosecutors and four DuPage County Sheriffs were indicted for conspiracy to suborn perjury and official misconduct for sending the two innocent men to Death Row.

The integrity and dedication of those ISP officers was one of the reasons Clutter came to my office that April of 2000. Clutter was again asking the Illinois State Police for help on behalf of Steidl, whose case was up on appeal. Clutter was steadfast in his conviction that Steidl was innocent. Clutter also provided a box full of documents to back up his claims. The box was filled with interview reports, intelligence reports, post conviction relief petitions, recantations by the two eyewitnesses, affidavits and one very damning police report.

Much of the documentation Clutter provided attacked the credibility of the two eyewitnesses, their bizarre stories and the alleged evidence used to convict the two men. It was this information, along with information in the State Police case file, that convinced me Clutter was right. The two men were wrongfully convicted, and maybe worse. Some of his documents would support my concerns of misconduct in the original investigation and prosecution of Steidl and Whitlock.

The ISP case file that sat before me was, without a doubt, the sloppiest piece of police work I had ever seen. The written reports contained a voluminous number of misspellings, run-on sentences, and poor grammar, but it was the details in the reports themselves that started to draw red flags and left more questions than answers. When I compared them with the information Clutter provided, I became even more suspicious of misconduct in this case. With each turn of a page, I got my notepad out.

The notes filled with one question after another. Why hadn't this lead been followed? Why had this lead been ignored? Reports filled with one contradiction after another. Lots of questions and lots and lots of red flags!

This was a capital murder case—two people brutally murdered, a man put on death row and another man sentenced to life in prison! As I read the file, my reaction was initially embarrassment and shame. Seven months into the investigation, investigators couldn't even spell the victims' names consistently right. Some reports identified Karen and Dyke as the "Rhodes" and others as "Rhoades" or "Rhoads." How pathetic was that? Not that you have to be an English professor to be a cop, but these reports weren't even at an eighth grade level. Given the seriousness of the crime, I was shocked at the unprofessional work—especially by one of my own. I learned that the State's Attorney's secretary had typed the reports for Eckerty. The same secretary he was caught-in-the-act with by her irate husband. She wasn't worth a damn behind a typewriter, but obviously she was good at other things.

As time went on, the more serious red flags in the Rhoads case file began to stand out. I couldn't believe the number of conflicting reports where Eckerty and Parrish would document something in one report and then contradict it later. Even a novice investigator would question the contradictions in the reports documented by them. The embarrassment and shame, though, eventually turned into the disgust I felt as I began to have definite suspicions of deliberate misconduct.

An investigator's job is to gather leads, find facts, corroborate those facts and conduct an unbiased, truthful and objective investigation. It's a search for the truth, no matter what or where the answers lead you. During the course of any investigation, information will come forward that turns up various leads and witnesses. It's an investigator's job to follow up on those leads and develop additional leads from that information. It's an investigator's job to seek out credible witnesses, ascertain the credibility of those witnesses and corroborate the information provided by the witnesses.

Information from witnesses may be truthful, embellished or filled with lies. It's an investigator's job to gather the information, investigate and corroborate what is fact and what is not. Furthermore, an investigator has a duty to be meticulous in recording that information. Every tidbit of information gleaned, every interview, and every piece of evidence must be documented, even if the information favors the suspects. An investigation is simply a search for the truth wherever it leads. This was definitely not the case in the Rhoads investigation.

If an investigator excludes or misleads the truth in a report by altering the facts, an unreliable witness can be made to look like a credible witness. By altering the truth it can make innocent men look guilty before the eyes of a jury. If a jury doesn't hear the truth and instead hears lies and believes those lies as the truth, it can lead to the conviction of innocent men. This was definitely the case in the Rhoads investigation.

Corroborating a witness's information solidifies the credibility of the witness. In the Rhoads case, using witnesses who obviously lacked credibility meant that investigators and the prosecutor had to turn to lying, manipulation and intimidation to make their witnesses believable. In this case, there were many witnesses developed through leads who investigators should have interviewed, but they ignored. There were also many witnesses who did come forward but for whatever reason, some of their information was partially or totally excluded, misrepresented and some was never documented. There were also witnesses who said they were intimidated, manipulated, or coerced by police into giving false information. This included the two alleged eyewitnesses, Darrel Herrington and Debbie Reinbolt.

It became obvious to me that investigators were picking and choosing what information they wanted to document and what information they wanted to exclude. When a case lacks physical evidence leading to any suspects, investigators will often times rely on making a circumstantial case. In a circumstantial case, one of the things an investigator will come to rely upon is the credibility of the witnesses used in making the State's case. The Rhoads case lacked physical evidence and there were no motives for the murders. That is, until Herrington and Reinbolt came forward. So the case file was filled with reports trying to provide the two key eyewitnesses with the credibility they so obviously lacked. And as I continued to review this case, I began to see the definite inclinations of intimidation of witnesses, manipulation of witnesses and a malicious distortion of the truth.

For the next five years of my career and long after that, I would learn exactly what I had gotten myself into. It was more than just the brutal and terrible murder of a beautiful young couple. More than the innocent men who had been wrongfully convicted for their murders. Even more than the misconduct by the original investigators and prosecutor who "railroaded" those two poor men into prison. It became even more frightening and egregious than the misconduct by my own command 14 years later who turned a blind eye to this terrible tragedy. In the end, it would all add up to the deceit, cover-up and power of a pathetic and corrupt State trying to maintain its image above all things, even over truth and justice. For most of my career, my adversaries had been the criminals I hunted down. Over the years I helped put more than my fair share of criminals behind bars, but little did I know my biggest adversaries were about to become those within my own department.

CHAPTER 4

THE FIRST EYEWITNESS

———————————■———————————

Two-and-a-half months after Dyke and Karen were murdered Darrell Herrington was the first alleged eyewitness to come forward. Herrington was known as the town drunk. His driver's license was revoked for several drunken driving arrests and the 45-year-old man resorted to pedaling his bicycle throughout town. Herrington claimed to be an eyewitness at the gruesome murder scene. Yet investigators never questioned why it took him so long to come forward about the terrible crime.

Not only was Herrington known as the town drunk, his many drunken driving arrests were compounded by two felony arrests for deceptive practice and a history of mental health issues. Despite this questionable credibility, the State used Herrington as one of the two main witnesses in the prosecution's case. The lack of physical evidence linking anyone to the crime made his testimony key in convicting the two men for the murders of Dyke and Karen.

"He knew certain things," State's Attorney Mike McFatridge arrogantly told *48 Hours*, "things, at least in our minds, that were not the things the town drunk would know."

Herrington linked Gordon "Randy" Steidl and Herbert Whitlock to the murders of Dyke and Karen Rhoads. But Herrington proved an unreliable witness from the first day he came forward. He spoke to police for the first time on September 19, 1986, when he "volunteered" to be an eyewitness in the Rhoads murders. In a 1998 interview report, former Paris Police Chief Gene Ray told Bill Clutter:

... it was raining like hell. I know it was fairly late [at night] or fairly early in the morning. Darrell was in the back seat of Jim Parrish's unmarked squad car, as they were pulling into the parking lot of the Paris police department, he blurted out, "just don't ask me about the murders."

Ray continued, "Being police officers they, of course, began to question him about his utterance once they got inside the police station." Efficient police work at its best, yet Ray couldn't remember the reason Herrington was in the back seat of Parrish's squad car in the first place:

> I don't recall the exact circumstances of how we came across him. Back in those days, Herrington was one of those guys who did a lot of drinking. If we saw him out, he was likely intoxicated ... the bulk of their contact with Darrell was fussing with his wife.

Regarding this first meeting, Ray stated officers "spent a lot of time with Darrell that night. We were trying to get him to tell us what he knew. Was he trying to confess? Was he a witness? Was he even there?" Ray added:

> Darrell was always hard pressed for cash when he was drinking. He drank a lot of money away. At the time, Darrell was riding a bicycle because he had just lost his license. He was trying to work, but was unable to drive. Herrington was a self-employed dry waller. Ray admitted that Darrell had told them, "I'd like to have my driver's license back."

That interview of Darrell Herrington on the night of September 19 was never documented by police even though it was the first time he came forward with knowledge of the crime. So why did police fail to document the first real break in the case? That question wasn't answered until 14 years later when Herrington's deceitfulness was finally disclosed. During that first undocumented interview, Herrington gave police the names of "Jim and Ed" as the killers of Dyke and Karen Rhoads.

Herrington's story changed two days later during his first documented police interview. That interview didn't take place at the Paris police station like one would expect—it occurred at Chief Gene Ray's residence. At that interview with Herrington were Ray, Jim Parrish, Jack Eckerty and Michael McFatridge, and after plying the town drunk with alcohol, Herrington changed the names of the two murderers to Randy Steidl and Herb Whitlock.

If it was true that Steidl and Whitlock committed the murders, then Herrington initially lied to police during his first interview about "Jim and Ed." Because of that lie, his credibility was questionable. When the police chose not to document his initial lie, they were obviously trying to hide his deceit and keep Herrington a credible witness. With no documentation concerning "Jim and Ed," Herrington's initial deceit could have been covered up forever. But because of the initial lie, Eckerty had Herrington polygraphed. If not for that polygraph, this deception by Herrington and the police would've never been uncovered.

Mark Murphy was the Illinois State Police examiner who administered Herrington's polygraph and he told Eckerty not only was Herrington lying, he was purposefully misleading police. In fact, Murphy later told me Herrington had failed his polygraph miserably. Mark Murphy was so convinced Herrington's story lacked credibility he strongly recommended a second polygraph exam.

Murphy's determinations and recommendations were ignored by the investigators. In fact, Herrington's negative polygraph was never disclosed to the defense. Instead, it was squirreled away and hidden in a court sealed envelope and acknowledged as an irrelevant report.

When I later questioned Eckerty as to why they never disclosed the negative polygraph disclosing Herrington's deceitfulness, his excuse was, "That's because Mike McFatridge didn't want anything negative in the case file that might show those two guys were innocent."

Instead the State hid that polygraph for almost 14 years ... a polygraph that definitely impeached Herrington's credibility. Years later, Mark Murphy acknowledged the State's deception in court by testifying, "The fact sheet he prepared based on Eckerty's information was no longer in his file at the state archives." Murphy continued, "That concerns me." If not for Murphy's notes and recollection concerning "Jim and Ed," this deceit would've never been revealed. In September of 1986, none of this mattered because it was just the beginning of a lot of deception on the state's part.

Of course, everyone has a price, and Herrington wanted certain favors in return. Another reason why that first meeting wasn't documented was Herrington's personal motives to cut a deal. His deal with the police included payment for his services, his latest DUI arrest taken care of and his revoked driver's license reinstated. Two days after this bartering session, on September 21, 1986, Herrington's first official version of the murders was documented by investigators and after plying him with alcohol, the police had their two murder suspects—Randy Steidl and Herb Whitlock.

Herrington began his wild story by telling investigators that on July 5, 1986, he started drinking around noon after a "domestic dispute" with his wife, Betty, at Jeanie's Place. Herrington said he left Jeannie's Place and went to Poor Robert's Tavern where he drank for approximately two more hours. After that, he went to the Horseshoe Club and drank for another two hours. During this time, Herrington said he drank seven-and-sevens (Seagram's 7 and 7-Up), and after the Horseshoe Club, made his way to Joe's Blue Lounge where he continued to drink for another 30 to 45 minutes when he said Randy Steidl came in the bar.

According to Herrington, Steidl said he didn't have any money, so he bought him several beers. Herrington said Elaine Armstrong was the barmaid that evening at Joe's Blue Lounge, and he remembered Beecher and Carol Lynch were in the bar and John Armstrong was in and out at different times. Herrington also remembered talking with Larry Temples. At some point in time, Herrington told investigators Herbie Whitlock came into Joe's Lounge and started talking to Steidl. Whitlock bought a round of drinks and Herrington heard Steidl and Whitlock discussing money.

Herrington said the three of them then went "barhopping" throughout Paris, leaving Joe's and going to the Horseshoe Club for another drink. There Whitlock excused himself and "went to the back of the bar" with bartender Mike Wilhoit for approximately five minutes. Whitlock returned to the front of the bar and allegedly asked Steidl if he wanted to get high on something. Herrington could not understand what they were talking about, but during this time he said Sherm Wright was also in the bar. After finishing their drinks, the three men left the Horseshoe and walked back to Joe's Lounge where Herrington bought yet another round of drinks.

While at Joe's Lounge, Herrington claimed Steidl left to make a phone call. Steidl returned and told Whitlock, "there was no answer." So Whitlock allegedly got up from the bar and left, stating, "I will go down and check things out." Herrington and Steidl continued to drink at the bar for another 45 minutes and Whitlock returned and told Steidl, "I think there is a light on in the house."

At this point, Herrington's story got even more bizarre. According to Herrington, Steidl asked him "to buy a six pack of beer and go for a ride." Darrell said, "Randy drove the vehicle" which he identified as, "a big type car . . . believed to be a Chrysler, cream in color." Then, according to Herrington, Steidl allegedly "drove to the house at the corner of Court Street and Clinton Avenue"—Dyke and Karen Rhoads' residence, and he said, "Randy pulled the car up beside the house on the north side of the residence closest to the front door." Whitlock got out of the car and knocked on the door. No one answered and they left and drove around, finishing the six pack of beer.

While they were driving, Herrington remembered he "heard Whitlock tell Steidl that, 'we are going to have to get that son of a bitch's money back'" and "we have to go back down there and do something." While Steidl and Whitlock were discussing money, Darrell said Dyke Rhoads' name was mentioned. Herrington's report continued that "after drinking the beer" they went back to a bar he thought was "possibly the Friendly Tavern. He was unsure though," because by this time, Herrington said he was "pretty drunk."

Eventually, Herrington said the three men ended the night at the Paris American Legion—still drinking. Herrington said at approximately midnight, around closing time, he asked Steidl for a ride home and the three men left in the same "cream-colored car." Herrington stated, " . . . after driving a short distance, he noticed that Steidl made a wrong turn . . . [and] told Steidl that he did not live down in this end of town." Steidl replied, "We have to check on something." They proceeded to the same house at the corner of Court and Clinton, and this time Herrington said he noticed a car in the driveway of the residence and the lights were on in the house. Steidl parked the car "close to the front door of the residence," and Whitlock exited the car and went to the front door and knocked. Herrington saw Dyke Rhoads answer the door and come out onto the front porch. Then he said Whitlock "waved to Randy and Randy left the vehicle and went up to what seemed to be a very heated discussion between Whitlock and the male subject." All three went into the residence. Approximately 10 to 15 minutes passed before Herrington heard loud voices, and he "could see what appeared to be a female silhouette through the upstairs window of the residence" and then he "heard a bunch of fighting upstairs and something breaking." Not too bad for a man who was drinking almost 12 straight hours and by his own admission was "pretty drunk."

Herrington's story continued with him exiting the car and going to the back door which he found locked. Using a credit card to slip the lock, he entered into the kitchen area where he "heard a female screaming like being tortured [and] saying, 'Please don't! Please don't kill me!'" Herrington said he continued through the house and then " . . . started up the stairs and that Randy stopped him approximately halfway up the stairs, in the bend of the stairs."

Herrington said Steidl angrily confronted him and said "What the hell are you doing in here, you son of a bitch? I told you to stay in the car." Herrington's account described Steidl with "blood on both arms and his clothes and that Randy was carrying a fish fillet knife with approximately a six inch blade." Steidl ordered Herrington "to get his ass back to the car" and he left the house with Steidl following behind. Once outside, Herrington told investigators, "Randy put a knife up to his neck and said, 'I will kill you in a minute if you say one word.'"

Herrington's unbelievable account continued, with Whitlock joining them outside covered in blood, and also threatening him in the middle of the night. Herrington said Whitlock "had blood all over him; it looked like someone had thrown blood all over him." Then surprisingly, Whitlock told them, "Everything is taken care of. I got to use the car, you guys stay out here."

Herrington told investigators the murders occurred sometime between 12:30 and 1:30 a.m. Yet over 15 people—some in their front yards or on their front porches—said they were sitting outside across the street in clear view of the Rhoads house during that same timeframe. Not one person saw nor heard the two men "covered in blood" standing outside threatening the falling down drunk. If you had just committed a heinous murder with the murdered woman's screams echoing throughout the neighborhood, why would you go outside covered in blood? Why would you take a witness back outside so you could threaten him out in the open? By threatening Herrington, they were obviously somewhat concerned . . . so, after brutally murdering two people, why didn't they just kill him, too?

Herrington's story got even more far-fetched when he said Whitlock left in the car, covered in blood, to get gasoline to burn the house down. Driving around town covered in blood after committing such a brutal and savage murder was a big risk for anyone to take. Even a Paris cop might have been suspicious.

While Whitlock was gone, Steidl allegedly took Herrington back into the Rhoads home and upstairs to the crime scene. When they entered the newlyweds' bedroom, Herrington "about fell across what he thought was a male subject laying on the floor with no clothes on." Herrington then observed a "female laying (sic) at a forty five degree angle across the bed with blood all over her." Herrington said the young woman "had no top on but had short pants on" and " . . . she had been cut all over the chest area." Herrington said, "he reached down to take the pulse of the female and Randy grabbed his hand and told him to not touch the bitch." Steidl threatened Herrington again: "This is what's going to happen to you and your family if you ever say anything . . . I should go ahead and kill you now but I don't know why I'm not." Before he left the room, Herrington told investigators "he looked at the female and, for some reason, put a pillow over the female's face . . . "

According to Herrington, Steidl took him back outside into the front yard and Whitlock returned in the car and removed "two milk jugs full of a dark colored liquid." Steidl told Herrington "to get the hell out of there" and threatened him once more, telling him if he said anything his "family would be like the people upstairs." According to Herrington, Whitlock chimed in, "you heard what Steidl said and that will happen to you." The report ended that Herrington "took off running from the residence" and "he fell down a couple of times running home and did not know if he passed out at these times or not because he was so drunk." That summarized Herrington's story from the two inconsistent reports written by

Eckerty and Parrish. I wasn't even a third of the way into the case file, and I was beginning to understand why Jack Eckerty was so concerned about looking like a "dirty cop."

One of the tools frequently used by investigators is a "consensual overhear" which is a body wire or recording device used to record conversations with a suspect of a crime. This tool is used especially in cases where there is an eyewitness or person who knows a suspect well enough to elicit incriminating information. To obtain a consensual overhear in Illinois an investigator must have a consenting party willing to have his or her conversations recorded and the investigator must get a court order signed from a judge. In the state police, specially trained technicians are called upon to conduct and monitor the eavesdropping.

Consensual overhears have specific requirements by law and infringements of this law can result in serious criminal or civil repercussions. Once an investigator obtains a consensual overhear, the case file should contain the signed consent from the participating party, the affidavit to the court, the judge's signed court order, a transcript of the conversation and an investigative report documenting the meetings, and investigators must write a detailed summary of each taped conversation. Upon completion, the overhear is reviewed by the issuing judge. By law, the overhear tapes must be kept for 10 years and if it involves a homicide, they must be kept forever.

On September 24, 1986, five days after Darrell Herrington came forward, Sergeant Jack Eckerty obtained an eavesdropping order from the Fifth Judicial Circuit Court in Edgar County. The order was issued to overhear conversations between Darrell Herrington, Herbert Whitlock and Gordon Randy Steidl. The ISP case file in the Rhoads homicide contained the court order for the overhears and only one short paragraph. The report indicated that on "9-24-86, at approximately 10:00 pm a surveillance video and eavesdropping device was used in a taped conversation between Darrell Herrington and Gordon Randy Steidl." Additionally, "On 9-25-86 at approximately 11:00 am, another eavesdropping device was used in a taped conversation again between Darrell Herrington and Gordon Randy Steidl" and "On 9-25-86, a second eavesdropping recording was taken between Darrell Herrington and Herbert Whitlock during a phone call from Herrington to Whitlock." That was it, despite protocol, the ISP case file I received contained no reports detailing the conversations overheard or the transcribed reports of these audio and video recordings. In April 2000 when I called Springfield, I was told neither the tapes nor transcripts could be located.

In a 1995 Post Conviction Relief petition filed on behalf of Randy Steidl, Attorney Michael Metnick acknowledged those overhears:

> The obvious purpose for placing Mr. Steidl on videotape was to elicit incriminating statements from him. Mr. Steidl's visual and verbal responses, while admittedly loud and crude, demonstrated a total lack of knowledge about the crime. Mr. Steidl's response of dismay, confusion and anger to Mr. Herrington's insistence that he was present and involved in the murders was clearly that of someone who had no connection with these offenses. These conversations which were never played in court and would have demonstrated that attempts to elicit incriminating statements from Mr. Steidl were unsuccessful.

Metnick was right and later I learned there were other more damning overhear tapes that were never disclosed to the defense.

The case file contained only two documented interviews with Darrell Herrington. The first was on September 21, 1986, and the second on November 24, 1986, when Eckerty and Parrish conducted a videotaped interview with Herrington. Obviously, investigators now had the break they needed—an eyewitness to the Rhoads murders and two "suspects," but they still lacked a motive. So investigators focused on making their one eyewitness as believable as possible by taping him. Like a character from a bad movie or detective novel, Herrington spoke with a fake larynx adding a strong, metallic, robot-esque quality to his voice. Years prior, throat cancer cost Herrington his larynx and the video depicts the state's key eyewitness as a thin, seedy looking barfly with dark red hair and mustache. The 10-page transcript of the November 24 interview basically contained the same information Herrington provided during his first documented interview.

Again, this account set the time for the murders of Dyke and Karen between 12:30 and 1:30 a.m. Herrington established the timeline by providing the time of the first trip to the Rhoads house, and his command of the English language was as butchered as his timeline:

> I was pretty, well, disconfused [sic]. I don't know. It was probably around 10 or 11. I don't know. It was getting pretty, well, late. We just drove around. Seemed to me like we just drove around and come back in from the North . . . We went to another tavern, but I don't know which one it was.

After the men went into the last bar, Herrington told investigators it was around "12 or 12:30" when they left. Herrington said, "They don't serve you nothin' to drink after 12:00, so I don't know. And I thought they was drunk. I asked Randy,

I said, 'Can you take me home?'" But when asked why Steidl drove to the Rhoads' home again, Herrington couldn't provide a reason, stating, "It was nothin' they had let me in on. I was pretty well loaded at the time, and I didn't give a shit where they was going or who they was going with or what . . . "

Herrington once again discussed the front porch confrontation between Steidl, Whitlock and Dyke Rhoads, but during this interview, just one month after the first interview, he changed this version of the story: "I don't know what happened. Evidently, I passed out or fell asleep or somethin' 'cause I don't remember. I didn't pay any attention after that. I just figured they went in to talk or so I just kinda sacked out, evidently." But something woke him up after he had passed out:

> I'd say somethin' woke me up. I saw somethin' by the car. I couldn't make out what it was so I got out and the closer I got to the house, I heard yellin' and screamin'. Someone was damned scared about somethin'.

This time, Herrington "could hear a woman screamin' and a man sayin', 'Please don't hurt me' or 'kill me' or somethin' like that."

Herrington repeated how he entered the home and met Steidl halfway up the stairway. Steidl "had blood on him. He had some on him, not very much on him, but some on the arms and hands." Between his metallic voice combined with his redneck dialect, Herrington's words were just as hard to understand as his story was believable.

As the tape continued, Herrington's account of the murder scene and the personal threats made by Steidl and Whitlock were much the same as in his first account, except for one deviation. This time, Dyke was no longer naked but partially clothed. "Yeah," Herrington said, "He [Dyke] must have had shorts on 'cause somethin' caught my eye and unless you know, evidently he had blood on his shorts 'cause I did have blood on my hands somewhere when I stumbled I can remember that. I was pretty drunk."

Twelve years later, in an affidavit provided to Bill Clutter by ISP Colonel Ken Metcalf, he stated, "I remember there was an alcoholic guy that didn't pan out." The "alcoholic guy" Colonel Metcalf was referring to was Darrell Herrington. Still this alcoholic was the same man the state used to eventually help convict Steidl and Whitlock for the murders of Dyke and Karen Rhoads.

Like Mike McFatridge said, Herrington "knew certain things . . . that were not the things the town drunk would know." And it's easy to know certain things if you're paid money, induced by alcohol and promises and then told by the police what to know.

Approximately one month after the trial and convictions of Steidl and Whitlock, Herrington came forward with the first of several recantations to the Paris Police regarding the Rhoads homicide. That recantation was instead hidden away and never disclosed by the police. Herrington's first official recantation occurred on November 21, 1988. Under oath, he recanted his testimony to Steidl's attorney at the time, Peter L. Rotskoff. The attorney started off questioning Herrington's reasons for recanting his prior testimony and he testified: "Well, there's a few things that came up there in trial at different times, some of them wasn't, wasn't even said at all."

Herrington began by telling Rotskoff the police provided him with alcohol prior to his interviews, "Yes, well, that was after I went to the police station. And they, two days after I told them what happened down there at the house, they brought me over here (Charleston, Illinois). And they just, they tried to get me drunk but I wouldn't get drunk."

"They bought you beer?" Rotskoff asked. And Herrington replied, "Beer and whiskey."

The investigators ferreted Herrington to the Charleston Motor Inn and had filled him with whiskey prior to his interview. So Rotskoff asked Herrington who the police officers were. Herrington said that, "Gary Wheat and Jack Eckerty brought me over that night," and "Jim Parrish came over." Herrington continued telling Rotskoff the Motor Inn incident was not the only time investigators plied him with whiskey and beer prior to being interviewed, " . . . They had me drinkin' . . . beer and wine and whiskey . . . at the police station," and at " . . . Jim Parrish's residence . . . The residence where he lives at . . . I was there day and night . . . They lied to my wife where I was. They told my wife they was taking me to Indianapolis."

Rotskoff asked Herrington, "Isn't it a fact that the police would tell you that you told them things when you were intoxicated which, in fact, later on you determine were not true?" And Herrington agreed by stating, "Right."

If what Herrington was telling Rotskoff was true, then the investigators had induced a witness to lie. Besides breaking the law, Eckerty also violated ISP policy, because the Rules of Conduct of the Illinois State Police forbids an officer from ". . . bringing into any police facility or state vehicle alcoholic beverages." A violation of this rule is Level 7 Misconduct; Level 7 Misconduct is termination. The Rules of Conduct also state that no officer will engage in the following actions:

> Officers will not induce a witness or any other person who has knowledge regarding any issue under investigation by the Department, or any other law enforcement agency, to make false statements, withhold information, conceal information . . .

That includes inducing a witness with false promises, promises of leniency, money, alcohol, drugs or by threats and coercion. Yet before this investigation was over, Eckerty and Parrish had induced the two eyewitnesses by using almost every one of these unethical tactics.

Randy Steidl's half-brother, Master Sergeant Rory Steidl was, at the time, a trooper with the ISP. When Rory learned Eckerty plied Herrington with alcohol, he reported the policy violation to the State Police Division of Internal Investigations (DII). The reply he received was, "You're just a young trooper starting out in your career. Do you really want to do something like that?" Despite this obvious warning, Rory wanted Eckerty's misconduct investigated and filed a complaint. No investigation was ever initiated by DII on Eckerty.

Nineteen years later, Eckerty would be called upon to testify. Whitlock was seeking a new trial and his defense attorney, Richard Kling, questioned Eckerty about plying Herrington with alcohol. A *Paris Beacon-News* article depicted Eckerty's testimony:

> Right from the start, Eckerty danced around Kling's questions if the first interview with eyewitness Darrell Herrington took place on September 21, 1986 at the police chief's house. "I can't remember the date," said Eckerty ... He did however recall providing Herrington with alcohol the night before he was scheduled to testify before the grand jury. "He was nervous and wanted to relax," said Eckerty. Kling probed Eckerty if he recalled another instance where alcohol was provided to Herrington at Parrish's cabin. "I can't recall," answered Eckerty. Kling was quick to produce a three page affidavit signed by Eckerty indicating the alcohol incident did take place. "I just don't recall," replied Eckerty. "If it happened, it happened." He also noted that he is not aware of any ISP regulation or standard operating procedure in regards to providing witnesses with alcohol.

Apparently the State Police's internal investigations didn't know about the policy regulations either.

Ironically though, an internal investigation was opened on Rory Stiedl at the request of Eckerty and McFatridge. The complaint accused Rory of interfering with an investigation. The basis of the complaint happened when Randy Steidl met with the FBI during his trial regarding narcotics trafficking and corruption in Paris. Randy requested his brother Rory sit in on his interview with FBI Special

Agent Ken Temples. Neither McFatridge nor Eckerty wanted Randy interviewed by the FBI. When Rory agreed to accompany his brother during the interview, Rory said Eckerty threatened, "You'd better think about this before you do it." Somewhat suspiciously, Eckerty and McFatridge repeatedly phoned during Randy's interview asking to speak with Special Agent Ken Temples. Temples confirmed the information Randy Steidl provided was about corruption in Paris. And Randy Steidl also claimed Darrell Herrington was paid off by Bob Morgan to become an eyewitness against him and Whitlock. According to Rory Steidl:

> S/A Temples told me a few days later that he had since been notified by the special agent in charge of the Springfield office, '. . . not to interfere with the Steidl case.' . . . S/A Temples told me that he was very suspicious of McFatridge, Eckerty and Parrish due to their highly unusual degree of curiosity about what Randy had said, the antagonistic approach they took with him and S/A Temple's prior experience with Eckerty and Parrish.

Two days after this interview, McFatridge and Eckerty filed a complaint against Rory that he was interfering in an investigation and an internal investigation was opened. Rory Steidl was eventually exonerated, but the message was loud and clear—keep your mouth shut.

Herrington also testified how once he was full of liquor, police manipulated his obviously fabricated and bizarre story. Rotskoff brought up how at trial Herrington testified he saw Randy with a knife in his hand, and he asked, "Did the police tell you to say that?"

"Yeah," Herrington replied, "they said that's what I said. They told me that's what I told them but I didn't say that. I know I didn't say it that way."

So Rotskoff asked, " . . . the police told you one thing and you knew something else?"

"Yes, I told them the bodies were a certain way," Darrell said. "They said 'no, laying this way.' I said no. We argued about that for about a day. . . . They just said, they say well, 'tell them Karen's body was laying on the floor at a 45 degree angle.'"

Herrington had told police Karen's body was on the bed at a 45 degree angle and not on the floor when he was brought into the bedroom. The police told him to say Karen's body was on the floor to go along with how she was found. Obviously, the investigators saw the flaw in Herrington's depiction of the crime scene and were trying to correct his contradiction. Herrington continued as he testified under oath about his prior testimony.

Rotskoff: So Darrell, what you're really saying is that from what you saw, you do not believe that it's possible that Randy could have been involved in the murder of Karen Rhoads?

Herrington: No.

Rotskoff: And you don't really know about the murder of Dyke Rhoads?

Herrington: Right.

Rotskoff: And as you sit here today, are there other matters that you testified to that you think you probably testified to incorrectly?

Herrington: I am sure there are. Seems like they told me everything to say.

Then Rotskoff questioned Herrington about the favors the police and prosecutor promised him and he admitted, "They promised me I'd have my driver's license back within two months. And they told me they would pay me $100.00 a day for every day I was off work. And they never done any of that."

According to Steidl's 1995 Post Conviction Relief petition, on July 21, 1986, Herrington pleaded guilty to his fifth DUI. He was sentenced to 30 days in jail, fined $200 and his driver's license was revoked by the Secretary of State on August 27, 1986. Less than one month later, Herrington met with Paris Police Chief Gene Ray on September 19, 1986. The agreement: "in exchange for providing eyewitness information to the Rhoads murders, [Herrington] would get his driving privileges restored and receive $100 per day for his services." More egregious than this was the failure of State's Attorney McFatridge to divulge the deal made between Herrington and Chief Ray to the defense attorneys. McFatridge's non-disclosure was just one of the many examples of misconduct by the State in this case. Twice convicted for felony deceptive practice, Herrington's 30 pieces of silver was a proverbial "Get Out of Jail Free Card" along with his driver's license reinstated and $100 a day for services rendered. Plus, all the beer and whiskey he needed to fabricate his outlandish story. When the State didn't meet their end of the bargain, Herrington contacted Peter Rotskoff and volunteered this recantation.

But State's Attorney Mike McFatridge was not through covering up the State's deceit, and on November 21, 1988, one week after the recantation to Rotskoff, Herrington met with McFatridge. In subpoenaed notes from McFatridge, Herrington admitted he agreed to give the recantation to Steidl's attorney because he was "upset about his failure to get his driver's license back."

McFatridge's notes further indicated he met with Chief Ray on December 20, 1988, regarding the promise to reimburse Herrington for "out of pocket expenses" and "lost jobs" during the Rhoads murder investigation. Chief Ray told McFatridge that while Herrington was paid $240 "for services rendered . . . he was probably owed additional monies." Notes indicate that on January 13, 1989, "Herrington received the benefits of his prior agreement with Chief Ray."

Not surprisingly, 11 days later, on January 24, 1989, Darrell Herrington recanted his recantation to Peter Rotskoff. And despite all of Herrington's DUIs, on May 18, 1989, McFatridge wrote a letter to the Illinois Secretary of State, and Herrington's driving privileges were reinstated. Ironically, Darrell Herrington became a pretty affluent man who owned a small fleet of business and personal vehicles that included expensive antique, classic cars.

But the most damning recantation by Herrington had already been made to the Paris police just one month after the convictions of Steidl and Whitlock. This recantation was eventually discovered 14 years later by private investigator Bill Clutter hidden away in the basement of the Paris Police Department. A recantation never disclosed by the police or prosecution, and a recantation that only aroused my suspicions even more and it wasn't just Darrell Herrington who was looking deceitful.

CHAPTER 5

THE SECOND EYEWITNESS

———————■———————

Seven months after the Rhoads murders and five months after Darrell Herrington offered his services, Debbie Reinbolt came forward as the second alleged eyewitness. Reinbolt's rough appearance was indicative of her equally hard lifestyle. She was a self-described drug addict and alcoholic who started drinking when she was approximately nine years old. By 11 or 12, she was using various drugs which, over the years, included marijuana, meth, cocaine, crack cocaine and prescription drugs.

Reinbolt had a history of numerous stays in rehab centers for both drug and alcohol abuse. When asked specifically about drug rehab, Reinbolt admitted, "I've been in Gateway about seven times" and in a second center "three or four times, probably." Reinbolt explained that, in the 1980s, " . . . I was drinking about every day to the point of being drunk," and in her own words, she admitted to having frequent "alcoholic blackouts." In addition to her drug and alcohol addictions, she also had a history with various mental institutions severe enough to warrant electroshock treatments.

Bill Clutter interviewed David C. Merritt, a counselor at Harmony House, a drug and alcohol treatment center in Danville, Illinois, who confirmed Reinbolt's mental instabilities. Merritt stated:

> I was astonished that her testimony would be given so much credibility. Reinbolt had a reputation for fabricating stories. She was delusional. She would say things that weren't true. She would say she was being followed, people bugging her phone.

Merrit stated that he knew of four mental institutions where Reinbolt sought treatment, one of which he referred to as "a hardcore psychiatric center." Like Herrington's failed polygraph, Reinbolt and Herrington's medical history of mental illness was also hidden away by McFatridge and never disclosed to the defense.

Not surprisingly, with all of these issues, Reinbolt had a criminal history that included arrests for felony theft, writing bad checks, aggravated battery to a police officer, resisting arrest, possession of hypodermic needles, and, of course, drugs. Like Herrington, Reinbolt was a witness most prosecutors would cringe at using in a capital murder case, but not McFatridge, because, like Herrington, Reinbolt knew things *they wanted her to know.*

There were several similarities between Herrington and Reinbolt's questionable history and involvement in the Rhoads murder investigation. Like Herrington, Reinbolt later recanted her testimony and recanted her recantations. Following the trials and convictions, Reinbolt, like Herrington, under oath, accused investigators of leading her in her testimony and inducing her to testify falsely. Reinbolt's coaching required more than a bottle of whiskey, and years later, she told the Illinois Attorney General's Office that investigators led her through several mock trials in order to make her story believable. Afterwards, investigators whisked her away to a detox center to keep her sober.

The same undisclosed bartering between Herrington and officials also occurred with Reinbolt. Her 30 pieces of silver was a $2,500 pay off from the Illinois State Police, an agreement not to be charged with the murders of Dyke and Karen Rhoads, and a recommendation for no prison time regarding her alleged participation in the homicides.

When Reinbolt first approached police, there were other haunting parallels to Herrington that would make even a rookie investigator question her credibility. Reinbolt stated she spent the evening of July 5, 1986, drinking for several hours, smoking pot and popping codeine pills. Despite her obviously impaired condition and that she admitted to several blackouts throughout the night of the murders, Reinbolt's testimony was key to helping prosecute Steidl and Whitlock.

Between February and April, police documented four interviews with Reinbolt, and each time she changed her accounts and versions of the murder of Dyke and Karen Rhoads. Her incredible stories were filled with countless contradictions and lies, but the investigators and prosecutor didn't care. In fact, they would go out of their way to corroborate her bizarre accounts by distorting the truth, fabricating evidence, creating other witnesses and even going so far as to intimidate some of the witnesses. Throughout the investigation, they resorted to manipulation, intimidation and lying to provide Reinbolt the credibility she sorely lacked.

The first documented interview with Reinbolt occurred on February 17, 1987, when she told police she encountered Whitlock at the Horseshoe Tavern approximately one week before the murders. According to Reinbolt, "Herb Whitlock stated that his dream girl was Karen Rhoades [sic] . . ."

Reinbolt worked the 4 p.m. to 12 a.m. shift at the Paris Health Care Center, and on July 5, 1986, she said she decided not to go to work, and called a co-worker named Beverly Johnson, asking her to clock her in and out of work. For most investigators, this would've been an immediate red flag since Reinbolt just admitted she purposefully deceived her employer, making her credibility an issue from the start.

Reinbolt then told investigators another co-worker at the Paris Health Care Center named Tammy was out of town that weekend, so she decided to borrow her car, a brown, small-type station wagon. Reinbolt knew Tammy kept the keys in the car so she just went to her residence and took it.

After taking the car without Tammy's permission, she drove to the home of Barbara Furry. According to the police report, it was around 4:00 or 5:00 p.m. when she allegedly arrived at Furry's residence and the two women smoked two "marijuana cigarettes." Around 8:00 to 8:30 p.m., the two women left, driving around town and smoked another "marijuana cigarette." At approximately 9:00 p.m., the two women arrived at The Tap Room Lounge in Paris where Reinbolt encountered Herb Whitlock. Eckerty's investigative report read verbatim depicting just one of Reinbolt's strange accounts:

> Reinbolt stated that Whitlock stated, "We're going to go out and have a good time [to]night" and asked if she wanted to go. Reinbolt stated at this time, someone walked by and gave Whitlock a letter which was sealed. Whitlock asked a male subject who was sitting next to him if he had a knife so he could open the letter. The male subject replied that he did not and by that time, Whitlock had taken a knife from his rear pocket, opened the knife, and opened the letter. Reinbolt described the knife as a black knife with a long blade. The blade and handle measured approximately thirteen (13) inches.

What a strange story, and why did Whitlock need to borrow a knife from someone if he had one in his back pocket? Especially a 13-inch knife, which was an awful big knife for anyone to carry in their back pocket! Yet Reinbolt's bizarre report continued:

Reinbolt stated that Whitlock read the letter. After reading it, Whitlock quite quickly borrowed Reinbolt's cigarette lighter and burned the letter and put the ashes in the ash tray. Reinbolt stated Whitlock again said, "We're going out to have a good time."

Reinbolt's account continued and the report read, "'What are you talking about? . . . are you going to beat the shit out of someone?' (Reinbolt explained to Detective Parrish and R/A [Reporting Agent, Jack Eckerty] at this time that in the past 'good times' to Whitlock was to beat someone up.)"

Whitlock then told Reinbolt, "I've got to take care of a few people. Some people know too much. It's got to do with drugs."

Was this the delusional fabrications Merritt told Clutter about, because I had never heard that "going out to have a good time" meant "beating the shit out of someone."

Despite the absurdity, Eckerty's strange and grammatically challenged report continued, "Reinbolt stated at that time, she got a few very weird feeling. Reinbolt stated Whitlock started to act very weird and act like he was on a trip from narcotics." Whitlock allegedly then told Reinbolt, "that he was going to get his dream girl that night" and repeatedly instructed, "If anyone asks you, you do not know anything. You do not know who I'm talking about."

Reinbolt told investigators that while she was talking to Whitlock, she saw Darrell Herrington and Randy Steidl "in the other part of the bar," and they were talking to " . . . a tall male subject who Reinbolt described as a very good looking subject." Shortly after the unidentified, good looking man left the bar, Herrington departed and when Steidl started to leave, Whitlock stopped him and told him, "I'll see you later. I'll be there in a little while."

One glaring contradiction in Reinbolt's story should have immediately stood out to investigators. Herrington never once placed himself, the two suspects or any "good looking man" at the Tap Room Lounge. Therefore, one of the eyewitnesses, if not both, was lying.

Approximately 15 minutes after the men left the Tap Room Lounge, Reinbolt claimed she and Barb Furry left and she, "took some codeine pills" and they ended up at the Paris American Legion where "she noticed Randy Steidl, Herb Whitlock and the same tall, good looking man who was at the Tap Room Lounge." While at the Legion, Reinbolt said she didn't speak to either Whitlock or Steidl, but then her story began displaying more of the delusional effects of Reinbolt's long history of drug and alcohol abuse. Already admittedly drunk and high on pot and codeine, Reinbolt said she suddenly " . . . felt that something weird might happen," and out of the more than 9,000 residents of Paris, she believed something bad was going to happen to Dyke and Karen Rhoads.

The report continued, "She asked her friend Barb Furry to find out from someone in the American Legion where Dyke and Karen Rhoades [sic] lived."

> Reinbolt stated that after awhile, Furry obtained the information about the residence. The police report continued: Reinbolt stated that she then drove from the American Legion in the direction of the Rhoades [sic] residence. . . . As she drove by, she observed Herb Whitlock outside the residence on the West side of the house, which would be the front of the residence. She stated that Whitlock was walking towards the left part of the house at this time. . . . she knew it was Herb Whitlock by the subject's hairdo and by the way he walks. . . . after going by the residence, she drove around for a while and said she just started to think. Reinbolt stated that after some time, she took the car back from where she had taken it earlier that evening. . . . after getting to the square, she heard several sirens. . . . at this time, she felt like something bad had happened. . . . she then walked to her house and sat in her car at her house for awhile.

So why did Reinbolt take Tammy's car if her car was sitting in her driveway? That question was irrelevant because Eckerty and Parrish never even bothered to identify Tammy, or the brown, small-type station wagon. A woman named Tammy Lewis was identified later, but police didn't interview her or even document her existence. Reinbolt's lie was just ignored by investigators, and McFatridge took care of the lie about Tammy and her car later in the investigation.

Reinbolt's first account continued when "days later," she saw Steidl and Whitlock "in front of the Horseshoe Tavern" and she asked Whitlock for "a gun or something because a girl was giving her some shit" and "she could not get a gun by herself because she had a felony arrest . . ." Reinbolt said Whitlock gave her the same 13-inch knife he had taken from his back pocket at the Tap Room Lounge and said, "Don't let anybody get their hands on that knife and don't get caught with it. When you're done with it, give it back to me if you have to get rid of it . . ." and "I can't afford for it to get loose." Reinbolt claimed she told Whitlock, "I don't want to know anything about the knife."

Reinbolt continued telling investigators, " . . . after getting home, she got to thinking about the knife and the murders of Dyke and Karen Rhoades [sic]. . . ." Reinbolt then graphically described how, " . . . she observed what appeared to be blood on the outside handle and blade portions of the knife. . . took the knife and put it in hot water for awhile. . . then took a toothpick and brush and cleaned the red substance from the knife. Then she "took a whetstone and sharpened the knife blade to give it a different appearance. Reinbolt stated the reason she didn't get rid of the knife was because she needed it at the time. . . . " She added that "on several other occasions," she spoke with Herb Whitlock who told her: " . . . that after Karen Rhoades [sic] was dead, now he was kissing and loving her all over."

Detective James Parrish also wrote a report detailing Reinbolt's first interview. Parrish's report, at times, mirrored Eckerty's, but as with Herrington's interview reports, there were several questionable inconsistencies.

Parrish's report began by stating that "Debra" had known Whitlock for "approximately 4-5 years" and had "several business transactions with him involving drugs" and she "has overheard conversations with Randy and Herbie talking about drug transactions with Jeb Ashley and Dyke Rhoads."

Also excluded from Eckerty's report, but included in Parrish's account was an important encounter Reinbolt said happened prior to driving Tammy's car over to Barb Furry's. Parrish's report indicated Reinbolt claimed she went into a bar called Jeanie's Place and saw Whitlock and Dyke Rhoads arguing and overheard Dyke say "that he wanted out." The report continued, "Debra then heard Herb state that you don't get out, you just don't get up and walk out of a deal. . . . " The alleged argument was taken outside but Whitlock returned and met with Reinbolt and Parrish's report indicated he:

> . . . told her that Dyke knew too much and he was going and would have to be gotten out of the way. Herb also said it was bad that Karen was in the wrong place at the wrong time because he liked her and was going to have to get her and at this time, he said Karen was his dream girl. Herbie stated that on several occasions during the conversation at Jeanie's Place that it didn't matter if Dyke was paid up or not. A short time later, Dyke came back into the bar and gave some money to Herbie and said, "Here is what you wanted" and at this time, Dyke left the bar. . . .

Why had Eckerty left such an important encounter like this out of his report during the same interview? And it brought up another interesting question, Herrington had told investigators that Whitlock and Steidl went to the Rhoads house, "to get that son of a bitch's money back." But here was Reinbolt telling investigators that Dyke came back into Jeannie's Place and paid Whitlock his money. Reinbolt's story also gave investigators several leads and potential witnesses to corroborate her incredible tale. Through Bill Clutter, I learned that every one of these witnesses refuted everything Reinbolt claimed about the alleged meeting at Jeanie's Place. And once again the investigators either outright ignored their information or purposefully distorted the truth in order to maintain Reinbolt's credibility.

Another omission from Eckerty's report found in Parrish's account also led to more questions:

> At approximately daylight on July 6, 1986, Randy and Herbie stopped by Debbie's house in Randy's car. At this time, Herbie told Debbie she doesn't know anything nor did she see anything. Herbie also told Debbie he saw her drive by the Rhoads' house and at this time, Debbie saw some blood on Herbie's neck and clothes. . . . Herbie made the comment that he would pay her some money to keep her mouth shut and Debbie's reply was, "I don't want anything to know or do with it," and then Herbie and Randy left Debra's house.

This painted yet another bizarre scenario. With firemen, police and citizens swarming the town in the wake of the Rhoads fire, did it make sense for the two blood-covered killers to be driving to Reinbolt's house during the early morning hours? Yet, despite the unbelievable tale, investigators finally found in Reinbolt's story exactly what they needed for a motive: a drug deal gone bad.

As with Herrington, investigators attempted to utilize a court-ordered consensual overhear with Reinbolt. On February 19, 1987, two days after coming forward to police, Eckerty obtained the court order. The case file reflected the same lack of documentation as in Herrington's recorded interactions with Steidl and Whitlock, and like with Herrington, the case file I was provided contained no documentation of the conversations overheard or any transcriptions.

The file, however, does read, "After the eavesdropping device was in place, Reinbolt drove to the First Christian Church in Paris . . . at which time conversations were overheard." Reinbolt wore the wire while attending a Narcotics Anonymous meeting which Whitlock attended. I learned about even more deceitfulness when during the recorded conversation that night, Reinbolt acknowledged she didn't even know who Herb Whitlock was. That, along with a witness named Stan Aklen who also came forward with this same information to police, which was also never documented or disclosed to the defense.

On March 29, 1987, Reinbolt's already bizarre story became more unbelievable when she wove a second account of the Rhoads murders. This time, her story conveniently started out "that she had been to Dyke Rhoads' house on prior occasions with Herb Whitlock on drug deals." The report read that approximately three weeks before the murders, " . . . she observed a red mark on the side of Mr. Whitlock's face and had made comment to Herb Whitlock that she had heard a story about Karen Rhoads slapping him" and "Whitlock stated that he had gone down to Dyke and Karen's house one night to talk to Dyke about drugs." Finding Karen alone, Whitlock said he argued with Karen and allegedly told her "that . . . he loved her and wanted to get in her pants." Karen then slapped Whitlock.

Reinbolt's story conveniently coincided with a July 11, 1986, interview by Detective Parrish. The interview involved 15-year-old Lisa Wheeler and an incident she allegedly observed. Wheeler told Parrish that on May 24, 1986, she was sitting on her porch around midnight waiting for her boyfriend, who happened to be a 36-year-old, married Edgar County sheriff's deputy, and she described a "male subject wearing blue jeans, tennis shoes, a white t-shirt and was a little bit taller than Karen . . . and one thing she does remember is that the subject had a very large chest." Parrish's report continued, "Lisa also stated the subject had brown collar length hair and was wearing a full mustache" and he knocked on the Rhoads' front door. Karen Rhoads answered the door and the man asked for Dyke. An argument ensued between Karen and the man for approximately an hour. Then according to Wheeler, the man called Karen a "fucking slut" and she slapped him and went inside the house. The incident Wheeler described was publicized in the local papers prior to Reinbolt coming forward to police, which may explain why she was able to add this to her story during the second interview.

Wheeler's description of the man didn't come close to Whitlock's physical description, but armed with this new information from Reinbolt, investigators didn't bother to corroborate with Wheeler that it was Whitlock confronting Karen. A simple photo line-up shown to Wheeler could have confirmed Reinbolt's new story, but they never bothered.

Reinbolt's second account continued to contradict her first version and the origin of the knife also totally changed. Reinbolt stated:

> On July 4, 1986, Herbert had talked with Debbie and wanted to borrow the knife that he knew that Debbie had carried in her purse. Herb also talked about Dyke Rhoads knowing to [sic] much and that he was wanting out. . . . Debra stated that Herb wanted to meet her at Jeanie's Place at 10:30 a.m. on July 5, 1986, and at this time, Debra was supposed to give Herb the knife. On July 5, 1986, Debra met with Herbert Whitlock at Jeanie's Place . . . Dyke Rhoads came

into Jeanie's Place also and he and Herbert had a talk. Dyke gave
Herb some money, amount unknown, and Dyke said, "That finishes
it, and I'm out." After Dyke left, Herb told Debbie, you just don't get
out of stuff that easy, and that Dyke knew too much. Herbert once
again asked Debbie about the knife and that he wanted it, but Debbie told Herbert that she wanted the knife back because the knife was
[her husband] Vick's and he would wonder where the knife was.

Herrington had lied in his first interview to police when he said "Jim and Ed"
had committed the murders. Now, Reinbolt's second account grossly contradicted her
initial interview with police. If her second story was true, Reinbolt had obviously lied
to police in her first interview when she gave them the elaborate story that Whitlock
provided her with his knife which had a red substance like blood on it . . . a knife she
said Whitlock inferred was used in the murders of Dyke and Karen. Now in this second version, it was Reinbolt who provided the murder weapon to Whitlock.

Her second story contained numerous other contradictions and Tammy's
brown, small-type station wagon also disappeared in this version, and now she
claimed she borrowed a car belonging to Della Wakefield.

Even more suspicious . . . just three days prior to Reinbolt changing her story
in the second interview, on March 26, investigators had already conveniently
interviewed Della Wakefield. This report indicated, "Wakefield stated that during that day [July 5, 1986], she received a telephone call from Debbie Reinbolt
. . . [who] requested . . . if she could borrow the Wakefield's personal automobile
for the evening . . . for the purpose of going out and partying." Wakefield agreed
and let Reinbolt use her dark green 1972 Ford Galaxy 500—a somewhat different
description than the brown, small-type station wagon from the first version.

Obviously needing to corroborate Reinbolt as much as possible, Wakefield's
report also indicated that some time in 1985 or 1986, "she witnessed a knife fall
out of Reinbolt's purse." Additionally:

> Wakefield stated that she remembered, on another occasion, in the
> Summer of 1986, seeing a similar knife or same knife in Debbie's
> purse at the Reinbolt residence. Reinbolt stated to Wakefield that
> the knife had been used by Herbie Whitlock in the murder of Dyke
> and Karen Rhoads.

Della Wakefield's interview conveniently backed up Reinbolt's second account, but what the investigators and prosecutor failed to report was that on

January 12, 1987, two and a half months prior to Wakefield coming forward to police in March, Della and her husband were arrested on two counts of aggravated criminal sexual abuse. After a meeting between State's Attorney Mike McFatridge and the Wakefields' attorney in February of 1987, a deal was cut, and Wakefield conveniently volunteered to speak to police on March 26, 1987, to corroborate Reinbolt's second story.

Wakefield testified at the trials of Steidl and Whitlock with the obvious purpose of bolstering Reinbolt's credibility, and two months after Steidl and Whitlock's convictions, on September 17, 1987, Wakefield's felony charges for aggravated criminal sexual abuse were dismissed by State's Attorney Michael Mc-Fatridge. Investigators and the prosecutor had now covered up another one of Reinbolt's previous contradictions.

Reinbolt's second interview continued weaving a whole new story. Contradicting Herrington's account, it was Reinbolt, not Darrell, who accompanied Steidl and Whitlock to the Rhoads' house from the American Legion when, as the report read, " . . . Herbie was still wanting the knife and was insisting on Debbie to go out with him that night. Herb said they were going down to discuss with Dyke about getting out of this." Then, despite one of Reinbolt's numerous black outs that evening, "The next thing Debra recollects is getting out [of] a car at Dyke and Karen's house and seeing noone [sic] around." The grammatically challenged report continued:

> . . . after getting out of the car, she remembers going into the house through a porch in to a kitchen and at this time, she stated that she could hear people screaming and a voice saying, "Oh, God, oh, God." Debra said it seemed like the screaming went on for a long time. . . . she remembers a doorway and almost tripping over something, then looking down and saw a body lying by the door and a lot of blood.

This was another dilemma for the State with the two eyewitnesses both placing themselves at the murder scene, yet neither Herrington nor Reinbolt ever reported seeing the other at the murder scene.

Reinbolt's second version continued at the crime scene where she told investigators she observed a body lying on the floor on the opposite side of the bed. She also saw " . . . a lot of blood everywhere in the room. The next thing she remembers was being back outside and getting back into the car." Reinbolt conveniently suffered another blackout at this point, but her memory quickly returned when

Parrish's report added, "Debbie remembers telling Herbie that she had to have the knife back and Herbie wanted to get rid of the knife, finally Herb gave the knife back to Debbie because it was Vick's and that Debbie insisted on getting the knife back."

Reinbolt said after getting home, " . . . Herb and Randy came down by the house and that Herb had blood on him and that Herb threatened Debbie not to say anything and if something happened he will say there was another woman involved and not use Debra's name."

Debbie Reinbolt wasn't nearly done fabricating more stories for police, and on April 13, 1987, she wove yet another version for investigators. Eckerty's report stated:

> In summary, Reinbolt added the following to her previous state-ments. Reinbolt stated that prior to the night of July 5, 1986, she remembers Herbie Whitlock saying something about setting a fire out in the country to cover-up for a fire that was going to be set in Paris. Reinbolt stated that sometime after the bars closed on late July 5 or early July 6, 1986, she (Reinbolt) remembers being at the Dyke and Karen Rhoads residence. Reinbolt remembers going into the residence, entering the residence through the back door and walking into the back porch area.

From the porch, Reinbolt made her way through the Rhoads' home and up the stairs. Now, in her third version, she "remembers something about a large vase and a broken table lamp . . . the vase and the lamp could be the same item but is not sure." Reinbolt recalled " . . . the lamp being broken and some person holding a broken piece of the lamp. . . . [and] remembers being in the bedroom with Dyke and Karen Rhoads and Herb Whitlock and Rany [sic] Steidl."

According to the report:

> Randy Steidl first having a knife and was cutting Dyke, while Whitlock was helping with Dyke . . . later, Whitlock had the knife and Steidl was helping Whitlock. Reinbolt stated that at this time, she remembers she (Reinbolt) was holding Karen on the left side of the bed. Reinbolt remembers telling Karen over and over ("It will be alright, it will be alright"). Reinbolt stated at the time she was saying this to Karen, she (Reinbolt) knew things were not going to be alright. Reinbolt stated that at some point, Dyke tries to get out of bed and ends up lying on

the floor between the bed and the door. Reinbolt stated that Karen was yelling and saying, ("Oh my God, Oh my God").

Reinbolt's story continued with Karen attempting to get out of bed and Reinbolt "grabbing Karen and holding her down." Uncertain as to what happened next, Reinbolt stated, " . . . that either Whitlock or Steidl cut Karen," and she had a "cut on the throat with a lot of blood."

Another bizarre and implausible twist to her story was the two intoxicated men—in the heat of a murder—taking the time to trade a knife back and forth so they could take turns stabbing the two victims.

Reinbolt's account also contradicted Herrington's story because he had the two men arguing with Dyke Rhoads on the front porch which continued with the three men going inside the house and upstairs. Is it plausible that Dyke Rhoads would go upstairs, get undressed, and get into bed next to his naked wife with two men still in the house arguing with him? Yet, Reinbolt's report specifically said both Dyke and Karen were lying in bed next to each other right before being murdered. The police report read:

> Reinbolt remembers being in the bedroom with Dyke and Karen Rhoads and Herb Whitlock and Randy Steidl. Reinbolt stated that as you are looking at the bed, standing at the foot of the bed, looking toward the head of the bed, Dyke was lying on the right side of the bed and Karen was lying on the left side of the bed.

According to Reinbolt, " . . . everything after this is a blank" and she "only remembers running out the back door." Although Reinbolt claimed everything went "blank," she later offered additional descriptions of the crime scene and something vague "about a shower in the house" but remembered nothing more.

Following Reinbolt's ever changing story, what happened after her third version to police was mind boggling and represented not only a severe breach of investigative procedure but a breach of the public's trust. Reinbolt had made a horrific confession to police in which she not only placed herself at the crime scene but also admitted to actively participating in the torture and murder of Karen Rhoads! Her violent criminal past, her alcohol and drug addiction, and her mental health problems already made her an obviously unstable person, but now her confession to this gruesome crime made her even more of a danger to society; yet, she was simply allowed to walk away from the Paris Police Station that evening!

Nineteen years later, Jack Eckerty was called to testify in Whitlock's attempt for a new trial and was asked why Reinbolt wasn't arrested for her part in the murders after confessing to police.

"If someone said they were holding down a body while someone else is stabbing that human being, would that be a crime?" asked attorney Richard Kling.

"I need to know more about the details before determining that," Eckerty testified.

"You are aware that she helped provide the knife and held the body down as the person was being killed, what more would you need to know?" asked Kling.

Eckerty ludicrously testified he would need to determine if the person was telling the truth. "Each case is different," he added.

Yet obviously, Eckerty and the others must have thought Reinbolt was telling the truth in 1987, because they used her to help put one man on death row and another in prison for life.

Reinbolt was eventually charged with concealment of a homicide, but, like Herrington, McFatridge cut her a deal, and, like Herrington, she grew disillusioned with the State's deal and recanted her testimony on two different occasions.

On January 13, 1989, she recanted her trial testimony in an affidavit to Steidl's attorney at the time, Peter Rotskoff. Reinbolt recanted this recantation 12 months later in December of 1989, after receiving a visit from Mike McFatridge, Jack Eckerty and Jim Parrish.

Reinbolt recanted her testimony once again on February 17 and 18, 1996. This time she recanted to Michael Metnick, Steidl's new attorney, in a four-hour taped statement. Her recantation was filled with allegations that police and the prosecutor had led her in her testimony. Reinbolt also gave chilling accounts of how police threatened and coerced her into some of her confessions, how they provided her with alcohol, monies and false promises, and how investigators lied to her in order to coerce and manipulate her into becoming their key eyewitness.

Reinbolt's credibility was immediately questioned by Metnick because, after all, she had already recanted her testimony once before and then recanted that recantation. When asked why anyone would believe her now, even if she was telling the truth, Reinbolt replied:

> Because after some consideration and thought, my goal is to get this over with, to end this with the truth about what transpired, just to clear my conscience . . . There were some things that didn't . . . weren't truthful in the testimonies and things of Randy's trial.

When asked how well she knew Whitlock and Steidl, she admitted barely know-ing them: "We were acquaintances, I suppose. That's about the extent of it," and she was unsure of how she ever met Steidl or Whitlock, admitting she saw them infrequently around town and did not know one better than the other.

Metnick asked her about her prior recantation, "Did you basically tell Rotskoff that you were not truthful when you testified at trial?"

"Yeah, I believe some of that was in there . . . I was feeling bad about this . . . I felt like I had been . . . I guess, manipulated in all of this," Reinbolt replied.

Reinbolt also gave Metnick another reason why, " . . . It was another fear thing . . . I'd talk to anybody, and here would come Mike McFatridge, Jim Parrish and Jack Eckerty . . . They're not giving . . . outright threats, but implied . . . [McFa-tridge said] I could be charged further . . . "

Metnick followed with a litany of questions which only strengthened Rein-bolt's obvious lack of credibility, "Where do you recall your whereabouts being the night of the murder?

" . . . I was at work for awhile . . . And I did skip out of work early . . . I only left early probably by approximately a half an hour, forty-five minutes . . . " she replied.

Reinbolt was admitting she was actually at work the evening of the mur-ders, thus making all of her prior stories to police obvious lies. She also testified that after leaving work, "I went to the liquor store . . . Drank four or five beers . . . I called Della Wakefield, asked about borrowing her car . . . I took the car for approximately two hours . . . drove around and drank . . . " approximately, "Eighteen beers, [then I went home and] took some codeine pills and smoked a cigarette. Laid down on the couch. Went to sleep, passed out, whatever you want to call it."

Reinbolt's evening of bar-hopping, her depictions of the crime scene, her participation in the murders were all fabricated and Metnick's questioning con-tinued addressing her deceitfulness when the following exchange took place.

Metnick: Did you have any knowledge of the crime?

Reinbolt: At the time, nothing other than what I have just told you.

Metnick: Were you at the Rhoads' house the night they were killed? Had you ever been in Dyke and Karen Rhoads' house?

Reinbolt: Nope. No.

Metnick: You were a witness to the murder, was that truthful testimony?

Reinbolt: No.

Metnick: Did you ever do drugs with Dyke Rhoads? Randy Steidl?

Reinbolt: No [to both questions].

Metnick: I'm asking you right now, was any part of what you testified to at trial regarding the events of July 5, 1986, or July 6, 1986, true?

Reinbolt: No.

Metnick: What parts were untrue?

Reinbolt: Oh, I don't know that Randy was there. I don't know that Herbie was there. Um, just everything . . . Because I wasn't there.

Debbie Reinbolt's recantation was 205 pages in length, much of it filled with allegations of misconduct on the part of the prosecutor and investigators who manipulated, intimidated and coerced her into confessing and testifying. Reinbolt recounted how one night at Jim Parrish's house, he told her he knew " . . . I had been involved or had information to do with the murders and that I might as well talk to him now because, quote/unquote, he would go to his grave trying to prove that I was involved." Reinbolt then added, "It was one of those deals where he [Parrish] said he didn't have to prove anything."

Reinbolt was actually right for once—Parrish hadn't proven anything in this investigation.

Continuing the recantation, Reinbolt elaborated on how her drinking often caused her to "black out" and how the investigators played on this weakness. "I have had so many bad dealings with police," she said:

> . . . and then when it all boiled down to it, and you have got cops sitting here saying, "Okay, you know, you're an alcoholic, you do drugs, you blacked out, you know, you had to have been there . . ." "Okay, well maybe during this blackout I was . . . " You know, they know more than I do, and you're caught in a catch 22 thing, I guess is the word for it . . . the word for it is the paranoia starts coming in and . . . because I've got a, you know, history . . . criminally.

The investigators used lies and coercion, coupled with Reinbolt's overall weak mental state, and were able to manipulate her. Exhibit # 48 in the Rhoads case file was a Bic lighter found at the intersection of Wood and Young streets. No fingerprints were ever taken from the lighter, and it was never linked to the crime scene; basically, it was a lighter on the street that anyone could have discarded. Reinbolt explained:

> They showed me a lighter they had in a bag and Eckerty asked me, did I recognize the lighter? . . . I've seen lighters like it. You can go right over here at the gas station and get you one, if you want one. And he said, Well, not with your fingerprints on it . . . We found it at the [Rhoads] house . . . therefore my story about driving by [the house] couldn't be correct, because here was the lighter.

Reinbolt told investigators that "this is craziness," but Eckerty said she could be charged with the murders and "the death penalty was brought up and that's when I asked for . . . and he read me my rights, and I asked for my attorney."

When Reinbolt asked for her attorney, she said investigators ignored her request. "They waited," she detailed. "It was a couple of hours or so before they even let me see [my attorney]. They had me up there all night . . . and then I gave that second statement."

"Were you ever shown any reports . . . that your fingerprints were on this lighter?" Metnick asked her.

Reinbolt explained the manipulation, "They didn't show me anything . . . I mean like they were trying to intimidate, scare me, whatever, which they did . . . I knew nothing about a cigarette lighter." Yet the manipulation had worked when she admitted she told police, "Okay, I had gave that cigarette lighter to Herbie, and maybe Herbie dropped it."

Metnick asked her if that was true and Reinbolt replied, "No . . . because I didn't give Herbie a lighter, number one, and I don't believe I was there, number two . . . like I said, I have not seen police reports, I have not seen anything, because they would never let me see those . . . but I wonder now even if there was police reports or anything else that . . . you know there was fingerprints even on that lighter."

Reinbolt was right to question the credibility of the investigators, there were no fingerprints and the lighter was not found in the house. This was just another example of the manipulation used to coerce a frightened and confused alcoholic, drug addicted, mentally disturbed woman into providing the fabricated stories the state needed to railroad two innocent men into prison.

There were only four documented interviews with Reinbolt. During an investigation, an investigator will *usually* document a report each and every time they meet with a witness or suspect. As with Herrington, this was also not the case with Reinbolt. So Metnick asked her, "From the time that you began meeting with the police . . . let's say from the time you gave them the knife . . . until the time of trial, on a weekly basis, how many times a week did you spend with Parrish and Eckerty?"

"Well, one or the other was around every day . . . normally at my house . . . there were occasions they'd take me to the detox unit or to the courthouse, sometimes the police station," Reinbolt replied.

Like Herrington, Reinbolt said she was also interviewed at Jim Parrish's home, and in my experiences, investigators don't usually conduct official police interviews at their residences . . . especially with murderers. The recant continued.

> Metnick: The first time, after you gave the knife, you met with Jim Parrish and Jack Eckerty. Is that correct?
>
> Reinbolt: I think that's when I told them that first story about going by the Rhoads house . . . that I had said that I had went by the Rhoads house, drove by and seen Herbie and Randy going in . . . I think that was my first story.

So Metnick asked Reinbolt why she told police the initial story in the first place and her answer reflected how easily she was manipulated by investigators when she replied, "Because they were hell-bent on the fact that I had been there, and me not liking and trusting police and figuring, well, hey, you know, I did black out. God knows what I did or didn't do . . . Okay my safest bet is to just tell them this, get this over with, and if I wasn't there, then I'm not involved."

Similar to Herrington's recantation, Reinbolt discussed how police got her to involve Randy Steidl in the murders.

"At first I didn't say anything about Randy . . . I very rarely mentioned Randy . . . then they would say to me . . . you need to bring it out, like leading. You need to bring out about Randy's involvement," said Reinbolt.

The investigator's intimidation and manipulation was evident when she continued her testimony about why she finally included Steidl, "Because that's who everybody was saying did it . . . the police had said that's who did it, and they said they could put me with them two . . . Jim [Parrish] broke his finger . . . he got mad at me . . . got mad when I didn't answer something the way he wanted it answered . . . Eckerty was sitting at the table . . . I was sitting at the table . . . Jim had been sitting at the table . . . Jim got up out of his chair and stood beside me and made a fist and went to hit me, and I guess he thought better of it and he smacked the table and then he got real mad, stomped in the other room, screaming about, "you made me break my God-damned finger."

And over the course of my review, Reinbolt was not the only witness in this investigation who relayed outbursts of anger and fear of being beaten by Detective Jim Parrish.

Debbie Reinbolt gave three separate stories to police over a two-month period, each time providing a little more information and a little more involvement in the murders. Instead of questioning Reinbolt's credibility, investigators used her instabilities and weaknesses to mold her into their witness. They failed to corroborate any of Reinbolt's constantly changing stories and ignored her lies. The police knew she had lied and Reinbolt acknowledged they knew it in her recantation, "They told me I did . . . And then by the time all the yelling and screaming and every other thing got over with, then I'd say okay, okay . . . then they'd inform me, well this is how it happened, this way . . . then I'd just go along with them."

Metnick asked Reinbolt why she went along with the police and she answered, "Still out of fear and out of confusion and whatever else was going on in my head . . . Jim and Jack, you know, saying, well I had to be there even though I didn't believe I was . . . listening to them going over and over it, to the point that they had me even convinced . . . during the times that the statements were changed . . . they would come and get me . . . we need to go over this so that everything that your testifying to is fresh in your mind . . . there were other times, like they sent me to detox, I had to go to detox, because they said I had to get my head together to be able to testify . . . If I didn't go, I could be charged further."

Investigators had induced Herrington, the town drunk, with alcohol during many of his interviews and Reinbolt was no different. Metnick asked her, "Was there ever a time that you met with the investigators when you were under the influence?"

"The story about driving by the house, it changed, because they came and got me one night . . . Parrish and Eckerty did . . . Took me up to the Police Department. I had been drinking that night, and I think I was doing codeine . . . And Parrish came back in and asked me if I wanted a pop or anything, and I told him no, you know, I'd do a beer, for real, and he did. I sat there and drank a few beers at the police station," Reinbolt said.

It seemed, at least during the Rhoads investigation, that the Paris Police Department doubled as a pub. The investigators and prosecutor knew both Herrington and Reinbolt were alcoholics, yet, they apparently had no qualms about plying them with alcohol when they wanted to manipulate their accounts of the murders before or during their interviews. It was obvious they knew their eyewitness had these weaknesses when they forced Reinbolt to go into detox to keep her sober prior to trial testimony.

Metnick addressed Reinbolt's third story to police and she admitted, "Yeah. That's my statement of fact. That I had been there. Randy and Herbie had been there . . . That I had seen Randy and Herbie stab Dyke and Karen. They tried to set the house on fire . . . Eckerty and Parrish kept badgering me about a frigging pillow, and I had no idea what they were talking about . . . they kept saying, you had to have seen a pillow, you had to have seen a pillow, to the point that I finally asked them, why, if I was there, did I have to have seen a pillow . . . that's when they informed me that Darrell Herrrington had come to them and said he had been there, and there was a pillow over Karen's face . . . no I said to them . . . bullshit. Because, I mean Darrell gets so drunk he couldn't even ride his bike, he'd fall off of it, let alone stand up."

It was astounding that one of these unbelievable eyewitnesses questioned the credibility of the other in this twisted and deceitful case. Reinbolt's recantation was in no way finished as she painted a vivid picture of investigators leading her deeper and deeper into her story. Reinbolt told Metnick, "They would question me, and I'd sit there and kind of do my little stupid look or whatever, and they'd say, well, didn't this happen this way?"

So Metnick asked her how his questions were different from the way the police questioned her and Reinbolt replied, "Because you're not telling me or hinting at any of the answers I am giving before I give them . . . It would be like . . . An example would be . . . wasn't Dyke in the doorway when you were at the top of the stairs?"

In the closing sentences of her recantation, Reinbolt acknowledged some concerns to Metnick: "I guess my main fear is just the repercussions from the State or whomever. I know McFatridge and Parrish and Eckerty are not going to be real pleased." And when Metnick asked Reinbolt what she thought she would get out of the recantation, she replied, "Probably a lot of trouble."

Not surprisingly, just five days after providing the recantation to Metnick, on February 23, 1996, Reinbolt recanted her recantation to the Edgar County State's Attorney. Obviously someone got to Reinbolt once again, either with veiled threats or veiled promises.

When interviewed by *48 Hours*, reporter Susan Spencer noted, "Over the years, Debbie Reinbolt has changed her story more than a half a dozen times."

"Why have you changed your story so many times?" Spencer asked her.

"Basically, wantin' to get out of this. Just wantin' it over. The bottom line is, I can't change a story that's true," Reinbolt replied.

Regarding Herrington's involvement, Reinbolt told *48 Hours*, "I thought somebody made this up—somebody's lost their freakin' mind. This is the town drunk. There is no way this man was there."

CHAPTER 6

TIMELINE OF CONTRADICTIONS

---■---

A neighborhood canvas turned up several witnesses who questioned the timeline of the murders, but investigators ignored the information and stood by the timeline established by Herrington and Reinbolt.

At approximately midnight on July 6, 1986, Tonya Lee Quinn returned home to the residence she shared with Loren Taylor; the Taylor house was located directly across the street from the Rhoads' home. Quinn told investigators she went to bed between 1:00 and 1:30 a.m. and observed nothing unusual occurring in the area.

Mark A. Knuth, a Department of Corrections officer, also visited the Loren Taylor home that night. In his interview, Knuth told investigators that between 12:30 and 1:00 a.m., he " . . . did not see anything out of the ordinary."

Terry Richey, who also lived across the street from the Rhoads, stated that at approximately 2:30 a.m. "she heard a noise outside her residence" and believed someone was attempting to steal her husband's motorcycle. Richey said she sat in the front room window and watched the motorcycle until 3:00 a.m. and "observed no one in the area of the Rhoads home." At approximately 3:30 a.m., Mercer A. Young and Kim Armstrong drove past the Rhoads home and "observed nothing unusual."

Ollie Campbell informed investigators that around 4:00 a.m. she was awakened by a woman screaming and heard what "sounded like a man and a woman . . . in a verbal argument." Another neighbor, Carla Tate, advised investigators that she was awakened at approximately 4:00 a.m. by the paper boy when she heard the paper hit her front porch. Paper boy William Sheperd advised investigators that at approximately 4:30 a.m. he was delivering newspapers in that area of town. When he went past the Rhoads house he "saw or heard nothing out of the ordinary ... and saw nobody walking or any vehicles on the street." Then, at approximately 4:45 a.m., Carla Tate heard a dog barking followed by an explosion. Tate looked out her window and saw a glow coming from the Rhoads' home. Tate ran to the residence and was the unidentified neighbor woman Terry Newman spotted outside the Rhoads home. After "screaming and yelling for someone to wake up," she returned home and phoned the fire department. At approximately 4:45 a.m., Maxine Elledge said she "heard two explosions" and "saw a red glow" emanating from the Rhoads' residence.

Bill Clutter provided several additional witnesses who also refuted the timeline set by the State's two star eyewitnesses. An affidavit from neighbor Ollie Campbell in March of 1992 was much more detailed than Detective Parrish's report. Campbell told Clutter:

> ... I was interviewed by Detective Parrish ... and told him that at approximately 4:00 a.m. I was awakened by a woman screaming and heard what sounded like a man and woman in a verbal argument. . . I was sleeping with an open window, and I was awakened by the sound of a woman screaming and a barking dog. I told my husband, "What's going on[?]" ... When it (the screaming) kept getting louder, that's when I got up. I heard loud shouting sounds of a man and woman arguing ... then the screaming and shouting suddenly stopped. I went out on the front porch but could only hear the sound of a big dog barking. . . . I did not see anyone. I did not see any cars parked in the street or hear any cars drive away. I saw no fire. I went inside and laid back down but could not sleep. Approximately 15 minutes later, I heard commotion and someone state[d], "Can you get the door open?"

Ollie Campbell's affidavit revealed, "I was never called to testify about the screams I heard shortly before the fire."

When Dr. Ben Light was interviewed in 2000, he stated that in the summer of 1986 he was seventeen, a senior in high school and living with his grandmother on Court Street, across the street and two doors west of the Rhoads' residence. Light advised he and his friend, Sean Newlin, set up lawn chairs in his grandmother's front yard. Light and Newlin were just "hanging out and talking" from approximately 11:30

p.m. until 1:30 a.m. that night. He stated he didn't remember seeing anything strange or unusual. Light said it was a "very quiet night," and he heard no verbal confrontations. Light was never interviewed by police, and he never went forward because he assumed that since the fire department had been called around 4:00 a.m., that investigators knew that's when the murders occurred. By the time the trials started, Light was away at college.

Likewise, Sean Newlin, a Deputy United States Marshall, was also interviewed in 2000. He confirmed that he and Light spent the evening and morning hours of July 5 and 6, 1986, sitting in Light's grandmother's front yard. He recalled sitting in the front yard right after midnight up until after 1:15 a.m. and possibly even as late as 2:15 a.m. The report read, " . . . he remembers hearing about the crimes later and the state's theory of when it happened and thinking, 'I was sitting there while they were being killed?'" Newlin stated that he:

> . . . didn't see anything unusual . . . He was surprised to hear about Darrell [Herrington's] testimony of screaming and that Randy's car had no muffler. He said [he] heard absolutely nothing, he didn't even remember any cars going by and if he'd heard anything, he would have gone to the police.

Newlin also stated that on that night, " . . . he sat there looking at the stars thinking what a clear, perfectly quiet night it was." When Newlin went home for the evening, " . . . his headlights shined on the Rhoads home and he saw nothing that struck him as unusual."

Investigators apparently missed these two key witnesses during the neighborhood canvas who had sat just two doors down from the Rhoads residence. Despite being outside on this quiet and clear night, neither Light nor Newlin saw nor heard anything unusual that night at the Rhoads' residence. At least not from midnight to a little after 1:30 a.m. during the time Reinbolt and Herrington claimed the murders occurred.

Monica Pitts was also interviewed by Bill Clutter. The report read, "Monica stated she vividly remembered the night of Saturday, July 5, 1986. She said it was the summer between her 7th and 8th grade year. She was spending the night with her friend, DeAnne Taylor who lived directly across from the Rhoads. The two girls went to see a late movie, and Pitts recalled walking back to the Taylor home and passing the Rhoads' house. There were no lights on at the Rhoads house and it "appeared that no one was home." After the girls went to bed, "Monica stated that she was awakened from a sound sleep by the sounds of screaming. By the time she propped herself up, the screaming had stopped. She thought the screaming sound she heard may have been a cat in heat. . . . Monica stated that it was still dark." Pitts woke up and could see fire trucks across the street at the Rhoads' house. Pitts told Clutter, " . . . she was interviewed by two police officers who asked her if the screaming sound she heard might have been a woman screaming. Monica told them it could be." Yet Eckerty's report reflected only that Monica was awakened when " . . . she thought she heard a cat screaming . . ."

Bryan Jones, who worked at the 24-hour Clark gas station in Paris, told investigators that at "approximately midnight" on July 5, 1986, he had a mysterious, late night customer. Jones described "a white male in his early 30's, approximately 6' tall with a stalky built [sic], unshaven face with fairly short hair down the middle of his neck." Jones said the man stood out to him because he had unusually "large hands." The customer was driving a white Oldsmobile Cutlass with Florida plates and appeared as if "he had been driving all night." The man bought gas, some sandwiches, Hostess cakes and a two liter bottle of Pepsi, and paid with a $50 bill.

Another report read, "On Friday, [July 4, 1986] or Saturday [July 5, 1986]," James C. Foley was " . . . working at the Freedom Oil Gas Station, downtown Paris." Foley told investigators he " . . . observed a male subject driving a cream colored car that he believed to be a two door. . . . the subject removed two or three gas cans from the rear of the vehicle . . . " and " . . . the subject purchased a total of twenty-one gallons of gas and paid cash." Additionally, the report read that "at the time of the purchase, it was dark and [Foley] was unable to describe the subject . . . [and] unable to give a more complete description of the vehicle." Foley stated, " . . . he was not sure about the license plate on the vehicle but he believed it to be an out-of-state license."

Actually, Foley gave investigators much more detailed information than what their report indicated. In 2000, Bill Clutter produced an interview report where Foley stated he specifically told investigators the car had "Florida" plates. Foley had also given a more detailed description of the man to the investigators. Like Jones, he described the customer as a stout, muscular man with blonde hair worn in a ponytail. The car was filled with candy wrappers and the man appeared to have been "living in his car."

I learned later that another witness came forward and gave information about a cream or white colored car and its blonde haired driver. This witness also told the original investigators about suspicious activity she witnessed at the Rhoads' house just prior to the murders. She was the same woman who appeared on *48 Hours* in May of 2000—silhouetted in darkness with her voice disguised because 14 years after the fact she was still too terrified to have her identity known. On *48 Hours*, she described:

... two men standing opposite the street light by Dyke and Karen's house. What caught my eye was that they had trench coats on in July ... one of them was a big guy with blonde hair and the other guy was small framed and looked like he had dark hair. And they were just standing there, lookin' towards Dyke and Karen's house.

Hours before the murders, she observed:

This car started coming around. And it was white with a gold stripe down it and it had Florida license plates. It would just go by in front of Dyke and Karen's house [and then] stop. I seen 'em lookin', you know, then take off. They did this about 10 times, I mean, continuously. Why would anyone do that?

This woman's information was also never documented in the original case file. When I asked Charlie McGrew why her information was ignored, his reply was: "We considered her '10-96.' She was nuts." When I asked McGrew why investigators never documented her information, he angrily bellowed, "What the fuck? You motherfucker! You working for the fucking defense now?" Later on, I learned this woman had actually provided the identity of the two men outside the Rhoads house that night. That information was also ignored and never documented by the investigators and prosecutor.

Frank E. Harris was a Paris resident and, at the time, the car he was driving had Florida plates. On the night of the Rhoads murders, Harris and Terry Brascher were at a party down the street from the Rhoads' home. Investigators had already received information about the cream colored car with Florida plates that was seen circling the Rhoads' home.

Since his car had Florida plates, Harris was pulled into the Paris Police Department on July 7, 1986. Harris told police he had walked by the Rhoads' house between 1:30 and 2:00 a.m. on his way home from the party, and he saw nothing unusual.

Harris said police had him stand in front of a two-way mirror in the interview room. He heard a voice on the other side of the mirror ask, "Is this him?"

Then he heard a voice answer, "It's not him." Harris was released by police, and of course they never bothered to document this incident.

Harris and Brascher were interviewed by Bill Clutter in 2000. They confirmed while coming and going to the party, they walked past the Rhoads' home. "I was pretty drunk that night," Harris said, but he remembered when he and Brascher walked past the Rhoads' home between 1:30 and 2:00 a.m., they saw nothing unusual.

This was amazing, the neighborhood canvas and additional interviews provided by Clutter identified over 18 witnesses who indicated nothing unusual occurred at the Rhoads' house between 12:30 and 1:30 a.m. The witnesses described a calm, quiet summer night. Many of these witnesses were sitting outside within eye and ear shot of Dyke and Karen's. Some were sitting on lawn chairs in their front yards, on their porches, in their bedrooms with their windows open, driving or walking past the Rhoads' house during this timeframe . . . and nothing unusual was seen nor heard at the house. No one heard any arguing, no one heard a woman screaming or crying out, "Please don't kill me!" or "Oh, God! Oh, God!"

No one saw two men covered with blood in the front yard of the Rhoads' house threatening Darrell Herrington, not once but twice. No one heard Herrington's metallic voice cutting through the night. Nor did anyone see the drunken man staggering off into the night after being threatened. No one saw Debbie Reinbolt in her blacked-out condition running out the back door.

Not a single person indicated anything unusual at the Rhoads' house until approximately 4:00 a.m. when several people reported hearing a woman screaming followed shortly by fire truck sirens around 4:39 a.m.

Most of the people interviewed in the neighborhood canvas would cause even a novice investigator to speculate the murders occurred sometime between 4:00 and 4:30 a.m. Yet investigators eventually excluded many of these potential witnesses from the case file witness list. This exclusion was most likely because the two alleged eyewitnesses, the town drunk and the convicted drug addict, placed the time of the murders between 12:30 and 1:30 a.m. Despite the alcohol and drug induced memories of Herrington and Reinbolt, despite all their alleged blackouts, the State stood by their timeline.

Herrington's account is that throughout the evening of July 5, 1986, he, Steidl and Whitlock frequented several bars in the Paris area. Not once does Herrington include Reinbolt as being part of the group or having seen her at any of the bars they frequented that night. In fact, when reading the case file, both Herrington and Reinbolt gave accounts to investigators they were both drinking with Steidl and Whitlock at the exact same time but at totally different bars.

In Herrington's account, he first met Steidl and Whitlock at Joe's Tavern between 6:30 and 7:30 p.m. They went to the Horseshoe Club and back to Joe's Tavern and at some point, the three men left Joe's Tavern in a cream-colored Chrysler driven by Steidl.

They went to the Rhoads' house, found no one home, and drove around town drinking a six pack of beer. The men went to the Friendly Tavern, and then around midnight, ended up at the American Legion. According to Herrington, the three men left together and returned to the Rhoads' residence when the murders occurred. Herrington identified over eight witnesses who he claimed saw him with Steidl and Whitlock that night. The majority of those witnesses were never interviewed—probably because the few who were interviewed denied ever seeing Herrington with Steidl or Whitlock that night.

Herrington told investigators that when he was at Joe's Tavern with Steidl and Whitlock, bartender Elaine Armstrong and patrons Larry Temples and Beecher and Carol Lynch were also present. When the men went to the Horseshoe Club, Herrington gave investigators the names of two other potential witnesses—Sherm Wright and Mike Wilhoit. Herrington indicated Whitlock met with Mike Wilhoit and then asked Steidl if he wanted something to get high on, but Steidl declined. Herrington made no mention of any witnesses at the Friendly Tavern or the American Legion.

The bartender at Joe's Lounge, Elaine Armstrong, was interviewed by Eckerty and Parrish on February 27, 1987, a little over five months after Herrington's first interview. Contradicting Herrington's account, Armstrong stated that on July 5, 1986, she did not remember seeing Randy Steidl "all that day in Joe's Lounge." She did remember "Darrell Herrington was in and out of Joe's Lounge all day long. Armstrong stated that usually at the end of the day, Darrell is so drunk that he does not know what is going on." There was no mention of Whitlock or Reinbolt in Armstrong's report.

For some reason, possibly because of Armstrong's denials, investigators never bothered to ask Larry Temples or Beecher and Carol Lynch if Herrington was with Steidl and Whitlock at Joe's Lounge that night. Likewise, Sherm Wright and Mike Wilhoit were never interviewed to corroborate Herrington's story of being at the Horseshoe with the two men. Twenty years later, when Mike Wilhoit was finally interviewed, the ISP report read:

> Wilhoit stated that incident did not happen and was not true. Wilhoit stated that he had never seen Herrington with Randy Steidl or Herb Whitlock. Wilhoit stated they moved in different circles and Steidl would not be seen hanging out with the town drunk, Darrell Herrington . . . Wilhoit stated that he never stepped outside with Whitlock on the night prior to the Rhoads homicide. Wilhoit stated he was never interviewed or testified in 1986.

No attempts were made to interview any employees or witnesses at the Friendly Tavern to corroborate Herrington's story. In interviews involving the American

Legion, witnesses Charles McClaskey, Beecher and Carol Lynch and Debbie Walton said they were at the American Legion around 11 p.m. and Randy Steidl was there but alone.

On February 24, 1987, investigators interviewed Charles McClaskey and their report read, "On 7/5/86 [he] . . . saw Randy Steidl at the American Legion at approximately 11 p.m. . . . It appeared as if he [Steidl] had been drinking quite a bit that evening." But when called to testify, McClaskey contradicted the investigator's report, stating he had seen Steidl at the American Legion at 11 p.m. but Steidl did not appear to be intoxicated.

On February 27, 1987, Eckerty and Parrish interviewed Debra Walton who told them she was at the Paris American Legion on the night of July 5, 1986. Walton told investigators she talked with Randy Steidl at approximately 11 p.m. and remembered dancing with Steidl who was wearing a Hawaiian flowered shirt and white pants. Several other witnesses interviewed also said Steidl was wearing a flowered Hawaiian shirt on the night of the murders. Yet, Herrington's version was Steidl was wearing a light blue shirt and jeans that night. Reinbolt was never asked what Steidl was wearing; investigators had already given her way too much information to remember.

Carol and Beecher Lynch said they also saw Randy Steidl at the Paris American Legion on the night of July 5, 1986. Their accounts were that Steidl was alone and they saw him leave from the bar in his vehicle alone. They weren't even questioned about Joe's Tavern. Each of these witnesses specifically told investigators they never saw Darrell Herrington, Debbie Reinbolt or Herb Whitlock at the American Legion that evening.

One witness the State did use to corroborate Herrington's story was Carol Robinson, who later claimed she was intimidated and coerced into lying on the stand. Carol Robinson was one of several women who claimed they were mentally and physically intimidated by both Parrish and McFatridge. Robinson was a bartender at the Horseshoe Club.

In 1992, Carol Robinson provided an affidavit and stated:

> I was interviewed on March 25, 1987, by Paris Police Detective James Parrish and DCI Agent Jack Eckerty. Det. Parrish asked me if I remembered seeing Darrell Herrington with Randy Steidl at the Horseshoe Lounge on the evening of July 5, 1986. I told him I couldn't remember the date I saw them together. Det. Parrish insisted that I had to have seen them together on July 5 because that's the date Herrington said I served them. Det. Parrish became

angry with me. Agent Eckerty then left the room. [Parrish then stated] "This is a murder case we're talking about. Do you want me to show you pictures of those kids?" I was frightened by Det. Parrish slapping his fist against his hand. I asked Det. Parrish, "Are you allowed to hit me?" I was scared and started crying and said, O.K. O.K. I agreed to sign a statement that I had seen Steidl and Herrington together on July 5, but I really did not remember when they came in. I remember only one occasion where Randy Steidl and Darrell Herrington were together in my tavern. It was unusual because Herrington is a known alcoholic but on the night I saw him with Steidl, he was sober and not drinking.

Herrington's own accounts of July 5, 1986, to Eckerty had him drinking for 12 hours and being "pretty drunk." But Carol Robinson told Eckerty that Herrington was uncharacteristically sober that night. This was just another suspicious contradiction never questioned by the seasoned investigator. Still, why would an investigator write two conflicting reports like this with Herrington self-admittedly drunk in one account, and Herrington "totally sober" in another witnesses account on the same night? Eckerty had been sloppy, but obviously it didn't matter to the state, because they only wanted to corroborate Herrington's story at any cost.

Also in Robinson's affidavit, she said Parrish told her Herrington claimed she had served him and Steidl that night. That was never documented in any of the interview reports with Darrell Herrington. In fact, Herrington had said it was Mike Wilhoit who served them at the Horseshoe Club that night, not Carol Robinson.

In total contradiction to Herrington's account of the evening was Reinbolt, who told investigators she and Barb Furry met Whitlock at the Tap Room Lounge at the exact same time Herrington claimed the three men were at Joe's Lounge. Reinbolt also placed Steidl and Herrington at the Tap Room Lounge. Herrington never once mentioned being at the Tap Room Lounge.

There were more than seven bar patrons and employees who refuted Reinbolt's story of drinking with Steidl and Whitlock that night. Yet, the information provided by these witnesses was factually distorted in reports or never documented—just as investigators did while checking out Herrington's story.

Reinbolt had also told investigators on July 5, 1986, she was scheduled to work at the Paris Health Care Center from 4:00 p.m. until midnight. Reinbolt claimed she asked co-worker Beverly Johnson to clock her in and out of work. Eckerty and Parrish interviewed Beverly Johnson on February 20, 1987. The report indicated:

Beverly stated that last summer she was an employee of the Paris Health Care Center and worked the second shift which was the 4pm to 12 shift at the nursing home. Beverly stated that on one occasion in the summer, that Debra Reinbolt called her at home and wanted Beverly to punch her in at work that day because she was not going to come to work. Beverly stated that she punched Debra in at approximately 3:45pm and punched Debra out at approximately 12pm [sic] midnight that night.

This report was used by the investigators to corroborate Reinbolt's story. Yet once again they failed to give a complete and accurate account about where Beverly Johnson actually was the night of July 5, 1986.

Beverly Johnson did tell Eckerty and Parrish that Reinbolt asked her once that summer to punch her in and out of work, but Johnson also later admitted she checked her timecards and knew it wasn't the night of July 5, 1986, because she was on vacation in Tennessee at the time. Beverly Johnson's timecard from the health care center also confirmed she didn't work that night. Investigators omitted this fact from their report thus distorting the truth by inferring Johnson clocked in Reinbolt on July 5, 1986. This inference instead corroborated Reinbolt's story. By omitting that Johnson was on vacation the July 5 weekend, investigators left out important information that discredited Reinbolt's story.

Reinbolt had also told investigators that after skipping work, she drove to Barbara Furry's house where they drank beer and smoked pot. According to Reinbolt, the two women drove around Paris smoking more pot and popping codeine pills. Then they allegedly started their evening of bar hopping, eventually meeting up with Steidl and Whitlock at the Tap Room and then later at the American Legion. At the American Legion, Reinbolt allegedly asked Furry to find out where the Rhoads lived because she had a "very weird feeling." Documentation provided by Clutter indicated investigator's had again manipulated and intimidated yet another witness who refuted Reinbolt's story.

In an affidavit, Barbara Furry said she told investigators Reinbolt's claim of being with her on July 5, 1986, was "absolutely not true." Yet, Furry's adamant denial to Eckerty and Parrish was omitted from their reports. Furry also told the investigator's Reinbolt "never came to my house" that night and "I never went with her to the Tap Room tavern that night or any night."

Furry's affidavit disclosed that at the time of the Rhoads murders, she was pregnant—another indication she was not out drinking with Reinbolt. She also stated that, at the time, she was a recovering alcoholic and had not had a drink in 10 years. She emphasized: "I have never gone anywhere to a bar with Debra Reinbolt."

Furry told the investigators, "... I don't smoke pot," and adamantly denied going to the American Legion with Reinbolt: "I told them the only time I went into any bars was with my friend Carol Wallace ... but I would not drink." Then Furry's affidavit addressed the intimidation by the two investigators when she was interviewed:

> My mother was out in the car waiting for me. I was so scared. They wouldn't tell me why I was there ... I asked if I could go now. They said no ... I began to cry. I remember thinking my water broke, and telling them, "I'll clean it up. I'll clean it up." I had peed my pants. As I was leaving, Parrish screamed at me, "Come back if you can ever tell the truth!" My baby was born five days later ... I remember Parrish coming back to my house after I had brought my baby home from the hospital. He was with a different man who he never introduced. I became ill because of the stress. . . . I was admitted to . . . St. Elizabeth's hospital ... suffering from a nervous breakdown.

Barbara Furry was never called to testify to contradict yet another lie by Reinbolt. Once again the investigators had again managed to manipulate the truth.

Years later, I had a phone conversation with a woman who wanted to give information about the Rhoads case. The woman said she was good friends with Barbara Furry who was still too terrified to ever trust the police again. Like Stan Aklen, this woman also questioned Reinbolt's credibility. She said she was a sponsor at the Paris Alcoholics Anonymous meetings, which Whitlock and Reinbolt attended in 1987. It was very apparent, she said, that Reinbolt and Whitlock did not talk or associate with one another, either before or after the Rhoads murders, something Reinbolt later admitted in her recantation.

Reinbolt even contradicted her own timeline when she gave two different versions of Dyke Rhoads and Whitlock arguing at Jeannie's Place. In one version, the incident happened at 10:30 a.m. on the morning of July 5. In the other version, the argument occurred after 4:00 p.m. after Beverly Johnson allegedly clocked her into work. This was a six-hour discrepancy that was ignored by investigators.

There was an even bigger discrepancy about this incident because investigators once again caught Reinbolt in another lie. Another lie they ignored and covered up.

Eva Jean Trover was the owner and bartender at Jeanie's Place, and was interviewed by Eckerty and Parrish on March 3, 1987. Trover emphatically told the two investigators neither Whitlock, Dyke Rhoads nor Reinbolt were in her bar that day. Just more conflicting information investigators never documented in their reports. On the day of the murders, Reinbolt had claimed she saw Dyke and Whitlock arguing at Jeanie's Place, Trover was working as the bartender.

In an affidavit to Bill Clutter, Eva Jean Trover stated:

> I knew Dyke Rhoads vaguely. . . . Herbie Whitlock used to go to school with my husband. I only remember him in [my bar] once watching a pool game. If they [Whitlock and Rhoads] had been in here, I would have remembered. That never happened. . . . I remember being asked this same thing by Detective Parrish and Agent Eckerty. I told them the same thing I'm telling you now. Dyke Rhoads was never in my tavern with Herb Whitlock or Debra Reinbolt.

Yet Eckerty and Parrish's interview report with Trover totally sidestepped Reinbolt's account of Whitlock being with Dyke Rhoads in Jeanie's Place on the day of the murders. The distorted report read:

> Eva stated that she had never seen Randy Steidl in [her] bar except one time and that was with a large framed, dark haired woman. Eva also stated she had never seen Randy in the bar with any other woman and never heard any arguments between Randy Steidl or anyone else while he was in the bar.

Reinbolt had never even mentioned Randy Steidl being in Jeanie's Place to investigators. Yet this was the only focus of their interview report with Trover, another purposeful distortion of the truth sidestepping Reinbolt getting caught in yet another lie. Once again the investigators were equally deceitful and manipulated the real information Trover provided them by distorting the truth and not reporting the real information that discredited Reinbolt.

In addition, Trover's husband and a bartender, Robert Marietta, worked the night of July 5, 1986, and were also interviewed by investigators. They also told investigators neither Dyke, Whitlock nor Reinbolt were in their bar that day or evening. Eva Jean Trover, her husband and the bartender were coincidentally omitted from the case file witness list as potential witnesses. It was becoming more and more obvious that Eckerty and Parrish had excluded several witnesses and their information which totally discredited Reinbolt.

It was no surprise that none of the bar patrons saw Debbie Reinbolt on July 5, 1986, because she wasn't at the bars at all that night, because like she admitted in her recantation, she was actually at work that night.

Investigators went to the Paris Health Care Center and obtained Reinbolt's timecards and the nurse's log which showed she punched into work at 3:45 p.m., and clocked out at approximately midnight. Reinbolt's own handwritten initials were on these timecards, and she had even signed the nurse's log. Investigators ignored this fact and never questioned if Reinbolt was really at work that night. Her immediate supervisor, Paula Cooper-Brlach, had also signed off on the timecards and the nurse's log and assigned Reinbolt to work sections A and B of the nursing home that night. Brlach was never interviewed by investigators, and in a 1992 interview with Clutter, she stated that:

> If [Reinbolt's] name is on [the nurse's log] then she would have had to have been there. I don't write people down that aren't there. If she hadn't shown up by 4:30, I would have definitely noticed her missing [and] it would have definitely been reported on the nurse's log.

If investigators had bothered to interview Brlach, they would have had yet another witness to refute Reinbolt's credibility. Apparently they didn't want that because they also could have easily obtained a handwriting analysis of Reinbolt's timecards and the nurse's log which would have either corroborated or discredited Reinbolt's story. That never happened and instead they ignored the possibility Reinbolt was actually at work that night.

The only attempt of corroboration by investigators was conducted on February 20, 1987, when Sgt. Eckerty called Nancy Davis, an administrator at the Paris Health Center. The brief report read, "At this time, the R/A [Eckerty] was advised by Davis that Debbie Reinbolt was employed at the Paris Health Center on July 5th and July 6th and both days, time cards showed Reinbolt working at 3:45pm to 12 midnight." This was the extent of the investigators' efforts.

This was all so amazing and by this time in my review, it was obvious the eyewitnesses had lied on at least one occasion under oath. They had both testified under oath in two trials that Steidl and Whitlock murdered Dyke and Karen Rhoads. They both recanted that testimony under oath in their recantations. So obviously, on at least one occasion while under oath, they had lied. Obviously this destroyed any of their credibility, but these were the two eyewitnesses used to convict the two men.

Imagine going to trial and having the likes of these two pathetic liars helping to determine your fate.

One eyewitness, the town drunk with a felony record, who admitted to drinking for 12 straight hours on the night of the crime, willing to come forward after he cut deals for money and promises. The other eyewitness, a woman with a history of mental instability, alcoholism and drug addiction, who is a violent felon and self-admitted murderess, who drank 18 beers, smoked three joints and popped codeine pills the night of the murders. Which one of them would you believe?

CHAPTER 7

THE FABRICATED EVIDENCE

———————■———————

President John Adams once wrote, "Facts are stubborn things; and whatever may be our wishes, our inclinations, or the dictates of our passion, they cannot alter the state of facts and evidence." Yet the state certainly tried to alter the facts when it came to the fabricated evidence provided by Reinbolt and Herrington.

After the suspicious evening of bar-hopping, Herrington and Reinbolt's stories got even more contradictory right before, during and after the murders.

Herrington said he asked Steidl for a ride home when the American Legion closed shortly after midnight, and the three men left in a cream-colored Chrysler driven by Randy Steidl. The same car he said they drove around town earlier drinking the six pack of beer, but police tried to manipulate Herrington into corroborating Reinbolt's contradictory story. In Herrington's recant, he pointed out the manipulation.

Q: So you told police that Herbie left in a Chrysler?

Herrington: Yeah. . . . I say probably a '66 or '67 beige Chrysler. . . . They said I must have been mistaken.

Q: You must have been mistaken? What did they tell you to testify to?

Herrington: Randy's car.

Q: What kind of car did Randy have that night?

Herrington: A red and white Buick. I say, probably '77 or '76.

Q: You couldn't have gotten mixed up on the two cars?

Herrington: I don't see how I could, but they said I did.

Reinbolt had spun a totally different story, and she had Steidl and Whitlock in Randy's car, the red and white Buick. Reinbolt also mentioned seeing Steidl and Whitlock at the Tap Room and American Legion with "a good looking man," but never once mentioned seeing Herrington at the American Legion, and in her version she was at the Rhoads house with Steidl and Whitlock, not Herrington.

Reinbolt's report read: " . . . she observed Herbie, Randy, and the unknown subject, who she could not identify, come out of the Legion, and Randy and the unknown subject walked towards Randy's car and Herbie walked over to Debbie." Reinbolt continued telling investigators " . . . Herbie was still wanting the knife and was insisting on Debbie to go with him that night. Herb said that they were going down to discuss with Dyke about getting out of this." Reinbolt then had one of her famous blackouts and the report continues:

> The next thing Debra recollects is getting out a car at Dyke and Karen's house and seeing noone [sic] around. Debra stated that after getting out of the car, she remembers going into the house through a porch into a kitchen and at this time she could hear people screaming and a voice saying, "Oh, God! Oh, God!"

Despite the eyewitnesses contradicting one another, investigators had another problem: numerous bar patrons also contradicted them. Many of those witnesses told investigators they personally observed Randy Steidl at the American Legion—*alone.* Not one of them mentioned seeing Herrington, Reinbolt or Whitlock at the Legion that night.

Throughout the night, Reinbolt and Herrington had Steidl and Whitlock covered in blood at the crime scene. Whitlock even allegedly drove around Paris covered in blood to get some gasoline in order to set the fire. Therefore both men would have been driving around at one time or another in either Steidl's red and white Buick or the cream-colored Chrysler, whichever eyewitness you wanted to believe, covered in blood. Whichever car it was, Steidl and Whitlock would've been dripping and smearing blood on the seats, steering wheel, carpet, pedals, and entire interior. Yet investigators never once attempted to obtain a search warrant for any vehicle. Of course, since they never established which car was used that night, it would've been hard to prepare a search warrant. But regardless of which car it was, a search warrant would have, more than likely, led to finding blood evidence in the car.

Another focus of Clutter's investigation was the knife Reinbolt provided as the alleged murder weapon. Like Herrington in his first story to police about "Jim and Ed," Reinbolt lied to police in her first interview. Her credibility was immediately brought into question because of the origin of the knife. In her first account, Reinbolt told investigators she borrowed a knife from Whitlock which he said was used to murder Dyke and Karen. Her elaborate story had her cleaning a "red substance" from the knife and incriminating herself when, " . . . she then took a whetstone and sharpened the knife blade to give it a different appearance."

In Reinbolt's ever-changing story, in her next version to police, it was she who provided the murder weapon to Whitlock. This knife was referred to as "the Reinbolt knife." If this were true, she had lied to police in her first story.

Exhibit #47 was the Reinbolt knife and she testified it was her husband Vick's pocket knife. Years later in her recantation, Reinbolt refuted the knife was the murder weapon used.

> Q: What did Parrish say to you that day and what did you say to him, with regard to the knife?
>
> Reinbolt: I know that you have, well actually, he didn't say knife, the murder weapon that was involved in the murders . . . I gave him the knife . . . this is one of those deals again where the cops are going to get me caught up in a bunch of bullshit . . . So I agreed to giving him the knife . . . Because my mind was telling me that, okay, you know, I'll end this . . . to get the law off my ass . . . they'll realize that it isn't a knife that was there. I wasn't there.
>
> Q: Was this the knife used, to your knowledge to kill Dyke and Karen Rhoads?
>
> Reinbolt: Not to my knowledge. No . . . they had, at this point, come back with this fantastic story that, yes, that knife was there and, yes, it matched the stab wounds so I had to have been there, blah, blah, blah.

When Reinbolt was asked if she gave Whitlock the knife or ever had any discussions with him about the knife, she emphatically stated, "No."

Scientific evidence also refuted the Reinbolt knife.

At Whitlock's trial, Dr. John Murphy, who performed the autopsies, testified, "The multiple stab wounds suffered by Dyke and Karen Rhoads were 'compatible' with the knife which prosecution eyewitness Debbie Reinbolt said was used to murder the couple . . ." Yet, Clutter provided documentation refuting Dr. Murphy and "the Reinbolt knife." Clutter turned to noted pathologist Dr. Michael Baden for help.

Clutter's report read, "The Reinbolt knife had a five inch blade and a pronounced hilt. The pathologist who conducted the autopsy measured the fatal wounds in both victims as six inches deep and noted that there were no hilt marks."

> Dr. Baden concluded that the Reinbolt knife was not compatible to the victims' wounds. Had the Reinbolt knife penetrated to a depth of 6 3/8 inches, the deepest wound identified, [Baden] would have expected hilt marks. A knife in the kitchen sink that was taken into evidence but never tested by police turned out to match precisely with the three wounds that were deemed fatal by the autopsy pathologist. The slits at the surface of the skin in each of the three fatal wounds measured 2.5 centimeters, which matched up nicely with the blade width of the kitchen sink knife, which measured 2.4 cm. The Reinbolt knife had a much narrower blade, 1.3 cm.

It wasn't just the investigators who were sloppy in this case. Dr. Baden's affidavit pointed out the overall sloppiness of the autopsies:

> . . . since there are discrepancies in Dr. Murphy's autopsy [report] concerning several of the wound measurements . . . I do not know which measurement is accurate . . . Dr. Murphy testified that wound #10 on Karen Rhoads extended deeply through the lungs and into the heart, however, the wound measurement of his [report] indicates that this wound had a depth of only '1' centimeter.

Despite Dr. Murphy's sloppiness, Badin's report also explained that the stab wounds were deeper and wider than the "Reinbolt Knife" could have caused. And looking at the autopsy reports, it seemed the killers knew exactly what they were doing because the location of the death blows were strategically placed as if it were the work of a professional killer . . . not two drunken men.

The majority of the stab wounds were less than one to one and one half inches in depth. The vast majority of stab wounds to Dyke were to his back. According to Baden, Dyke was most likely lying in bed on his stomach when he was first stabbed. Karen had defense wounds, indicating she fought with her killer or killers.

I imagined Karen being held down while the killer plunged the knife, calculatingly, an inch to two inches at a time, into her body. Was Karen tortured? Had she seen something she shouldn't have, as the case file indicated? Did the killers want to know if Karen had talked or were they worried she might talk? Did they want to silence her and Dyke before they could or was this just an evil, malicious random act? Karen wasn't sexually molested, so rape wasn't the motive. Their house was not burglarized . . . so why were they killed? *A drug deal gone bad?*

Dyke and Karen's lifestyle didn't reflect any involvement in any type of narcotics trafficking. At the time of their deaths, they only had around $200 in the bank—not the type of money one expected from a drug trafficker. Witnesses, some who were Dyke's best friends, revealed that prior to his marriage, Dyke smoked pot and used cocaine on a limited basis. They also said that once Dyke met Karen, he distanced himself from them and any type of drug use. No one interviewed ever saw Dyke deal any drugs. At the time of his death, no drugs were found in Dyke's system. Yet, the State used Reinbolt's story to establish the murders were over a "drug deal gone bad."

Another significant piece of evidence used at the trials by McFatridge was Exhibit #26—a broken lamp from Dyke and Karen's bedroom. McFatridge used Reinbolt's knowledge of the lamp to prove to the jury she was actually in the Rhoads' home during the murders. In Debbie Reinbolt's constantly changing accounts, she suddenly and conveniently remembered a vase or lamp. She remembered going into the Rhoads residence through an unlocked door and walking into the kitchen. This even though Herrington told investigators he found all the doors locked—another unanswered contradiction, but Reinbolt continued, telling investigators she made her way into a hallway, up the stairs and into Dyke and Karen's bedroom. The report read:

> Reinbolt stated that sometime, either before going into the bedroom or right after entering the bedroom, Reinbolt remembers something about a large vase and a broken table lamp. Reinbolt stated that the vase or the lamp could be the same item but is not

sure. Reinbolt remembers the lamp being broken and some person holding a broken piece of the lamp.

There was a broken lamp in the bedroom, but no fingerprints were found on any broken pieces of the lamp.

Clutter noted that in Reinbolt's first two stories to police, she never mentioned anything about a broken lamp. In the third report, Reinbolt suddenly remembered the broken lamp. Clutter discovered an even bigger discrepancy. When looking at the crime scene photos, he discovered that the inside of the broken lamp was "bone white." Clutter stated, "If the lamp had been broken before the fire was set, one would expect to see blackened soot stains" on the inside of the broken lamp.

Clutter's discovery was verified by State Certified Arson Investigator Terry Brown. Brown's conclusion: "Based on the lack of smoke damage on the inside and edges of the broken pieces of ceramic lamp . . . the lamp was not broken during the commission of the crime, as Reinbolt described in her testimony . . . " Brown stated the lamp had to have been broken " . . . after the fire had been suppressed by firemen."

According to Clutter, "Even the State Fire Marshall who conducted the original investigation concurred that the lamp had been broken after the fire in the kitchen had been extinguished." When Karen and Dyke's bodies were removed, there was an outline of soot around their bodies. One would expect that the soot would also have covered the inside of the lamp and outlined it on the floor too if it had been broken before the fire, as Reinbolt testified, but it hadn't.

Twenty years later, ISP investigators obtained additional information questioning Reinbolt's testimony about the lamp. Investigators interviewed a man named Phil Sinclair, who was a close friend to Reinbolt and who also said one of his relatives was a fireman who responded to the Rhoads murder scene. Sinclair told investigators his relative admitted it was his ax which actually broke the lamp after the fire. The same lamp Reinbolt claimed was broken during the murders and prior to the fire. If what Sinclair was saying was true, this was just another example how the state used fabricated evidence to establish Reinbolt's credibility.

Just like the knife, Reinbolt testified in her recantation it was the police who manipulated her trial testimony regarding the lamp.

"Mrs. Reinbolt, do you recall you giving trial testimony regarding the vase or the lamp that was in the Rhoads house? Tell me how the vase got into this?" Metnick asked.

"Yes, I did . . . because the police . . . Well actually, it was Jim Parrish who did that. They kept asking over and over about a vase or a lamp being broken, and I'm like . . . Since I'm not knowing anything, don't know. It would be like I'd say, I don't know what your talking about, and then they would come up with, well, there was a broken vase or a broken lamp there. And then I'd say okay, so there was, and then they'd go on and say, well, there was a piece by the door, or Herbie had a piece in his hand, or Dyke had a piece of this broken vase or lamp in his hand. And that's how that came in," Reinbolt admitted.

Franklin D. Roosevelt once said that, "Repetition does not transform a lie into the truth," and in 2004, Reinbolt told the Illinois Attorney General's Office, McFatridge and the two investigators manipulated and fabricated her testimony about the lamp. Reinbolt admitted they put her through several intense mock trials in order to get the lamp story straight for her trial testimony, telling the Attorney General's Office, "It didn't much matter to me what it was . . . I got tired of arguing with them."

McFatridge used the same tactics to give Herrington credibility in order to establish he was in the Rhoads' bedroom that night. Herrington claimed while he was in the Rhoads bedroom, he reached down, grabbed a pillow and "throwed [sic] it" on Karen's face. During closing arguments, McFatridge claimed Herrington's knowledge of the pillow therefore made him a credible witness. Dr. Michael Baden's affidavit also refuted Herrington's account of the pillow:

> I am of the opinion, based on a reasonable degree of medical certainty, that it is highly improbable for Darrell Herrington to have "throwed" the pillow over the face of Karen Rhoads, as he described in his trial testimony, after he was allegedly shown the dead victims. It is my opinion that the pillow was forced over the face of Karen Rhoads <u>while she was alive</u> and was used by her attacker to suppress the screams . . .

Baden based this assumption around several facts including neighbor Ollie Campbell's 4:00 a.m. report of a woman screaming that suddenly stopped. Baden's theory was further evidenced by the existence of defensive wounds on Karen's "left hand, wrist and arm," and since Karen was able to fight her attackers, " . . . she would have been able to scream and would have likely called out," but couldn't because the pillow was suppressing her screams. Additionally, Baden said the crime scene diagram and the disarray of the bed " . . . is consistent with a struggle that took place on the bed." And finally:

> A woman's pair of broken eye glasses, smeared with blood splatter, was found on the bed quilt relative to the location of Karen's head

and indicated that the pillow was applied to her face with sufficient force to cause her glasses to break during the attack.

This brought up yet another contradiction—the screams. When Herrington was outside, he reported hearing a man screaming, "Please don't kill me!" In another account, Herrington placed himself in the downstairs hallway, hearing the murders in progress, with Karen screaming, "Please don't kill me!" At the very same time, Reinbolt claimed she was holding Karen down, and Karen was screaming, "Oh, God! Oh, God!" So whose account was accurate? Or better yet, was either account accurate?

Reinbolt also suffered from several convenient "blackouts" during her depiction of the crime scene. Despite her blackouts, "Reinbolt described the bedroom before leaving as seeing the mattress on some angle for some reason and Dyke lying on the right side of the floor between the bed and the bedroom door.... Karen was lying off the bed towards the foot and left side of the bed." Reinbolt then told investigators that "... she also remembers something about a shower in the house but remembers nothing more about the shower."

A direct contradiction to this was Herrington's account: "Herrington stated that Steidl took him into the bedroom at which time he walked through a door and about fell across what he thought was a male subject laying on the floor..." Herrington then told investigators that he "... observed a female laying at a 45 degree angle across the bed with blood all over her.... [He] observed that the female had no top on but had short pants on."

Herrington's depiction of the crime scene vastly contradicted Reinbolt's because in her version, she had both Dyke and Karen's bodies lying nude on the floor immediately after she allegedly watched them get murdered. That concurred with how the firemen found the couple, both were nude and both on the floor.

Herrington said he was shown the crime scene after the couple was already murdered. He said Dyke was on the floor and Karen was on the bed partially clothed. So how did Karen's nude body that Reinbolt saw during the murders go from the floor back up to the bed and get partially clothed? After murdering the couple would the killers take the time to put clothes back on the victim and put her back on the bed?

Illinois State Police Crime Scene Technician Gary Knight's report confirmed the depiction of the crime scene. Knight's report read that firemen found "... the bodies of [Dyke and Karen] ... lying on the bedroom floor in the upstairs southwest bedroom." This placement of the bodies was confirmed by the outline created by the smoke damage and soot from the fire that outlined the bodies on the carpet. Another unanswered contradiction in this questionable investigation.

Still the biggest thing gnawing at me was why didn't Herrington or Reinbolt ever report seeing one another at the murder scene? They said they were both present in the house during the murders, yet never once do they mention seeing one another and not one report documented either eyewitness ever seeing one another at the murder scene.

In a phone conversation, I asked Charlie McGrew why, and as usual, I received the same reply I always got from McGrew, "What the fuck? Are you working for the fucking defense, now?" Ignoring his hostility, it was a question I wanted answered, and McGrew had an excuse ready. He claimed they never saw one another because Reinbolt was taking a shower. In fact, McGrew claimed, "They all took showers." He was referring to an interview report with Penny Cash, an ex-girlfriend of Steidl's, who told investigators, " . . . she had heard Randy Steidl make the comment to Herbert Whitlock that they had taken a shower in the basement of the Rhoads residence after the homicide." The shower was in the Rhoads' basement but Reinbolt still would've had to walk down the stairs past Herrington. So, was this shower scenario even plausible, and after all the screaming and fighting, would the killers actually take the time to shower in the victims' home?

My next series of questions infuriated McGrew even more when I asked why didn't the investigators document Reinbolt taking a shower and what did she do with her bloody clothes after taking the shower?

The same questions applied to Steidl and Whitlock, too. Given the accounts of arguing with Herrington outside the Rhoads' residence, covered in blood, Whitlock driving around, covered in blood, to get gas . . . when did they have time to shower, I asked?

"Fuck you, motherfucker! Fuck you! You'll see! We got the right guys!" McGrew angrily lashed out.

I saw no use in continuing to talk to McGrew about his unbelievable scenario and knew it was useless to ask any more questions. If they took a shower though, investigators could've had crime scene technicians look for evidence of hair or blood in the shower. This evidence would have definitely placed the defendants at the crime scene if they were really there. I didn't need to ask McGrew that question, because Reinbolt's own story already answered that and contradicted McGrew's outlandish shower scenario. In her interviews with investigators, Reinbolt had claimed:

> [The morning after the murders] Debbie stated that Herb and
> Randy came down by the house and that Herb had blood on him
> and that Herb threatened Debbie not to say anything and if some-

thing happened he will say there was another woman involved and
not use Debra's name.

So, with McGrew's and Cash's account of how they all took showers in the Rhoads'
basement, Reinbolt's own report contradicted the State's undocumented shower
scenario, because hours after the murders, Reinbolt, in her own words, said Whitlock came to her house and had "blood on him." Then again, maybe Reinbolt had
used all the soap.

At the time of the Rhoads murders, DNA was not available, and future DNA
testing of blood and hair fibers found at the crime scene never linked Steidl or
Whitlock to the Rhoads murders. But for now, as I continued to read the case
file and compare it with Clutter's information, I was amazed the investigators
and prosecutor had used these two eyewitnesses and their fabricated evidence
to prosecute the two men. The two eyewitnesses obviously lacked any credibility
whatsoever; and as far as I was concerned, by this time, neither did the original
investigators or prosecutor.

CHAPTER 8

GUILTY BEYOND A REASONABLE DOUBT?

———————■———————

While writing about the Rhoads case, noted *Chicago Tribune* columnist Eric Zorn observed:

> I'm told I'm naive to expect prosecutors in an adversarial system of justice to seek the truth rather than victory and to go wherever the evidence leads them. Until now, this story seemed to underscore that naiveté and serve yet another frightening example of how the engine of the State, once in motion can roll right over the innocent as well as the guilty.

Eric Zorn was right, and despite the many contradictions in the eyewitness' stories, the lack of corroboration, the fabricated evidence, the leads ignored, the blatant distortion of the truth and the witnesses who were ignored, Randy Steidl and Herb Whitlock were charged with the murders of Dyke and Karen Rhoads.

Both men were arrested for the murders on February 19, 1987. Without one piece of legitimate evidence, a fingerprint or a drop of blood linking either man to the scene of the crime, despite alibi witnesses and despite their adamant denials, the case against them was made based on the statements of the two eyewitnesses, Darrell Herrington and Debbie Reinbolt, and on the theory of a "drug deal gone bad" between Dyke Rhoads and the two men.

Initially, other than Reinbolt, there was never any physical or circumstantial evidence to indicate the murder of Dyke and Karen Rhoads was over any drug deal gone bad. There were rumors spread that Dyke was involved in clandestine drug running trips from Florida to Paris, but family members said Dyke never went to Florida except once when he was a little boy on family vacation. Not one person claimed Dyke ever dealt drugs. One witness, a self-admitted drug dealer in Paris, stated, " . . . the media surrounding the case suggested Dyke and Karen Rhoads were killed because they were involved in the distribution and trafficking of illegal drugs. [He] stated that was so far from the truth that it was laughable."

However, State's Attorney Mike McFatridge used unsubstantiated testimony from Steidl's estranged ex-wife to infer otherwise. While Randy had no history of drug involvement, his ex-wife was no stranger to the cocaine or methamphetamine crowds and was self-admittedly associated with the Sons of Silence motorcycle gang. In an ISP investigative interview, she admitted, "she is an addict," and her drug of choice was meth.

Debbie (Hopper) Steidl, Randy's ex-wife was interviewed by Eckerty and Parrish twice during the investigation—once on October 1, 1986, and again on February 20, 1987. During those interviews, she never once mentioned any drug involvement by her ex-husband, Randy. Yet interestingly, while Randy's trial was in progress, she was interviewed a third time on June 9, 1987, by Detective Parrish. Now Debbie Steidl *suddenly and conveniently* remembered that, in either May or June of 1986, Randy told her he was planning to drive a semi to Florida for a drug deal that was arranged by Herb Whitlock. She also *suddenly* remembered Randy once walked into the tavern where she worked and showed her a gun and a bag of cocaine.

These were first time accounts, and investigators never questioned why she failed to mention these incidents before and why—all of a sudden—*her* drug-induced memory had conveniently improved.

McFatridge also utilized another ex-girlfriend who testified Steidl once made a statement he sold cocaine "to all the bigwigs in Paris." These accounts by both women were unsubstantiated, yet McFatridge used this information at trial to impugn Randy Steidl's character. Other than Reinbolt's wild story, these unsubstantiated allegations were the extent of linking Steidl to any type of drug trafficking, but by creating this image, McFatridge was able to infuriate the jury into accepting the motive for the Rhoads murders as a drug deal gone bad.

Margaret Lynn Magers, a juror during Steidl's trial, believed the unsubstantiated allegations of drug dealing deprived Steidl of a fair trial. According to the

Post Conviction Petition, "At one point during the deliberations, she [Magers] expressed an opinion that the State had failed to prove Mr. Steidl guilty beyond a reasonable doubt," but another juror replied, "What difference does it make if he killed those people? How many other people has he killed with his cocaine?" McFatridge's strategy obviously worked.

Yet, Randy Steidl, the alleged drug dealer, just two weeks prior to the Rhoads murders, had gone to the FBI with information of corruption and narcotics trafficking in Paris.

The FBI report I read was filled with names and allegations of political corruption, gambling and narcotics trafficking. In fact, many of Steidl's allegations were directed at State's Attorney Mike McFatridge, the man who was prosecuting him. If Randy Steidl was a drug dealer, why did he go to the FBI about narcotics trafficking and want to draw attention to Paris? And then two weeks later commit a murder over narcotics? In the Post Conviction Relief Petition on behalf of Steidl, his attorney, Michael Metnick, stated:

> An all encompassing police investigation failed to reveal any evidence, physical, eyewitness or circumstantial, of Mr. Rhoads and Mr. Whitlock being involved in drug dealing with one another. The Rhoads telephone records, bank accounts, lifestyle, and personal belongings do not reveal any involvement of any drug trafficking. The prosecution, however, seized on Ms. Reinbolt's uncorroborated testimony and used it to inject highly prejudicial testimony regarding alleged other drug usage and dealing by Mr. Steidl.

Upset that Dyke's name and character were impugned as a drug dealer, the Rhoads family concurred with Metnick's assessment. During the investigation, family members approached McFatridge with these concerns, but they were ignored. Instead, they said McFatridge intimidated family members by waving the bloody crime scene photos of Dyke and Karen in their faces. He didn't want their questions, because they were already on their way to railroading the two local barflies.

"Do you want the guys who did this to get away with it?" McFatridge chastised.

How ironic. I reflected on all of the reports I had seen regarding State's Attorney Mike McFatridge and his *alleged* cocaine use and trafficking. I personally sat in on an FBI interview when a man we interviewed said McFatridge was a heavy cocaine user. The man, who wished to remain anonymous, said McFatridge was associated with known local drug dealers and one of his friends, he claimed, had a picture of McFatridge snorting cocaine.

On September 20, 2000, one of my own agents wore a body wire for ATF in another Paris murder investigation. During the recorded conversation, I listened to an upset father telling my agent he would blow the lid off Paris if his two sons were convicted for the murder, and he threatened that he even had pictures of Mike McFatridge snorting cocaine with one of his sons, Jerry Board.

In 2001, Secretary of State Police interviewed a subject who claimed he had delivered a kilo of cocaine to an attorney named "McFetridge" in Danville, Illinois. The attorney was driving a red Pontiac Grand Am. Coincidentally, McFatridge went to work in Danville after he was the Edgar County State's Attorney and—not that it infers any guilt—the ISP intelligence profile on Mike McFatridge indicated he owned a 1995 Pontiac Grand Am.

In 2002, we received a report from Inspector Troy Wesley regarding the interview of a former Sons of Silence biker named Scott Gones. The report read in part, "Gones said he has been previously told by Donny Comstock, Jerry Board, Dale Peterson and possibly Mike Plew all from the Paris, Illinois, area they have sold or otherwise been involved with State's Attorney McFatridge in distributing controlled substances."

Even in 2004, McFatridge's name was again linked to alleged cocaine use. When state police investigators interviewed Mike Dunlap, his report read in part:

> Whitlock maintained he was set up by the State's Attorney, Mike McFatridge and Jim Parrish, Paris Police Department. Dunlap recalled that sometime between 1987 and 1989, he attended a party at a home on Pembroke Street, in Paris, Illinois. While at the party he had occasion to observe Mike McFatidge snorting what Dunlap believed to be cocaine. Dunlap stated that the cocaine was located on the top of a baby grand piano.

Even more ironic were two FBI reports from 1986 and 1987, one from approximately two weeks before Dyke and Karen were killed when Steidl and Whitlock went to the Danville FBI office. The reason was to file a report against McFatridge and others regarding corruption, gambling and narcotics trafficking in Paris. A partially censored FBI report read, "Concerning drugs in the Paris area, Steidl advised that in August, 1985, he went to a party on East Crawford in Paris . . ." and witnessed a cocaine transaction between McFatridge and the party's host. The report, filled with redacted names, continued:

> Steidl advised that it was his understanding from [censored name] that [censored name] got his cocaine supply from McFatridge and

[censored name]. Steidl advised McFatridge and [censored name] are the main suppliers of cocaine in the Paris area, and that McFatridge is a user of cocaine himself. Steidl advised that the cocaine brought in by [censored name] and McFatridge is distributed through [censored name], another friend of McFatridge. Steidl advised he feels [censored name] who is a businessman with many connections, is the one who actually gets the cocaine brought into the area, and McFatridge gets a percentage on the sale of the cocaine in the area in exchange for McFatridge not pursuing any criminal investigations.

Years later Randy Steidl confirmed to me that the "censored name" of the businessman he gave to the FBI was Bob Morgan. Like McFatridge's allegations against Steidl, these were all unsubstantiated reports which were never investigated or proven true. Yet ironically, McFatridge used the unsubstantiated testimonies of a pissed off ex-wife and ex-girlfriend to link Randy Steidl to narcotics trafficking and a subsequent death penalty.

It was the blatant omission of information never documented by investigators that also continued to make me suspect Steidl and Whitlock were railroaded. On September 9, 1986, James Parrish interviewed Mike Dunlap regarding an incident he observed shortly after the murder of the Rhoads. Parrish's report read: " . . . that he [Dunlap] and his sons were at a creek next to his residence. Mike stated that Herschel Wright and two other male subjects were at the slab doing cocaine."

Herschel Wright was a member of the Sons of Silence motorcycle gang. His brother, Randy Wright, also a member of the motorcycle gang, was arrested for the murder of an Edgar County Deputy. The sheriff's deputy was bound and tied to railroad tracks—the power of a huge locomotive used as the murder weapon to scatter his body parts for miles. Randy Wright was arrested but later acquitted for this heinous murder and the deputy's death remains yet another unsolved homicide to this day.

Parrish's interview with Dunlap continued:

Mike stated that Herschel had fingernail scratches on his chest . . . [and] a very large gash between his nipple and left arm pit. . . . the wound was very fresh because the wound was red and inflamed. Mike stated that the wound appeared to be serious enough for stiches [sic] but Herschel appeared not to have had any treatment for the wounds. . . . the gash was approximately 3-31/2" in length.

Mike stated the two subjects with Herschel were described as No. 1 subject, heavy set, long hair and dirty; No. 2 subject was clean shaven, fairly short black hair with a small amount of grey [sic] and dark complected. Mike stated the two subjects were in a new Dodge window van with a luggage rack on the top [that] had two or three different colors and he did not know the other two subjects with Herschel Wright at the time.

Despite Dunlap's information of what he observed just days after the Rhoads murders, investigators never bothered to interview Herschel Wright and they never attempted to identify the two men doing cocaine with Wright. They didn't need to, because Mike Dunlap had actually told Jim Parrish and Mike McFatridge the identity of the two men—information Parrish purposefully excluded from his report. Eckerty had told me once Darrell Herrington came forward, "McFatridge steered us away from all the other suspects." So why did McFatridge want to steer investigators away from all the other suspects? Years later, maybe I learned why . . . and I also learned about Parrish and McFatridge's deceitful omissions from Dunlap's 1986 interview.

Dunlap's report had always bothered me, and in 2004, state police investigators interviewed Michael Dunlap a second time. It was a lead I had always wanted to explore, and what Dunlap told investigators only confirmed my suspicions about the obvious misconduct I suspected in the original investigation.

ISP investigators learned Dunlap had actually identified the two men doing cocaine with Hershel Wright to Parrish and McFatridge. According to the report, one of the men he described to Parrish and McFatridge " . . . was dressed in a Hawaiian type flowered shirt . . . " and Dunlap identified " . . . this person to be Bob Morgan." The third man was "another biker-type person" who Dunlap was not sure but whose description fit that of another Sons of Silence enforcer named Dale Peterson. Dunlap said McFatridge wanted nothing to do with this information, and they turned him away as McFatridge told him "they already had the right guys." One of those "guys" was Herbert Whitlock.

At one time, Whitlock was a close friend with Mike Dunlap. Dunlap told the ISP investigators in 2004 that shortly after the Rhoads murders, Whitlock showed up on his doorstep—distraught and crying, and said he thought he was being set up to take the fall for the Rhoads murders. When Dunlap told Whitlock he should go to the State's Attorney's office or the police, Whitlock responded that they were all part of the set up. Mike Dunlap was never called to testify, and Parrish's interview report had purposefully excluded information identifying Bob Morgan who was already identified as a suspect in the original investigation. A suspect who, for whatever reason, investigators continually seemed to ignore. A suspect who Steidl and Whitlock had gone to the FBI and linked to cocaine trafficking with McFatridge. Obviously, Dunlap's testimony would have shed doubt on the guilt of Steidl and Whitlock, but Parrish and McFatridge had once again deceitfully altered informtaion.

It was no secret Bob Morgan was a suspect in the initial stages of the investigation, and here was a man giving police specific information that Bob Morgan, an affluent businessman, was doing cocaine with two Sons of Silence bikers just days after the Rhoads murders and they ignored this information. The encounter also divulged a suspicious wound across the chest of Herschel Wright. Yet even after the 2004 interview with Dunlap, the question still remained why did McFatridge and Parrish purposefully exclude Morgan's name from Dunlap's report?

In the years following the trials, several other witnesses came forward and said their information was also ignored, never documented, or altered by police. Some witnesses claimed they were intimidated. Some said they were intimidated into lying.

Carol Robinson was one of the witnesses who claimed she was manipulated and intimidated by Parrish and Eckerty into corroborating Herrington's bar-hopping accounts. She said McFatridge also took part in the manipulation. In her 1992 affidavit, she stated:

> During the trial, I had to meet with State's Attorney Michael McFatridge prior to testifying. I told the State's Attorney I didn't think I could remember what date I saw Herrington and Steidl. I told the State's Attorney I didn't think Randy could have been involved in the murders on the night I saw him with Herrington because he was so drunk. Mr. McFatridge replied, "Hey, young lady, you just answer the questions." He was trying to get me to say the date was July 5. I said, "No, I can't remember the date." I told him, "I'm not going to lie." Mr. McFatridge replied, "Never mind about that; I'll give you the date. You just testify about seeing them together that one time." Mr. McFatridge said, "You'd be telling the truth, right? It's up to the other attorney to see through it." I was very upset about it. . . . I was too worried about lying. I remember waiting for Randy's attorney to question me if I was certain of the date, but he never did.

The State's Attorney's scheme was supported by trial testimony. Under direct examination, McFatridge asked Carol Robinson:

McFatridge: Now, calling your attention to the evening hours of Saturday, July 5, 1986, were you tending bar at that time?

Robinson: I work every night except for Sunday.

McFatridge: And do you recall serving Darrel Herrington and Randy Steidl?

Robinson: Yeah.

McFatridge: And were they together?

Robinson: Yeah.

McFatridge's manipulative questioning inferred to the jury that Robinson saw Herrington and Steidl together on July 5, 1986, thus, corroborating Herrington's deceitful tale. In actuality, Robinson told McFatridge, "I really did not remember when they came in; it is possible I witnessed this incident in September of 1986. But again, I cannot be certain of the date." But the truth didn't matter to McFatridge. His strategy was to distort the truth.

McFatridge was equally manipulative in utilizing the testimony of witnesses like Elaine Armstrong and Charles McClaskey. A report by Eckerty reflected that Elaine Armstrong saw Whitlock at her bar, Joe's Lounge, in the early evening hours of July 5, 1986, but she never saw Randy Steidl. She remembered Herrington was "in and out" of Joe's Lounge and " . . . he was pretty drunk." Yet in Herrington's account, he was drinking with Randy Steidl at Joe's Lounge for most of the evening. Ignoring this contradictory information, McFatridge instead used Armstrong for more devious purposes. Eckerty's report stated that sometime before the murders, Steidl told Armstrong, "There is something big coming down next weekend and it's so big that [no one can] stop it." Another report from witness Charles McClaskey stated Steidl told him, ". . . he [Steidl] was leaving town because there was going to be some heavy shit coming down around the 4th [of July]."

When McFatridge called Armstrong and McClaskey to testify, it was for the specific purpose of making inference about Steidl's statement that something big was coming down meant the murder of Dyke and Karen Rhoads. McFatridge used Elaine Armstrong's trial testimony to make this point.

"Steidl said something was going to happen the next weekend, something terrible, that it would scare the whole town." Armstrong testified.

This testimony embellished what Armstrong was quoted as saying in Eckerty's report, and Steidl's attorney failed to address Armstrong's exaggerated version.

When Steidl said "something big" was about to happen, he was referencing his recent meeting with the FBI, and his remarks to McClaskey and Armstrong expressed his belief the FBI was going to act on the information he had provided them.

After Steidl and Whitlock were arrested, even the FBI agent they went to, Special Agent Ken Temples, admitted it was " . . . odd that two guys would come in like that and then be accused of a double homicide." And Temples was right . . . why would two men go to the FBI, providing allegations of narcotics trafficking, if they were involved in it, too?

Coincidentally, the man Steidl and Whitlock accused of corruption and narcotics trafficking, Mike McFatridge, ended up prosecuting them for the Rhoads murders. And Steidl and Whitlock were not suspects until Herrington came forward and after that, like Eckerty said, "McFatridge steered us away from all the other suspects." Coincidently, one of those suspects was Bob Morgan, who Steidl and Whitlock claimed was the businessman McFatridge was protecting in narcotics trafficking. In fact, Steidl later told the FBI he believed that Morgan was paying a large sum of money to Herrington to testify against them. If this were all true, this could be a huge conspiracy of corruption, and Bill Clutter later provided me with chilling evidence that Steidl might be right.

McFatridge had also cut deals with criminals charged with heinous sex crimes—such as Della Wakefield—to corroborate Debbie Reinbolt's testimony. And he used jail house snitches to testify against Steidl. According to the June 10, 1987, *Paris Beacon-News*:

> Lester Wells, an inmate at the Edgar County Jail, testified for the prosecution . . . According to Wells, Steidl did not specifically admit he was responsible for the deaths. However, Steidl said the young couple died because they failed to pay for some drugs brought back from Florida, and the fire was set not to destroy evidence of the murder but "to give a message to others who were trying to rip them off."

McFatridge and the investigators also spent a lot of time manipulating and coaching their two eyewitnesses. Herrington was not only caught in a lie in his initial story to police, he failed his polygraph "miserably." McFatridge purposely manipulated this evidence of Herrington's deceit and never disclosed it to the defense. Prior to the trials of Steidl and Whitlock, McFatridge took—along with various other reports—Darrell Herrington's failed polygraph report, and placed them in a court sealed envelope. This sealed envelope—filled with other exculpatory information, like the eyewitnesses' mental health records—was never disclosed to the defense. Years later, in 2005, an investigator from Bill Clutter's office discovered all those reports hidden away in that sealed envelope.

Besides McFatridge's blatant manipulation and failure to disclose exculpatory information, he also failed to inform the defense that Herrington and Reinbolt were promised compensation for being the State's witnesses.

In Steidl's Post Conviction, Attorney Michael Metnick stated, most " . . . egregious, however, was the failure of Mr. McFatridge to divulge to the defense that the local chief of police agreed to pay Mr. Herrington $100 per day for his assistance, and that Mr. Herrington was seeking help from the chief to have his driver's license reinstated."

Reinbolt also cut a deal with the State—a deal to stay out of prison and money from the prosecutor who, according to Metnick, " . . . had an absolute obligation to reveal these promises of payment to defense counsel. They failed to do so."

Debbie Reinbolt was promised and paid a good chunk of money for a woman who helped murder a young girl by holding her down while two men tortured and stabbed her to death! Why would anyone ever pay any amount of money to a murderer—a person who confessed to participating in such a brutal and horrible crime? State's Attorney McFatridge later testified about the money paid to Reinbolt and " . . . that he made the decision to give $2,500 in relocation money to Deborah Reinbolt."

A receipt entitled "Witness Protection Relocation" read as follows:

> The undersigned, Deborah I. Reinbolt, agrees that $2,500.00 constitutes the full and complete amount of monies received and reasonably necessary for the relocation of herself and family to be allocated as follows:
>   1. $600.00 to be received . . . by Deborah Reinbolt.
>   2. $900.00 to be paid to her landlord for past-due rent.
>   3. $1,000.00 to be retained by Detective James Parrish paid to Deborah I. Reinbolt . . .

Despite the money being provided allegedly for relocation purposes, some of it was used to pay back rent, not relocation. Also, Reinbolt was headed to prison; her relocation was a five-year sentence at Dwight Correctional Facility. McFatridge and Parrish also stumbled over their testimony regarding who actually paid her. Under oath, Detective James Parrish testified:

> . . . that the relocation money came out of the State's Attorney Office and he believes it was paid to Deborah Reinbolt's husband and

daughter and not directly to Deborah Reinbolt. He has no recollection regarding paragraph three of the [above] receipt nor does
he have any recollection as to whether he held any money pursuant
to that paragraph.

McFatridge testified he " . . . categorically denies that Deborah Reinbolt was
promised any money before or during trial and denies that she was ever provided
compensation in exchange for her trial testimony." Yet Reinbolt's recantation contradicted McFatridge and Parrish regarding the monies given to her.

"The only money that was ever received, and I guess you can say I received
it, I turned it over to my husband, the day I was sentenced . . . I think it was before
the trial . . . I think, because they [McFatridge and Eckerty] gave it to Jim Parrish
to lock up in the safe at the police department . . . If anybody asked me was I to be
given any money from them, just to say, 'not to my knowledge,' because I hadn't
been given any money," Reinbolt explained to Michael Metnick.

There was other evidence McFatridge and Parrish lied about the payment
to Reinbolt. The proof sat right in front of me in the state police case file: a payment of $2,500, not from State's Attorney McFatridge's office—as he and Parrish
testified—but from the Illinois State Police to Debbie Reinbolt. The payment receipt of $2,500 in the ISP case file was signed by Jack Eckerty, badge number 1208,
and Charlie McGrew, badge number 1593. And the money was paid to Reinbolt
on August 20, 1987, five days before she was sentenced.

Never in all my years in the state police had I ever seen or heard of my
department paying any money to a person who confessed to helping brutally
murder anyone! But, right there in front of me was the signed receipt by Eckerty
and McGrew. I was dumbfounded and ashamed that they paid $2,500 to this
drug-crazed woman who admitted holding Karen Rhoads down while the poor
girl was stabbed 26 times! That certainly wasn't Integrity, Service and Pride in
my book.

It was State's Attorney McFatridge's duty to disclose to the defense that both
witnesses were compensated for their testimonies, but the State never revealed
this information to the defense. The *Paris Beacon-News*, covering Herb Whitlock's
trial, stated:

According to the instructions to the jury given by presiding Judge
James K. Robinson . . . a person is guilty of murder if he or she "aids
or abets" in the act. In other words, according to Edgar County
State's Attorney Michael McFatridge, even if someone simply is

"there" or participates in any manner—even detaining a victim—
that person can be found guilty of murder.

Yet ironically, the article continues, "Reinbolt, who pled guilty to the concealment
of a homicide, testified, 'I was there. I participated,'" adding that she, " . . . loaned
Whitlock the knife used to murder the couple."

But according to Reinbolt's recantations, the prosecution promised to cut
her another deal at sentencing.

"What did you plead guilty to?" Metnick asked Reinbolt.

"Concealment of a homicide by destroying or altering physical evidence, with
the knowledge that Dyke and Karen Rhoads died by homicidal means . . . The plea
agreement arose out of, you know, if I would agree to testify against Herbie and
Randy, then they would enter into this plea agreement with me . . . Jim and Jack
just kept saying over and over, well you are probably going to come out smelling
like a rose on this," Reinbolt responded.

McFatridge had recommended Reinbolt avoid any prison time for her part
in the Rhoads murders, but his promise of probation backfired. An outraged citizenry circulated a petition pressuring the judge to sentence Reinbolt to five years
in the penitentiary.

In Reinbolt's words, " . . . they [the Paris citizens] felt that I, having been
involved in the murder, I was getting special treatment from McFatridge, Parrish
and Eckerty, and . . . I wasn't being prosecuted like they thought I should have
been, or charged like they thought I should have been."

The citizens' outrage that Reinbolt received "special treatment" was not as
far-fetched as her statement inferred. And another red flag in this case shocked me
once again when I learned Eckerty, Parrish and McFatridge made sure they stayed
in touch with their star eyewitness during her incarceration. Not only did they
occasionally visit Reinbolt in prison, they corresponded to her with personal letters. I was astounded at the correspondence I read between Reinbolt and her law
enforcement buddies. A two-page letter addressed to "Debra Reinbolt [at] Dwight
Correction Center" from Detective Jim Parrish read in part:

> Dear Debbie, Yes, I know I haven't written, and yes I know you're
> upset. What can I say, I'm sorry. We have been very busy with
> burglaries, but I should have taken time. How have you been do-
> ing? I hope fine, from all reports that I've heard, you are doing
> fine and working for the warden. . . . Sometime in the near future,
> Eckerty and I are going to drive up and see you and spend some

time.... Darryll [sic] is doing fine and going about town as nothing ever happened and working every day. Darryll [sic] is still drinking as if who thought he would stop.... I am thinking about you even though I don't write very often. See you soon. Sincerely, Jim.

This was unbelievable! Here was a convicted felon who allegedly helped in a brutal double murder and the detective who helped put her in prison was writing her *sympathy* letters. "I am thinking about you even though I don't write very often"? "What can I say, I'm sorry"? "Sincerely Jim"? In all my years in law enforcement, I never stayed in touch with or wrote one letter to someone I helped put in prison. Especially a murderer! Parrish's letter reeked of sentiment, and later I learned there might be more than just sentiment to their obviously close relationship.

Shockingly, it wasn't only the investigators who also visited Reinbolt in prison. An excerpt from a second letter dated May 6, 1988, from Reinbolt to Mike McFatridge read:

> Mike, I want to thank you for your recent visit [April 27, 1988] ... I would like to apologize for my attitude and for not making much sense the day you were here ... it just seems to get harder for me by the day, and I'm slowly losing hope ... is it possible to go before the prison review board and have my time cut ... have you approached Judge Pearman yet?

That summer of 1987, McFatridge arrogantly went to trial using the words of Herrington and Reinbolt to help convict Steidl and Whitlock. In his closing arguments at Steidl's trial, McFatridge stated, "What makes Debra Reinbolt and Darrell Herrington so believable is what they don't say. Sure there were 10,000 rumors at that time. How was it they picked out the 10 rumors that were right? Why weren't they wrong?"

By this time in my review, it was pretty obvious the police and prosecutor had induced, manipulated and intimidated these two pathetic alcoholics into their bizarre and contradictory stories. And with some beer, whiskey and promises of money and favors, along with several mock trials, Herrington and Reinbolt were indeed able to pick out "the 10 rumors that were right."

CHAPTER 9

THE DEFENSE RESTS

———————————■———————————

Gordon Randy Steidl was described as a rugged-looking barfly who had gotten into his fair share of barroom scuffles. No one interviewed depicted him as a bully or someone they feared. When he spoke, it was straight forward, mincing few words. Most of the people interviewed considered him a friend, and he appeared to be well-liked in the community. With blonde hair and blue eyes, he also dated his share of the local women. At the time of his arrest, he was just 35 years old. Prior to the murders, he was never charged with a felony and his criminal convictions consisted of six misdemeanors over a 10 year period from 1974 to 1984. The convictions were offenses typical of a barroom brawler, such as breaking the public peace, criminal damage to property and assault. Randy Steidl was never arrested nor had any history linking him to any type of drug involvement.

Herbert R. Whitlock, Jr. was born and raised in Paris and was 41 years old when he was arrested for the murders. He was also depicted as a local barfly and was known around town as a small time drug dealer. According to some, he was good for picking up some pot, a gram of cocaine, or maybe even an eight ball now and then. Whitlock had a felony cocaine possession charge at the time of his arrest for the Rhoads murders.

Whitlock had no criminal history for violence. Instead, he was described by many as a man who walked away when faced with a physical confrontation. Whitlock was a thin and wiry man at 5'9" with only 150 pounds on his lean frame. Other than the felony drug charge, he had one misdemeanor arrest for obstructing police and one for a verbal assault.

Steidl and Whitlock also had alibi witnesses for the night of the murders. On the day of July 5, 1986, Steidl was in Peoria, attending a family function where more than 150 family members were present. Randy wanted to stay the night, but his mother insisted they drive back to Paris so she could attend church the next morning. Randy reluctantly drove back to Paris that evening.

Years later, he told me if he had only stayed in Peoria that night, he would've had 150 alibi witnesses, then he good-naturedly joked, "But this was Paris, so they probably still would've convicted my ass." Randy said he didn't arrive back in Paris until later in the evening, and he didn't make it out to the bars until later that night. Several witnesses confirmed that.

On December 1, 1986, investigators interviewed Marcia Edwards, a bartender at the Barn Tavern. Edwards remembered seeing Randy Steidl that night, and he was drinking rum and coke. Edwards also recalled Steidl was with two heavy set girls from Marshall, Illinois. She did not recall seeing Herrington, Reinbolt or Whitlock at the bar that night. Edwards identified Kathy Walters as the second bartender in the Barn Tavern that night, but investigators didn't bother to interview her.

Charles McClaskey said he saw Steidl at the Paris American Legion that night around 11:00 p.m. He said the two of them had a beer together, and he never saw Whitlock, Herrington or Reinbolt at the Legion. Deborah Walton also told investigators she danced with Randy Steidl at the American Legion between 10:30 and 11:00 p.m. Beecher and Carol Lynch said they saw Steidl at the American Legion and they also saw him leave the bar alone around 12 to 12:30 a.m. in his car.

The two heavy set girls from Marshall, Illinois, were identified as Chris Farris and Nanette Klein. An interview report indicated that on the night of July 5, 1986, Chris Farris told investigators she and two friends, Nanette Klein and "Julie Pershil," drove from Marshall to Paris. Both Klein and Farris told investigators they met Steidl and a Dennis Uselman at the Barn Tavern between 9:00 and 9:30 p.m. Herrington nor Reinbolt ever mentioned drinking at the Barn Tavern with Steidl or Whitlock that night.

Both girls said Steidl left the Barn an hour later for the American Legion, telling them he would meet them at the Horseshoe Club later that night. According to the girls and Dennis Uselman they met Steidl at the Horseshoe Club sometime after midnight, after other witnesses had Steidl leaving the American Legion. The four left the Horseshoe and went to Uselman's apartment where they sat around, drank beer and smoked "a marijuana joint."

Chris Farris told investigators that she and Randy went next door to his apartment where they split another beer and had sex twice. Nannette Klein told investigators that later on she went to Randy's apartment to get Farris, and had to wake the two of them up. She said Randy got up and told her he needed to mail his unemployment papers right away. Klein said Steidl left for approximately 5 to 10 minutes in his car, and then he returned. The two girls left his apartment around 3:30 a.m. and headed back to Marshall.

Dennis Uselman was also questioned by investigators, and he confirmed the same accounts given by Klein and Farris. The investigators' report also indicated that "Julie Pershil" was also with Klein and Farris at the Barn Tavern when they met Steidl. The investigators not only failed to interview "Pershil," they didn't even correctly identify her. Her real name was Julie Perisho.

One of the things McFatridge used was the information Steidl left his apartment on Sunday morning, July 6, 1986, to mail his unemployment papers. McFatridge suggested to the jury Steidl left his apartment to go and see why the fire had not started at the Rhoads' house. An important lead was to verify if Steidl did mail his unemployment papers, and investigators did go to the unemployment office and learned that Steidl's actions were nothing out of the ordinary.

In 1992, Bill Clutter confirmed this when he interviewed Deborah Geir, office manager of the Mattoon office for the Illinois Department of Employment Security, who stated that the earliest time an applicant can mail their unemployment certification is 12:01 a.m. on Sunday. Geir stated that in order for applicants to receive their checks faster, it was not unusual for people to mail their paperwork at the earliest possible time.

With no holes in the alibi witnesses' statements, McFatridge instead focused on the sex, drinking, drug use and the fact that Uselman was a "deaf mute" to cast doubt on their alibis, and it worked. Years later, Chris Farris " . . . stated that she remembers being told by McFatridge that if she and Klein were going to help the defense, he, McFatridge, was going to paint her and Klein as whores." Farris said "this was intimidating" and "characterized McFatridge as a 'Worm.'"

Herb Whitlock also had his share of alibi witnesses. Eva Jean Trover had refuted Reinbolt's allegations she witnessed an argument between Whitlock and Dyke Rhoads at her bar on July 5th.

"I remember being asked the same thing by Detective Parrish and Agent Eckerty. I told them the same thing I'm telling you now. Dyke Rhoads was never in my tavern with either Herb Whitlock or Debra Reinbolt," she later told Bill Clutter. Instead her information was purposefully distorted by investigators, and she was never called to testify.

Herb Whitlock's main alibi witness was Nancy Land. She advised investigators that on the night of July 5, 1986, around 9:30 p.m., she was having a beer at the

Friendly Tavern when she got a call from Whitlock. They met outside in the parking lot, and after that she drove them to the Whitlock family farm outside of Paris. They stayed there until approximately 12:30 to 1:00 a.m., and after showering and cleaning up, Whitlock asked Land to drive him to his parent's house in Paris. Land's interview obviously conflicted with both Herrington and Reinbolt's accounts and the timeline the state established for the murders. So Land was interviewed by investigators not once but three times, and she never once deviated from her story. Not happy with her unwavering account, investigators had her take a polygraph, one of only a few witnesses polygraphed during the entire investigation, and Nancy Land was much more truthful than Darrell Herrington ever was.

Whitlock's father, Herbert Whitlock, Sr., also corroborated Land's story when he said he was watching the Goodwill Games in the early morning hours of July 6, 1986, when his son arrived home. Father and son talked for a while and then he said Herb Jr. fell asleep on the sofa.

During his 1987 trial, Steidl was represented by attorney John Muller. Muller's performance as a defense attorney was pathetic if not somewhat suspect. I was shocked when I read Steidl's Post Conviction Relief Pettition. By 1995, Randy Steidl had a new attorney, Michael Metnick, and his Post Conviction Relief petition was 137 pages in length and was filled with witnesses never called who could have refuted Herrington and Reinbolt's weak and contradictory stories. Citing gross mistakes and negligence on the part of Muller, Metnick's motion asked the Supreme Court of Illinois to re-try Randy Steidl based on inadequate representation during his initial trial.

Muller's testimony addressed one of his inadequacies when he explained why he met so infrequently with Randy prior to his trial. Muller said he refused to visit Steidl at the Edgar County Jail because, "I prefer talking to them (clients) at the courthouse and it is a thirty mile drive from Charleston to Paris." Muller was paid a $32,000 retainer by Steidl's family, and he couldn't afford the gas to Paris? But Muller gave another reason why he didn't want to go to Paris.

> Muller: I would prefer to talk to him in a jury room, just the two of us than I would in a jail because I don't know who is listening in a jail.
>
> Metnick: Why?
>
> Muller: I don't know if they have the room bugged where I'm talking to him or not.
>
> Metnick: Were you concerned the room was bugged?

Muller: In Edgar County, I'm always concerned about that.

"Bugging" a room is a serious offense, yet here was a defense attorney in a capital murder case afraid to talk to his client because he feared the jail may be bugged! Was this Paris and its lawless reputation or just Muller's paranoia?

Muller's fear went well beyond his concerns that his conversations were being illegally bugged. During the trial, "Muller expressed a concern to Mr. Steidl and his family that he was being followed by a yellow Cadillac with Florida license plates." Muller testified that he was so "unnerved" he kept two guns with him during the trial for protection. Randy's half-brother, Rory Steidl, confirmed Muller once showed him a semi-automatic Tech-Nine machine gun he carried in his briefcase. So why would a defense attorney need to carry a gun in his briefcase?

Muller also related an account that not only unnerved but obviously terrified him. Muller was staying at a local motel outside of Charleston and "One night, at his hotel, Mr. Muller heard an engine racing." Muller looked out his motel window and observed the same yellow Cadillac El Dorado that had been following him— its bright lights shining into his motel room with the driver revving the engine. Muller testified, "I had a weapon with me and I opened the curtains and I held the weapon out, pointed to the vehicle at which point it dimmed its lights and backed out of the driveway."

Paula Myers, another potential witness who was ignored, said she met Muller at the courthouse during Steidl's trial. Myers wanted to tell him that Carol Robinson felt McFatridge and Parrish were intimidating her into lying on the stand. Myers said Muller was too unnerved to listen to her. In a recorded interview with Clutter, Paula Myers described her weird conversation with Muller:

> He said, Paula, I've had it. This is when I say I know he knew my name because he said, Paula, and he said, Paula, you know, I have had a yellow El Dorado come up to my motel room and pull onto the curb and point their lights into my window and flash their lights, and he said it had scared him and he had put the barrel of a gun outside the curtain to let them know that he had a gun in there because he thought it was someone trying to intimidate him or scare him and he told me that it had got to the point that his wife was walking around the house with a gun in her purse . . . scared.

"Did he sound scared on the phone?" Clutter asked her.
"He sounded terrified," she replied.

Unnerved and terrified certainly doesn't make for a very good defense attorney, especially in a capital murder case. Besides being terrified, Muller was also sloppy.

While representing Steidl, Muller used a former client, Michael Patrick Malone, as his "investigator" in the case. Malone owed Muller several thousand dollars for representing him on a misdemeanor charge and divorce case. Malone was introduced to the Steidl family as Muller's investigator, but after that first meeting, they never saw him again.

Malone was an investigator who, according to Muller " . . . doesn't write. He's dyslexic, he doesn't write very well. He speaks to you." In addition to the amateurish investigator, Muller refused to hire a forensic pathologist to refute "the Reinbolt Knife," and an arson expert who could've easily refuted Reinbolt's lamp testimony. With Muller ill-prepared and unnerved, McFatridge maneuvered his lies and cover ups right under the defense attorney's nose.

Herb Whitlock's 1987 trial attorney was Ronald Tulin from Charleston. Tulin is acknowledged as an accomplished, respected and well-known criminal defense attorney.

In 2005, Herb Whitlock, with his new defense team, Attorneys Richard Kling and Susana Ortiz, sought a new trial in Edgar County, and during that hearing Ron Tulin took the stand for the defense.

The *Chicago Tribune's* Hal Dardick reported on Tulin's testimony when he told the court, " . . . prosecutors failed to turn over documents they were required to reveal." Additionally, Tulin " . . . conceded that he made two significant mistakes at trial" regarding the evidence. Tulin was referring to the alleged murder weapon, the knife provided by Reinbolt, and the broken lamp. According to Tulin's testimony, "It would have been scientific evidence that what Reinbolt said was not true." Tulin said, "It has bothered me all these years. I just came over and told the truth today."

Tulin also didn't know that in 1987 the ISP was aware of another serious flaw in Reinbolt's story which affected his client. Stan Acklen was a sponsor for the Narcotics Anonymous meetings in Paris and was at the February 19, 1987, meeting attended by Reinbolt just two days after she came forward to police with her first story. Acklen witnessed Reinbolt ask two men to point out Herb Whitlock to her because she didn't know him. Acklen questioned how Reinbolt could know Whitlock on the night of the murders in July 1986 yet was unable to recognize him seven months later on February 19, 1987. Acklen said he didn't trust the local police so he reported his concerns to a state police investigator who also ignored him and his information was never documented.

Ron Tulin did call Acklen to testify during Whitlock's trial, and when referring to Reinbolt, he told the jury, "I wouldn't believe anything that woman told you!" But the judge intervened and "ordered the jury to disregard Acklen's observation about Reinbolt's believability."

During the Narcotics Anonymous meeting, Reinbolt was wearing a concealed body wire and recorded the conversation Acklen overheard between Reinbolt and the two men. In 2004, ISP investigators located and listened to that taped conversation and it confirmed Acklen's concerns, with Reinbolt plainly asking two unidentified men to point out Herb Whitlock to her. Reinbolt had admitted in her recantation she barely knew who Steidl or Whitlock were, and the overhear tape confirmed this, but that taped conversation was never disclosed by the police or prosecution. Instead the judge "read to the jury a partial transcript . . . of the 'eavesdropping'" operation which detailed the brief conversation between Reinbolt and Whitlock. While the transcript showed that Whitlock continually denied any involvement in the Rhoads murders, nothing was read from this transcript about Reinbolt not being able to identify Whitlock.

During an interview Tulin told me the only overhear tape he listened to was garbled and indiscernible. When I told him about the taped conversation where Reinbolt asked two men to identify Whitlock, he said that was never disclosed to him. Tulin said that information, along with Acklen's, would have definitely discredited Reinbolt to the jury. Tulin exclaimed that the investigators and McFatridge "did not play the game like it was supposed to be played. They withheld a lot of information. There are rules, Mike, and they broke them."

Ron Tulin was right. Withholding information favorable to the defense is a Brady violation and violates the Constitution of the United States. In 1963, the United States Supreme Court ruled in *Brady vs. Maryland* that any and all evidence, favorable or unfavorable, must be disclosed by the prosecution to the defense. And as I continued to review the Rhoads case, it was full of such Brady violations.

Steidl and Whitlock both took the stand during their trials and professed their innocence. Whitlock adamantly told the jury, "I did not stab anybody. . . . I did not kill Dyke Rhoads. I did not kill Karen Rhoads." He continued to vehemently maintain his innocence over the next 20 years.

Like Whitlock, Steidl adamantly maintained his innocence. Reports stated, "Steidl remained calm while on the stand . . . and maintained, 'I did not kill Dyke and Karen Rhoads.'" McFatridge countered to the jury, "What is Randy Steidl's defense? His defense is simply he denies everything."

The jury stalemated on a decision in Herb Whitlock's trial, so they eventually found him guilty of the murder of Karen and not guilty for the murder of Dyke. The jury wasn't convinced he had killed either one, so their rationale was to find him guilty of killing only one. Herb Whitlock was sentenced to life in prison.

Weeks later, on June 15, 1987, Randy Steidl was found guilty for the murders of both Dyke and Karen Rhoads. Upset over the verdict, Steidl declared, "It wasn't a trial. It was a lynching," and promised to appeal the verdict. Steidl also reacted physically.

The *Paris Beacon-News* headline for June 16, 1987, reported: "Defendant Attacks State's Attorney in Judge's Chambers." According to the article, "Steidl landed one blow on the side of the head of . . . Mike McFatridge . . . and was quickly wrestled outside the courtroom area."

Years later, when I finally met Randy Steidl face-to-face, he told me about the incident of slugging McFatridge in the judge's chambers. Randy snickered as he told the story. After landing the blow to McFatridge, he said the judge looked at him and said, "Son, you're in big trouble, now!"

Randy laughed, "Big trouble *now*? I was just convicted for a double murder and sentenced to death! What could be bigger trouble than that?"

Randy Steidl spent the next 12 years on Death Row, vehemently claiming he was innocent yet powerless to do anything about it. He lived each day wondering when the state was going to place him on a gurney and murder him, too. Randy said oftentimes when he went to sleep, he prayed for God not to let him wake up the next morning. Yet each morning, he woke up to the same fears and frustration, and continued to fight for his freedom.

In news reports following the trials, McFatridge praised Eckerty and Parrish for " . . . putting the case together." "These two men," according to McFatridge, "worked literally thousands of hours to make this guilty verdict possible."

McFatridge was right, by manipulating and juicing-up the two alcoholics, lying in reports and withholding evidence favorable to the defense, they had certainly put "the case together." And with the likes of Herrington and Reinbolt, I'm sure it probably took "thousands of hours."

Darrell Herrington and Debbie Reinbolt both recanted their trial testimony in 1989. This evidence was presented before the honorable Judge Paul C. Komada in a Petition for Post Judgment Relief filed on behalf of Steidl, but prior to the hearing, after McFatridge got to them, both Herrington and Reinbolt recanted their recantations.

Randy Steidl's appeal was subsequently denied by Judge Komada, but he was granted a substitution of judge after the Illinois Supreme Court ruled, "Judge Ko-

mada considered information outside the record which is prejudicial error" and
" . . . should be recused from further consideration of this case." There was also
more to this—a conflict of interest arose when it was disclosed that Judge Komada
had purchased two houseboats from his good friend, retired ISP Sgt. Jack Eckerty.
I was upset—Eckerty would only offer me one houseboat.

Steidl's request for a new trial was denied, but his death penalty was commuted to a life sentence. Unbelievably, when referring to the credibility of Herrington and Reinbolt, Judge Tracy Resch stated:

> While the evidence was closely balanced, this was not a case where
> Deborah Reinbolt was the only witness upon whose testimony the
> jury based its verdict. It was not a case of the "I said/she said" vari-
> ety. The State's case included important testimony from witnesses
> in addition to Deborah Reinbolt, including Darrell Herrington,
> Ferlin [Lester] Wells, Debra Steidl and Elaine Armstrong. The de-
> fendant attempted to discredit Reinbolt's testimony with the testi-
> mony of newly discovered . . . witnesses, including Barbara Furry
> . . . and Eva Jean Trover. None of these witnesses were credible.

How incredulous that the judge attacked the credibility of the defense's alibi
witnesses—Furry and Trover—noting their alcohol and drug history as the basis
for his logic. How ironic that the judge deemed these witnesses weren't credible
because of alcohol or drug use, but Herrington and Reinbolt *were,* despite their
extensive drug and alcohol abuse? As I finished reading the irrational opinion,
I was again reminded of columnist Eric Zorn's comments: "Another frightening
example of how the engine of the State, once in motion, can roll right over the
innocent as well as the guilty."

Zorn's words took on an even more sinister meaning when Bill Clutter disclosed still more damning information the state had kept hidden for 14 years—a
scandalous confession Clutter found in the basement of the Paris Police Department! What sat before me were four pages—one page, a Paris Police Department
offense report, with an additional three pages of handwritten notes. The documents revealed that on August 19, 1987—just weeks after Steidl and Whitlock's
convictions—Darrell Herrington made a monumental confession to police.

The report indicated that the Paris Police Department responded to a domestic battery involving Darrell and his wife Betty. Both Darrell and Betty Herrington were interviewed separately by police. According to the handwritten
notes attached to the police report, the interviews were conducted by "Gene,

Jim, and Gary at Darrell's house." In Clutter's interview with Paris Police Chief Gene Ray, he confirmed this incident when shown these documents. Ray identified the notes as Detective Jim Parrish's handwriting and that "Gary" could be Paris police officer "Gary Cash or Gary Wheat." Attached to the police report were notes taken on a separate piece of paper with the heading "Herrington Dry Wall and General Construction." The note read, "August 19, 1987. 11pm. Darrell, Gene, Gary, Jim at Darrell's house. Since then has remembered had conversation with Paula Myers said there was more that Darrell knew but didn't say in court." The notes stated that when Herrington entered the Rhoads house the night of the murders, he:

> Saw Bob Morgan standing at bottom of stairs . . . Bob told Darrell, "You didn't see me." And Darrell said, "Okay." Darrell talked to Morgan at post office three days later. Bob met Darrell at Darrell's shop and offered Darrell $25,000 cash and $25,000 property to keep his mouth shut.

The last page of notes had the name "Paula Myers" written and underlined in the upper right-hand corner. The page was a transcript of a conversation Herrington related between himself and Paula Myers:

Darrell: I went up and saw Randy.

Paula: I think there's more to it than what has been said.

Darrell: There is. I'm going to see to it the big guy is put away. Herb and Randy are set free. I seen something at the bottom of the stairway before I saw Randy or Herb. Nobody knows about that.

Paula: I think they walked in on what you walked in on.

Darrell: Yeah.

Paula: Debbie [Reinbolt] had to be morbid to hold them down.

Darrell: It didn't happen like that at all. Somebody had offered [me] $50,000 to testify to something [I] knew. What it is is true.

The notes continue on the same page regarding an interview of Betty Herrington by Paris Police:

> Betty (within two weeks ago) said Darrell told her that Bob Mor-
> gan had offered him a bunch of money to keep his mouth shut.
> He [Morgan] also told him [Herrington] he could have a job and
> wouldn't have to do anything. [And that the] police aren't smart
> enough to catch him . . . Darrell said that Bob M. was shipping
> dope in the bags of dog food. One bag of dog food would have
> dope in it. Betty said Bob M. is always speaking to her and asking
> how she is.

Later Clutter interviewed Paula Myers to determine if Herrington ever made any of these statements to her after the trials. Myers recalled she was at a bar called Poor Robert's when she spoke with Herrington. During a game of pool, Myers asked Herrington about the Rhoads case, and he told her, "There ain't none of it true." Herrington said investigators had him hypnotized and "They put that in his head." Herrington asked Myers "would you do something to help me?" and then Herrington asked her to "contact an outside authority, like the FBI. [and he] . . . specifically told me, 'Do not to contact anyone in Edgar county.'" Herrington told Myers, "What I testified to was not the truth."

Herrington said he was "offered money by Bob Morgan and he was afraid he was going to get in trouble about the money. Herrington said he would rather they keep him busy with jobs." According to Myers, Herrington said "there was another person in the house" the night of the murders, but he never revealed the name to her. Myers said she told Herrington she didn't want to get involved, and told Clutter she never contacted the FBI. "I've never told anybody 'til now," said Myers. She also told Clutter that the Paris Police never interviewed her about what Herrington had told police on August 19, 1987. Not only had the Paris police ignored Herrington's confession, they never interviewed Paula Myers. Why not? Why did they keep information like this hidden?

Over the next 20 years, police and prosecutors adamantly claimed and judges ruled Darrell Herrington was a credible witness. In the original investigation, Mike McFatridge and investigators portrayed Herrington as an eyewitness credible enough to put one man on death row and a second man in prison for life.

"He knew certain things," State's Attorney Mike McFatridge said of Herrington, "Things, at least in our minds, that were not the things the town drunk would know."

Yet, one month after those convictions, the State's credible witness, Darrell Herrington, proclaimed to police that Steidl and Whitlock were innocent, and admitted he was untruthful in his testimony. He also made accusations that Bob

Morgan was in the Rhoads' home during the murders, and Herrington told police Morgan paid him $50,000 to "keep his mouth shut."

Herrington was admitting he committed perjury to the police and had possibly aided in the concealment of a homicide, and he named a suspect whose name had continually came up in the initial investigation—a man police acknowledged was a suspect but failed to investigate! Instead Herrington's confession to police that night was ignored and hidden away!

In 2006, Bob Morgan was interviewed by State Police and the FBI about Herrington's statements. The state police report read:

> Morgan stated he first met Darrell Herrington in the late 80's or early 90's when Herrington worked at Septimus, putting up drywall. Herrington worked at a dairy farm called New Milk in Georgia for Morgan in 2001. The Boards also worked at the same location. . . . Morgan never offered or paid Herrington the twenty-five thousand dollar reward moneys. Morgan trusts Herrington and does not know why Herrington would have made statements to police about Morgan being at the Rhoads at the time the homicides took place.

Bob Morgan also denied even knowing Herrington during the time of the Rhoads murders and to confirm this told the investigators to ask his secretary, Norma Pruitt, and she "would not lie for food, sex or money."

They did and Norma Pruitt's interview contradicted Bob Morgan when the FBI report read, "Norma stated Bob Morgan and Darrell Herrington had a long-standing relationship which pre-dates the Rhoads homicide. . . . Norma remembers Darrell doing drywall jobs for Morgan even before Karen Rhoads came to work at Morgan Manufacturing."

It was no secret Bob Morgan was a suspect in the original investigation, and the Rhoads case file revealed Eckerty was suspicious enough to have run indices checks on Morgan, an intelligence database investigators used to link individuals to other crimes or see if they were connected with any other criminal cases.

Karen Rhoads worked for Bob Morgan, and she had reported to friends and family suspicious activities she saw at work that troubled her, things she questioned like the machine guns and cash she saw in the trunk of Morgan's car, and the creamers she was concerned might be "full of dope" from Morgan's office. Karen told several family members she was going to quit her job.

Carol Robinson told Clutter some workers from Morgan Manufacturing were in her bar shortly after the murders and one of the workers said, "There was a big argument between Karen and Bob and Bob told her that she couldn't walk out. She said she was walking out and Karen said if he tried to stop her, she would open her mouth."

During a 1995 interview with Clutter, Bob Morgan " . . . admitted giving Herrington work after the trial but denied giving him any cash."

In the years since, state police intelligence analysts determined Herrington became pretty affluent after the trials of Whitlock and Steidl. Not only did Darrell eventually own a fleet of personal and work vehicles, he obtained expensive antique cars and other properties. Pretty good for a man who, at one time, had his driver's license revoked and was forced to pedal his bicycle around town. Much of Herrington's work was accrued through doing jobs for Bob Morgan.

As my review of the Rhoads murders continued, I found Morgan's name inextricably linked to the case, but I still had more questions than answers.

It was disturbing that the original investigators failed to explore Karen's concerns that helped identify Morgan as a suspect in the first place. The information about the guns and large amounts of cash warranted a serious look.

Equally disturbing was the apparent effort of Parrish and McFatridge to at least limit, if not exclude, Morgan's name from reports. Mike Dunlap had told police he saw three individuals doing cocaine at a remote location just days after the murders. Dunlap positively identified Morgan and Sons of Silence gang member Herschel Wright as two of the men he observed. Yet Parrish's written report deceitfully changed Dunlap's information to indicate he could not identify the other two men doing cocaine with Herschel. Here was a young woman murdered after expressing concern her boss was involved in narcotics, and just days after the murder he is seen consorting and doing cocaine with an outlaw biker, who was an enforcer for the Sons of Silence. Wasn't a meeting between an outlaw biker and affluent businessman days after the murder of one of his employees somewhat suspicious? My biggest question, though, was why the police and prosecutor ignored this information and purposefully excluded Morgan's name and hid the information away?

I found it unbelievable that investigators in 1986 either failed to see or had deliberately ignored this connection to Karen's murder.

Still, Clutter's discovery of the August 19, 1987, police statement in which Herrington alleged seeing Morgan at the Rhoads' house on the night of the murders and he was subsequently paid $50,000 was another in a long list of incidents where the police failed to act regarding Bob Morgan's possible involvement in the case.

During my review I questioned if Herrington was even at the Rhoads' house the night of the murders, but I also remembered how Steidl and Whitlock made allegations to the FBI alleging McFatridge was involved in narcotics trafficking with Bob Morgan. Was Herrington, the desperate town drunk, approached and offered big money to testify untruthfully against Steidl and Whitlock as his statement to police indicated that August? Did he assume that because it was Bob Morgan who offered him the money, he was behind the murders and was told to "keep his mouth shut"? Was this all a huge conspiracy?

Why did police ignore Herrington's admission of being deceitful? It certainly wasn't the first time police caught him in a lie. Instead, the reports indicating his perjury were just hidden away in a cardboard box in the basement of the Paris Police Department for 14 years!

Fourteen years later, in 2000, the upper command of the State Police would also ignore these documents and the scandalous cover-up in 1987. The ISP command also ignored all the documentation and indications of intimidation, manipulation and outright lying that occurred in the original investigation by the investigators and prosecutor. It didn't matter to my command that the original jury didn't hear the truth. It didn't matter that two men were possibly wrongfully convicted based on a conspiracy of lies. It didn't matter that two innocent men may be in prison, while the real killers remained free. Because all of this information was about to be deemed "too politically sensitive" by the politically compromised upper command of the Illinois State Police!

Chapter 10

Too Politically Sensitive

---■---

As the new Investigations Commander, my responsibilities were significantly more than I had previously handled. I oversaw the operational and administrative functions for a nine-county area in East Central Illinois. My administrative duties included anything from overseeing budgets and federal grants to the case management of past and current criminal investigations. I was also responsible for oversight on the day-to-day field operations of five different units. Not a day went by that one or more of the units weren't involved in some type of criminal investigation, and it was my head on the chopping block if one of them screwed up. Given these responsibilities, I spent long hours at work, and when I wasn't at work, my cell or home phone was constantly ringing. It seemed like I was at work seven days a week, 24 hours a day, and I loved it.

My experiences from up north were somewhat different than some of the investigations we encountered in downstate Illinois.

I remember an Amish mother bringing in her teenage son because she caught him having sex with his brother's horse. The red faced agent I sent in to interview the young man was barely able to keep his composure while the teenager confessed to screwing several of the other family farm animals. The agent lost it though when the young man finally confessed to screwing his brother's horse, tearfully explaining, "But you don't understand. I love that horse!" Things were definitely different in downstate Illinois.

I enlisted the aid of Sgt. Greg Dixon and put him in charge of the General Criminal Investigations Squad. Dixon was one of the best criminal investigators

I had ever met, and he was a conscientious, hard-working cop with the utmost integrity.

One day, Greg came into my office holding a case file that was neglected since 1997. For three years, the file sat in a cardboard box in the corner of the former supervisor's office. The case involved the possible murder of a one-year-old baby girl named Madyson Nicole Smith. When we reviewed the case file, we both concurred the little girl was likely murdered and identified the potential suspect as the child's mother, Kelsey Smith. We learned that following Madyson's death, Kelsey Smith moved to Florida, where she was convicted for attempting to murder her second child.

We contacted Florida officials who told us how they caught Kelsey Smith in the act of trying to suffocate her second child, a six-month-old baby girl. Hidden cameras had captured Smith placing a plastic bag over her baby's head and subsequently she was imprisoned for that until her release date in 2006.

"It's about time someone from the state of Illinois got off their ass and did something about this case!" the Florida prosecutor's scathing words chastised us.

The prosecutor explained that, in 1997, they contacted our district regarding their suspicions that Kelsey Smith had murdered her first child, Madyson Nicole. The state police master sergeant in charge back in 1997 told the Florida officials the ISP was interested in pursuing the case. Yet when Florida officials made a special trip to Illinois, they were ignored by the master sergeant who suddenly advised them, "We're too busy."

When I looked at the file, I knew immediately why they were "too busy." The file indicated the master sergeant assigned a female sergeant in his squad as the Kelsey Smith case agent. It was well known that the master sergeant and female sergeant were having a torrid affair at the time. Therefore, when the master sergeant said they were "too busy," it was because he and his female sergeant were "too busy" cheating on their spouses to investigate the heinous murder of little Madyson Nicole. I was livid and ashamed that these two ISP officers had so blatantly and negligently ignored such an unforgivable crime.

Despite being blown off by the ISP, the Florida officials still provided documentation of over 60 interviews they conducted during their trip to Illinois. Those interviews, along with other files, sat in that cardboard box from 1997 until Greg Dixon discovered them in 2000. We re-opened the investigation and caught a break when Kelsey Smith's Florida cellmate agreed to wear a wire and record Smith describing how she murdered her one-year-old daughter.

The cellmate—a notorious serial killer herself—told us Kelsey Smith had actually confided to her once before about murdering Madyson. Even this heartless serial killer was appalled at the mother's brutal accounts and said, "Something has to be done about this monster."

The wired conversation I listened to between Kelsey Smith and her cellmate was one of the most disturbing confessions I heard in my career. Tears welled up in my eyes, and I became furious as I listened to the recorded conversation as Smith talked with absolutely no remorse and bragged on tape how she tortured and murdered her little girl.

Her voice sounded gleeful as she recalled how she tortured the little girl, first describing how she would take a wet kitchen towel, tightly roll it up and then chase her one-year-old daughter around the trailer beating her. With contempt and hatred, she described how the little girl ran to the locked screen door, clawing at the screen with her little hands and crying for her daddy as Smith repeatedly snapped the helpless child in the back with the wet towel. There was no doubt this woman was a monster.

Kelsey Smith's unwitting confession on tape then turned to the disturbing murder of Madyson. Smith bragged how she calculatingly and step-by-step murdered her daughter. With absolutely no remorse, she told her cellmate how she placed her one-year-old daughter on the kitchen counter and placed a plastic bag over Madyson's little head and then suffocated her. Graphically, she described how when she put the bag over her little girl's head, the tears began flowing down Madyson's cheeks. As the life was being sucked out of the little girl, she grasped up at her mother, fighting for her life.

Kelsey Smith described her feelings as little Madyson fought for her life: "I wish you'd hurry up and die, you little bitch." Smith's cold and disturbing words continued:

> And then, when she took the last little gasp, I put my hand over her face, and I was like, "Well, fuck, okay, that's it." It didn't make a fuck to me. As a matter of fact, after I knew she was gone, I picked her up, took her into the living room, laid her on her nap time blanket to make it look real good. Yeah, it was real quick. It was like five minutes. But I waited. I waited 15 minutes before I called anybody. I smoked a cigarette and then I put on my Hollywood face.

As I listened to this monster, I couldn't help but picture this little one-year-old baby girl lying there helpless and crying, too young to understand why her evil mother was suffocating the life from her. And I also couldn't comprehend how two ISP supervisors had so callously ignored her murder.

The disturbing conversation didn't end with Madyson's murder. When her cellmate mentioned Smith's future release, she asked her if Kelsey planned on having any more children. Smith matter-of-factly replied: "Yeah, I'll most likely have more babies. And I'll probably kill them, too. Well, maybe I won't if it's a boy, but who knows."

Kelsey Smith was eventually charged in Illinois with the murder of little Madyson Nicole, and she pleaded guilty and received a 55-year sentence in the Illinois Department of Corrections. As far as I was concerned, for a monster like Kelsey Smith, she got off way too easy.

Others did too, like the two ISP supervisors who ignored this terrible crime for all those years, because they were too busy screwing in cheap motels. They had *all* gotten off way too easy. Eventually, the master sergeant and his female sergeant divorced their spouses and married, and in 2002, Captain Fermon rated these two officers as highly skilled investigators and highly skilled supervisors. Both were eventually promoted to the rank of Lieutenant and one eventually to the rank of Captain. At the expense of the Illinois taxpayers, these two people—who are supposed to protect and serve—earn a combined salary of almost a quarter million dollars a year, but I knew the shame those two brought onto the Illinois State Police, and each time I think about the unmerciful murder of little Madyson Nicole Smith, the anger still wells up inside of me. Integrity, Service and Pride my ass!

Years later, Dusty Rhodes of *The Illinois Times* discussed my ISP career. Rhodes stated " . . . the nonchalance of [Callahan's] tone also demonstrates the depth of his dedication to the Illinois State Police. He doesn't tell it to show how tough things can get; it's much like an anecdote proving that things can always get worse."

And as the year 2000 progressed, things were about to get much worse, and with each passing year after that, the words "Integrity, Service and Pride" became even more meaningless.

The Rhoads case review was, at the time, just one of the many things on my plate, but I took the director's letter to heart: "Please be assured, the foremost interest of the Illinois State Police in this and any case is to seek the truth and ensure justice is served."

The Rhoads case also intrigued me. I had never seen a criminal investigation conducted as sloppily as this one. It amazed me how the State believed enough evidence existed to even arrest Steidl and Whitlock, let alone get a conviction.

As I dug into the case, I enlisted the aid of Sergeant Dixon to evaluate my review of the Rhoads case. I also planned on going to Paris during my review of the Rhoads case. With the *48 Hours* show just around the corner, I felt this would be a great time to go and listen to the gossip among the locals. In late April, Greg and I received an invitation to attend a meeting in Edgar County to address the meth epidemic that was hitting the area. I was sure the upcoming *48 Hours* show had revived attention to the Rhoads case and when we arrived at the meeting, we were not disappointed.

The Rhoads case was the topic of discussion when we walked into the meeting room. Ted Todd, an Edgar County Sheriff's Deputy, was telling the group, "They used the town drunk and a lying bitch to railroad those two guys."

"Hell, we all know who did it . . . God dammit! But he owns half the town," the Chrisman police chief responded.

Todd responded, "They asked for my help, but I refused to have anything to do with that case. I wasn't about to put my name on any of those reports."

Years later, I learned Todd was good to his word when Clutter interviewed a woman who said she had given him some important information about Whitlock's whereabouts the night of the murders, and Ted Todd, true to his word, never documented that information.

The meeting continued when a Barney Fife-type made a remark that makes all cops look bad—that mentality you know exists in some cops but you're still always shocked when you hear it firsthand. The officer's callous words addressed the group, "Who cares? Steidl and Whitlock were both assholes! And they would have ended up in prison on something else anyways!"

During the meeting I noticed the Paris Police Chief seemed to be watching me closely.

When the meeting ended, I found it strange that he singled me out. The Police Chief's name was Tom Boren and I wasn't mistaken about him watching me throughout the meeting. It turned out Boren was not a local cop from Paris, but was from Kansas City. Maybe he sensed we had similar law enforcement backgrounds since we were both from big cities. He certainly didn't know me, but he was easy to see through and it quickly became apparent he was a troubled man.

Chief Boren took me outside away from the rest of the group and we walked down a little dirt road. It was obvious he didn't want anyone to hear what he had to say. He told me how excited he was when he was first hired as the new Police Chief, and he talked about the innovative ideas he attempted to introduce into the small town.

Then quietly, almost as if he feared someone was listening, he began telling me how frustrated he was and in Paris, there were certain people who were above the law. Boren talked about attending morning coffee meetings with local Paris businessmen, but he quit attending because he viewed them as "inappropriate."

123

What a strange comment from a chief of police who, in most towns, is expected to network with the local community businessmen, but Boren never bothered to tell me what was "inappropriate." But he kept spilling his guts and warned that I needed to be careful if I was going to be working in Paris.

"You need to be careful of certain officers," he said, revealing concerns that some of his officers were "spying" on him.

It seemed strange that Boren was confiding in me so quickly, but he was no fool. He had already guessed my real reasons for being in Paris that day, and suspected I was there because of the new interest in the Rhoads case. When he asked, I didn't deny it, and I asked him what he knew about the case. Boren explained he knew very little about the murders since they happened well before his time, but he had heard all the familiar rumors and innuendoes. Then nervously, he related concerns he was going to "look dirty" in the upcoming *48 Hours* telecast.

Boren explained he allowed a private investigator to snoop around the basement of the police department and he had found some documents in the old chief's file. Boren was concerned because the documents were mysteriously destroyed when someone burned the box containing those documents without his authorization. His concern was *48 Hours* was going to blame him for the suspicious destruction of the documents.

Boren was, of course, referring to the August 19, 1987, police report and notes hidden away where Herrington told police he had lied when he testified and been paid off by Bob Morgan to keep his mouth shut. Boren didn't know that the private investigator, Bill Clutter, made and kept copies of the documents and that I also possessed copies of those same police reports.

As I prepared to leave that day, Boren said he still had two years left on his contract with Paris, but was thinking about breaking it and moving on to another job. He looked extremely depressed and said, "I just need to get out of Paris." And when I met Boren a second time, he was good to his word and had quit his job as the Paris Police Chief.

FBI Special Agent Nate Williams was also interested in pursuing some things in Paris so I reached out to him early on. The FBI had already pursued successful criminal investigations in the Paris area, including the infamous Mafioso Pizza Connection Case and the Sons of Silence motorcycle gang, so Paris and its criminal element were no strangers to the feds.

On May 2, 2000, my review of the Rhoads case was completed in a 10-page memorandum. The memo was forwarded through my chain of command to the Region Commander, Lieutenant Colonel Diane Carper, on May 3, 2000. The memo summarized my review of the case file and stated:

Steidl and Whitlock were subsequently convicted based on the eyewitness testimony of Darrell Herrington and Debbie Reinbolt. Based on the case file and documentation provided by Mr. Bill Clutter, I have found many discrepancies in this case which warrant the Illinois State Police re-evaluating this case.

I concluded that neither Steidl nor Whitlock were proven guilty beyond a reasonable doubt, and I added there were other viable suspects, such as Bob Morgan, who were never thoroughly investigated and new information indicated a need to take a closer look at those suspects.

There was no doubt in my mind I was reopening the investigation, and it didn't occur to me I would encounter any opposition. In my 20 years as a cop, I had never needed permission to conduct a criminal investigation, and I didn't think I needed it now. We had already successfully re-opened other cold cases, like the murder of little one-year-old Madyson Nicole Smith, without needing permission.

With the *48 Hours* episode fast approaching, Lt. Col. Carper forwarded my memo to Captain Steve Fermon, who was in his newly created position as State-wide Investigations Officer. He e-mailed a response to Carper on May 9, 2000:

> Thank you, I would also suggest that before we take Mr. Clutter's (findings) as truth we establish contact with the person responsible for the appeal. This case has been tried and through a series of appeals over the past 14 years, much info has been documented through testimony. Transcripts may/should be available. Any thing we do should be coordinated with the Appellate Prosecutor's Office. They too may have concerns or a need for follow up, etc. Just a few thoughts. SMF.

Fermon was somewhat misinformed. Since this was a capital murder case and Steidl was, at one point, sentenced to death, it was actually the Illinois Attorney General's Office, not the Appellate Prosecutor's Office, handling the appeal. Despite Fermon's innuendoes about "Mr. Clutter's findings as truth," Captain Strohl defended my review of the Rhoads case. Strohl's e-mail read:

> Callahan brought up several issues in his May 2nd memo regarding some discrepancies in the Rhoads homicide . . . that warrant further investigation. I concur with Lt. Callahan . . . We need to re-open this case ASAP, I would also recommend the FBI be included

to assist/facilitate in some aspects of this investigation. I realize this is a sensitive issue particularly with the issue that Randy Steidl was sentenced to death.

But Carper still insisted we reach out to the prosecutor's office.

Following the Colonel's instructions, I contacted the Illinois Attorney General's Office on May 12, 2000. James Ryan was the Illinois Attorney General at the time and I had met him on a few prior occasions. I also knew some of his assistants from the days when he was the State's Attorney for DuPage County. I called the general number and asked to speak with the Assistant Attorney General assigned to Steidl's appeal. After being transferred, I explained to the female assistant on the other end of the phone that I was asked to review the Rhoads investigation. Her response was one I already anticipated. She readily admitted it was a very poor case and should they lose the appeal, they likely wouldn't re-try the case. Her only concerns were with the appeal and not my reinvestigation of the Rhoads case. I informed Captain Strohl about the conversation and in turn, Strohl e-mailed Carper and advised her:

> Lieutenant Callahan has reached out to the Attorney General's Office. It should be noted that many of the issues Lt. Callahan identified in his memo are not issues/questioned raised by Mr. Clutter. These issues are the ones he identified as he reviewed the ISP case file.

May 12, 2000, was a Friday afternoon, and I actually had hopes of getting home at a decent hour that evening. Before I could leave though, I received a call from Assistant Attorney General Bob Spence. I knew Bob from when I was a young agent and he was an Assistant DuPage County State's Attorney. I always liked Bob, and from my experiences he was always a straight-forward, aggressive and fair prosecutor.

We exchanged the usual pleasantries and caught up on our lives the last few years. His interest though was Steidl's appeal, and I explained to Bob how I was assigned to review the Rhoads case to see if it warranted being re-investigated. Then I went over the concerns I had with the original investigation and my intentions of re-investigating the case.

Not one to pull any punches, Spence replied, "You're right. This case is a piece of shit and if we lose the appeal, we'd never re-try this case. We could never win it."

Spence ended our conversation with, "Good luck and good hunting, Mike. I know you, and I know your persistence."

After hanging up, I started getting ready to call it a day, but my day wasn't over by a long shot. Shortly thereafter, I received another call from Spence. This time, it was a conference call and the third person on the phone was introduced as Assistant Attorney General Joel D. Bertocchi, who was higher up on the Attorney General's food chain than Bob Spence. I rehashed almost verbatim the same information I told Bob just minutes earlier. At the end of the call, Spence asked me to fax him a copy of my memorandum. I called Captain Strohl who said, "You heard the colonel. Send it." So, I faxed my May 2 memo to the Illinois Attorney General's Office in Chicago.

I didn't know it at the time but all hell was about to break lose.

That evening, Lily and I were preparing to go out to dinner when I received the first of two strange phone calls from Captain Strohl. The first call was baffling and troubling. John said we were both "in big trouble" and were being called to Springfield the following Monday. He had no clue why we were in trouble and was told we'd find out on Monday. I spent the next couple of hours wondering what we had done wrong.

Then the second call came from Captain Strohl, and this time his demeanor had changed, and he said we were no longer in trouble and "the Attorney General's Office applauded us for saving them some embarrassment." Apparently, we were now out of hot water, but neither one of us still had a clue as to what had happened, and I spent the entire weekend in the dark.

The first thing Monday morning, May 15, 2000, I received a phone call from Bill Clutter who said a small bombshell went off when the Attorney General's Office received my memo. Clutter said because of my memo, a conflict of interest was identified and the Illinois Attorney General was filing an emergency motion to withdraw from Steidl's appeal. I had to wait until the next day to learn what the conflict of interest was.

That night, *48 Hours* aired the program on the Rhoads case. There were no questions from any Mike Wallace types and no embarrassment for the state police. They had dodged a bullet this time, and the show highlighted many of the same unanswered questions a lot of us had.

The next day, on May 16, 2000, Assistant Attorney General Joel D. Bertocchi made an emergency motion for the Attorney General's Office to withdraw in Steidl's appeal. Bertocchi's motion advised the appellate court that the Attorney General's office recently became aware of information that made it a conflict of interest for their office to continue the role as prosecutor in the appeal. The motion added the Attorney General was unable to provide specific information because the conflict concerned a criminal investigation.

My memo had identified Bob Morgan as a suspect, and it turned out he was a campaign contributor to Attorney General James Ryan. That was the conflict of interest.

Chicago Tribune columnist Eric Zorn wrote about the Attorney General's withdrawal in his May 17, 2000, column, "State shies away from defending murder conviction":

> The only clue why the state took the highly unusual step of suddenly distancing itself from a prosecution it has been defending since mid-1987 was the fifth paragraph of the seven page motion . . . but a translation of the legalese in [the] motion might read like this: "The state is now in the middle of a promising criminal investigation into other suspects, and under those circumstances it wouldn't be right for us to go to court and argue that the previous convictions are valid."

Shortly after the Attorney General's withdrawal I received a call from Lt. Col. Carper. Her words were stern, direct and short, like always. She said I was going to be receiving a call from the ISP Deputy Director of Operations.

"If you know what's good for you, just listen to him. Don't respond and don't ask any questions and everything will eventually be okay." Then she added, "You're a young command officer and just learning."

At first I had no idea what she was talking about. The impression she was giving was I had done something wrong and I had no clue what it was I had done.

Deputy Director Dan Kent considered himself the ISP's "Mr. Integrity, Service & Pride," as he liked to be called. Those of us in the ranks considered Kent, like Carper, one of the politically correct commanders who had little operational experience and had spent the bulk of their careers in administrative posts or the State Police Academy where playing basketball or reading text books was the extent of their daily police work.

The Governor of the State of Illinois was George Ryan. During his administration, the Illinois State Police upper command took on a completely new identity as these politically correct academy brats rose to power. Many appointed to the upper command of the State Police were regarded as the "yes" men and women Ryan preferred. This was the type of leadership George Ryan wanted. Ryan's administration was also one of micro-management with a goal of minimizing scandal. Those of us in the ranks were often apprised, through subliminally threatening memos, of the ramifications if we failed to report even the slightest of scandalous newsworthy information. The memo's message emphasized: "The Governor's Office considers the Illinois State Police the eyes and ears of the State." Many of us took it to mean the Governor's office considered the state police as his own personal KGB or his own personal "snitches."

These Commanders fit the George Ryan mold. Some of them, I judged willing to sell out their integrity and their oath for the power their new positions provided.

For now, "Mr. Integrity, Service and Pride" was a powerful man within the Illinois State Police, and when Kent called he immediately began giving me an ass-chewing I knew I didn't deserve. His first words were, "How dare you send an official state police document outside our agency?"

The realization immediately hit me—apparently, Carper and Fermon had told Kent it was my idea to send the May 2 memo to the Attorney General's Office. Carper was obviously setting me up to take all the blame. Not one to be taken advantage of, I interrupted his highness during the reprimand and blurted out, "But, sir, I was just following orders from Captain Fermon and Lieutenant Colonel Carper."

"*What*?" Kent replied, obviously taken aback by my defense.

I explained Fermon's e-mail and Carper's subsequent orders. Kent's only reply was "I'll get back to you." He never did.

Carper was the one who called back, "You just don't get it, do you? You just don't see the big picture here, do you?" she spewed out in anger.

I smirked on the other end of the phone and thought to myself, "Oh, yes I do, Colonel. I see the big picture," and I saw through her back-stabbing set up, too.

This was a dangerous time for me, though, as I was still on probation as a new lieutenant—a promotion that could be snatched away if my upper command determined I wasn't capable of handling the job. Captain Fermon had gained an unbelievable amount of influence in Springfield, especially with Deputy Director Kent. No one understood Fermon's instant rise to power, but everyone feared it. I also knew Fermon had it out for me, and I needed to cover my ass on everything I said or did.

My concerns were confirmed just a few days after I received the angry call from Kent. Greg Dixon knocked on my door and came into my office and confided that when I initially received the Rhoads case file, he received a call from Fermon's best friend, Danny Reed. Dixon said Reed delivered a personal message on Fermon's behalf, warning Greg not to assist me in reviewing the Rhoads case.

According to Dixon, Reed said, "You're fucked if you do. You're sitting on a mountain of shit, you'll get fucked. It's going to be hell if you do."

Greg Dixon's integrity was too strong and despite the warning, he helped me with the case, and we would both learn in the years to come, it wasn't a mountain of shit we were sitting on—it was the whole damn sewer system in the State of Illinois.

Not long after Kent's butt chewing, I received another call from Jack Eckerty.

"How are you doing? I heard you ran into some rough waters. Are you okay?" he asked in a consoling tone.

For a man who had been retired for years, Eckerty was certainly in the know, and I admitted I was weathering some rough waters, but I'd manage to get through it.

Then he stunned me: "You found out about all the politics in this, didn't you?" he asked. The first thought in my mind was that perhaps something similar had happened to Eckerty when he was investigating the Rhoads case. I definitely sensed he was a troubled man about this case and was dealing with some sort of guilt. The conversation reminded me of two browbeaten kids sitting in the corner of the classroom, consoling one another, but it also alerted me that Eckerty knew a lot more than what he was telling me.

I told Eckerty I knew about the conflict of interest, and asked, "You know, Jack, speaking of campaign contributions, I read the case file and at some point, it seemed as if Bob Morgan was a suspect."

"Bob Morgan was always a suspect in my mind, Mike, and still is to this day. But McFatridge steered us away from him and all the other suspects when Herrington came forward," he said.

I didn't ask him why he thought McFatridge would do something like that. I didn't need to; I already knew about Steidl and Whitlock's visit to the FBI alleging McFatridge's involvement with the local Paris businessman. I also had the police reports where Herrington said he lied in his testimony and was paid to keep his mouth shut by Bob Morgan. Eckerty's comment led me into asking him about the two eyewitnesses.

"Why wasn't the negative polygraph on Herrington disclosed?" I asked.

Eckerty confirmed the state's deception when he replied, "That's because Mike McFatridge didn't want anything negative in the case file to indicate that either of those two guys were innocent." Unbelievable! Eckerty was actually admitting the negative polygraph was never disclosed!

When I asked about Reinbolt, his only reply was simply, "I never believed Reinbolt." Here was one of the lead investigators admitting his two key witnesses—Herrington and Reinbolt—were liars! Shocking since he knew full well Herrington and Reinbolt were used to convict Steidl and Whitlock.

A few days passed, and Eckerty called me again. This time, his tone was more upbeat, and I sensed a sort of relief in his voice. CBS's *48 Hours* had already aired, and the Attorney General's decision to withdraw was no longer a subject in the media. I had a strange feeling Eckerty figured the Rhoads case was going to go back into hibernation, and since I had my hands slapped, I wouldn't want to pursue the investigation anymore. His demeanor was overly friendly, and he acted like we were the best of buddies.

"Hey, do you like boating and water sports and stuff like that?" he asked.

"I can take them or leave them, why?" I replied.

Eckerty said he sold expensive houseboats on Lake Shelbyville and asked if I wanted one, explaining he would "take care" of me.

"I won't make a dime off of you," he promised.

I graciously declined his generous offer—but Eckerty assured me if I ever changed my mind, the offer was always there. He didn't know it, but I was already aware of his houseboat deals with Judge Kamada. As far as I was concerned, the Rhoads investigation was going to be re-opened, and I didn't want any conflicts of interest with my alleged new-found buddy, Jack Eckerty.

On May 18, 2000, Captain Strohl and I were summoned to Springfield to discuss the Rhoads homicide. The meeting was held on the second floor of the Illinois State Police Headquarters—"the Armory Building" as it was known. The Armory Building housed all the anointed top brass of the state police. These were all of the politically correct cronies George Ryan had placed in power and I was told a lot of top brass from the Division of Operations were attending the meeting. In my entire career, I had never gone through so much effort just to reopen a case and conduct a criminal investigation.

Those attending the meeting were Lt. Col. Diane Carper, Lt. Col. Edie Casella, and Captain John Strohl and myself. Casella was in charge of Operational Services Command or as some referred to it, our Intelligence Division. She also brought three intelligence analysts with her to listen to my briefing of the Rhoads investigation. Also attending was Assistant Deputy Director Andre Parker, the number two man in the Division of Operations.

Andre Parker was another one of the former Academy brats who specialized in playing basketball but rose to power under Governor George Ryan's administration.

Prior to George Ryan's gubernatorial election, he was the Illinois Secretary of State, and that office was embroiled in an investigation known as "the License for Bribes Scandal." The Illinois State Police commenced an investigation and it was no secret the Public Integrity Squad investigating the scandal was prohibited from conducting a real investigation.

Once Ryan was elected as governor, it became even worse. ISP Colonel Earl Hernandez, who was in charge of the investigation, stated in a newspaper interview that the executive branch exerted more pressure to stop any legitimate investigation.

"The man who is going to be your boss doesn't approve of what you're doing," Hernandez told the *Chicago Sun Times* about the clear message he received.

Col. Hernandez retired from the state police rather than buckle to the pressure and cover up of the investigation. Andre Parker was the supervisor of the ISP Public Integrity Squad that eventually cleared Ryan and his cronies of any misconduct, as Jim Dey of the *News-Gazette* reported, "The politically compromised leadership of the Illinois State Police looked the other way when it came to George Ryan."

For his loyalty to Ryan, Parker was appointed to the upper echelon of the state police and was now a very powerful man in the department.

George Ryan and his cronies would not fare as well in the coming years when the feds picked up the case and continued the investigation under the direction of U.S. Attorney Patrick Fitzgerald's office.

I spent that afternoon on May 18, 2000, briefing Parker and the rest of the group regarding my concerns about the two eyewitnesses, the suspicions of misconduct I had about the original investigators and prosecutor and the other suspects who were seemingly ignored. For approximately two hours, the people in that room sat spellbound.

"This is an intriguing case," Parker declared when I finished. "It sounds like a made for TV movie." And Col. Parker assured everyone, "we will do the right thing."

Parker gave his blessing to reinvestigating the Rhoads case and added it was so intriguing he wished he could help in the investigation. Since the biggest portion of his career had been playing basketball at the ISP Academy, I really didn't want or need his help. After giving his blessing, he excused himself. As he was leaving the room, almost as if it was an afterthought, he looked back and asked me why the Attorney General had withdrawn from Steidl's appeal.

"Because there was a conflict of interest; Bob Morgan is a campaign contributor to Ryan," I replied.

Parker stopped dead in his tracks and wheeled around. There was shock on his face when he asked, "Not *George Ryan?*"

"No . . . Jim Ryan, the Attorney General," I replied.

The shock left Parker's face, and he appeared relieved. "Oh, okay," he said, and he quickly exited the room. That was my first and last contact with Andre Parker involving the Rhoads case, though I wondered why it mattered if Jim or George Ryan received campaign contributions from Morgan. Politics shouldn't have anything to do with a murder investigation.

When I got back to Champaign that afternoon, I called Dixon in and told him about the meeting. Mystified by Parker's obvious concern over the campaign contributions, I asked Greg to research Morgan's campaign contributions. His search uncovered that Morgan had contributed even more significant sums of money to George Ryan, numbering in the tens of thousands of dollars.

After already taking a lot of heat over this case, Parker's concern over campaign contributions was obvious, so I informed Captain Strohl about our latest discovery. Strohl wanted to err on the side of caution and told me to send the information regarding Morgan's political contributions up the chain of command. It didn't take the ISP brass long to react and Captain Strohl and I were once again summoned to Springfield by Lt. Col. Diane Carper.

Being a police officer can be a thankless job, but if you believe in the oath you take as a police officer and do your job to the best of your abilities, it's also very rewarding. It's about men and women who want to make a difference. It's a job where you're never going to be rich, and at any given time, can risk losing your life to protect the lives of others. It's an oath you take to serve mankind:

> To be honest in thought, word and deed; to maintain unimpeach-
> able integrity; to be just, fair, and impartial; to be steadfast against
> evil and its temptations; and to give my utmost to protect the rights,
> property, and lives of our citizens. . . . I will never compromise with
> crime and shall, at all times, uphold the Constitutions and laws of
> my country and the state of Illinois.

Some officers live by that oath and some don't.

Standing there that spring day in 2000, I was looking at Lieutenant Colonel Diane Carper, her colonel clusters all shiny—a symbol of her power that she liked to flaunt. Carper could be described as a matronly, if not manly, woman in her mid-40s. Never married, Carper's spouse was her job. Short of demanding genuflecting when entering her office, she exuded a paramilitary persona. With a dry personality, she was all-business. Her rank and power were used to disguise her lack of knowledge and experience as a real cop.

We didn't know what to expect and were not told the reason for the impromptu meeting. Shortly after we had walked onto the second floor of the Armory Building, Carper came out and escorted us into her plush office. Carper was quick to get to the point like always, and her stern words just about destroyed my faith in the department I had believed in for all those years.

"You cannot re-open the Rhoads case. You cannot touch it," she ordered. "It's too politically sensitive."

Carper's words bit into me as I stood there helplessly in her office. I was in total disbelief and when I looked over at John, I saw the same shock. It felt like a sledgehammer had just struck me in the stomach—and the air was sucked from my lungs. At first, I couldn't respond, I just stood there dumbfounded and the room seemed to start spinning around. In all my years as a police officer, I would have bet my life I'd never hear the orders Carper spoke that day, especially from someone in the Illinois State Police.

A surreal feeling overcame me . . . everything the ISP stood for, all the men and women who had risked their lives, all the sacrifices we make suddenly seemed so pointless. Was everything I believed in just a meaningless lie? You dedicate your life to an ideal and then your faith in everything is destroyed by three words. For the first time in my career, I began questioning my own department's integrity.

I had just been told a murder was too politically sensitive to investigate. A murder with so many unanswered questions. A murder where two men might be wrongfully convicted and maybe even worse, railroaded into prison with help from one of our own. A murder where the real killers were still running around free. How could any murder investigation be too politically sensitive to investigate?

My mind was reeling as I tried to speculate on what was too politically sensitive. Was it the misconduct I brought out in the original investigation, was the department afraid its image would be tarnished? Were they afraid if the truth came out and the two men were freed, expensive lawsuits would follow? Was it the connections between George Ryan and Morgan that Parker seemed so concerned about? Maybe George Ryan couldn't afford the scandal with the feds breathing down the governor's neck. Regardless, is it right to leave innocent men in prison for those reasons?

Captain Strohl and I just stood there for what seemed like endless moments, unable to speak. Then the shame and anger began to clear my mind. Yes, I realized, I had really heard those three words. The shame hit me full force. We were letting a lot of people that believed in us down, and they deserved better than this.

Just one week earlier, we were given the go-ahead to reopen the Rhoads case, but now, for reasons not shared with us, it was too politically sensitive.

I suddenly remembered the FBI's interest in looking at Morgan, so I asked Carper, "What about the FBI, they're still interested in investigating this, what if they run across something on the Rhoads case? What if they find something and we turned our backs on all of this? Won't it make us look like we tried to cover something up?"

Carper stood there with a deep concern etched on her brow. She already knew ATF was in Paris and had made connections to the Board brothers and the Rhoads murders. They were also interested in all the suspicious arsons in Edgar County. Standing there in silence for what seemed like forever, she finally replied, "Okay, you can go along with the FBI, but you can only gather intelligence."

Her orders became more specific and she vehemently reiterated we still couldn't "touch the Rhoads case." Carper's orders were specific and she wanted no reports written, only periodic updates on what the FBI or ATF was doing. We were "absolutely forbidden" from doing anything operational or proactive. Carper reiterated that we could only gather intelligence. Carper was also very clear that if the FBI or ATF got operational on anything in Edgar County and especially if any information came up on the Rhoads case, she wanted to be immediately notified, and they would address it at her level or the levels above her.

I still couldn't open an investigation, and it seemed pretty obvious, Springfield wanted me as their little snitch so they could alert the governor's office if anything scandalous or embarrassing came up from the feds.

But despite these roadblocks, I looked at it as an opportunity to keep my foot in the door on the Rhoads case. I reasoned that perhaps one day, under new leadership, I'd eventually get a chance to investigate the Rhoads case and without any restrictions. I had a short leash to walk on, but at least I could still walk, especially if I stayed under Springfield's radar.

We left the Armory building that day feeling dejected and ashamed. Carper and whoever else had violated the oath we had all taken. Captain Strohl and I began that day proud of the Illinois State Police and its reputation, but by the time we left the Armory that afternoon, neither one of us had much pride anymore.

I remember sitting in the passenger seat of his squad car, watching the flat, seemingly endless cornfields of East Central Illinois whisk by. For the longest time, I just looked out the window at the shimmering light reflecting off the green fields. Distraught, a thousand things were running through my mind . . . "too politically sensitive!" I finally broke the silence, turned to John and asked, "Can you believe what we just heard?"

Three years later, after I filed a lawsuit against the ISP command, Captain John Strohl testified about his feelings when we were told the Rhoads case was too politically sensitive:

" . . . I guess you could take it a couple of ways. But I took it to mean it was too politically sensitive. That we were not to go there as opposed to being too politically sensitive, be careful how you proceed. The message to me was clear . . . don't go there . . . it was kind of a shock to me to be honest with you . . . it seemed to me like it wasn't the right thing to do. I mean, there were concerns that Mike had identified that . . . may or may not have proved that somebody was innocent . . . And to me, I mean, no matter what information you have, you should share it with the prosecution or other side so that justice is served. Good or bad," Strohl testified.

Q: . . . did you talk to Mike about it when you were driving back?

Strohl: I am sure we did. I mean, I remember that we were both dazed by the information. I mean, I was dumbfounded. I just couldn't believe what I had heard. . . . it seemed like, one day, we're on this track where we're going to . . . do the right thing. And [the] next thing you know, stop the presses, you're not going there. . . . I had never been in that situation before in my career.

After that meeting with Carper, I often reflected back on the letter from the Director of the Illinois State Police to Bill Clutter: "Please be assured, the foremost interest of the Illinois State Police in this and any case is to seek the truth and ensure justice is served." For myself and others in the ISP, over the next few years, the mighty leadership of the Illinois State Police would continually prove those words weren't worth the paper they were written on.

The FBI and I eventually set up a meeting with the brother and sister of Dyke Rhoads—Andrea Trapp and Tony Rhoads. I arranged for the meeting to take place at my office. As long as the feds were snooping around Paris, Carper said I could go along and gather intelligence with them, so this was an opportunity to still participate and not openly violate her orders.

Andrea and Tony are two of the strongest and most dedicated people I'd ever meet. For years, they were unconvinced and had questioned the State's version of the motive behind Dyke and Karen's murders. They still had questions and still wanted answers. For 14 years they tried to get someone in law enforcement to listen to them . . . but no one would. Some families would have been happy with the closure the State provided, but Andrea and Tony wanted the truth and they wanted real justice for Dyke and Karen.

At first, they were leery of us and Andrea later explained that they had lost their trust in government. Sitting there and listening to them, it seemed to me this frustration had almost turned into hopelessness, but once again, they came forward. When they realized we were genuinely interested, you could see the hope return in their faces. Eventually they dropped their guard, and the conversation flowed. At times, it was very emotional, but as we talked back and forth, I could see their hope return because someone was finally listening and someone finally cared.

One of their biggest questions over the years was the "drug deal gone bad" motive McFatridge used to convict Steidl and Whitlock. Andrea and Tony didn't have an opinion whether Steidl and Whitlock were guilty or innocent, but they were deeply upset McFatridge characterized their brother as a drug dealer. Tony acknowledged that prior to his marriage, Dyke was an occasional pot smoker and had used cocaine. Embarrassed and fighting back tears, Tony admitted he was Dyke's supplier—a fact he wasn't proud of, but he said the concept of Dyke being killed over a "drug deal gone bad" was unfathomable. As Tony told 48 Hours, "There's a difference between somebody who's an occasional pot smoker and somebody who gets involved with a drug deal that's gone bad, that's going to cost you your life."

Dyke's mother, Carolyn Rhoads, had gone to McFatridge and questioned the State's motive, but Andrea and Tony said he ignored their mother's questions, and instead waved the grisly photos of Dyke and Karen's mutilated bodies in her face. McFatridge shooed Mrs. Rhoads from his office with, "Do you want the guys who did this to Dyke and Karen to get away with it?"

But even with the convictions, there were too many questions and too many things that didn't make sense for any real closure. Andrea told us about a strange visit from Darrell Herrington just months after the convictions. She was a young teenager, and it was the spring of 1988—not even a year after the trials—when Herrington rode up to their house on his bicycle in his usual drunken state. Andrea and her mother were the only ones home that evening and she described his visit as kind of surreal since by this time the family was trying to go on with their lives.

Andrea said Herrington started rambling about the events of July 5 and 6, 1986, and things didn't happen the way they were made to appear. He told Andrea and her mother he had a letter in a safety deposit box and when he died, the letter would "tell the truth about everything that had happened that night." Herrington said the letter was for his "protection" and told them Dyke's name would be cleared one day and he was "not a doper." This strange meeting was approximately one year prior to Herrington's recantation to Peter Rotskoff, and was even more evidence Herrington had never told the truth. Herrington's drunken visit only caused more questions and suspicions for the Rhoads family.

For almost two hours, I sat there and listened to Andrea and Tony. At times, they fought back tears and at other times, anger welled up in their voices. I let them talk freely, only occasionally interrupting to ask a question. One thing was obvious throughout the meeting, they loved their brother and I saw the hurt and anger for what had been done to his name. They were not afraid and only wanted the truth, no matter what it was.

Police and politicians take an oath to serve and protect our citizens—people like the Rhoads family. For years, they were let down by both the system and the men and women who swore to protect and serve them. The meeting with Andrea and Tony touched me and it made me ashamed. They had definitely been let down, and I made a promise I would spend the remaining years of my career fighting for the opportunity to answer some of those questions for them. Touched by the meeting that evening, I was definitely not going to give up my concerns about the Rhoads case.

CHAPTER 11

PARIS: TOWN OR PRISON?

---■---

For such a small town, Paris has an inordinate amount of honky-tonk drinking establishments. Many of these "watering holes" were, at one time or another, filled with rough and rowdy bikers, including members of the Sons of Silence motorcycle gang. The roar of their Harleys reverberating throughout the streets of Paris, the Sons of Silence were, at one time, one of the most feared biker gangs. Paris also has an inordinate number of unsolved homicides. More than a few of them involving drug deals gone bad.

From my experiences, some of the local residents were afraid to talk to law enforcement. Those who did insisted on remaining anonymous. It's all about self-preservation in Paris, and I really didn't blame them; no one wanted to become just another unsolved homicide—butchered in the middle of the night and their house burned down. And for such a quaint town, Paris has a violent history. An anonymous letter written to the FBI reflected one mother's fear:

> I'm writing to you instead of calling, due to the fact I don't want to leave my name. I live in the small town of Paris, Illinois. There is a lot of things going on in this town that's not right. I know every town and city has it's problems with drugs and deaths. But, this place is awful. Plus, there's a lot of the local police department involved. . . There has been several unexplained deaths in this town over the past several years. . . I don't know why people haven't done something a long time ago. I have a five month old son now and I

don't want him to grow up with all this garbage around him. I do
hope and pray that things can change for the better.

The letter was signed, "Sincerely, A Worried Mother in Paris, Illinois."

This letter caused me to reflect back to my teenage years. I was 17 at the time, and I grew up in Terre Haute, Indiana, about 20 miles northeast of Paris. One of my friends' father owned a small cabin just outside of Paris and we had planned on heading over for a weekend of partying. We also had plans to go into Paris and check out the local female talent.

My dad was half-asleep on the sofa while I was loading up my car. Half interested and half-asleep, he asked what I was up to. When I told him about our plans, he shot straight up off the sofa. Wide awake now, he sternly said, "You're not going! You're not going to Paris!" His words shocked me because I wasn't used to being told I couldn't do something. When I tried to reason with him, he wouldn't bend—"You're not going to that lawless town! You'll only get into trouble over there!" My dad left no room for any debate and I didn't go to Paris that weekend. It wasn't until 30 years later that I finally understood what my dad was talking about. Like the "worried mother in Paris," he was right—and there were certainly a lot of unexplained deaths in and around the sinister little town.

One incident involved a man found floating face down in an isolated, rural pond, linked to an oil well scam with local, affluent Paris businessmen. The police ruled the man's death a suicide with little to no investigation. I remember discussing the alleged suicide with a special agent from the FBI years later and telling him it was hard to imagine someone just walking out into a pond and drowning themselves. Smirking, he replied, "Yeah, and it's hard to believe it was from drowning when the autopsy showed no water in his lungs."

Then there was the murder of a local Paris woman named Betty McNay, who was found strangled to death on the other side of the state in Pike County. There were rumors McNay threatened to go to police after becoming another victim of the same oil well scam that had befallen the suicidal man found in the pond. When I learned about her murder, I asked Eckerty if he had heard of Betty McNay. After all, he seemed to be the man Paris police reached out to whenever they *actually* decided to investigate a homicide, but Eckerty claimed he never heard of her. A somewhat suspicious remark since I had already run her name in our indices system and had received the report detailing Eckerty and Parrish's interview of Bob Morgan in the murder investigation of Betty McNay. Ironically, after this interview, it was also Jack Eckerty who advised the case should be closed because of a lack of leads. Her murder remains unsolved to this day.

There was a deputy rumored to have interrupted a biker's drug deal; so he was tied, bound and gagged to some railroad tracks, the power of a locomotive used to scatter his body parts for miles. His head was found in Ohio still lodged in the locomotive.

There was a young college girl who was lured to a biker party, gang raped and then beaten to death, her body left in a surrounding forest preserve. The FBI report I read identified Herschel Wright, a name I was already familiar with, as the prime suspect.

There were men found bound and shot in the back of the head execution style with no motive for their deaths. A woman chopped up and her body burned in a steel drum. Rival motorcycle gang members who came to Paris and were never seen again. There were all of these and many other murders which all remain unsolved, just like the murders of Dyke and Karen Rhoads. Yet some of these other murders had associations to the Rhoads homicide.

Another case involving an alleged drug deal gone bad involved the 1984 murders of Gary Landsaw and Ronald Gilbert. Gary Landsaw was a member of the Diablo motorcycle gang from nearby Terre Haute, Indiana. The two men's disappearance was originally investigated as a missing person case. Indiana and Paris Police suspected foul play, but they were never able to build enough connections to take the case beyond a missing person's matter.

Renewed attention was given to the case in 2000, when guns from the Paris Police Department's evidence vault mysteriously vanished and surfaced in Indiana. The Bureau of Alcohol, Tobacco and Firearms (ATF) and Indiana State Police were able to acquire information about the murders of the two men. Finally, after 16 years, with this new information, a homicide investigation was initiated.

When Bill Clutter wrote to the ISP Director, some of his new information came from that ATF investigation involving the murders of Landsaw and Gilbert. Clutter's letter also reflected an association to the Rhoads case:

> A year ago last spring, ISP Sgt. Michael Britt . . . interviewed a witness at the U. S. Attorney's Office in Peoria. The witness gave Sgt. Britt information concerning the unsolved disappearances of two Diablo motorcycle gang members believed murdered in 1984, and also provided information concerning the murders of Dyke and Karen Rhoads of Paris . . . This witness informed Sgt. Britt that an innocent man, Gordon "Randy" Steidl, had been convicted of the Rhoads homicide.

Shortly thereafter, I received a copy of Sgt. Britt's report which implicated two Paris men, brothers Duke and Jerry Board, in the murders of Landsaw and Gilbert.

Sgt. Britt had interviewed Sonya Board, the ex-wife of Duke Board, and she stated that during their marriage, Duke admitted he, his brother, Jerry Board, and Dale Peterson, an enforcer for the Sons of Silence motorcycle club, murdered the two men over a drug deal in which Jerry Board allegedly owed the Diablo's money.

According to Sonya's statement, Duke said he and Dale Peterson "tried to burn the bodies and then buried them on the [family] farm." Sonya also indicated that Duke's first wife, Debbie Board, witnessed the murders. Sonya claimed she spoke with Debbie who admitted to witnessing the murders.

According to ATF, Debbie's interview mirrored Sonya's account and verified Duke burned the bodies and buried the two men on their farm after the victim's fingers, toes and other small body parts were cut off and fed to pigs.

Britt's report also mentioned the Rhoads case and indicated Debbie told Sonya, Duke admitted he was also involved in the murders of Dyke and Karen. According to Sonya, Debbie said a subject named Steidl was convicted for the Rhoads murders, but it was actually Duke who had committed the crime. Britt's report continued, "Duke had reportedly stabbed Dike Rhodes [sic] thirty-one times because this occurred on Rhoads' [sic] thirty-first birthday then cut his penis off and stuffed it in Karen Rhodes [sic] mouth who had also been stabbed."

With the possible association to the Rhoads murders, I contacted ATF case agent Eric Jensen that April 2000. This all occurred before I received the disturbing orders from Carper that the Rhoads case was too politically sensitive.

Jensen informed me ATF was close to arresting the two Board brothers for the murders of Landsaw and Gilbert. Besides Britt's information, ATF had gained other potential leads in the Rhoads murders. Jensen said ATF had interviewed a man named Donnie Comstock who claimed he was Jerry Board's former roommate. Comstock told ATF that Jerry Board confided to him he was hired to assist in the murders of Dyke and Karen and it was his job to burn the Rhoads house down. With ATF's information, both Jerry and Duke Board could also be considered potential suspects in the murders of Dyke and Karen Rhoads.

For the next few months, we had little interaction with ATF other than sharing information while they continued putting the final touches on their murder investigation. In the interim we were told we could not touch the Rhoads case because it was too politically sensitive, but I still had my foot in the door as long as the feds were snooping around and we stayed below Springfield's radar.

ATF contacted us later that summer and requested our assistance, and on August 2, 2000, we assisted them with the arrests of Jerry and Duke Board. We met the small army of ATF agents on the outskirts of Paris at the Edgar County fairgrounds.

Prior to making the arrests, we met with the Edgar County Sheriff who expressed his concerns, exclaiming, "You can't arrest the Boards!"

I listened in disbelief at his concern over retaliation from the Boards, and an ATF agent reasoned, "Sheriff, no one is above the law."

Frustrated, the sheriff replied, "You don't understand—I have to live in this town!"

We split the small army of agents into two groups, with each group assigned to arrest one of the brothers. I was with the ATF agents who spotted Duke Board driving his pickup down the highway moments before his arrest. Jerry Board was also taken off quietly by the other group of agents. Both men were taken back to the Edgar County Jail.

Jerry Board was the first brother interviewed. I watched him through a one-way mirror sitting in the interview room—his big frame handcuffed to the wall with his long greasy blonde hair pulled back into a ponytail. He sat there cockily while ATF and Indiana State police agents hammered away at him regarding his involvement in the Diablo murders. Throughout the interview he arrogantly denied any involvement in the murders and they were getting nowhere with him.

Violating Carper's orders, I couldn't resist and asked one of the agents to ask Jerry Board if he knew anything about the Rhoads murders. Board's cocky and arrogant composure dissolved when agents asked him if he knew who killed Dyke and Karen. He became visibly upset—nervously fidgeting in his chair, his smugness turned into a feigned sadness, with big crocodile tears welling up in his eyes. When he was asked why he was crying, Board claimed it was because he was "close to" and "best of friends" with Dyke and Karen. He rambled on defensively interjecting, "I bet you think it's me because of the *48 Hours* show! Everyone knows I wear my hair in a ponytail and I always wore trench coats back then."

Board was alluding to a segment of the *48 Hours* telecast where an unidentified woman witnessed suspicious activity prior to the murders. Her face and voice digitally altered, stating, among other things, she " . . . noticed two men standing opposite the street light by Dyke and Karen's house. What caught my eye was that they had trench coats on in July . . . one of them was a big guy with blonde hair and the other guy was small framed and looked like he had dark hair . . . " Her description physically matched Jerry and Duke Board.

This woman was another one of the several people who provided information to investigators in 1986, but whose interviews were ignored and never documented. When I asked Charlie McGrew why, his excuse was because this woman was "10-96" or "nuts."

Following the *48 Hours* telecast, McFatridge also acknowledged the authorities knew about this woman but had ignored her information. According to the *Paris Beacon News*:

> Former State's Attorney Michael McFatridge said that the mystery woman is not a new witness, if he identified her correctly. He could not recall specifically what she told the police, but the woman he remembered was interviewed during the investigation.

This all went back to the one central flaw of the original investigation that information identifying other suspects or pointing to Steidl and Whitlock's innocence was not documented or made available to the defense.

I eventually learned the identity of this woman through Bill Clutter and used this information to try a second time to get my command to reconsider and let us reinvestigate the Rhoads murders.

This same neighbor woman was also interviewed by ISP investigators years later in September of 2004 and this time her interview was documented. The report chillingly referenced the Board brothers' possible connection to the Rhoads murders:

> [The neighbor woman] stated on July 4, 1986 she had returned from a Bingo game in town and arrived home at approximately 9:00 p.m. [The neighbor woman] stated it was on a Friday night. . . . she went out on her front porch to sit and observed two men standing across the street from the Rhoads house, under the street light. [She] stated that it was not completely dark and she noted the two men were wearing trench coats. [She] described one of the men as a white male, approximately 6'00" to 6'03" tall, long sandy blonde hair, mid-thirties and big looking. [She] stated that she could not be absolutely sure but the subject strongly resembled Jerry Board. [She] described the second man as male white, shorter, dark hair and mid-thirties.

The report continued and on the next night, July 5, 1986, the neighbor woman:

> . . . was at her residence taking care of her terminally ill husband . . . [and] stated that her husband had a bad day and remembered it was very hot . . . . she was setting [sic] on her front porch around 6:00 p.m. when she observed a white Camaro or Pontiac Trans-Am with a gold stripe down the side . . . the vehicle looked newer. [She]

144

stated the vehicle had Florida plates and was occupied by two male whites. [She] described the men as the same men she had seen on July 4, 1986. . . . the vehicle circled the block approximately ten to twelve times and would drive past the Rhoads house very slowly and would stop in front of the house.

But the neighbor woman's account continued when she described to investigators an encounter she had with Jerry Board:

. . . several months later, she saw Jerry Board in the restaurant where she worked and payed [sic] attention to his profile. [She] stated she almost fainted . . . [and] she flashed back to the subject she saw standing outside the Rhoads house and stated she thought he was the person she saw standing under the street light next to the Rhoads house.

Coincidentally, Clutter learned that shortly after the 1984 murders of the Diablos, Duke and Jerry Board had moved to Florida. And they returned to Paris before the murders of Dyke and Karen Rhoads. Jerry also admitted he had a "cream colored" car back then. Despite the information from the neighbor woman and despite other witnesses linking a cream or white colored car with Florida plates to the Rhoads murders, Jerry and Duke Board were never looked at as suspects by the original investigators. In fact, they were never even interviewed. Jerry Board had even fit the description of the man buying the gasoline the night of the Rhoads murders with the white or creamed colored car with Florida plates. Yet police had never tried to identify this man.

After listening to Board's interview with ATF, I contacted Andrea Trapp and asked her if Dyke and Karen were really "best of friends" with Jerry Board.

Andrea was shocked, and said, "Dyke might have known who Jerry Board was but he would never associate with him," and she added, "Dyke was somewhat of a snob and would have refused to hang around the likes of a Jerry Board and I don't think Karen even knew who he was."

Almost two months later in mid-September of 2000, our office received a strange phone call from Herbert Board, Sr., the father of Duke and Jerry Board. He wanted to speak with Special Agent Jeff Marlow in our General Criminal Investigations squad. Marlow was related to the Boards and the elder Board wanted to meet with Marlow to discuss the arrest of his sons, who were locked up in the Edgar County Jail awaiting trial. I immediately contacted ATF, and it was decided to put a body wire on Marlow and have him meet with Board Sr.

The meeting took place September 20 in Paris. Board Sr. was upset about his son's arrest for the murders and threatened if his boys were convicted of the crime, he would expose a lot of things that would "blow the lid off" Paris. He claimed on the wire he even had pictures of former State's Attorney Mike McFatridge snorting cocaine with his son, Jerry.

Then the elder Board showed Marlow ATF's reports. The ATF agents were stunned because their reports hadn't been disclosed in discovery. The only others that should have had them were the Edgar County State's Attorney and the Paris Police Department. This was a serious issue for the agents. Here was the father of the two defendants with their official reports, including the names of witnesses. Witnesses who later claimed they were harassed and intimidated. I learned that in Paris, confidential reports were never really confidential.

Sometime later Andrea Trapp contacted me with another piece of troubling information. Andrea said she encountered one of the sisters of Duke and Jerry Board who was just coming from visiting Jerry at the jail. According to Andrea, the sister claimed her brother was upset because of a visit he received from a Paris detective. The sister told Andrea that Jerry was offered immunity from the Diablo murders if he could provide any information about Bob Morgan. The sister said Jerry vehemently denied knowing anything about Bob Morgan.

ATF's Eric Jensen blew a gasket when I forwarded this information to him, and he said no one had the authority to talk to or grant immunity to Jerry Board. The alleged visit was suspicious, and Jerry Board had periodically worked for Morgan over the years. I couldn't help but wonder what the real reason for the visit was, and if it did occur, did someone want to know if Board was willing to spill his guts or was there an investigation we didn't know about? Since this was ATF's investigation it wasn't my business to find that out.

Still a red flag went up the next day when Jensen called and told me a mysterious $25,000 defense fund was set up anonymously for Jerry Board at the Edgar County Bank & Trust—a financial institution coincidentally owned by Bob Morgan. And the Edgar County judge, for some reason, blocked ATF from finding out who the anonymous donor was.

During this same time, FBI Special Agent Williams, Sgt. Dixon and I made two trips to the Marion Federal Correctional Center. ATF said an inmate at Marion had provided them with information about the murders of Landsaw and Gilbert. Since he was at one time a high ranking member of the Sons of Silence, they felt he could be a good source of information.

The inmate went by the name of "Cricket." He started the interview by describing his life as a Sons of Silence and his vivid stories of biker lore depicted a wild and carefree life of drugs, alcohol, sex, violence and recklessness. It seemed the more violent and reckless you were the more respect you received.

The discussion eventually turned to the murders of Lanslaw and Gilbert, and Cricket bragged Jerry Board had initially hired him to do the hit. He said Jerry wanted this done because he owed a lot of money for drugs, and the initial hit was set up for a Saturday afternoon at the Board's farm outside Paris. Their plans went awry when Cricket said the Diablos "showed up in force and we were badly outnumbered." The hit was called off and Board agreed to pay the debt at the next arranged meeting.

Cricket wasn't available the next time Jerry wanted to try the hit, and the Board brothers reached out to Dale Peterson—another enforcer with the Sons of Silence.

"Dale was a pretty good shot, but not as good as me!" Cricket bragged.

According to Cricket, Dale said the ambush went as planned, and Peterson claimed he and Duke Board shot and killed the two men as they came to meet with Jerry Board.

Cricket's story conflicted somewhat with Sonya and Debbie Board's with the events that allegedly occurred right after the murders. Cricket said Dale Peterson told him they put the bodies in the trunk of an old Lincoln Continental and drove to Indiana, and dumped the car in a quarry at the Peabody Coal Mines.

Cricket laughed and said Peterson panicked afterwards because he realized he left the headlights on, but Cricket told him not to worry because the quarries are deep and the car would just disappear or the battery would eventually die out. He ended his version of the murders with the story that in the late 80s, Peterson showed him a human finger bone he made into a lanyard which he proudly hung around his neck. Peterson, however, never told Cricket whose finger it was.

Despite my orders from Carper, I asked this colorful figure if he had any information about the Rhoads murders. He mentioned the same rumors and pointed out the same suspects we already had, but piquing my interest, he added, that some time after the Diablo murders in 1984, he remembered Peterson telling him he was hired to do another double murder in Paris. Peterson also told him others were with him when he participated in this double homicide.

Cricket said Peterson never mentioned the Rhoads name, but in 1990, Peterson told him he had a "blackened heart" over something he had done. The reference apparently referred to something from Peterson's past and was so upsetting he often talked about getting a "black heart tattoo." Cricket speculated Peterson's remarks could be connected to the second double murder.

With all this, now there were even more suspects and even more suspicious associations to warrant looking at the Rhoads case once again. Now all I had to do was convince my command to quit turning a blind eye to all of this information—a task I learned was easier said than done.

Dale Peterson ended up committing suicide in 1990 and Cricket described his death in detail because he was on the phone with Peterson moments before he shot himself. Cricket said Peterson had popped an enormous amount of Valiums "which always made Dale depressed."

In the background, Cricket heard Peterson popping off rounds at Debbie (Hopper) Steidl, Randy Steidl's ex-wife. Cricket laughed at the memory of Debbie screaming, but added, "Dale was just messing with her. If he wanted to, he could have shot her right between the eyes." Seconds later, after hanging up the phone, he said Peterson turned the gun on himself.

Debbie Steidl refused to discuss a confession Peterson allegedly made just before shooting himself. Coldly and without emotion, she told Clutter, "That's between God and Dale, now." Debbie Steidl was wrong for I doubt it would ever be between God and Dale.

Jerry and Duke Board were eventually tried before a jury in Edgar County and were acquitted for the murders of Landsaw and Gilbert. Frustrated, dumb-founded and upset, Eric Jensen called and told me the verdict. He was beyond words. He was confident of a conviction. Upset with the decision, he said they polled the jurors after the trial and one female juror spoke up for the jury. "Oh, we all thought they were guilty," she said, "but you don't understand. We have to live in this town."

Now where had I heard that before? And after all, this was Paris. Ironically, just one day after their release, Duke and Jerry Board went to work again for Bob Morgan.

It wasn't long after the Boards' acquittal that I received another call from Eric Jensen. This time, he wanted to refer another possible homicide to us which also had associations to Jerry Board. Frustrated, Jensen wanted nothing more to do with the town of Paris, "They should just build a wall around that damn town and make it a prison," he said.

The potential homicide referred by Jensen resulted from an interview by Investigator Ken Fryman, Jr. from the Illinois Secretary of State Police. Fryman was working with the FBI on a federal investigation involving the Sons of Silence, and he received information about another possible unsolved homicide in Paris that was ruled "an accidental or intentional" drowning. Fryman's information came from a man named Richard A. LaBaume, who was incarcerated at the state's Hill Correctional Facility in Galesburg, Illinois, and he provided information about the death of a Paris bar owner named Conrad "Connie" D. Wilhoit.

On June 22, 1999, Connie Wilhoit was found dead, floating in his son's swimming pool. The death was ruled an "accidental or intentional" drowning, but LaBaume provided information that Wilhoit's death was definitely intentional.

LaBaume explained the sequence of events and the motive leading to Wilhoit's murder, which allegedly occurred because of another drug deal gone bad.

On October 6, 1996, the Paris Police executed a search warrant at the 230 Club on North Main Street in Paris. The 230 Club (a.k.a. The Horseshoe Club) was owned by Connie Wilhoit, and police discovered 32 grams of cocaine during the search. Wilhoit was charged with possession of a controlled substance with the intent to deliver.

According to Fryman's report, Wilhoit learned from a Paris policeman that the informant was Jerry Board. Angry because of the set up, Wilhoit enlisted the aid of LaBaume to find someone to do a "hit" on Jerry Board. LaBaume said he introduced Wilhoit to a man named Michael A. Stine, a.k.a. "Gunner." Stine was a high-ranking member in the Northsiders motorcycle gang and it was arranged he would kill Board for $10,000.

After the contract was finalized, LaBaume admitted he started to get nervous and warned Jerry Board "that Wilhoit was going to have him snuffed." Board in turn, arranged a meeting with Stine. According to LaBaume things changed after that meeting and now Wilhoit was the target. Stine, in the presence of LaBaume, phoned Wilhoit on the morning of June 22, 1999, and learned Wilhoit was going to his son's house that day. LaBaume said that after the call ended, Stine bragged, "he was going to kill the punk bitch today." Although LaBaume denied being present during the murder of Wilhoit, he was able to provide Fryman explicit details of the murder.

According to LaBaume, Stine went to the house of Wilhoit's son and at gunpoint, forced him into the swimming pool, where he intended on shooting him. The report continued that " . . . Wilhoit grabbed his chest, complaining of a heart attack," and then, "Wilhoit went down in the water. Stine then held Wilhoit's head under the water until he was dead." Labaume added that Stine took Wilhoit's "black hat with the red feather and was wearing it when LaBaume picked him up and took him back to Indiana." Several days after Wilhoit's death, LaBaume said Stine was still wearing the hat and telling everyone Wilhoit had traded him the hat for a tattoo.

Other than LaBaume's story, there was little else to go on to investigate Wilhoit's death as a murder. LaBaume's release from state prison was pending, but he was looking at additional federal time so he agreed to cooperate and wear a wire in hopes of getting recorded, incriminating conversations from both Jerry Board and Michael "Gunner" Stine.

Unfortunately, before the FBI initiated the first wire, the same old problems in Paris happened. LaBaume made a preliminary phone call to Jerry Board to set up a meeting, and shockingly, Jerry Board began sarcastically reading Fryman's report back to LaBaume. We were baffled how he had gained access to the police report, but unnerved by the leak, LaBaume refused to cooperate anymore, figuring he was better off going to federal prison than ending up dead. The Wilhoit investigation came to an end before it could even get off the ground. Wondering how the report was leaked, I called Kenny Fryman. Kenny was dumbfounded and had no idea, commenting that other than the feds and state police, he had only given his report to the Paris Police Department. Wilhoit's death remains an "intentional or accidental" drowning.

These were not the only two cases with associations to the Rhoads murders. Another strange death occurred on January 2, 1987, during the Rhoads homicide investigation.

Phillip Stark was a Paris resident who worked by day as a loan officer at Citizen's Bank and was also a part-time police officer at night. Stark was married and had two daughters. Although a banker, policeman and family man, he had a dark deviant side.

Paris neighborhoods were haunted by a prowler and Peeping Tom during the summer of 1986. Karen Rhoads, a few days before her murder, reported to her sister-in-law, Andrea Trapp, " . . . a chilling tale of a Peeping Tom peering through her window." Margaret Newman, who lived across the street from the Rhoads, described the prowler as " . . . wearing what appeared to be a police officer's hat with a small build carrying a portable radio." Paris Police Detective Gary Cash said, "Stark was known to suffer from insomnia and could be seen driving around town in his blue Maverick in the wee hours of the morning." Cash added, "Phil Stark was suspected of being the Peeping Tom whom neighbors reported seeing in the Rhoads neighborhood in the days leading up to the murders."

Stark's deviant side went beyond possibly peeking in darkened neighborhood windows. There were innuendos that the 36-year-old Stark liked young teenage girls. According to former Edgar County Deputy Mike Heltsley, Stark confided that he " . . . was screwing a 14-year-old nympho that lived across the street from the Rhoads."

"That's where he was the night of the murders," Heltsley said.

This was not the first time allegations of sexual misconduct surfaced against Stark. He resigned from the Chrisman, Illinois, police department under a cloud of suspicion of sexual misconduct with yet another 14-year-old girl. Chrisman Police Chief Steve Moore investigated those allegations. The police report with the 14-year-old girl and her family indicated she had been walking down an alleyway and was stopped by Phil Stark in uptown Chrisman. The report indicated that, "Phil told [the 14-year old girl] he would pay her $5.00 to suck Phil's penis. [The 14-year-old girl] stated no. Phil then asked [the 14-year-old girl] if he payed [sic] her $10.00 if he could have oral sex with [her.] [The girl said] no."

Despite these serious allegations, no formal charges were ever brought against Phillip Stark. Instead, he quietly resigned from the Chrisman Police Department and went on to become a part-time deputy for Edgar County. On the night of the Rhoads murders, Phillip Stark was working as an Edgar County Deputy.

Seven months after the Rhoads murders, on January 2, 1987, Phillip Stark allegedly committed suicide by shooting himself not once, but twice. His death was ruled a suicide from one shot to the right side of his head with a .22 automatic and another shot to the left side of his chest from a .357 magnum. Stark's wife, Nancy, reported hearing only one shot. Because of a potential association to the Rhoads murders, Detective Jim Parrish and Sergeant Jack Eckerty investigated Stark's death. Days after her husband's death, Nancy Stark was interviewed by Eckerty and Parrish. Nancy Stark told the investigators:

> ... the day of or the day after (she could not remember) the Rhoads homicide ... Phillip woke up in a cold sweat. Phillip told her that he had dreamt of stabbing someone. ... from that time on, Phillip was continuously worried about whether he had committed the homicide. Nancy stated that she would sit and talk with Phil many times about the homicide and they agreed that Phil could not have committed the homicide because he had been working at the Edgar County Sheriff's Office Department as a radio dispatcher on the day of the homicide. ... she knew that her husband, Phil, had talked to Deputy Dick McDaniels of the Edgar County Sheriff's Department and Trooper Terry Hackett of the Illinois State Police about his worries about the homicide.

McDaniels and Hackett were never interviewed by Eckerty or Parrish, if they were, it was never documented. Other colleagues also came forward with information indicating suspicions of Stark's possible involvement in the Rhoads murders.

Edgar County Deputy Mike Heltsley was interviewed years later by Bill Clutter and he stated that, "Phil Stark became real paranoid after the murders, it was more than just a mild nervousness. It was like he had done something criminal. He was visibly shaking."

Regarding the Rhoads investigation, one night, Stark asked Heltsley, "Mike, is my name coming up? Is my name coming up?"

When Heltsley asked Stark why his name would be coming up in the Rhoads investigation, Stark replied, "I may have problems. Well, I was there that night."

Heltsley said that it was "almost like he was making a confession to the crime." Heltsley also added Stark was concerned he may be questioned by the state police in the Rhoads murders. After the murders of Karen and Dyke, Heltsley said he "observed a change in Stark" and he was "as nervous as a whore in church." Deputy Mike Heltsley was never interviewed by Eckerty or Parrish.

The FBI had issued a report about the murders of Dyke and Karen Rhoads on February 2, 1987, and McFatridge commented on the FBI report by stating in a news article, that while the report "has not sparked any major developments in the case," according to McFatridge, it "has got us thinking about different areas." The article continued:

> The report does emphasize the person or persons who may have committed the crime "is likely someone who has undergone a personality change since the murder," McFatridge said. This person may display opposite personality characteristics. . . . "This would be a 180 degree change."

With this information in mind, Phil Stark definitely fit the profile from the FBI analysis. According to several witnesses, Stark had definitely undergone a notable personality change after the Rhoads murders. His apparent suicide more than supported that.

Corroborating the wife's story, Eckerty and Parrish also interviewed the brother and sister of Phillip Stark. Both confirmed Stark told them he "dreamt that he was stabbing someone" and "from that time until the time Phil died, he was constantly worried that he was the one who killed the Rhoads." While describing this dream, Stark claimed "he saw a knife going up and down."

Eckerty and Parrish obviously considered Stark a viable suspect in the Rhoads murders, because Parrish testified that at the time of Stark's death, "we recovered hair from him and blood samples which we sent to the [Illinois State Police] Crime Lab. . . . And after that, we conducted an investigation to see if any of the rumors were true." Oddly, in the very same report identifying Stark as a potential suspect though, Eckerty cleared him by the end of the four-page report. His report read:

> On 1-7-87, [I] went to the Edgar County Sheriff's Department
> and obtained . . . the radio log that had been typed on 7-5-86 and
> 7-6-86. The log reflects that on 7-5-86, Stark reported to the Edgar
> County Jail at 3:51 P.M. and left the jail at approximately 2:00 A.M.
> on 7-6-86. It is believed by the R/A [Eckerty] who investigated the
> Rhoads homicide that the homicide could have occurred around
> 12 midnight on 7-5-86. It is believed from the investigation of the
> Rhoads homicide that Stark had nothing to do with it.

When I discovered this report existed, I was astonished Eckerty would clear
Stark as a suspect by mere speculation. ISP protocol is to gather facts, report the
facts and never voice personal opinions. Eckerty's report was the first time in my
25 years I saw an investigator interject his opinion that a potential suspect had
nothing to do with it. The reason why was easily answered.

Eckerty and Parrish conducted the Stark investigation throughout the month
of January. Eckerty didn't write any reports regarding Phil Stark until weeks later on
February 20, 1987—coincidentally, just three days after Debbie Reinbolt first came
forward as an eyewitness and one day after Steidl and Whitlock were arrested. Reinbolt corroborated Herrington's timeline of the murders. With the arrests already
made, an investigation into Phil Stark would only muddy the waters for the prosecution. Eckerty acknowledged that records indicated Stark worked at the Sheriff's
Department until approximately 2:00 a.m. on the morning of July 6, 1986. Since
Eckerty was accepting the alleged timeline for the murders from the two drunken
eyewitnesses, he cleared Stark's name. Yet neighborhood canvases already refuted
the timeline set by the two eyewitnesses and made the time of the murders more
likely around 4:00 a.m. If the murders occurred later in the night as the neighborhood canvas indicated, Stark could definitely be considered a viable suspect.

Even more suspicious is the fact Eckerty wrote the Stark reports under a bogus Illinois State Police file number "87L0072" which was, according to Eckerty, a
"suicide watch file." In my 25 years with the ISP and after talking to several other
investigators, no such thing as a "suicide watch file" ever existed. The investigation
into Stark had uncovered significant associations to the Rhoads murders making
him a viable suspect. Protocol required writing those reports to the Rhoads case
file number, but they weren't; instead Eckerty wrote the reports and information
concerning the new suspect to a bogus ISP case file number. Despite these reports
indicating a definite association between Stark and the Rhoads murders, with no
further investigation by Eckerty and Parrish, these were the only investigative reports documented by them. The investigator's one mistake was they had already

sent off Stark's blood and hair samples to the ISP Crime Lab under the Rhoads case number. Therefore, Stark's name still surfaced in the Rhoads case file on the ISP lab documentation, but this was the only link in the Rhoads case file to Phil Stark.

McFatridge also participated in the deception to hide Stark's name from the Rhoads investigation. Like other pieces of exculpatory evidence, the prosecution never disclosed these reports to the defense. McFatridge even filed a motion during the trial of Randy Steidl " . . . requiring that the defendant make no reference or mention of Phillip Stark and any evidence pertaining to him in that Phillip Stark is now deceased and any evidence would be immaterial and irrelevant . . . "

Regardless of what detectives learned, who knows what Stark actually knew about the Rhoads murders. One could speculate that if Stark's dreams were a reality, then he could have been the killer—first stabbing Dyke in the back while he was sleeping and then turning his attack on Karen. Or maybe Stark was just a Peeping Tom, and he saw the murderers that night.

Maybe Phil Stark's death was not a suicide after all, maybe his death was just another unsolved homicide in Paris, Illinois.

CHAPTER 12

A FAILURE TO COMMUNICATE

○ne of the all-time classic films from 1967 is *Cool Hand Luke*. Actor Paul Newman portrayed Cool Hand Luke, a colorful and rebellious convict in a Southern prison. Throughout the movie, Newman's character repeatedly tries in vain to escape. As each attempt fails and he is re-captured, the warden, played by Strother Martin, exclaimed, "What we have here is a failure to communicate!" In Cool Hand Luke's last, ill-fated attempt to escape, as a guard raises his gun, Luke delivers his final words: "What we have here is a failure to communicate!" In 2001, we also continued to have a failure to communicate with the politically compromised Illinois State Police upper command.

By January 2001, approximately seven months had passed since Lt. Col. Carper issued her shameful and disturbing orders. Still, because of the FBI interest, there was a small window of opportunity for me to stay involved—as long as my involvement was only in gathering intelligence. So, when I went along with the FBI, if we were interviewing someone and they happened to give information on the Rhoads case I couldn't just ignore it. I was careful though not to document the information in reports since I would have been violating Carper's direct order, and that would have been an instant excuse for her to get rid of me. The FBI wrote reports, and I continued to fly below Carper's radar, hoping something would break wide open that couldn't be ignored. After all, Carper wasn't going to tell the FBI they couldn't conduct an investigation because it was too politically sensitive.

During this time, the Illinois State Police was undergoing another change. Investigations and patrol were being separated. Instead of a lieutenant running investigations and answering to the patrol captain, a captain was going to be assigned over newly formed investigative zones. Two lieutenants, one in charge of narcotics and one in charge of general criminal would answer to the new investigations captain. It wasn't as complicated as it sounds—it just meant the Illinois taxpayers were paying for three times as many command officers at around $100,000 a person. Therefore in January 2001, my title changed from District 10 Investigations Commander to the Zone 5 Narcotics Commander. Instead of overseeing all of investigations, I now shared those duties with another lieutenant and captain. In late January of 2001, Major Edie Casella became my new commander.

Edie Casella was the former Lieutenant Colonel at the May 18, 2000, Rhoads meeting with Col. Andre Parker, but Edie hadn't fit in with the politically correct command anointed by Governor George Ryan. She had fallen on hard times and was the victim of the politics that now ran rampant through the Armory Building. She refused to be one of the "yes" men and women who were, during that time period, a necessary requirement to be an ISP Colonel.

I had met Edie in 1984 when we both went through training to become Special Agents in the Division of Criminal Investigations, but aside from that May 18, 2000, meeting, I hadn't seen her in approximately 16 years. Edie lived in Springfield, and with this new assignment she was being forced to drive to Champaign—around a three-hour daily commute.

The Illinois State Police command were experts at retaliation by adeptly removing those they found to be too candid or not politically correct enough. When these transfers occurred, everyone in the ranks knew the command's intension was to vindictively dole out both humiliation and punishment. The teletypes announcing these changes would go out—eloquently written—from the director, assuring everyone the officer would continue to be a valuable asset to the Illinois State Police in his or her new assignment. In actuality, in cases like this, the teletype's real subliminal message was: "Please join us in congratulating Commander So-and-So on their new assignment of cleaning the shit houses at the State Fairgrounds. I'm sure Commander So-and-So will continue to be a valuable asset to the Illinois State Police."

At the time of her removal, Edie was the senior ranking Lieutenant Colonel in the Illinois State Police when the George Ryan administration took over. After years of sacrifice, dedication and unselfishness, her removal was definitely a humiliation. She had stood up to the new ISP Director's son who was given a six-figure job in the state police by daddy and George Ryan's "pay-to-play" politics. This was the same

ISP Director who assured Bill Clutter "that the foremost interest of the Illinois State Police in any case was to seek the truth and ensure justice is served."

Since Edie was not "politically correct" enough for the new administration, they called upon the Division of Internal Investigations (DII) to do her in. It was well known that DII's Public Integrity Squad had covered up for George Ryan in the License for Bribes scandal. That's how DII worked. When called upon, DII had no problems covering up a scandal for those with clout. On the other hand, if someone with clout wanted someone out of the way, they could be ruthless and would go out of their way to make a case against the person. After 25 years of dedication to the department, Edie Casella had her one and only internal investigation opened on her.

Despite providing documents to defend her innocence, she told me how the DII Colonel callously dropped them into a nearby trashcan as he smugly told her, "You don't understand. They want you done."

As a result of the one-sided internal investigation, Edie was demoted from her position as Lieutenant Colonel and reassigned as my commander. Many would have taken the reassignment hard. Because of her character, she put the betrayal and lies behind her and came over with a positive attitude and put all her efforts into her new job. As time progressed, along with Sgt. Greg Dixon, Edie Casella was one of my biggest allies to get the Rhoads case reopened.

It was in early February when Casella e-mailed me asking the status of the Rhoads investigation. I immediately suspected this was a test from Springfield to check if I was complying with Carper's orders. I didn't know Edie well enough to trust her, and before Carper's orders, an intelligence analyst under Casella's command put the Rhoads case in a Rapid Start database often used in homicide investigations.

After Carper's orders, I called the analyst to stop the project, "I already know. I guess some people are above the law," she said before I could even get a word out.

I rationalized since my lieutenant colonel ordered me to cease on the Rhoads case, I assumed the analyst's lieutenant colonel, Edie Casella had issued the same order to her. With this in mind, I carefully responded to Edie's e-mail. We met that afternoon at a local coffee shop and after talking, it became apparent she was unaware the case hadn't been reopened. I told her about the meeting Captain Strohl and I had with Carper. When I described how we were told the case was deemed too politically sensitive, Edie looked at me in disbelief.

"Oh, my God! What the hell does that mean?" she exclaimed.

I'm not sure she even believed me, and later I learned she went to Strohl for his version, but he confirmed Carper's disturbing orders.

Faced with the unbelievable information from both myself and Strohl, Edie forwarded a carefully worded e-mail to Carper regarding both the Rhoads case and Bob Morgan. The e-mail read, "In short, I was not sure what the initial ground rules were . . . but if you allow, a repository case to be opened, I would also like to track this [with an ISP intelligence program] at the most restricted access level."

Carper replied:

> With regard to the Steidl case and Morgan:
> 1. Lt. Callahan reviewed the case file and identified areas of concern.
> 2. Analytical support was solicited from [Operational Services Command] (OSC); the case file was submitted to OSC for scanning and analysis. STATUS UNKNOWN?
> 3. If, after proper review of the matter, it was determined that the aforementioned case should be reopened or a new case opened on this matter then a meeting should be held at the Regional and Divisional level first to discuss recommended action and direction. It was emphasized the Department would do the right thing.
> 4. We were also awaiting the outcome of Steidl's appeal. STATUS UNKNOWN?
> With regard to other cases involving Morgan:
> 5. There was no prohibition put on opening new cases on Morgan, except for the one listed above . . .

Obviously, the prohibited case listed above, to which Carper referred, was the Rhoads investigation. Still Carper's e-mail seemed to open the door that we could revisit the Rhoads case, at least, "at the Regional and Divisional level."

With this small glimmer of hope, Casella, Dixon and I started to quietly form a game plan to once again request reinvestigating the Rhoads case. Certainly we had learned more disturbing information since Carper's May 2000 orders—Herrington's failed polygraph which was never disclosed; McFatridge's decision to keep information favorable to the defense out of the case file like the neighbor woman on *48 Hours*; and the potential involvement of others like Dale Peterson and the Board brothers along with their association to Morgan.

There was also new technology available, DNA testing was not available in 1986, but DNA was now a factor in solving many crimes and in helping free many wrongfully convicted men and women throughout the country.

The evidence in the Rhoads case had long been either refuted or questioned, and revisiting the evidence was important. Between the case file and Clutter's information, there were certainly several leads and witnesses to follow up on that were either ignored or excluded which could shed light through a renewed investigation. These were just a few of the things we felt we could take back to the upper command. So Major Casella arranged a meeting to discuss the Rhoads case at Carper's "level." However, with no criminal investigative experience, I wasn't sure what Carper's level was other than being a political hack.

On April 4, 2001, a second attempt was made to reason with the upper command of the Illinois State Police to reopen the Rhoads investigation. This time I had Major Casella, Sgt. Dixon and Master Sergeant Danny Reed with me; all seasoned investigators to help in the effort.

The meeting took place in a conference room on the second floor of the ISP Armory building once again. When the meeting ended, Carper looked across the table at the four of us. She was annoyed, and I detected a look of irritation on her face, and then her biting words were just as stern and direct as before—like a general scolding her soldiers.

"You cannot reopen the Rhoads case," Carper ordered, her tone was meant to intimidate. "It's too politically sensitive, and that comes from above me."

Obviously fed-up with our efforts, Carper reiterated her shocking message.

"And just so I'm perfectly clear here, so you understand . . . you cannot reopen the Rhoads case," she said in a cold and stern voice. "It's too politically sensitive, and that comes from above me. Am I understood?"

We all sat there in stunned silence, with no idea how to respond.

Up to this point, I think Edie and Greg thought I was embellishing about Carper's orders. Now, they were hearing those shameful orders for themselves. I looked at Edie and saw the stunned look on her face. Greg was sitting there with his head hanging down, fidgeting in his chair. Reed just sat there with a blank stare on his face. I suspected they were experiencing the same surreal feeling I had the first time I heard Carper's orders. My eyes met Edie's, and I gave her a look of "I told you so." At first, she didn't even acknowledge me. She was still in shock. When Edie refocused, her eyes quickly darted to me, and her thoughts were clear—"Oh my God! I can't believe she just said that!"

Greg still had his head down. He was either still in disbelief or too ashamed to look up. Danny Reed showed no emotion. What could we say? We had pleaded our case and it had made no difference.

Then Carper gave us the same worthless spiel about how we could still go along with the FBI and gather intelligence, but we could not be operational in any way. Carper was arrogant enough now to stand in front of five ISP officers on two different occasions and tell us a murder case was too politically sensitive.

159

And her power was the support from the command above us and our fear of all of them.

Afterwards, Edie, Greg and I went for coffee. Three decorated officers—proud of their jobs, proud of their department and now that pride was being questioned. Here were three cops devastated by three little words, and those words weren't "Integrity, Service & Pride."

Four years later, in 2005, Edie Casella testified under oath in federal court about that meeting with Carper. Casella was asked about her feelings after Carper said the Rhoads case was too politically sensitive. Edie replied, "I just think what I took out of that meeting was I want to use the term shell-shock or, you know, something similar. I was surprised that someone would say that in a group environment."

> Q: Is that the philosophy of the Illinois State Police to be careful about investigating things that are politically sensitive?
>
> Casella: No. I mean, I have not run into that in my experience.
>
> Q: Anyone ever before in any other case either before or after told you that a case was too politically sensitive?
>
> Casella: No.
>
> Q: Were you and Mike and Greg collectively, were you frustrated by what Carper had said to you?
>
> Casella: I think frustration is one term. I think disappointed, surprised that we didn't actually accomplish our goal which was to change her position.

Likewise, Sgt. Greg Dixon also testified about the April 2001 meeting:

> Q: You indicated that Edie Casella told Colonel Carper that she wanted to proceed and become operational with the investigation?
>
> Dixon: Correct.
>
> Q: What was the response of Lieutenant Colonel Carper?
>
> Dixon: . . . to our surprise, Colonel Carper basically . . . set some real strict limitations on what we were going to do and what we were not going to do regarding the case . . .

Q: What about with the Rhoads murder?

Dixon: We hit a brick wall on the Rhoads. She basically said that ... we were to cease and desist on that case. That it was too politically sensitive and that that [came] from above her. That this was a serious issue and that [came] from above her and she said it a couple of times. That it was too politically sensitive, it [came] from above her, and that we would not investigate that case.

Q: So it was clear?

Dixon: Very clear.

Like John Strohl, these two decorated officers—despite internal pressures and intimidation from within the ISP—took the stand and testified. Instead of the state police command applauding them for their integrity and protecting the ISP's good name, they were silently ostracized for the rest of their careers. These were brave people who had nothing to gain—only to tell the truth. There were other brave men and women from the ISP who also came forward and told the truth, but not one of them was from the politically compromised upper command of the Illinois State Police.

Carper once again left a small window open for us—we could still gather intelligence, as long as we didn't get operational. There is a difference between gathering intelligence in a case and being operational. While both intertwine, there is a definite distinction. When one only gathers intelligence, they take in all information—fact, fiction and hearsay. One gets operational when they try to separate the fact from fiction and then corroborate the facts to build a prosecutable case. Intelligence gathering is simply taking down information, fact or fiction, and doing nothing with it. Operational is actually proactively seeking information, searching for facts and verifying them as the truth. It's gathering information and then corroborating it, developing and following leads, collecting physical evidence, obtaining credible witnesses and informants to prove a prosecutable case.

Our fear was what the upper command would do if we crossed that line? Greg Dixon would put it succinctly in his testimony:

I think the fine line was that it was so specific, that Col. Carper made it so specific if we did something that was considered operational in that case that we—I could see us getting charged or getting a DII case put on us and we were violating a direct order.

> So, I mean, so there you go. You have a direct order from a Colonel and to some degree, it's up to her discretion of what she's going to consider intelligence gathering. That if you go out there and the phone starts ringing and they're calling the Governor's office or they're calling the director's office and she just told you to stay in the shadows and be intelligence only and you're doing something overt or operational, you're in trouble. You'll get in trouble.

Greg had summed up our main fear—the fear of retaliation if we took things too far and actually investigated the case. Despite being limited in our efforts, we still persisted. We came up with some creative ideas to allow us to fly below Springfield's radar but still sell it as intelligence gathering if the question ever arose. This was all occurring during the summer of 2001.

It was the July 4th weekend, and my family was invited to a house boat party on beautiful Lake Shelbyville. There were two house boats hooked up next to one another, and we were ferried from the shore out to the party. Once on board, I walked around, admiring the detail and extravagance of the house boats. I was standing by myself on the bottom deck of the smaller house boat, watching my son playing in the water, when I was approached by the owner of the house boat—an affluent businessman in Southern Illinois.

I told him how much I admired his boat. He replied that he bought the boat from a good friend—Jack Eckerty. My look of surprise prompted a small smirk on the man's face.

"Yeah, I know Jack Eckerty," I replied, realizing he might have a hidden agenda.

Then it came out, "I just had dinner with Jack and his wife the other night. He's sure nervous you were looking at that Rhoads case." His agenda was now obvious.

"Yeah? Well he should be," I retorted.

The man was taken aback by my sarcastic reply, and our conversation ended quickly. Not feeling very welcome on the boat, I made my way to the top deck of the second house boat where I found Lily.

The day was hot, and we were sweating profusely and drinking bottled water as I told Lily about my strange encounter. Then suddenly a strange middle-aged woman approached us and said, "Hi, Lieutenant Callahan, I'm Sergeant Jack Eckerty's wife."

This was beginning to feel like deja vu. I'm in the middle of a frigging lake and now I run into Mrs. Jack Eckerty. She obviously knew me, but I had never met the woman before in my life, and before I could even say a word, Mrs. Eckerty started rambling about the Rhoads case and how it had "troubled Jack for years." She said he still had nightmares over the case and wanted me to know her husband was a good man, adding, "Jack always hoped that he put the right boys in prison."

I heard in Mrs. Eckerty's voice the same guilt and concern I had heard in her husband's. She continued rambling on, talking about how, just recently, McFatridge came over to their house and they spent four days pouring over boxes of information on the Rhoads case. And she wanted me to know they came to the conclusion they "got the right boys." I couldn't help but wonder why Jack was still having nightmares then.

Here I was, trying to enjoy the July 4th weekend with my family and out of nowhere, two strangers approach me to talk about the Rhoads case, and everyone was so concerned for poor Jack Eckerty. This case had troubled me for over a year now, and obviously it was haunting others too.

That summer, one thing I learned about Edie Casella is she isn't afraid to buck the system if she thinks it's wrong, and Edie simply refused to take no for an answer when it came to trying to reopen the Rhoads investigation. In August of 2001, despite Carper's orders, she asked me to prepare another memorandum, voicing our views and concerns to try yet a third time to get the Rhoads case reopened. Wanting to make an even stronger argument this time, Edie went to the Illinois State Police crime lab in Springfield to meet with forensic scientists to inquire about the use of DNA in reviewing the Rhoads murders.

When I initially reviewed the case in 2000, I had asked for the crime scene photos and overhear tapes in the Rhoads homicide. I was told they couldn't locate them and forgot about the missing photos and tapes once Carper stopped the reinvestigation. When Edie went to the lab in 2001, I asked her to inquire once again about getting the crime scene photos, but her inquiries had the same results as I had.

Our seemingly innocent inquiry was most likely one of our biggest mistakes, but I wouldn't learn why until January of 2008 when I saw the discovery in Whitlock's request for a new trial. The Illinois Appellate Prosecutor's Office turned over almost 3,000 documents which only furthered my convictions about the state police's cover-up in this tragic case. As I filtered through the reports, I was quick to point out to Clutter the numerous documents that were either negligently or purposefully withheld, and I was shocked by the unethical boldness of the state police investigator who had surreptitiously recorded attorney-client privileged conversations between Steidl, Whitlock and several of their legal counsel. But it was the destruction of key evidence that brought back memories of Edie's visit to the ISP lab that summer of 2001.

Besides the crime scene photos, the state had made a crime scene videotape. And the evidence destruction document that sat before me was only more proof of the state's lengthy attempts to cover-up this travesty. There it was in writing—the videotape of the Rhoads crime scene was destroyed for no apparent reason by the state police. The destruction of the evidence was against policy and against the law.

The state police was already looking bad enough in this case and the destruction of this videotape was more proof of potential misconduct. The videotape was actually destroyed on February 26, 2001, shortly after Edie e-mailed Carper about the Rhoads case. This was a capital murder case which was still on appeal in 2001, and evidence like this should never have been destroyed, especially with appeals still pending. Even more suspicious, the person destroying the evidence wasn't even assigned to our zone and had no authority to destroy the evidence. The person destroying the videotape was a master sergeant assigned to Tech Services, a bureau responsible for conducting overhears and wiretaps for the department. During the original Rhoads investigation, this master sergeant was the same Tech Services Agent who had put the body wires on Herrington and Reinbolt, and 15 years later he suspiciously destroyed evidence of the crime scene. Apparently the state police didn't care because they never bothered to investigate why.

A second document in the discovery also explained a lot of other questions. It was a memorandum written by Lieutenant Jill R. Hill on January 8, 2004. Hill, at the time, worked in the Division of Forensics, and according to the memo, she was directed by someone she failed to name to pull the Rhoads crime scene photos from the Forensics Archives. The same crime scene photos I had requested.

"Upon review of the file, I discovered that there were no crime scene or autopsy photographic negative envelopes in the file," Hill wrote. Hill's memo further revealed that on May 16, 2000: "A check of the archive book revealed that the file had been requested by Inspector Tommy Martin," and was not returned to the Forensics Archives until January 31, 2003. Inspector Tommy Martin had kept the file for almost three years and when the file was finally returned, Hill discovered in 2004, it contained no crime scene photos or negatives.

Lieutenant Hill's memo indicated she contacted Martin about the missing photos, and he admitted taking the file in 2000. Martin told Lt. Hill when he pulled the file, he also discovered the crime scene photographs and negatives were missing. Martin admitted he never bothered to report the photos missing and instead held onto the file for almost three years. He alleged he was the one that told me they couldn't find the crime scene photographs in 2000. The case was attracting a lot of attention in May of 2000 and there were still appeals; missing evidence like this was a serious matter. Martin claimed the reason he pulled the file was because retired crime scene tech Gary Knight asked him to pull it. Gary Knight was the crime scene technician during the Rhoads investigation. Knight was also one of Martin's best friends and I learned so was Charlie McGrew, the supervisor over the Rhoads case. Protocol was still for Martin to report the missing photos immediately, but he hadn't.

Hill never bothered to inquire why Martin failed to report the photographs missing. In fact, Lt. Hill and the state police command ignored this suspicious conduct. And Lt. Jill R. Hill, despite no investigative experience, ironically became the new captain over Zone 5 Investigations overseeing an allegedly renewed Rhoads investigation in 2007.

All this made me flashback to Edie's visit to the forensic lab back in August of 2001. When she inquired about the Rhoads crime scene photographs, Edie was approached by Tommy Martin, and he asked why she was "snooping around" and asking for the Rhoads crime scene photos. At the time, Edie didn't give his question much thought and neither did I. In 2001, neither of us knew about the friendship between Tommy Martin and Charlie McGrew. The same Charlie McGrew who had told me, "Don't make us old guys look bad."

Tommy Martin eventually left the Illinois State Police and he got a new job— Tommy Martin became the Chief Deputy of Douglas County, under Sheriff Charlie McGrew.

Later that summer, a third meeting with Lt. Col. Carper occurred Monday, August 20, 2001. During that meeting, Major Casella advised Carper she was having a Rhoads Homicide Assessment done by our intelligence people, and she told her she had gone to the forensics lab to inquire if evidence in the Rhoads case could be scrutinized with new DNA technology. Edie was careful to cover our asses and tell Carper we had only been gathering intelligence but was once again seeking permission to reopen the Rhoads case. Once again, Carper reiterated we could not reopen the Rhoads investigation. We had now been stonewalled three times by the ISP upper command.

We had already contacted the U.S. Attorney's Office, the FBI and the IRS, and garnered interest from them, but after September 11, 2001—9/11—the federal government's focus turned mostly to terrorism. Time after time, it seemed like we had one roadblock after another put in front of us, with the biggest obstacles coming from the upper command of the Illinois State Police, but we were about to encounter the biggest setback of all.

During Major Edie Casella's command, other than the frustration of the Rhoads investigation, our zone thrived and was extremely successful. Audits and inspections showed vast improvement in our narcotic task forces, and operationally, they were some of the top task forces in the state. Likewise, our general criminal unit handled a significant amount of high-profile murder investigations which had culminated in successful arrests and convictions. Colonel Carper even acknowledged this in her testimony years later:

> When Major Casella was over Zone 5, there seemed to be a lot of good things happening. I mean, certainly, there's positives and negatives . . . for anyone in charge of any command. . . . It seemed like we were handling a lot of homicides. . . . but Major Casella was covering a lot of ground and working a lot of hours and accomplishing, I think, some good things.

Despite this positive feedback, changes occurred.

On October 10, 2001, our intelligence bureau finished the Rhoads homicide assessment and forwarded their analysis to Major Casella and myself. This document was forwarded to Lt. Col. Carper and the ISP upper command. The 17 page analysis mirrored both my concerns and recommendations over the past two years and was summarized in the last section:

> A review of the information contained in the rapid start database promoted more questions than it answered. The eyewitness testimony provided by Darrell Herrington and Debbie Reinbolt is suspect at best. Their stories contradict each other and could be refuted by the available alibi witnesses. Several witnesses who could have confirmed or denied portions of Herrington and Reinbolt's accounts were never interviewed. Other witnesses provided legitimate leads that deserved additional follow-up by investigators. In hindsight, investigators should have conducted these additional interviews and followed up on others. In conclusion, the events surrounding the murders of Dyke and Karen Rhoads do not . . . lead one to assume beyond a reasonable doubt that Steidl and Whitlock committed these gruesome murders. . . . It is safe to assume that if the events occurred in the exact manner as prescribed by all the witnesses and at the approximate times, it would have been almost impossible for Steidl and Whitlock to have committed these murders.

Fourteen days after the homicide assessment was completed, Edie Casella was called to Springfield by Lt. Col. Carper. During that meeting, Carper callously informed Edie she was being removed as the Commander of Zone 5 Investigations and replaced by Captain Steve Fermon. Edie told me how shocked and upsetting her sudden and unexpected removal was, and barely able to hold back the tears, she said she sat there dumbfounded and then finally asked Carper why she was being removed.

"You obviously have a communication problem," Carper coldly replied.

Major Edie Casella had a communication problem alright. Her problem was she had refused to take "no" for an answer from the politically compromised command of the Illinois State Police. What we had here was definitely a failure to communicate.

CHAPTER 13

TWO SETS OF RULES

---■---

The teletype announcing Major Edie Casella's removal announced her successor as Captain Steve Fermon. The teletype also acknowledged he would maintain his position as the Statewide Investigations Officer. One man doing two jobs while Edie was relegated to a cubicle at the crime lab.

Fermon's assignment meant I was going to have to watch my ass more than ever, and shortly after his return, I heard he was bragging about getting get rid of me. So I confronted him to address the rumors. I could tell he was irritated, and of course, he denied the rumors, but unwittingly confirmed them with a threat.

"I want you to know, I can make one phone call, and you'll be gone! Do you understand that?" Fermon arrogantly threatened.

I replied I understood, but he repeated his verbose threat, sharply reiterating, "Do you understand me? Do you understand I can make one phone call and you'll be gone?" His message was very clear that he had that kind of power. It was well known throughout the ISP that Fermon had close ties to Deputy Director Dan Kent. Their relationship was obvious from the suck-up e-mail Fermon sent Kent shortly after becoming the commander of Zone 5:

> I have a very good "mentor" who has taught me how to do the tough things. I am an expert at adapting, adjusting and overcoming. You have been very good to me and very good for the ISP. Please make no mistake, I am on the home team. Thank you

for your support, past, present and future! I would also like to seek your counsel regarding future "opportunities" within the ISP . . .

Kent's return e-mail only re-enforced their close relationship: "I have never doubted your loyalty or questioned what team you were on. When I look back next year, I will still be proud that I was able to better position you for the future. It was a good thing."

When I left Fermon's office that day I knew he could pull the trigger anytime he wanted.

The situation began deteriorating almost immediately at the zone and things were destined to only get worse. Fermon began transferring people and never even bothered to consult with me, oftentimes, I was the last to know some of my own people were transferred. It was futile to broach any subject with Fermon because it was always his way or no way.

The zone quickly reverted back to the days of no accountability, and I was powerless to do anything but sit back and watch Fermon's vindictive ruthlessness. For me and a lot of people in Zone 5, it was one of the most miserable times of our careers in the State Police.

Dave McLearin was one of Fermon's first targets. McLearin was always one of the "go to" guys whenever the shit hit the fan in the area; he was the guy the local or county police called whenever they needed our help. During his career, Dave took four bullets for the department—a man brave enough to stand at the wrong end of a gun and almost lose his life. Dave had supported my becoming the new Lieutenant back in 2000, and shortly after my promotion, it was Dave who warned that Fermon was gunning for me.

In 25 years of police work, Dave McLearin never once had an internal investigation opened on him, but that all changed when Steve Fermon became Zone 5 Commander.

On February 9, 2002, Dave was out to dinner with his wife and neighbors for her birthday when Douglas County authorities contacted him about a suspected meth lab. Subsequently, he contacted me and we made arrangements to handle the meth lab by calling out another supervisor and other zone personnel. Our guys ended up arresting the meth cook before he even got his lab started.

Four days later, Sgt. Tony Snyder went to Fermon behind closed doors to complain that McLearin had showed up at the scene with his neighbor. Illinois State Police policy allows command officers to use their squad cars for personal use but only with immediate family members. Snyder said an agent at the scene named Bill Kroncke wanted to file a complaint. I called Dave when I saw Snyder sneaking into Fermon's office and he told me about Kroncke's complaint.

So after Snyder left, I met with Fermon about the complaint, but he said, "I'm too busy. Don't worry about it. I told Snyder to handle it man to man with McLearin and if Kroncke was so upset, he shouldn't have waited almost a week to file a complaint."

All of this occurred in mid-February and the matter seemed to be dropped since Fermon never brought it up again. McLearin's violation was a minor infraction, and in fact, Fermon often made it a habit to borrow my task force pick-up trucks for his personal use, and he even had the balls to charge the gas to my task force accounts.

Two months passed, and on April 2, 2002, Fermon sent me the following e-mail:

> I have recently received information indicating that on Saturday February 9, 2002 . . . in processing a clandestine meth lab, that unauthorized personnel were allowed access to the lab site by on-scene supervisor personnel. Were you aware of this?

What a hypocrite and liar! Fermon knew about this incident well before this April e-mail, in fact, he knew about this incident through Sgt. Snyder before I did. In 25 years of police work, neither Dave McLearin nor I ever had an internal investigation opened on us, but on May 30, 2002, Fermon signed an internal investigations complaint against Dave and I. The complaint against me was for failing " . . . to make proper notification to your supervisor regarding an incident involving a subordinate officer's unsatisfactory performance during a February 9, 2002, investigation of a clandestine methamphetamine laboratory."

Fortunately for Dave and I, Sgt. Snyder put his February visit to Fermon in writing, which not only saved our butts, but made Fermon out to be the liar he was! DII Deputy Director Harold "Skip" Nelson was later asked and testified:

> Q: Is that a violation? Mr. Fermon's placing false charges against Mike Callahan? Is that a violation of DII—forget DII. Is that a violation of ISP policy?
>
> Nelson: Yes. If we knew that it was malicious.
>
> Q: So, for example, if he knew at the time he was filing the charges that they were not truthful and he went ahead and filed them, that would be a violation.

Nelson: Correct.

But Fermon still continued his attacks on me when, one day, my son's school called and said Tanner was sick. Lily was away on a trip and it was up to me to take care of him. As usual, Fermon wasn't around and wouldn't answer his pager or cell phone, so I left a voicemail that I was leaving for the day. I also took personal time off, despite spending the rest of the day working at home. It was no surprise when Ruby informed me the next day that Fermon wanted to open a DII case against me for taking care of my sick son on state time. Fortunately Ruby showed him my timesheet where I had taken the personal time off.

Even more hypocritical, during that same summer, Fermon attended a blood splatter seminar at beautiful Lake Shelbyville. He also took his 17-year-old high school daughter on the taxpayer's dime. For two days, his high school daughter took part in the training until Fermon was confronted by the Deputy Director of the Division of Forensics and was forced to take his daughter home. Skip Nelson confirmed Fermon's inappropriate behavior, "Yes. I believe that was confirmed. . . . my conversation was only with [the Deputy Director of the Division of Forensics] . . . I do vividly remember that conversation because she was uncomfortable that she had attended that training and saw Captain Fermon's daughter there . . . she told [Fermon] that she didn't think that it was appropriate or professional to have his daughter sit in on that type of training. . . . Because she was not a member of the State Police and then also because of the content of the training."

> Q: . . . was it appropriate for Mr. Fermon to [take his daughter to the training]?

Nelson: No.

Despite the fact two Deputy Directors believed this was inappropriate conduct, no DII case was ever opened on Fermon. Yet he had wanted to open a DII case on me for caring for my sick son! That year, I learned time and again there are definitely two sets of rules in the Illinois State Police.

Fermon should've learned though, when you live in a glass house you shouldn't throw stones. Fed up with more continuing baseless attacks against him, McLearin turned Fermon in to internal investigations (DII) for having the Zone 5 range officer, Special Agent Bill Kroncke, falsify his departmental qualification shoots. Illinois State Police policy mandates officers qualify yearly:

> . . . in firearm safety and marksmanship, officers are required to train quarterly and demonstrate proficiency . . . Any officer who fails to

> qualify . . . or does not complete the number of annual qualifications, may, at the discretion of the Director, be: relieved from duty, subjected to disciplinary action, or assigned to non-enforcement activities.

After DII's investigation, the final report read, "Fermon admitted during the calendar year 2000 he falsified a shoot record. . . . Fermon said Kroncke came to his office, the card was fictitiously filled with shoot scores, and Fermon signed the completed record."

When I was interviewed in the DII investigation, the master sergeant in charge of the investigation confided that Dan Kent wanted them to handle Fermon's case "as an administrative issue only." But in my eyes, Fermon had lied, a terminable offense in the state police. Still, despite the deceit, Fermon's case was handled only as an administrative case, and at his disciplinary board hearing, the newly appointed Deputy Director of Operations, Chuck Brueggemann, commended Fermon for telling the truth to DII.

A good friend of mine, Col. Jim Fay, said he sarcastically interjected, "Yeah, it only took him two years and DII catching him to finally come forward and tell the truth!"

In my civil lawsuit years later, DII Deputy Director Skip Nelson testified about Fermon's infraction of untruthfulness and if he considered it a serious offense.

"Yes, it is. . . . It goes to integrity, number one. It goes to safety, officer safety, safety of the public. And more importantly, it goes to leadership. Because he is in a leadership position."

Col. Nelson's testimony continued and he was asked and answered:

> Q: I want to talk to you a little bit about truthfulness, honesty and those sorts of issues . . . To you as deputy director over DII, what does Giglio mean?
>
> Nelson: Giglio is a court ruling where . . . an officer, if they have in their personnel file, if there's been a finding in the past that they [an officer] have been dishonest or untruthful, that it can adversely impact their ability to testify in court because that information can be subpoenaed or petitioned and then their credibility is in question.
>
> Q: . . . Is this the sort of violation that would rise to the level that would have to be disclosed pursuant to the Giglio decision?

Nelson: Yes, sir.

Q: Now, a related subject to untruthfulness would be falsification of documents . . . I guess if you're falsifying documents, you're being untruthful, but you're sort of taking it one step further? . . . but it's also having someone else falsify those documents or bringing someone else to do this for you.

Nelson: Yes, sir.

Q: And the determination essentially was that Mr. Fermon had falsified his records . . . Submitted records to the department knowing that they were not true? . . . He had instructed someone else to participate in that with him . . . that he had failed to qualify?

Nelson: Yes, sir.

Q: Have you seen people terminated for falsifying documents?

Nelson: Yes.

Q: And if an officer had not qualified with a weapon and was involved in a shooting and there was a tragedy that occurred, that would be very detrimental to the department, I would assume?

Nelson: Yes.

Yet Fermon's punishment was a slap on the wrist and then it was business as usual with Fermon continuing his relentless witch hunts against several other zone personnel. And he wasn't afraid to lie, manipulate or use his obvious power with Deputy Director Kent to get his way. The hypocrisy continued when Fermon removed Special Agent Lance Dillon from investigations for, above all things, being untruthful and Giglio issues. Talk about the pot calling the kettle black!

Dillon was at one time assigned to VMEG, a narcotic task force Fermon ran as a master sergeant and was now the captain over. Dillon had brought forth allegations of perjury against VMEG agent Lou Shanks, a close friend of Fermon's. Dillon was also instrumental in the removal of another one of Fermon's friends he had hired years earlier at VMEG, a man with a criminal history. Fermon was eventually forced to terminate his friend from VMEG.

After Dillon's allegations against Shanks, it was no surprise that he became another victim of Steve Fermon. I was there the day Fermon gloatingly called Dillon into his office and told him he was being transferred to patrol. When Lance asked for a reason, Fermon arrogantly replied, "We've documented some performance deficiencies, and that's all I can say."

This was the same bureaucratic crap we all expected from the state police hierarchy and an e-mail from ISP legal Kevin Eack to Fermon confirmed this:

> I have reviewed the documentation provided . . . and the proposal to transfer [Dillon] to patrol. While I do not see the underlying documentation . . . it is clear [Dillon] is no longer suited, qualified or eligible to serve in investigations. Please . . . Ensure that at no time, either verbally or in writing, that the transfer [to patrol] be characterized as disciplinary in nature. Rather, it should be, at all times, characterized as a re-assignment (not demotion) based upon "operational need" and the "best interests of the Department."

It also became obvious Fermon had used his power and influence with Kent to get rid of another one of his intended victims when his short e-mail to Kent referencing Dillon's removal read: "I could kiss you, but I will not, thanks so much!"

During this time frame, probably the only thing that saved me was Fermon was too busy attacking others at Zone 5. Val Talley, an African American master sergeant was assigned as Fermon's new Staff Officer. Fermon went ballistic when he got the news, so he vindictively gave the one remaining private office in the zone to a white trooper, a man two ranks below Talley. Master Sergeant Talley was put in a cubicle in the squad room with the agents in the zone. Despite being a command officer, he never once complained.

I couldn't say this was racial discrimination by Fermon or just his anger, but I certainly felt uncomfortable with his treatment of Talley. And Fermon continued, relentlessly attacking Talley while he was at the zone, publicly belittling him with scorn or deriding comments and eventually, he transferred him out of the zone. Val Talley didn't take the abuse lying down, and he eventually filed a human rights complaint against Fermon.

There were others who suffered Fermon's wrath when he became the commander. People were transferred from units for no apparent reason, and against their wills, oftentimes my own people were transferred and I didn't even know about it until they called and told me. Carper acknowledged this in her testimony:

. . . I would call and talk to Lieutenant Callahan . . . and it didn't seem Lieutenant Callahan would be knowledgeable of things that I thought a commander would have passed on to a lieutenant. . . . one of the things that I had spoken to [Fermon] about is the need for him to communicate downwardly better and within his work group.

Master Sergeant Mike Bernardini was another to suffer the wrath of Fermon. Bernardini was one of the most accomplished criminal investigators in the state police, and his expertise was acknowledged zone wide from several local and county departments. During 2001, Zone 5 was called in to investigate three homicides: the rape and murder of a young college co-ed at Eastern Illinois University, the attempted rape and murder of a young flight attendant at a rest area, and the murder of a Vermilion County Sheriff's Deputy. That year we also handled several death investigations and assisted with two local cold case homicides. Thanks in part to the expertise of Bernardini, those crimes were solved and culminated in successful convictions.

Under Fermon's command, Bernardini was forced to move to a small satellite office, and would sit back and also be falsely accused of policy violations. It was no secret Fermon was out to get Mike Bernardini, and again, Fermon broke protocol and went around Lt. Col. Diane Carper as usual to use his clout with Dan Kent to get rid of Mike. Fermon even boasted to others in the department how he used Kent's power. An e-mail from a lieutenant to Fermon acknowledged this:

> Subject: problem child
> We talked a couple of weeks ago about how to transfer a difficult and obstreperous Master Sergeant. You told me you had rid yourself of Bernardini by going to Col. Kent . . .

And like so many others that year, Mike Bernardini became another victim of the vindictiveness of Steve Fermon, thanks to Mr. Integrity, Service and Pride.

Fermon was also instrumental in taking care of a lot of his inept cronies he had brought into the zone. The type of police officers who had no problem committing perjury on the witness stand, violating the Constitution or running amok like lawless cowboys in the Old West. And the department and DII did nothing but cover that up, too.

The master sergeant who had neglected the murder of little one-year-old Madyson Nicole Smith back in 1997 was once again brought back into Zone 5 to run the general criminal unit. In fact, with less than three years of investigative experience, Fermon helped get him promoted to Lieutenant. Likewise, the female sergeant who had the affair with the master sergeant and also ignored the Madyson Nicole Smith case was promoted to master sergeant. Fermon appointed her as the Director of VMEG, his old narcotics task force. According to Fermon's ratings, she was a highly skilled investigator and a highly skilled supervisor—even despite several occurrences which Lt. Col. Carper and DII would deem as "just management issues."

In March 2002, a VMEG agent e-mailed a friend who worked at St. John's Hospital in Springfield. The e-mail was "flagged" by hospital security personnel due to some very derogatory statements made by the agent. Hospital security contacted the Sangamon County Sheriff's Office who initiated an investigation. The Sangamon County Chief Deputy contacted Fermon after determining the e-mail originated from a VMEG agent in the Danville office. The e-mail, lengthy in its entirety, contained a significant amount of profanity, but it wasn't the profanity that had alarmed officials. The e-mail read, in part, "I have another case going to Federal court that week. Another fuck thinks he is going to beat us. What a fool. I am also going to buy a new gun—AR-15. It is pretty cool. I can't wait to put it in the Niggers' faces on search warrants."

Faced with this egregious conduct, especially from an outside department, Fermon had no choice but to contact DII. Before he did, he called a meeting with me and the VMEG master sergeant. I was shocked at their utter disregard for this man's racial slurs and their sympathy for his racist actions. Both were emotionally distraught with having to face the inevitable duty of terminating the agent. The VMEG master sergeant began crying uncontrollably about having to remove him, and she was oblivious to the racial slurs or violence the officer had threatened in that e-mail. It was obvious—neither one of them thought his actions or words were wrong. Instead of feeling disgust and shame for his behavior, they were upset over having to remove him. But Fermon had an idea, and he instructed the VMEG supervisor to tell the agent about his pending DII case and if he wanted to ever be a police officer again, he should resign before they were forced to fire him. An e-mail from Fermon to Carper confirmed this which read, "I anticipate that [the agent] will realize the gravity of the situation and tender his resignation."

The agent took Fermon's advice and resigned, and eventually went on to become a fireman in Central Illinois.

This was not the only scandal that emanated from VMEG under Fermon's command. In January of 2002, VMEG agents initiated two separate search warrants—one in Vermilion County and one in Ford County. Subsequently, two individuals were arrested. Likewise, in February and again in May 2002, VMEG agents executed three more search warrants, all in Vermilion County. And again, two other people were arrested. In each of the five search warrants executed by VMEG, hearings were conducted questioning the truthfulness of the affidavits used to obtain the search warrants. The defense attorneys alleged that investigators and " . . . other members, including Director of VMEG, have engaged in a number of instances where intentionally false and misleading information was used to obtain search warrants; intentionally false and perjures testimony was given." Additionally, " . . . no action has been taken except to attempt to cover up or excuse the criminal behavior of the agents involved. [VMEG] is operating without supervision or oversight and outside the bounds of the law."

In November 2003, the chief judge vehemently concurred with the defense attorney's accusations. One ruling, in part, stated: "In this case, there is clearly a problem of law enforcement going overboard, exceeding their authority prevaricating, absolutely ignoring the Constitutional mandates, which prescribe the actions of this particular police officer, and perhaps the entire organization." Additionally, the court stated:

> Before we get to the meat of it, the first thing I would really kind of like to get to is that this court, for approximately 30 years, had been going through pretrial orders pursuant to Supreme Court Rule . . . In defense, they call it Brady material. And how an agency can . . . of its own volition, keep information from the State's Attorney thereby keeping it from defense attorneys absolutely befuddles me. . . . This particular outfit seems to have gone the next step to decide what [the State's Attorney] can see and what it can't based on some policy somewhere developed by someone unknown to anyone. . . . [The VMEG investigator] was impeached today probably 20 times and not on inconsequential issues.

Additionally, the judge ruled:

> . . . the agent and the office he is employed by, VMEG, intentionally withheld from the State's Attorney discoverable materials and therefore prevented the defendants complete discovery. The effects of the agents withholding said discovery is to deny the defendant's constitutional rights under the Illinois and United States Constitutions.

By the time the courts ruled on the VMEG search warrants, Captain Strohl was named the interim Zone 5 Commander. On November 25, 2003, Captain Strohl met with Lt. Col. Diane Carper and DII Area Commander Lance Adams, one of Fermon's best friends. Captain Strohl provided a four-page memorandum outlining the perjury, Brady violations and all the Constitutional violations identified by the chief judge. Strohl specifically brought up four supervisory policy violations against the VMEG master sergeant and Captain Fermon. Yet no DII case was ever initiated from Strohl's complaint. In his deposition, Strohl was asked about his complaint to DII and Lt. Col. Carper.

> Q: Do you recall meeting with Carper and DII about this matter?

> Strohl: Yes. It was subsequent to this memorandum after I sent this in.

> Q: What happened in that meeting?

> Strohl: The meeting involved Lance Adams, who is in DII, Col. Carper and myself. You know, they had reviewed this and felt that this was not a supervisory issue. . . . Something that had been going on a long time in VMEG. They had kind of indicated that they didn't want to investigate it as a DII matter, and they didn't. They felt it was just a management issue.

The rules of conduct of the Illinois State Police state, "Officers will uphold the Constitution of United Stated and the state of Illinois, obey all federal, state and local laws in which jurisdiction the officer is present and comply with court decisions and orders of courts having jurisdiction." But according to two of the ISP's upper command—despite a judge's order that the VMEG supervisor and its agents violated the Constitution of the United States and the State of Illinois— this was just a "management issue"! The female master sergeant was eventually promoted to the rank of lieutenant in the Illinois State Police. Like David Letterman once joked about the George W. Bush administration, the same could be said for the Illinois State Police: "Let no cronies be left behind."

There are definitely two sets of rules in the Illinois State Police.

The nepotism continued, and in 2001, Fermon recommended his good friend from VMEG, Lou Shanks, for a lucrative job in the Illinois State Police's Financial Crimes Unit. Fermon's influence evidently got his good buddy the job when a state police interview report with the Financial Crimes supervisor read:

> . . . Captain Steve Fermon referred Shanks to Lieutenant Patrick
> Keen as a viable candidate for the position. Lt. Hill and Lt. Jiannoni
> advised they made the decision to hire Shanks based on the follow-
> ing: Shanks was referred and endorsed by Fermon . . .

Lou Shanks began working for the ISP but still had to pass a background investigation. When someone is hired into the state police, a comprehensive background
investigation is mandated. Obviously, this is done to cut down the risk of handing
guns and badges over to serial killers, other felons or incorrigible types. When Fermon hired Shanks at VMEG, he never bothered to initiate a background investigation, probably because they were good old buddies. However, with Shanks' new
position in the state police, a background investigation couldn't be overlooked.

Oftentimes, former ISP officers are hired to conduct background investigations.
In Lou Shanks' case, retired Master Sergeant Ron Haring was assigned his background
investigation, and Haring took the job of doing backgrounds very seriously.

Two months after Shanks was hired, Haring completed his background investigation and his recommendation read in part, "Due to the negative and factual
information documented in this complex background investigation, it is the opinion of this special investigator representing the people that this applicant is not suit-
able or recommended for any position with the Illinois State Police." Haring based
his recommendation on derogatory character references, untruthfulness by Shanks
during his background interviews, violations of VMEG policy, personal character
issues which forced his resignation at the Danville Police Department, and alleged
criminal violations of perjury and unlawful use of a weapon. Haring's background
investigation was thorough—something you would expect from a command officer
in the state police, at least most command officers in the state police.

Haring's investigation disclosed that prior to Fermon hiring Shanks at VMEG,
he was a Danville Police officer, and after admitting to having "sexual intercourse
with a woman, not his wife" while he was a "shift sergeant on official police duty,"
he resigned after an internal investigation was initiated. Haring also questioned
Shanks' truthfulness regarding his past drug use and his report stated Shanks answered "no" when asked if he ever used any illegal drugs. Yet Shanks' applications
to the Vermillion County Sheriff's Office and to VMEG disclosed he admitted
using marijuana in the Navy. Additionally, Haring's reports noted two other times
Shanks was untruthful during the course of the background investigation. Other
issues of untruthfulness also arose in Haring's investigation about the perjured
testimony by Shanks in an Indiana drug trial. And Haring's report included the
Indiana prosecutor's account:

... that he did not believe Shanks answers were material to the issue for a perjury charge, but thought Shanks was a questionable person and made him very uneasy. . . . He advised . . . perjury charges possibly could be filed through July 2005 on Shanks.

Haring's file also included Shanks' violation of VMEG policy by utilizing his assigned squad car for personal use and then lied telling Haring he was not aware of any VMEG policies prohibiting officers from using their squad cars for personal use. Shanks was caught when Haring provided a copy of the VMEG policy prohibiting this, with Shanks' own signature on the document.

The most damning finding by Haring was that, while employed with the State Police Financial Crimes unit, Shanks was detained at the Sangamon County Court House for being in possession of a switchblade. According to Illinois Criminal Statutes, carrying a switchblade is illegal, and it's a felony. What Haring's background investigation seemed to indicate was the ISP had a potential felon and liar working in our fraud unit. Maybe they needed his expertise.

While Haring was completing his investigation on Shanks, all hell broke loose when Fermon came to the aid of Shanks by complaining to several upper command officers, including his good buddy, Mr. Integrity, Service and Pride. It meant nothing but trouble. Not for Lou Shanks, but for Ron Haring.

The flurry of e-mails generated from Fermon only re-enforced his powerful influence:

> Please monitor this situation closely . . . for feedback to DII re Mr. Haring's conduct, methods etc. If his words are NOT appropriate I will send info to DD Kent for forwarding to DD Murphy.

Haring's fate was sealed after an e-mail from Fermon to Kent reflected, " . . . Mr. Haring requires close supervision and follow-up. My recommendation is to sever this relationship when practical." The axe eventually fell, and despite the enormous amount of paperwork he provided, it was Haring and not Shanks who was removed from working for the state police. Later, DII Deputy Director Skip Nelson testified about the Shanks background:

> Q: Were there allegations made that somehow Mr. Fermon was attempting to get Mr. Haring removed as a background investigator?

> Nelson: Yes.

Q: Was that something that was looked into?

Nelson: Yes.

Q: Was there a determination made?

Nelson: Yeah . . . Haring was taken off of doing backgrounds as a result of this whole confrontation between him and Captain Fermon . . .

And Nelson added, "Haring was removed because he was overzealous in his pursuit of Mr. Shanks."

Had Fermon let his Deputy Director buddies do his dirty work and get rid of Haring, life would have went on in the ISP as usual. Fermon's arrogance was his own worst enemy though and before Haring was removed, he made a series of intimidating phone calls to Haring filled with threats and profanity. At the time, Haring had no clue that the stench of the ISP upper command was already in the process of removing him—he had more faith in the state police leadership than that. So, upset by the unprofessional conduct of Captain Fermon, Haring made an official complaint to the Director of the State Police and DII.

During this same time frame, Zone 5 secretary Ruby Gordon-Phillips filed a hostile work environment complaint against Fermon accusing him of " . . . nepotism, bias, favoritism, intimidation, untruthfulness, racial prejudice, manipulation, and abuse of authority." Ruby's three page complaint to DII stated:

> . . . the majority of Zone 5 personnel do not have faith in the department in doing the right thing when it comes to Steve Fermon. Steve Fermon has indicated that he has been given full power through Dan Kent to do anything he very well pleases. Fermon has indicated to me that . . . he can make a simple phone call and things will go his way . . . That he is fully protected and non-touchable. That the department will cover this up for Fermon. So this is why I've indicated that Zone 5 will tell you all the facts, but have no faith that anything will be done about this individual who is out of control with abuse of power and nepotism.

Ruby's complaint specifically cited others who suffered the brunt of Fermon's wrath: "The intimidation that Fermon displays on personnel who will not play his game is very blatant. Val Talley as Fermon's staff officer has been treated inhumane and with malice and prejudice."

Another allegation by Ruby involved Fermon's relationship with Tracey Reed, the wife of his best friend, Danny Reed. Tracey had mysteriously gone from an employee at VMEG to getting a lucrative state police position when Fermon went to Springfield. Now he had brought Tracey back to the zone as his administrative assistant which blocked a well-deserved promotion for Ruby. Earlier in his career, it was common knowledge Fermon had an affair with Tracey. So Ruby's allegations were Fermon used his influence to get his ex-mistress a lucrative state job without the proper qualifications.

Despite DII misrepresenting Ruby's complaint that "Fermon is having an ongoing sexual relationship with Administrative Assistant II, Tracey Reed," her three-page complaint actually read:

> Whether this guy is having an affair at this time is not the question. It is common knowledge that he did have an affair with Tracey Reed in the past. . . . Is it normal for a Captain to take his AA on most business trips? Is it normal for a Captain to give his AA nearly a 16% raise within a two year period? What Captain do you know transfers his AA with him wherever he goes?

Ruby was referring to several e-mails she had provided to DII showing Fermon and Tracey Reed, along with Dan Kent, taking trips together to resorts like Snow King, Wyoming—all on federal funds. It was my experience not too many Captains took their secretaries on trips like this, yet the e-mails Ruby provided were proof of the overnight stays at the taxpayer's expense. The first e-mail from Deputy Director Kent to Fermon read: "Can we pay for it with Meth money? There is no General Revenue."

Fermon's reply to Kent read:

> We should be able to fund this travel with Federal Meth Grant Funds, however, I will get the ball rolling to *ensure* [italics added] we have 'approval or authority' . . . My records reflect that the conference/lodging will be at the SNOWKING RESORT, Jackson Hole, Wy. This is a beautiful area, 62 miles from Yellowstone Nat'l Park, minutes away from Grand Tetons, excellent shopping, fishing, rafting etc. I plan to build a few days of vacation into my trip and enjoy the great outdoors . . . Tracey will fly to Jackson at some point probably around Wednesday . . . No one knows this stuff, but it will be a good time!

Despite the unorthodox protocol of Fermon traveling with his secretary to Snow King Resort was the added hypocrisy of Kent violating his own directive. In February 2002, Kent had issued a directive that Federal Meth Grant monies could be utilized for the "dismantling of meth labs only." Yet six months later, here he was violating his own directive by using these monies to attend a conference in "beautiful Snow King Resort, Wyoming."

Ruby's complaint also disclosed Tracey was allowed by Fermon to do her own performance evaluations, and an e-mail from Tracey Reed to Fermon confirmed this:

> Subject: Performance Evaluation.
>   Print these [attachments] and look at them. My brain is too tapped to do much more on it right before close of business. Change what you wish . . .

The lengthy attachments showed, through her evaluations of herself, Tracey Reed had quite a high opinion of her work performance. At least enough to get 16% in pay raises from Mr. Integrity, Service & Pride over the next two years when everyone else was getting far less.

In 2004, Colonel Jim Fay told me how the Illinois Inspector General came to the ISP Division of Administration and pulled all of Tracey's employment files. Soon after the Inspector Generals' visit, Tracey Reed mysteriously resigned, and her last e-mail read: "Remember that you have to take care of yourselves and those close to you first, this is only a job!"

As for Fermon, DII totally disregarded the real issues of Ruby and Haring's complaints, and as everyone expected, he skated on everything.

When I read through the DII file regarding Lou Shanks, it was evident DII also tried hard to whitewash as much as they possibly could. But they couldn't get away with whitewashing everything, and although most of their reasoning for not sustaining many of Haring's complaints were ridiculously humorous, DII had no choice but to find him guilty of being untruthful on at least one occasion. Likewise, DII had no choice but to find Shanks guilty of carrying a switchblade into the Sangamon County Court House. The department couldn't afford to cover this up since there were Sangamon County reports showing the criminal activity. With that glaring evidence, they had no choice but to sustain the allegation. Lou Shanks had committed a felony in the State of Illinois. But Shanks was never charged with the crime or even punished. The DII report from Skip Nelson read:

> . . . the investigation confirmed Shanks was in possession of a switchblade knife at the Sangamon County Courthouse on October 17,

2001. The fact Shanks was carrying this weapon while employed as a
civilian investigator with the ISP is a significant concern.

Despite Nelson's significant concern, Shank's kept his lucrative state police job for
another nine months on the taxpayer's dime. He had committed a felony in the
State of Illinois, yet he stayed on the state police's payroll and worked as an investigator . . . or, as I saw it, a felon investigating felons.

Despite the huge amount of paperwork provided by Haring and Ruby to back
up their allegations, DII ruled every single charge against Fermon as "unfounded"
or "not sustained." Shanks too suffered no repercussions. Yet, Ron Haring did, and
he was removed from doing backgrounds until the new Deputy Director of DII
took over. Ruby Gordon-Phillips also suffered consequences, and the remaining
few years of her career were spent being ostracized and attacked by the ISP upper
command. She was subjected to so much internal pressure and stress she took an
early retirement for health reasons.

I learned that Fermon had more than his share of DII cases throughout his
career. Interestingly, after what seemed to be considerable whitewashing in each of
the DII investigations, he was exonerated in each and every case. Yet the individuals who made the allegations always suffered retaliation and were removed from
their positions or transferred. I too was destined to suffer that same fate.

The Division of Internal Investigation is mandated to thoroughly investigate
allegations to "absolve the innocent and identify the guilty." I came to learn their
real intent in many instances was to "absolve the guilty and punish the innocent."
And the cover-ups by DII for Fermon and other ISP commanders in the years to
come were about to get even more egregious.

Newlyweds Dyke and Karen Rhoads; 1986.
(Photo courtesy of the Rhoads family.)

Crime scene photo: Dyke and Karen's bedroom.
(Photo courtesy of *48 Hours*.)

Burning Rhoads residence, 433 E. Court Street, Paris,
Illinois.
(Photo courtesy of *Paris Beacon-News*.)

Family members Tony Rhoads and Andrea Trapp at the gravesite of
Dyke and Karen.
(Photo courtesy of *48 Hours*.)

Edgar County State's Attorney, Mike McFatridge.
(Photo courtesy of *48 Hours*.)

Edgar County courthouse,
Paris, Illinois.
(Photo courtesy
Mary Anne Lipousky-Butikas.)

Paris Police Chief Gene Ray.
(Photo courtesy of
Paris-Beacon News.)

Paris Beacon-News.
(Photo courtesy Jake Aurelian.)

Eyewitness Darrell Herrington during November 1986 police interview.
(Photo courtesy of *48 Hours.*)

Eyewitness Debbie Reinbolt in 1987.
(Photo courtesy of *48 Hours.*)

Randy Steidl being led away by police; convicted and sentenced to death
for the murders of Dyke and Karen Rhoads, 1987.
(Photo courtesy of *48 Hours*.)

After a jury stalemate, Herb Whitlock was convicted for the murder of
Karen Rhoads and sentenced to life in prison without parole, 1987.
(Photo courtesy of *48 Hours*.)

ILLINOIS DEPARTMENT OF STATE POLICE

CASE ACTION REPORT

Division No.	Case Title:		Case Agent:	Officer	Date of Action:
86-L-3365	Homicide - Dyke Rhoads		Eckerty 1208	20L210	8/25/87

County	Court/Hearing	Docket No. (s)		This Action Closes Case?
Edgar	5TH Circuit	87-CF-38 87-CF-20 87-CF-21		☒ Yes ☐ No

I. ADJUDICATION

Proceeding Codes
A. Complaint (16,17)
B. Prelim Hearing (1,4,8,6,7)
C. Grand Jury (2,3,6)
D. Information (16,17)
E. Plea (10,11,12,13)
F. Bench Trial (8,9,10,11,12,13)
G. Jury Trial (8,9,10,11,12,13)
H. Civil (7,14,15)
I. Steward Hearing (7,14,15)
J. Other (5,6,7,19,20)

Action Codes
1. Bound Over
2. True Bill
3. No True Bill
4. Waived
5. Nolle Prosequi
6. S.O.L.
7. Dismissed
8. Acquitted
9. Mistrial
10. Felony Conviction
11. Felony Conv. (Reduced)
12. Misdemeanor Conviction
13. Misdemeanor Conv. (Reduced)
14. Civil Finding For State
15. Civil Finding Against State
16. Warrant Issued
17. Summons/Notice Issued
18. Juvenile Hearing
19. Motion Hearing
20. Continued

Defendant	Date of Arrest & No.	Charge(s)	Crime Code	Prcdg Code	Action Code	Sentence/Fine/Action
1. GORDON R. STEIDL	2-19-87 A-17606	Murder	0110	GJ	10	DEATH SENTENCE
2. Herbert R. Jr. WHITLOCK	2-19-87 A-17607	murder	0110	G	10	LIFE - WITHOUT PAROLE
3. DEBORAH I. RIENBOLT	4/29/87 B-6135	Concealing Homicide	3745	F	10	5 YEARS AT D.O.C.

The Illinois State Police case action report on the adjudication
of Steidl, Whitlock and Reinbolt, 1987.

CONFIDENTIAL SOURCE'S RECEIPT OF FUNDS

Purpose: Purchase of Evidence [ ], Information and Services [ ], Protection Expenses [X]   Division No. 86-L-3365

I hereby acknowledge the receipt of Official Advance Funds in the amount of Two Thousand Five Hundred Dollars
and 00/100 dollars ($ 2,500 00), provided to me by Special Agent ___J. R. Eckerty___ 1208
(Name and ID No.)

Provided by: J R Eckerty 1208   Date 8/20/87   Confidential Source: Deborah J Rienbolt 8/20/87
(Signature and ID No.)   Witness   Date

Witnessed by: Charles E McGrew 1593   Date 08/20/87   C/S No. 86L 3365
(Signature and ID No.)

269

IL 493-0126   ADMINISTRATIVE USE ONLY – DO NOT DISSEMINATE

File in 86L 3365   DSP 4-14 (8/85)

433

Illinois State Police receipt for payment of $2,500 to Debbie Reinbolt signed
by Sgt. Jack Eckerty, M/Sgt. Charles McGrew and Debbie Reinbolt, 1987.

December 10, 1987

Dear Debbie,

Yes I know I haven't written, and yes I know you upset. What can I say, I'm sorry. We have been very busy with Burglaries but I should have taken time.

How have you been doing? I hope fine, from all reports that I've heard you are doing fine and working for the warden. I figure in a year you will be the warden.

Sometime in the near future Eckity and I are going to drive up and see you and spend some time.

Daryll is doing fine and going about town as nothing every happened and working everyday. Daryll is still drinking as if who thought he would stop.

I'm not much for writing so I will say good bye and take care of yourself. I am thinking about you even though I don't write very often. See you soon.

Sincerely
Jim

```
Date: 04/14/00
From: MSgt. James Wolf
  To: Lt. Colonel Diane Carper          WOLFJAM  - ISPHOST
Subject: Clutter letter                 CARPERD  - ISPHOST
-------------------------------------------------------------------------
```

I think Callahan should take the lead on this and work with Rollings (who is more familiar with this case) to determine if CLutter's information warrants additional investigation. I also think having the Investigations Commander review the case file etc, gives us additional credibility if this should get to a Mike Wallace type.
Bottom line, we do not want anyone to be embarrassed or put in the hot seat for not investigating this or contacting individuals who state they have information about the incident.

Pressure from a forthcoming episode of *48 Hours* and rumblings from Private Investigator Bill Clutter caused deep concern within the ISP command as evidenced by this excerpt from Lt. Col. Diane Carper's staff officer.

Private Investigator Bill Clutter talking to *48 Hours'* Susan Spencer about the state's flawed evidence: exhibit #26, the broken lamp.
(Photo courtesy of *48 Hours*.)

HERRINGTON
Drywall and General Construction
1307 S. Central St.
Paris, IL 61944
(217) 466-4510

YOUR SHOPPING LIST

SAW BOB MORGAN STANDING AT BOTTOM OF STAIRS when he entered the residence. Bob told DARRELL "you didn't see me." AND DARRELL SAID "OKAY."

DARRELL TALKED to MORGAN AT Post Office 3 days LATER

Bob MET DARRYLL AT DARREll's SHOP AND OFFERED DARRYLL $25,000 CASH $25,000 PROPERTY TO "KEEP HIS MOUTH SHUT.

BOB MORGAN
MIKE MORGAN
JOHN ARMSTRONG

Since Trial less remembered

AUG. 19, 1987 11:00pm

DARRELL, GENE, GARY Jim AT DARRELL'S House

Had CONVERSATION with PAULA MYRES SAID there was more that DARRELL KNEW but DIDN'T SAY IN COURT

Detective Jim Parrish's notes found hidden away in the basement of the Paris Police Department by Bill Clutter 14 years after the convictions of Steidl and Whitlock.
The notes were taken during a domestic dispute between Darrell Herrington and his wife on August 19, 1987, just one month after Steidl was sentenced to death and Whitlock to life in prison.

Diane Carper's handwritten notes: "Steidl case not to be reopened."

Photo of Lt. Col. Diane Carper, promotion ceremony of Mike Callahan.

Steven Fermon
12/18/2002 02:47 PM

To: Diane Carper/IlStPolice@IlStPolice
cc:
Subject: Rhoads Homicide

THIS IS REGARDING THE STEIDL CASE. LT. CALLAHAN HAS BEEN ADVISED THAT DEP. GOV. BETTENHAUSEN HAD POSSIBILY SOLICITED THIS CLEMENCY PETITION.

OBVIOULSY WE NEED TO DISCUSS BEFORE ANY MEETINGS, THIS IS THE PLACE BETWEEN THE ROCK AND THE HARD PLACE. SMF

Captain Steven M. Fermon
ISP Zone 5 Commander
█████████ Champaign Office
█████████ Pager
----- Forwarded by Steven Fermon/IlStPolice on 12/18/2002 02:44 PM -----

E-mail from Captain Steve Fermon to Lt. Col. Diane Carper regarding the clemency petition for Steidl and Whitlock to Governor George Ryan.

Captain Steve Fermon.
(Photo courtesy of *Illinois Times*.)

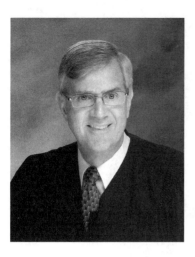

Federal Judge Michael McCuskey, on June 17, 2003, gave the state of Illinois 120 days to retry Randy Steidl or free him. Judge McCuskey ruled "acquittal was reasonably probable if the jury heard all the evidence."

Illinois Attorney General Lisa Madigan. In 2004, her office refused to retry Randy Steidl and he was eventually freed after her office determined, "information favoring the defense was never disclosed."
(Photo courtesy of *Chicago Tribune*.)

Randy Stedil walking out of prison a free man once again, May 2004.
(Photo courtesy of *48 Hours*.)

Mike Callahan meeting Randy Steidl in October 2007.
(Photo courtesy of WCIA-TV, Champaign, Illinois.)

Mike Callahan, Lily Callahan and his attorney John Baker walking out of the Federal Court House in Urbana, Illinois after a jury agreed the Illinois State Police violated Callahan's 1st Amendment rights (April 2005).
(Photo courtesy of *48 Hours.*)

Mike Callahan speaking to the media after winning his trial.
(Photo courtesy of *48 Hours.*)

Mike Callahan and son Tanner playing basketball.
(Photo courtesy of *48 Hours.*)

Herb Whitlock with his daughter the day he was freed after spending almost 21 years in prison.
(Photo courtesy of *Chicago Tribune*.)

Herb Whitlock with his attorneys, Richard Kling and Susanna Ortiz.
(Photo courtesy of Bill Clutter.)

Mike Callahan meeting Herb Whitlock on the day of his release from prison.
(Photo courtesy of *Chicago Tribune*.)

Governor George Ryan, convicted and imprisoned for 6 ½ years on federal racketeering charges in 2006. Assistant U.S. Attorney Patrick Collins said, "Deterring corruption in Illinois is a difficult job. It is a mutating virus."
(Photo courtesy of *Chicago Tribune.*)

```
Date: 04/03/01
From: Diane Carper                          CARPERD - ISPHOST

I cannot emphasize enough how important it is to report issues that may be
construed as significant.  The Governor's office considers the Illinois State
Police the eye's and ear's of the state.
```

Excerpt from an e-mail issued by Lt. Col. Diane Carper to the ISP commanders in her region.

On December 9, 2008, Governor Rod Blagojevich became the second Illinois governor in a row to face federal criminal charges. On January 30, 2009, Blagojevich was removed from office after a 59-0 vote from the Illinois senate. Robert Grant, special agent in charge of the FBI Chicago office, declared of Illinois: "If it isn't the most corrupt state in the United States, it's certainly one hell of a competitor."
(Photo courtesy of *Chicago Tribune.*)

CHAPTER 14

CLEMENCY: HE GIVETH, HE TAKETH AWAY

---◼---

President Ronald Reagan once said, "Politics is supposed to be the second oldest profession. And I have come to realize that it bears a close resemblance to the first oldest profession." Reagan's observations were especially true for the State of Illinois with all its political corruption and pay-to-play politics. The U.S. Attorney's Office under Patrick Fitzgerald, along with several federal agencies, made that apparent in their fight against the political corruption that arrogantly abounds in the State of Illinois. But for now, George Ryan was still governor and the state police command was still his guardian.

One of my concerns with Fermon taking over command was what was going to happen to the Rhoads case. I knew he was aware of the case so I broached the subject about reopening the case with him. Fermon, however, wasn't too supportive from the start. This was emphasized in an e-mail dated December 12, 2001, to Lt. Col. Carper, when Fermon reported:

> I have asked Lt. Callahan and, M/Sgt. Reed and Sgt. Dixon to work out a mutually acceptable time for us to discuss this. At this point in time, applying VALUE, RESOURCES and SUPPORT [is something that] I don't really think that we can support . . . however, I will reserve decision until I have heard the facts.

Before we sat down and met, I divulged to Fermon our previous orders from Carper about the Rhoads case being too politically sensitive to reinvestigate. With this information, Fermon e-mailed Carper on January 11, 2002, inquiring:

> On January 22, 2002, I will meet with Lt. Callahan, M/Sgt. Danny Reed and Sgt. Dixon to discuss the [Paris] investigation. We will then determine what direction we are going. I would like to discuss this with you BEFORE the meeting so that I have a full understanding of the previous direction given.

Carper's "previous direction" was only reinforced in some handwritten notes she later gave up in discovery three years later, in bold print, the notes plainly indicated, "STEIDL CASE NOT TO BE RE-OPENED." Of course, we weren't aware of these communications between Carper and Fermon, so Greg and I continued to try and seek Fermon's support in reopening the Rhoads case.

Greg and I met with Fermon later that January and shared every piece of information we had gathered, every person who gave us information, every person who was still giving us information and also about the hidden camera location. I had no reason to be concerned about the confidentiality of the things we discussed, but a lot of the information divulged at that meeting was eventually compromised.

Even Danny Reed supported us.

"Steve, you need to listen to those guys. They have something," Reed said. "Those two boys [Steidl and Whitlock] are innocent."

At the conclusion of the meeting, Fermon said he felt we had neither the resources, time or support to address any of these concerns, but said he would reserve his final decision for a later date. So we still had a glimmer of hope when we left that night.

That hope disappeared when Fermon sent out a memorandum mid-February reassigning Sgt. Dixon without my knowledge and despite his intimate knowledge of the Rhoads case. Shortly after Dixon's transfer, Danny Reed came into my office and told me that from that point on Fermon wanted all of my attention focused on my narcotics task forces. I was to cease on anything involving the Rhoads case or anything else, and if I received any information, I was to forward it to either Reed or Sgt. Ben Halloran. Since there was still federal interest in Morgan, Reed advised I could sit in on any meetings with the feds, but tin 2002, despite the federal interest, we never met with them.

During 2002, I was still receiving some information through Andrea Trapp and others, but Reed and Halloran ignored any of the information I forwarded. Halloran's token response was, "The Captain said this case is too big for us. We need federal assistance." Halloran showed absolutely no interest and I came to think that's what Fermon wanted all along.

Except for one incident in May, I was stonewalled once again when it came to the Rhoads case in 2002. The incident occurred when I was asked to conduct an inspection of our evidence vault. During the inspection, I found a brown paper sack on a top shelf in the vault. The bag had the Rhoads case number on the side and contained the name Gordon "Speidle." The vault custodian admitted she had questioned the evidence and the poor documentation involving the poor chain of custody.

According to the exhibit card, the brown bag contained the bloody underwear of Dyke and Karen Rhoads and bloodstained bedding. What was most interesting was that the evidence bag not only had Steidl's name misspelled, but the exhibits were submitted to the vault on July 11, 1986, by Sgt. Jack Eckerty. Something wasn't right about this evidence. Steidl wasn't a suspect until late September 1986, but here was his name on an evidence bag dated just a few days after the murder. I was ordered to stay out of the case, so I took the questionable evidence and turned it over to Reed, and after watching him open the evidence bag, I turned and went back into my office. Of course, the evidence issue was ignored and nothing was documented about the discrepancy.

For most of 2002, I was totally frustrated and assumed the Rhoads case was dead in the water, maybe forever. That October, I was at a local Champaign County chiefs' meeting when Assistant U.S. Attorney Tim Bass pulled me aside and asked why the ISP was no longer interested in starting a joint federal and state investigation.

"I don't know," I said in frustration, "Ask Captain Fermon."

However the issues surrounding the Rhoads case were not over, and on December 2, 2002, I received a surprise phone call from one of Whitlock's new attorneys, Richard Kling. I had talked to Kling several times before, and he was calling to tell me he had spoken with Deputy Governor Matt Bettenhausen and Governor Ryan was considering clemency for both Steidl and Whitlock.

Kling asked if I would be willing to meet with the Governor's Office on behalf of the two convicted men and I told him I was more than willing. I knew I would still have to contend with my chain of command, so I advised Kling it would be better if he requested a meeting through the Governor's office. By now, I had no trust in my command and knew they would probably block any meeting with the governor. Almost a year had passed as I sat back helplessly watching the Rhoads case get ignored. This phone call was great news, finally Whitlock and Steidl had a chance for freedom after almost 15 years.

It was also good news because if they were given clemency, it made the Rhoads case an unsolved homicide. The Illinois State Police couldn't ignore reinvestigating the case then—no matter how politically sensitive.

Approximately two weeks later, I received a call from Ed Parkinson from the Illinois Appellate Prosecutor's Office. Parkinson said he was asked to respond to a clemency petition filed for Steidl and Whitlock. Kling was right and Parkinson confirmed George Ryan was considering clemency for both men and he wanted to meet with me. We talked quite awhile, and I told him about my concerns regarding the original investigation. I had no problem telling Parkinson I felt the two men were innocent. Parkinson said he also believed Randy Steidl was innocent but felt differently about Herb Whitlock.

"Whitlock knows something," Parkinson said. "I don't think he was involved in the murders, but I think he knows something."

I was floored when Parkinson said he wanted to keep both men in prison "to keep a hammer on them." His reasoning was if they knew something, this would force them to talk. This was unbelievable; here was a prosecutor telling me he believed these two men were not involved in the murder, but he wanted to keep them in prison because they may "know something"?

"Ed, this isn't Communist China!" I responded. "We're not supposed to keep innocent people in prison because they may know something about a murder!"

I didn't understand his logic, because if it meant getting out of prison, they could've made up a story a long time ago. Parkinson's attitude softened a little when I didn't back down.

"Mike," he said, "there have been a lot of roadblocks in this case with this administration, but we have a new governor coming in, and I promise you I won't let this go."

I certainly about roadblocks in this case, but no one seemed to give a damn about the two innocent men sitting in prison or the murdered couple laying six feet under the ground who deserved some justice! I never talked to Ed Parkinson again and I learned later from an internal e-mail from the ISP command why I didn't:

> ISP is being asked by Ed Parkinson, Appellate Prosecutor's Office, to give input as to whether or not Herbie Whitlock and Randy Steidl should be given clemency for the 1986 murders of Karen and Dyke Rhoads of Paris, Illinois. . . . Mr. Parkinson contacted Zone 5 and advised he was recently given the case to review and wanted ISP's input.

The e-mail continued, explaining why Ed Parkinson never called me back:

> [Lt. Col.] Carper contacted Mr. Parkinson and advised him any such
> opinion, if given, would have to come from Director Nolen. . . .

It was obvious my command didn't want me talking to anyone and an e-mail from Fermon to Carper illustrated just how much turmoil these new developments caused. The e-mail, written in all caps to Diane Carper, exclaimed:

> Subject: Rhoads Homicide
> THIS IS REGARDING THE STEIDL CASE. LT. CALLAHAN
> HAS BEEN ADVISED THAT DEP. GOV. BETTENHAUSEN HAD
> POSSIBLY SOLICITED THIS CLEMENCY PETITION.
> OBVIOUSLY WE NEED TO DISCUSS BEFORE ANY MEET-
> INGS, THIS IS THE PLACE BETWEEN THE ROCK AND THE
> HARD PLACE.

Whatever the place between the the rock and the hard place was, it was obviously upsetting enough that Fermon and Carper needed to meet and discuss it before any other meetings. But neither one of them would ever explain what this strange e-mail meant.

Lt. Col. Carper testified how important communication was to her, and I could speak from experience about her anal expectations of communication.

I remember when we handled the tragic accidental shooting death of a local police officer's young son. The man told us his knee struck a nightstand and his service weapon fell from the table, and as he tried to grab his weapon, it discharged. The bullet went through an adjoining wall and struck his young son in the chest. What a nightmare. Sobbing, the man told our agents how he rushed into the next room and saw his son standing there looking up at him for a brief moment, and then he slumped to the ground, lifeless before his eyes. I couldn't imagine anything worse than this.

After receiving a briefing, Carper criticized that we failed to determine which knee the man bumped the nightstand with. For Chrissakes, a man had accidentally shot and killed his son! What could be worse than that, and this anal bitch wanted me to call the heartbroken man and ask him which knee hit the nightstand! What the hell did it matter, it wouldn't change a damn thing!

The suspicious e-mail between Fermon and Carper was intriguing, so during my civil trial years later, Carper was asked to explain what Fermon was referring to in his e-mail about "the place between the rock and the hard place."

Q: What did you understand that to mean?

Carper: I did not ask him what he meant by that.

Q: Did you think it was strange?

Carper: I didn't give it any thought.

So much for Carper's expectations of communication.

It was crunch time now, and the ISP upper command were running around like a bunch of frightened roosters and hens in a hen house—and the fox stirring up trouble was the clemency petition. Lt. Col. Carper e-mailed Fermon with an order to be prepared to discuss all aspects of the Rhoads case. That task eventually fell to me. I had been away from the Rhoads case for the better part of a year, and the details were not as vivid in my mind as they once were. I began reviewing the case in anticipation of a meeting.

During all this, Andrea Trapp called me one day upset and confused regarding a phone call from Ed Parkinson. He had advised her about the clemency petition and said it was his job to fight against the petition. Andrea was confused and asked him if Steidl and Whitlock were innocent, why would he fight against their clemency? Reassuring her, as he did with me, Parkinson told her "this case has been met with nothing but roadblocks by the Governor's Office but a new administration is coming in, and I'll see that something gets done."

Andrea was upset and asked me, "Are those guys innocent, Mike? All we want is the truth."

Silently, I thought, "Join the club." And I told Andrea I believed the two men were innocent and if released, the State would have no choice but to reinvestigate Dyke and Karen's murders.

Parkinson had requested a meeting with the ISP on or before January 3, 2003. So the plan was for Fermon and I to meet with the new Deputy Director of Operations, Col. Chuck Brueggemann and Lt. Col. Carper before they met with the prosecutor. But our first meeting was cancelled, and a second meeting for January 2, 2003, was also cancelled. I had a strange feeling we were never actually going to meet to discuss any clemency issue. I had the gut feeling the ISP command didn't want to get involved because of all the misconduct I brought forward, and they just wanted this to quiet down, go away and they could go back to covering it up.

Time was ticking away and Governor Ryan was set to leave office. He designated January 11, 2003, as the day he was going to address his issues on the death penalty. If not for a call from the Deputy Governor to my home on the night of January 8, I think the ISP command would have let that time tick away.

It was a Wednesday night, and I was curled up on the sofa with Lily in front of the fireplace. The phone rang and the caller identified himself as Deputy Governor Matt Bettenhausen. I was stunned at first; not many cops at my level got personal phone calls from a Deputy Governor.

Bettenhausen's voice and demeanor reflected the arrogance of a man who knew he was important. He was calling regarding the clemency issue for Steidl and Whitlock and informed me Richard Kling said I was "the man to talk to at the Illinois State Police regarding the Rhoads homicide."

His words were short and to the point: "So tell me, are they guilty or innocent?" As much as I wanted to blurt everything out to Bettenhausen, I had little trust with anyone in state government—especially in this administration. So I explained to him that I definitely had an opinion regarding their innocence, but I had to go through my chain of command in order to speak to him officially.

"Do you know who I am?" he said in an intimidating voice. Certainly I knew who he was, but I explained how I had gotten into trouble once before for speaking outside the department and expressing my views on Steidl and Whitlock's innocence.

Bettenhausen said he had ISP First Deputy Director Doug Brown on hold.

"That's great," I said, and told him if Brown gave permission, I would gladly talk to him about the Rhoads case.

Bettenhausen put me on hold for what seemed like forever and when he finally came back on the line, he abruptly ended our conversation, telling me he would talk to me later. Apparently, Doug Brown didn't want me talking to our Deputy Governor either and for all I knew, maybe he was the one who had deemed this case too politically sensitive. Maybe Brown knew about the misconduct in this case and was part of the cover-up. At this point, I didn't trust any one of them, but I knew I needed to make some phone calls before the shit started rolling downhill.

I called Fermon and then Carper who told me I had done the right thing in not answering the Deputy Governor because he often used his position to bully people into breaking the chain of command. Then she cut our call short, saying she needed to report up the chain of command immediately. Shortly after midnight, Carper called back and told me to be in Springfield the following morning by 6 a.m. and to be prepared to provide a briefing on the Rhoads case to the ISP brass so they could meet with the Governor's Office on the clemency issue.

That night, sleep wasn't a factor. I was meeting with the top command of the Illinois State Police, and as intimidating as that was, I had the added pressure that I knew what I said or didn't say could affect the freedom of Steidl and Whitlock. At this point, I had little faith in my department's leadership. Especially when it came to this case, and I didn't know just how high up the cover-up went.

I arrived at the State Police Academy the next morning at around 5:45 a.m. and I ran into Carper who, suddenly, seemed humble. Maybe it was the guilt she was feeling for ignoring this case for almost three years now that it had surfaced once again. I couldn't help myself and remarked.

"I hope something's finally going to get done," I said. "I know you deemed this case too politically sensitive."

Carper snarled and shot back, "No, I didn't! You didn't hear me correctly!"

"Don't ever say that!" she snapped.

Carper couldn't look me in the eyes though, she knew what she had said, and she had said it more than once, and in front of others besides me. Instinctively, I knew I had better let the issue go and walked out of the room.

By 6 a.m., everyone arrived for the briefing. There were a lot of top brass there, including Col. Chuck Brueggemann who had just taken Kent's place. Brueggemann was another one of those commanders who was a legend in his own mind. From the very start of his career, he was considered one of the politically correct annointed ones, and could be very charismatic and polished, more like a politician than a real cop.

Two of my old commanders from up north were also present—Lt. Col. Rick Rokusek and Major Joe Gryz. Brueggemann also invited Lt. Craig Koehler and a retired ISP investigator named Dennis Kuba, who I didn't know. Fermon and Carper rounded out the group and Brueggemann said First Deputy Director Doug Brown and a few other Colonels would be in attendance later that afternoon.

It was a little overwhelming at first because it wasn't very often one got called in to talk before the top brass like this. So I was pretty nervous—especially with what was at stake. Obviously, I was hoping someone was finally going to do the right thing in this case, but I still had reservations about trusting my command. Someone had wanted this case covered up for a long time now, and Carper had said the orders came from above her.

George Ryan was on his way out and a new governor was coming in, Rod Blagojevich, who was preaching ethics and reform. So, maybe, the department was going to be forced to quit ignoring all the deceit and misconduct in this case. Still, I couldn't shake the feeling that I needed to be very careful. What I said at this meeting could cost a chance of freedom for Steidl and Whitlock.

The meeting that Thursday, January 9, 2003, started a little after 6 a.m. and I didn't get home until late that evening. I started out by providing the group with a large stack of the documents that were accumulated over the years. I spent time carefully going over the contradictions and concerns I had with Herrington and Reinbolt's bizarre stories. Eventually, I brought up the potential Brady violations by the original investigators and prosecutor who I believed had withheld key information. I pointed out my suspicions of intimidation and manipulation of various witnesses, and I went into the suspicious phone calls from McGrew and Eckerty.

That was a big mistake. Dennis Kuba jumped out of his seat and angrily bellowed, "I know those two men! They're friends of mine! I won't sit here and listen to them badmouthed like this!"

I saw that I had hit a raw nerve and needed to be careful. My remarks about the ISP personnel were not being taken well by some of the people in that room.

"I don't think we need to go there," Brueggemann advised.

I quickly changed directions and dropped my suspicions of misconduct. I trusted Joe Gryz and Rick Rokusek, but I didn't know the others . . . or just how politically compromised they were. Later, I learned Dennis Kuba was not one that should get offended about misconduct or cover-ups, since he himself was sued in a civil wrongful conviction case. But this was obviously a sensitive subject that could also work against Steidl and Whitlock. I re-focused my efforts for the better part of the day, going over all the other discrepancies in the case—all the contradictions, the leads ignored and the evidence that had since been refuted.

During a break, I saw Fermon and Brueggemann in a corner of the classroom with their heads together. Later, while sitting in the cafeteria, Fermon mentioned seeing me watching them. Fermon admitted he asked Brueggemann, "It's my understanding that this is a politically sensitive case?"

"Yes, it's a very politically sensitive case," he said Brueggemann responded.

As the briefings continued, the more information I provided and the longer I spoke, I saw the people in the room becoming overwhelmed. This was a vast amount of information to digest in such a short period of time. Some of the commanders were in awe, some intrigued, but no one, other than Dennis Kuba that one time, ever attacked what I said. There were a lot of tentacles to this case and it was an impossible situation for anyone to sit there and digest it in only one day.

I identified the other suspects, like Morgan and the Boards, and how they were ignored in the original investigation. I provided the police reports that were hidden away for all those years by the Paris police where Herrington admitted he had lied at trial and been paid $50,000 by Morgan to keep his mouth shut. I supplied them with the FBI reports and Clutter's documentation. It was a long and grueling session.

By the afternoon, all the other bigwigs had shown up, including First Deputy Director Doug Brown. I concluded the briefing by voicing my opinion that I didn't believe Steidl or Whitlock were proven guilty beyond a reasonable doubt, and the two men were innocent. Fermon interjected and told the group that two juries had found Steidl and Whitlock guilty, their cases had went through appeals, and he argued we didn't have the right to contradict what the juries had decided.

I vehemently disagreed with his rationale and countered that the stories the juries heard from Herrington and Reinbolt were built on lies; evidence presented at trial had long since been refuted; and evidence of their innocence was withheld from the defense. And I reasoned if the original jurors never heard the truth, how could they make the right decision based on believing a bunch of lies. Certainly history had shown several examples of men and women who were wrongfully convicted by juries. Individuals who were convicted by a jury but later exonerated, freed through DNA technology, confessions by the real killers, or the uncovering of police misconduct. I specifically pointed out the case of Rolando Cruz and Alejandro Hernandez as a prime example. Here were two men convicted twice by two different juries but later found to be innocent. No one in that room could question that.

"Would anybody in this room want your life to depend on the likes or credibility of a Darrell Herrington or Debbie Reinbolt?" I challenged the group. And no one in that room spoke up and answered my question.

First Deputy Director Doug Brown was another one of our politically correct commanders who had never conducted a criminal investigation. Yet it was Doug Brown who advised the group that either he or Brueggemann was going to meet with the Governor's Office the next day to discuss the clemency issue, and looking back, the more I think about it, Steidl and Whitlock never had a chance.

After the briefing, we took a break, and Rokusek and Gryz took me out into the hallway. They said I had impressed the First Deputy Director, and he was going to give me a chance to look at the Rhoads case again. They also informed me Doug Brown was going to ask me a series of questions and I needed to be very careful how I answered them. I didn't understand at first, but it soon became apparent what Brown was concerned about, and it wasn't any clemency issue.

When we returned, Brown asked me a series of questions based strictly on the concerns of misconduct I had raised in the original investigation. Despite the issue of clemency and freedom for two wrongfully convicted men, this was Brown's only focus. I knew I had to be careful now, but I wasn't going to hold back either. It became obvious the ISP command was only concerned over the misconduct I had brought forth when Doug Brown asked me if I had *proven* any of the misconduct I claimed.

How could I prove anything if I was never given the opportunity to investigate it in the first place?

"No. I haven't *proven* any misconduct," I carefully replied, but then I added, "there was definitely misconduct in this case, I have more than enough suspicions to justify that, it's just a matter of proving who was responsible for what misconduct." Then I explained my rationale to the group. I didn't know if it was only one of them, a combination of or all of the original investigators and prosecutor together that had conspired to withhold evidence and information from the defense. Certainly evidence was withheld, and there were people that claimed they lied or were intimidated and manipulated in the investigation. Not only were the eyewitnesses' stories riddled with suspicion, so were the investigator's reports. Still, I couldn't prove my suspicions for who was responsible unless I actively investigated those issues.

I knew I had to be careful and if I said the wrong thing, there would be no reinvestigation into the Rhoads case or anything else in Paris. I was convinced that Brown's only concern was to keep the misconduct under wraps. For hours I had just briefed all these commanders on all the concerns in this case and now all Brown wanted was to hide the misconduct.

I don't know if my answer satisfied Brown or not because Brueggemann broke in and asked me if there was still any federal interest in Paris, and I told him about my recent conversation with Assistant U.S. Attorney Tim Bass. Brueggemann asked me to reach out to Bass once again, and then he instructed Fermon and I to put together proposals for resources we would need. In front of the group, Brueggemann declared he wanted "a full court press." I believed Chuck Brueggemann was sincere, but he would also prove to be just another politically compromised hack. I didn't know it then, but his facade of a full court press was going to be my last attempt at reinvestigating the Rhoads case forever.

I left that evening exhausted yet filled with hope that good things were finally about to happen. Steidl and Whitlock would get clemency, we would reinvestigate the Rhoads case and find the real killers and give everyone the closure they deserved. That night, for the first time in a very long time, I slept well again.

The next morning Andrea Trapp called me in tears, extremely upset. She asked if I had heard about Steidl and Whitlock getting clemency. I told Andrea about my meeting with the ISP brass the day before and told her I knew they were supposed to meet with the Governor's Office that afternoon, but I had heard nothing about clemency being granted. Andrea said information was circulating around Paris that Governor Ryan had signed off on clemency for Steidl and Whitlock that morning.

Andrea said she called the Governor's Office and asked to speak with Governor Ryan. She was upset and angry because his office hadn't bothered to give the victim's family the courtesy of the news first, if clemency was granted. Andrea said if Steidl and Whitlock were innocent, then they should be released, but the family wanted some answers from the Governor's Office as to why they were being released. They simply wanted to know if Governor Ryan believed Steidl and Whitlock were guilty, and he was just shortening their sentence, or did he feel they were wrongfully convicted and the real killers were still free? And if so, what was Ryan's office going to do about the murders of Dyke and Karen? The family wanted and felt they deserved some answers.

Andrea said her call to George Ryan was intercepted by a young woman in the Governor's Office who blocked her from talking to Ryan. Andrea explained to the woman that she had young nephews who had never been told Dyke and Karen were murdered, and she didn't want them to find out about the murders from a press conference. Andrea told me how the woman callously replied to her questions.

"Then you'd better tell your nephews because clemency has been granted," she said and then curtly hung up.

Andrea said she was incensed and persisted in calling Governor Ryan's Office until she was finally put in touch with Deputy Governor Matt Bettenhausen. The Deputy Governor confirmed with her that Governor Ryan had granted clemency to Steidl and Whitlock that morning. According to the Deputy Governor, the families were being Fed-Exed a package that would explain the reasons for clemency. Bettenhausen told her to expect the package that evening and hung up.

"Mike, if those two guys are innocent, are you going to try and find out who killed Dyke and Karen?" Andrea asked.

I was confident again and reassured Andrea I was going to try my best to solve the case. This was my second promise to Andrea Trapp, and a second promise I wasn't able to keep.

I was ecstatic with the news of the clemency. It seemed as if everything I had said and been fighting for was finally coming to the forefront, and it appeared I would no longer be impeded by any politically sensitive issues.

Late that Friday night, I got another call from Andrea. She told me how her family had gathered that evening at her parents' house to await the package from the governor's office. Around 7:00, a Fed-Ex truck started down the long, private lane leading to their home. Andrea said all their wounds were being reopened, and her father started crying at the sight of the truck. As the tension mounted, the truck suddenly stopped halfway up the drive, sitting there momentarily and then backed up and left. The package from the governor's office was never delivered.

Confused, Andrea began making calls to the Governor's Office leaving numerous messages with no luck. Then Bettenhausen finally returned her call at 10:50 p.m.

"You don't have to worry anymore, clemency for Steidl and Whitlock has been taken off the table," he brusquely told her, and then abruptly hung up.

During his 1999 inauguration, George Ryan exclaimed, "I hope very much to be a hero." On Saturday, January 11, 2003, Governor George Ryan pardoned four condemned men and commuted the death sentence for every Death Row inmate in Illinois.

Obviously, George Ryan wanted to be a hero, but many thought his cause against the death penalty was nothing more than a deflection from the corruption and scandal that was ingrained in his political career as Secretary of State and Governor.

Ryan made history when he left office, stating, "Our capital system is haunted by the demon of error: error in determining guilt, and error in determining who among the guilty deserves to die." Because of that rationale, George Ryan commuted the sentences of all Death Row inmates—163 men and 4 women. It didn't matter to Ryan that many of these men and women were actually guilty of terrible crimes. No, this was a package deal that was obviously devised to make his inaugural dreams of becoming a "hero" a reality. But George Ryan was nothing more than a hypocrite, because that same day clemency was not granted to Randy Steidl or Herb Whitlock.

There were others besides Andrea who were told clemency was granted for Steidl and Whitlock that previous Friday morning. Eric Zorn and Steve Mills of the *Chicago Tribune* were also told by Deputy Governor Bettenhausen that George Ryan had given clemency to Steidl and Whitlock.

Yet when the journalists broached the subject with George Ryan before his Saturday morning press conference, Ryan said he didn't know what they were talking about.

"Clemency for Steidl and Whitlock wasn't even close," Ryan claimed. The journalists persisted, noting their information came from the Deputy Governor.

"Then go talk to Matt Bettenhausen!" Ryan exclaimed.

It was obvious that sometime between Friday morning and Friday evening, clemency was given and then taken away from Steidl and Whitlock. And it remains a mystery why there was a change of heart about clemency for them.

I speculated—did Chuck Brueggemann or Doug Brown actually make a visit to the Governor's Office that Friday afternoon? Under oath, they both denied they ever met with Governor Ryan's Office on the issue of clemency for Steidl and Whitlock. After receiving a personal call at my residence from a Deputy Governor, the huge uproar it caused by upper command which resulted in a 12-hour briefing on Thursday . . . the ISP upper command denied ever meeting with the Governor's Office the following day. I reflected on the e-mail from Lt. Col. Diane Carper that read: "The Illinois State Police is considered the eyes and ears for the Governor's Office."

So I asked myself, "What would a Governor who was brought up in the age old corruption of Illinois politics do if state police upper command told him there was misconduct and corruption in the original investigation and convictions of Randy Steidl and Herb Whitlock?" Certainly he would realize if the two men were freed, multi-million dollar lawsuits would be filed at the state's expense. Certainly the image of the Illinois State Police would be tarnished along with the people's trust. Since one of the suspects was a major campaign contributor throughout the years to good old George, what would George Ryan do then? Were these enough things to change the mind of a man later convicted on 22 counts of fraud and racketeering?

George Ryan wanted to be a hero. A scandal like this would muddy the waters for our want-to-be heroic governor. For a while, George Ryan got his wish and he was a hero. But the hero was really a hypocrite. Years later, after his convictions on racketeering and fraud, a *Chicago Tribune* editorial chastised:

> This was a man acclaimed by many people for his moratorium on capital punishment—congratulated by world leaders such as Nelson Mandella, honored by the lighting of the Colosseum in Rome, nominated for the Nobel Peace Prize. Yet this also is a man hounded from office because, by the end of the term as governor, the stench of corruption on his watch rendered him untouchable. The people of Illinois, though long and inured to their state's culture of political sleaze, saw his reelection as intolerable. . . . Corruption is his epitaph.

CHAPTER 15

FULL COURT PRESS

------------------- ■ -------------------

It was disappointing news when Steidl and Whitlock were denied clemency. Another roadblock from the mighty engine of the state, but at least something positive seemed to come out of the long briefing with the ISP upper command—finally, we had permission to initiate an investigation and with no restrictions. According to Col. Brueggemann, "My understanding was that we were going to, [in] my term, kind of put on a full court press . . . " In reality, Brueggemann's "full court press" was nothing more than the hypocritical and bureaucratic hype from another politically compromised ISP commander.

Still, at the time I believed him and I wasted no time contacting Assistant U.S. Attorney Tim Bass. Together we garnered quite a bit of interest from several state and federal agencies. The first meeting in January 2003 included the U.S. Attorney's Office, FBI, IRS, ATF, DEA, Illinois Department of Revenue, Illinois Department of Insurance, Illinois Securities Commission, an Indiana drug task force and, of course, the Illinois State Police.

Brueggemann said his goal was to make this an OCDETF case, which stands for Organized Crime Drug Enforcement Task Force, and meant the feds would pick up the tab for the investigation, and he pompously explained.

"Yes . . . I, having worked numerous OCDETF cases, I know that once a case is adopted—that's my term, adopted—as an OCDETF case, that brings to bear resources such as transcription, office space, overtime and federal attention," Brueggemann testified.

And Fermon acknowledged in his proposal that the feds were also interested in making this an OCDETF case: "The United States Attorney's Office . . . Tim Bass, DEA Resident Agent in Charge, Dave Lenartowicz, and the FBI supervisor, Special Agent Nate Williams, have indicated they would support a Federal OC-DETF."

At our first meeting, a former Edgar County police officer named Dick McDaniels provided us with a colorful depiction of Paris and some of its citizenry. McDaniels told us how some of the Paris businessmen rose overnight from poverty to become powerful men worth millions of dollars. It was obvious McDaniels had a lot of background information and we were lucky to have him on board, but Fermon's response and treatment of McDaniels was shocking. With deriding sarcasm in his voice, Fermon verbally attacked him, belittling his input.

"I think that's a pack of lies! And until you bring me something more concrete than that, I'm not going to support that!"

Fermon rudely interrupted at one point, with a callous smirk on his face, rolling his eyes—"All we have is a bunch of baseless allegations!"

I was embarrassed at Fermon's conduct and negative attitude. Someone will always play the Devil's Advocate in meetings like this, but this was much more than that and Fermon was not good at hiding his displeasure about this investigation. Greg Dixon agreed when he later testified:

> We were asking Dick McDaniels questions and he was there on his own time, he was there to assist us. And I'm sitting right on the left side of Steve and while Dick was talking, Steve was looking at his watch and rolling his eyes. Dick McDaniels took offense to it and said, "You know what? If you don't need my help, fine. I won't come back. And I will not participate . . . "When I left the meeting, I just had a feeling that we were kind of fighting a losing battle. That we didn't have great support from the command on this issue.

Fermon had certainly opposed the reopening of the Rhoads case and this new investigation was no different when he sarcastically testified:

> . . . from Lieutenant Callahan's standpoint . . . this investigation is the only thing happening in the world at this point in time. . . . we had ongoing homicide investigations, we had death penalty cases, we had a lot of other things, and as I'm sure, most everyone would agree, we had very limited resources.

From Fermon's perspective, I guess some homicides are more important than others, and I didn't realize it was okay for the police to pick which homicides should be investigated and which ones shouldn't. I would have liked to see him explain that to the families of Dyke and Karen Rhoads or any other family who's loved one was brutally murdered and the police chose to ignore it because of "limited resources." As far as I was concerned, we weren't limited by resources . . . just limited by integrity and dedication.

Fermon's proposal also reflected his obvious lack of support and negative attitude towards the investigation:

> Many claims have been made reference [certain Paris citizens], and [their] alleged involvement in narcotics trafficking, money laundering, tax evasion, arson, extortion, intimidation, racketeering and homicide. These assertions have been made by citizens of Edgar County, past and present associates [of these individuals] as well as local, state and federal investigators. However, at this time, the Illinois State Police is in possession of very little documentation which provide factual information . . . [on] any of these alleged crimes.

Fermon was right. The Illinois State Police didn't possess enough factual information to make a case on anyone. How could we possess any factual information when he and the ISP upper command had spent the last three years impeding a criminal investigation?

In my proposal I asked for Greg Dixon and another agent to be assigned to the investigation, but Fermon wanted his old buddy from the shooting range, the agent who had falsified his qualification shoots. Given his Giglio issue, I couldn't believe he wanted him on an important federal investigation; the man was caught lying, and his credibility would definitely be an issue in a federal investigation. I couldn't help but wonder if Fermon was deliberately trying to sabotage this case from the beginning.

Lt. Col. Carper also continued her resistance to the investigation when Brueggemann had us submit proposals for the resources we needed. She didn't submit a proposal until almost three months after his orders, and Carper also ordered, "You cannot share any of the documents you have on the Rhoads case with the federal task force." And I began to think that maybe the Rhoads case was still too politically sensitive.

Despite Fermon and Carper's obvious lack of support, I didn't feel there was much they could do anymore with Col. Brueggemann's alleged backing—and especially with the added interest and support by the feds.

Paris was no secret to the feds. According to ATF, Paris had more than its share of suspicious arsons. The FBI had investigated the Sons of Silence for years, and Paris was part of their nine year investigation in the Mafia Pizza Connection case. The FBI had also been receiving several suspicious FDIC audits that were conducted on some of the local businesses and their owners. The IRS had also conducted a few criminal investigations in Paris, and they were interested in looking at others who had gained unexplained wealth and affluence.

There were mysterious businesses identified that no one knew exactly what they did, but they claimed millions of dollars in profit each year. And the IRS indicated some of those profits were shared with men from Chicago with "definite mob undertones."

Nate, Greg and I had conducted surveillances on some of these mysterious businesses. We had been given information about suspicious truck traffic in and out of two separate businesses during late night hours. The trucks always arrived at the businesses between 2 a.m. and 4 a.m., with only a skeleton crew of employees working. The trucks were never seen unloading and the employees were told to stay away from them. Shortly after their arrival, a supervisor showed up and checked out the contents of the truck, and once satisfied, the truck would continue on its unknown journey.

One late evening, around midnight, I asked Greg Dixon to go into one of the businesses—feigning being lost and looking for directions. Greg came out and described the spacious warehouse, empty except for a card table, phone and two metal folding chairs at the entrance. In the back of the warehouse, Greg described a big conveyer belt with small mounds of white powder on it, so he asked one of the men what they did there. The man laughed and told Greg, "We pelletize corn starch."

We had never heard of pelletizing corn starch before, but it was certainly profitable because we learned it made the businessman a $4,000,000 profit that year. And since the business only claimed $150,000 in sales tax to the Illinois Department of Revenue that same year, we regarded it as a somewhat suspicious profit.

There was a second business we learned about with the same suspicious late night truck traffic back when Edie Casella was the zone commander. Greg had came up with the idea of secretly renting and utilizing a trailer in a Paris trailer park and setting up a time-lapsed video surveillance of that business. We had agonized if Carper would construe this as more than intelligence gathering, but we did it anyway, without her knowledge. We suspected the late-night truck traffic was possibly involved in drug trafficking. The information was again that the trucks surreptitiously arrived in the early morning hours between 2:00 and 4:00 a.m. Sometimes the trucks were unloaded and the contents were put in a tobacco barn, oftentimes they were not unloaded and would leave as stealthily as they arrived.

One of the difficulties we encountered was installing the thousands of dollars worth of camera equipment in the trailer without attracting attention. We finally accomplished the task, but didn't know our clandestine surveillance was destined to become compromised soon after it got started.

It was FBI Special Agent Nate Williams who first raised concerns to Greg and I that not long after Fermon became the new commander, the camera location was mysteriously compromised. One night someone broke into our trailer containing the thousands of dollars worth of surveillance equipment, but the equipment was not disturbed. The equipment represented quite a haul if it were a common burglar, but whoever broke in seemed content with letting us know they were aware of the surveillance.

This was just one of the many things, along with Fermon's negative attitude about the investigation, that started to draw our suspicions to his strange conduct.

The FDIC audits also definitely questioned some of the business practices going on, and one report acknowledged a source that said, "that there have been several suspicious murders involving persons associated with financial transactions involving" some of the local businessmen. There were certainly several unsolved homicides in and around Paris since 1973 and even more recent suspicious deaths also surfaced during our task force meetings.

A Douglas County businessman was found dead in his home shortly after he filed bankruptcy. Just before his death, he had complained to his bookkeeper that he had gotten mixed up with the wrong people—the Mafia. He had borrowed money from a Paris businessman and couldn't pay it back. After filing bankruptcy, he was found mysteriously dead in front of his television one morning. The coroner, who himself suddenly came into a lot of money, failed to conduct an autopsy to determine the cause of death and the man was buried before he was even cold.

There were businessmen mentioned who had numerous off-shore bank accounts in British St. Kitts, and for such a small town of only nine thousand, there were an awful lot of wealthy people. Ironically, we learned that one of my neighbors who lived only a few houses down from me had sold his insurance company to one of the Paris businessmen. Later, he confided to me that he was offered a suitcase full of laundered money as part of the negotiation for his business, and with instructions on how to launder it. I never bothered to ask if he took the suitcase . . . I left that for the FBI.

At the tail end of these meetings, Fermon would walk in flippantly interjecting, "You have nothing! These are just good businessmen," and like a line from the *Sopranos*, he would exclaim, "They're just good earners." His outbursts embarrassed me, and looking around the room, I saw others who had just heard those reports puzzled by Fermon's remarks. Again this was just one of the many things, along with Fermon's negative attitude about the investigation, that would draw our suspicions about his conduct.

The FBI shared an intelligence report about the suspicious takeovers of several car dealerships in Illinois and Indiana surrounding Paris. Some of the extorted businessmen were afraid to talk after being told their families would be murdered and their houses burned down in the middle of the night if they did. Some of these businessmen involved in the alleged business extortions had criminal histories. One had a criminal history for bootlegging from the south side of Chicago to East St. Louis. Another one of the prominent businessmen was a convicted child sex molester. But according to Fermon, these were just good businessmen and just "good earners."

There were reports of suspicious business trips to Colombia, South America in the early 1990s, with rumors of narcotics trafficking and gun running.

Paris was already established as one of the "meth capitals" in the state, but there were also rumors of large scale heroin, cocaine and cannabis trafficking. There were stories of individuals who called themselves "The Company," and other associations to the infamous Mafia Pizza Connection case. We had unsubstantiated reports from witnesses who allegedly saw large amounts of drugs in the back of semi-trucks. There were also stories about truck drivers who drove their unknown cargos from Paris to the outskirts of Chicago and were met by men who took their trucks and, after a few hours, returned them empty.

A former waitress wrote a letter about the mid-eighties referencing secret meetings in the back of her boyfriend's bar, the Horseshoe Club. She claimed a local businessman met every few months with businessmen from Chicago, and her job was to serve them food and drinks. She described how she witnessed large exchanges of money at these meetings, but was told by her boyfriend, Connie Wilhoit, to mind her own business. In the letter to Whitlock's attorney, Richard Kling, she described one of these meetings where one of the men from Chicago approached the local businessman and asked if his "problem was being taken care of." The local businessman said a call was made and the problem was being taken care of that weekend. Her letter chillingly added that was the weekend Dyke and Karen Rhoads were murdered.

Since 2000, we had received a lot of information, and because of the restrictions that we could only gather intelligence, a lot of this information wasn't verified or corroborated. What we possessed was some fact, some hearsay and a lot of small town lore; we had nothing criminal we could prove yet, but there was certainly plenty of smoke. And from my experiences, where there's smoke, there's usually fire.

Fermon continued showing an outward opposition to the case, and along with his negative demeanor, other things came to light which seemingly compromised some of the things we had done in Paris. Weird coincidences had occurred that at the time didn't cause any suspicion, but now, with Fermon's behavior, did.

Over the last few years, Andrea Trapp had given us a lot of information. There were only a few people who knew Andrea was giving us information and Fermon was one of those few people. From 2000 until 2002, other than a few of her family members, no one in Paris knew Andrea was talking to the state police. After Fermon arrived, Andrea received two strange visits. One was from the Paris Chief of Police and the other was from a girlfriend whose uncle worked for Bob Morgan. Andrea believed these visits were meant to intimidate her and the message was clear: she should be aware that certain people knew she was communicating with the state police and they weren't happy about it. Around that same time, she said Smoke Burba began following her around town or sitting outside her home. Now the question arose whether someone had compromised the confidential association with Andrea. Her visitors had specifically identified the Illinois State Police as who she was talking to. Why not the FBI, as they were certainly much more visible in Paris than we had been?

Then another incident occurred which started to add to a long list of growing concerns that the case was being compromised. When Edie Casella was Commander, she had asked for intelligence analyst Tim Harney to assist us. Harney had gathered intelligence for us since 2001, and he was located in Springfield only an hour from our zone. He also became part of our new task force here in 2003.

One day Harney called and said Fermon had removed him from the task force investigation.

"Did you want this?" I asked him.

"No. I want to stay involved in the case," he replied, and then added Fermon said he was going to replace him with an intelligence analyst from Peoria.

This was ridiculous; Peoria was one and a half hours away from Champaign and it didn't make sense. Tim had intricate knowledge about the case and he wanted to stay involved, so why would Fermon replace him with a guy who had absolutely no knowledge of the case and who lived farther away? Fermon wasn't even Harney's boss and had no authority to remove him, either. Harney's boss was Captain Ken Kaupas, so I e-mailed Kaupas and asked if Harney could stay on the task force investigation. Kaupas wasn't aware Harney was even removed, and said Tim could certainly stay on the case.

Afterwards, I went to Fermon's office and told him I talked to Harney and then called Captain Kaupas who said Harney could stay on the case.

"You did *what*?" Fermon bellowed as he turned a deep crimson.

Before I could reply, he angrily stormed out of his office. Fermon had tried to pull a fast one and it didn't work this time, but I couldn't help wonder why he was doing all of this.

From January through mid-April 2003, additional concerns continued to surface that Fermon was compromising the investigation. I continued to catch Fermon in more lies and more attempts to impede the investigation. In an e-mail to me, he stated, " . . . a case having this potential magnitude is best served by you personally serving as the case agent." Yet, at the same time, I learned he really had a different agenda. Captain Strohl called and said Fermon asked him to take me as his lieutenant in patrol. Here was Fermon secretly trying to get rid of me behind my back. Strohl later testified about Fermon's real intensions.

"He kind of inferred that he would like to get rid of Mike. I can't recall the specific words, but it was not a positive thing. It was, 'I'd like to get rid of Callahan.' . . . it was somewhat derogatory." Strohl said.

I learned it wasn't just Fermon trying to get rid of me, either. Strohl's testimony identified a second person trying to get rid of me:

> Col. Carper asked me a couple of times if I thought Mike would like to come to patrol. And without asking Mike, I always said no. Mike has been in investigations the bulk of his career. That's what he knows, that's what he does. . . . And that really wouldn't make a lot of sense to have him come to patrol and have him learn new tricks, so-to-speak. I mean Mike was well versed in investigations and patrol is just different. . . .

It was now becoming apparent that both Fermon and Carper were trying to get rid of me, and obviously this case *was* still too politically sensitive.

Concerned about Fermon and Carper still impeding my efforts, and no longer trusting my department enough to bring any concerns to them, I made arrangements to meet with an attorney named Mary Leahy. She had experience dealing with the darker side of the State of Illinois, but never to the extent that a murder case was deemed too politically sensitive by the state police upper command. She was appalled by the state police's conduct, and advised me that a new Governor was elected and would soon take office. Mary Leahy was asked to be an advisor in his administration, and she assured me she would take the misconduct to the new governor, suggesting, " . . . that we put off meeting for a couple of months to see if the issues that you raised with me are solved under the new administration."

Mary Leahy was referring to the new administration of incoming Governor Rod Blagojevich, a governor who campaigned with the promise he was going to clean up corruption and restore ethics back in Illinois government. Unfortunately, neither Mary Leahy nor I realized the ethics reform Blagojevich touted was just another false political promise, and it became very clear over the next few years that I couldn't rely on anyone in the State of Illinois to do the right thing.

It wasn't only Greg and I who developed suspicions about Fermon. FBI Special Agent Nate Williams also had suspicions, and when you started adding things up, Nate said, Fermon wasn't "passing the smell test."

Fermon had openly opposed the re-opening of the Rhoads investigation when he first became the zone's commander. We didn't have the resources, he said, and then he transferred Greg Dixon and told me to address my narcotic task force business only. All of a sudden, people in Paris knew Andrea Trapp was talking to the state police and Fermon's demeanor and open opposition for the new investigation was obvious.

Also in 2001, Nate and I had interviewed the wife of a one-time prominent Paris car dealer. His dealership was taken over by some local Paris businessmen. The woman said her husband was so terrified from threats he had received, he still slept with a chair propped under their bedroom door. She related rumors of semi-trucks making clandestine trips to Chicago, and rumors of a business with "a mountain of cocaine" inside one of its warehouses. The woman said she was so concerned, she had gone to an ISP Commander who supervised a local drug task force and who lived just north of Paris. That commander was Steve Fermon, and at the time he was the master sergeant in charge of VMEG. She added that he had ignored her information. In 2001, this didn't give me any significant concerns, as a lot of people get frustrated if police don't act on their information. Now, here in 2003, it just added more suspicion to a long list of concerns.

I remembered back when I initially reviewed the Rhoads case, Fermon, through Danny Reed, had told Greg to avoid helping me because I was "sitting on a mountain of shit" and I was "going to get fucked." Nate Williams had said something definitely "wasn't passing the smell test"—he was right, and maybe it was something much bigger than "a mountain of shit."

CHAPTER 16
MOB TOWN IN A MOB STATE

Al Capone, "Bugs" Moran and the St. Valentine's Day Massacre are synonymous with Chicago and its storied history of organized crime. These infamous figures and events have been immortalized and glamorized in books, TV and film. We have come to expect organized crime in major metropolitans such as New York and Chicago. Yet, a farming community like Paris, Illinois—in a rural, isolated area—harboring the Mafia would, to most, be unbelievable.

I don't know if the citizens of Paris considered their town a "mob town," but it certainly has a history of violent crime and unsolved murders. Some of the town's residents were also documented members of the Sicilian Mafia. I remember sitting in briefings, with federal agents telling us how certain Paris residents had "definite mob undertones," with mob connections "to Chicago, Detroit, St. Louis, Las Vegas, New Jersey, New York and even to Italy." The Paris community profile bragged it's, " . . . one of the Midwest's best kept secrets," and up until 1984, Paris was also one of the Sicilian Mafia's best kept secrets.

On April 8, 1984, a young U.S. Attorney named Rudolph "Rudy" Giulianni indicted 31 Mafia figures in the Pizza Connection Case. The Pizza Connection involved a nine-year federal investigation of international narcotics trafficking and a money laundering conspiracy estimated at $1.6 billion per year. This was a sophisticated operation reaching from Sicily to New York and yes, even quaint little Paris, Illinois.

In 1975, Gaetano Badalamenti, considered "the boss of bosses," was the head of the Sicilian Mafia. The Pizza Connection originated when Badalamenti formed an alliance with the New York Bonanno Crime Family, lead by Salvatore Catalano. This international union created a narcotics distribution and money laundering network between the United States and Sicily.

Sicilian mobsters—known as "Zips"—immigrated into the United States and went into business, starting Ma and Pa pizzerias in small Midwestern towns. In actuality, pizza pies weren't the Zips' main source of income; their pizzerias were nothing more than drug and money laundering fronts. These Zips were "made Sicilian Mafia members," and were depicted as clannish and secretive, and some of the meanest killers in the business. Many of the Zips were fugitives fleeing Italy on charges ranging from narcotics to murder. A 1978 intelligence report read:

> The typical immigrant is stereotyped as follows: He is a male between 25 and 40 . . . He is married to a Sicilian and has several children. His English is broken and he isolates himself socially, associating only with other Sicilians whom he introduces to outsiders as a relative. He owns and operates a pizzeria (usually named Alfano's, Joe's, Maria's, Roma or La Roma) which is generally in a small town.

Many of these Ma and Pa pizza parlors ended up in the State of Illinois. At one point, a little over 50 pizzerias were identified as having possible connections to this powerful syndicate in Illinois alone.

In *The Pizza Connection: Lawyers, Money, Drugs, Mafia*, Shana Alexander reported:

> The Bureau put the Midwest pizza parlors under surveillance and struck gold. The Midwest men were not a heroin outfit for the Brooklyn Zips. They were acting on the instructions of a powerful, mysterious telephone caller from someplace overseas. The caller, code-named, "The Uncle," was using the Midwest Sicilians to work out some sort of deal with the Zips of Brooklyn. Then, the FBI discovered the caller's identity. He was no less than Gaetano Badalamenti, former *capo di titti capi* of the Sicilian Mafia, the Boss of Bosses, and since 1978, the most wanted man in Italy. . . . All the Midwesterners were his relatives.

How was Paris, Illinois, connected to this international crime syndicate? When the Pizza Connection Case went to trial, among the 31 people initially charged by the federal government was Guiseppie "Joe" Vitale, " . . . owner and operator of Joe's Pizza in Paris, Illinois." A January 22, 1987, news account report states, "The federal case against Vitale . . . [was] based on wiretapped conversations between the defendants and members of their families carried out in the Sicilian dialect of the Italian language." After Vitale's conviction:

> A spokesman for U.S. Attorney Rudolph Giuliani, who led the federal prosecution, said they viewed Joe Vitale as a "major member" of the group. [Vitale was] Convicted on one count of conspiracy and 10 counts of involvement on racketeering-influenced corrupt organizations . . .

Federal prosecutors hailed the convictions of the men indicted in the Pizza Connection Case as what " . . . may be the most significant victory ever in the international effort to end the Mafia." As unbelievable as it seems, there were actually small Midwestern towns like Paris connected to the secret society based on "omerta." The Pizza Connection Case proved this a reality.

Through the years I had listened to former Paris police officers talk about Joe's Pizza and how sometimes they received late night orders to stay away from the pizzeria. Curious, despite the orders, they still drove by and would see a black limousine parked in front of the pizzeria. After a few hours, they said the limousine disappeared as quickly as it had appeared, and shortly after that, they were told they could resume their normal patrols. Consistent with their stories, an Intelligence Report from the Pizza Connection Case files read, "Out of town or out of state cars may be observed at . . . [the] place of business on Sunday nights, but seldom will anybody be seen."

There were other intriguing stories surrounding Mafia lore in Paris.

FBI Special Agent Nate Williams and I interviewed a man whose wife was a former housekeeper for the Vitale's. His wife described to him a huge cherry wood table covered with "stacks of cash from one end of the table to the other" in the Vitale dining room. On occasion, she said, a big black limousine would pull up in front of the Vitale home. Joe would run to the dining room table and put stacks of money into a bag and then hurry outside to the limo, the window would roll down, and he would hand the bag of money inside. The limo left as quickly as it arrived.

Sgt. Dixon and I also interviewed a criminal justice instructor at a Danville community college, who, at one time, lived directly across the street from the Vitale home. After Joe Vitale was incarcerated for his conviction in the Pizza Connection Case, he said he often saw a big black limo drive up to the Vitale home. When Vitale family members ran out to the limousine, again the window would roll down and two or three boxes were handed over to the family. This occurred throughout Joe Vitale's imprisonment, he said.

Another informant related how a man named Guiseppe "Joe" Galbo opened another Joe's Pizza in nearby Georgetown. According to the informant, Joe Galbo "muled" suitcases of laundered money for Vitale to Chicago and Detroit. At some point, an argument ensued between the two "Joes" over money and hard feelings arose. A former Georgetown cop even told us Galbo approached him and asked to borrow his police uniform so he could ambush and kill Joe Vitale. The former officer said he refused the request, but it was Galbo who ended up on the wrong side of a bullet when he was shot outside of Joe's Pizza in Paris. Galbo was lucky and survived the gunshot wound, but he apparently got the message and left the Paris area.

Another amusing story occurred when Nate Williams and I sat down with a former employee of Joe Vitale. It was a Friday night, and at first the man was somewhat leery to talk with us; his concern was he might be arrested for saying the wrong thing. We assured him it was not his past we were interested in, and during the course of the evening he became pretty comfortable with us. When it came to talking about Joe Vitale though, he flat out refused to talk.

Eventually I asked him if he knew anything about the Rhoads murders and he claimed he didn't have any first-hand knowledge, however, he had heard from some "reliable sources" that the prosecutor and investigators were "paid off" in the Rhoads investigation. He also said he heard former State's Attorney Mike Mc-Fatridge was a heavy cocaine user, and he even identified a friend who claimed to have photos of McFatridge snorting cocaine.

"The key to solving the Rhoads case is Darrell Herrington," he added.

Apparently, feeling at ease with us, maybe even momentarily forgetting who we were, he added, "You know what you do? You do what we used to do. You take Darrell way out into the woods where no one can hear you. Then you hang him from a tree by his arms, put a meat grinder under his toes, and you start grinding away, and believe me, he'll tell you everything you want to know about the Rhoads case."

I remember the smirk of amusement on Nate Williams' face from across the table. Obviously, the man seemed to forget who we were and I also tried to hold back a laugh.

"You know, we can't do that. We're the police," I replied.

Realizing his incriminating remark, the man defensively exclaimed, "I'm not saying we ever did that! I'm just saying that if you did something like that, it would work!"

There was never any doubt in my mind that something like that would probably work, and after that night, every time I went to Paris, I couldn't help but look for people who limped.

The Mafia lore surrounding Paris was certainly intriguing. That spring in 2003, I was watching my son's Little League game, and standing next to me, leaning over the center field fence, was Federal Judge Michael McCuskey. Judge McCuskey later that summer played a big part in righting many of the wrongs done in the Rhoads case. As we watched our sons playing baseball, we began discussing Paris and its dark history. At the end of the conversation, the judge looked over at me and said, "You know, Mike, the Pizza Connection never really ended."

Not long after that conversation with Judge McCuskey, other major developments unfolded which indicated the judge just might be right. Nate Williams had submitted thirteen phone numbers for toll analysis in 2001 and now he was calling to tell me about some breaking news regarding those phone numbers. He explained a satellite had intercepted approximately nine of the phone numbers and there were also phone calls being recorded by Italian authorities regarding the murder of a South American Ambassador involving narcotics trafficking. The phone calls were being recorded at a pay phone in Italy. But the most shocking news was the calls were originating from Joe's Pizza in Paris, Illinois!

This was big news and at the next meeting, Assistant U.S. Attorneys Tim Bass and Rick Cox had DEA Analyst Ron Swigman brief the group about the recent developments. Swigman reaffirmed everything Nate had told me, and since the phone calls from Joe's Pizza to Italy were still being intercepted by the Italian authorities, Swigman said DEA wanted to start tapping the phones on this end. The problem, he said, was Joe's Pizza had high security T-1 phone lines and DEA didn't have the technology to tap the pizzeria's phones, so they were reaching out to the FBI. With these new developments, everyone became pretty excited, so we decided to start meeting on a weekly basis.

One week later, the phone calls from Joe's Pizza were still the main topic of discussion and Swigman told the group the calls were still being intercepted in Italy. As the meeting broke up and everyone started leaving, Fermon made a startling comment.

"I was just at Joe's Pizza last weekend eating pizza," he blurted out.

Only Greg Dixon, Nate Williams and I heard the comment. I was shocked and couldn't believe Fermon just admitted to patronizing a convicted felon's pizzeria. And not just any convicted felon, Joe Vitale was a documented member of the Sicilian Mafia and a man U.S. Attorney Rudy Guiliani had said "played a significant role" in the Pizza Connection. To make things worse, Fermon visited Joe's Pizza knowing there was a potential federal investigation and Italian authorities were wiretapping phone calls in Italy.

I saw the look of concern cross Nate's face when he heard Fermon's comment. Later Greg and I were discussing Fermon's behavior, and he also acknowledged Nate's look, so I picked up the phone and called Nate.

"I'm glad you called because I would've been suspicious if you hadn't. You know, an FBI agent could be fired for doing what Fermon did. That was definitely unprofessional conduct," he exhorted.

Nate was right; it wasn't something anyone could argue about, at the very least, Fermon's conduct was a serious policy violation. It didn't mean he had done anything criminal, but it was certainly questionable and suspicious behavior, especially when you added in all the other concerns we had.

One week later, things worsened when Ron Swigman said the phone calls from Joe's Pizza to Italy had abruptly and mysteriously stopped! Hearing this suspicious news, Nate started pushing me to go to the Division of Internal Investigation and report Fermon's conduct. Nate had a lot more faith in my department than I did, so I put it off.

In the interim, Greg and I began researching the old Pizza Connection case. The ISP was involved in helping the FBI gather intelligence, so our archives were full of investigative reports and the mobsters associated to the case, including Joe's Pizza in Paris.

Greg also began looking at old newspaper articles on the Pizza Connection case and other organized crime figures and associates. From these old newspaper articles Greg's memory was tweaked. One of Central Illinois' most colorful organized crime figures had been a man named Frank Zito. According to a 1999 article from the *State Journal-Register*:

> . . . syndicated columnist Drew Pearson listed Zito among "Illinois' worst hoodlums . . . Outside of Chicago, the most powerful underworld figure in Illinois is Frank Zito, whose balding, grey-fringed head, conservative clothes, and scholarly appearance belie his violent background . . . He controls gambling, prostitution and bookmaking in the Springfield and Sangamon County areas." Zito came to the United States from his native Sicily in 1910, and by the late 1920s, he appears to have been pretty firmly in control of organized crime activities in Springfield.

The article continued:

> There are, for example, rumors that Zito may have ordered the May 1929 assassination of Caesar Sansone, who had been a close

advisor to John Picco, the Italian Consular agent in Springfield and a close associate of Zito's. The belief is that Sansone may have come to "know too much" about Zito's business affairs and may have been a little too talkative for his own good.

The name Picco sparked Greg's memory and a second article read:

> . . . John Picco, a Springfield businessman . . . would himself be the victim of a gangland murder three years later. Picco, in turn, had been closely associated with figures in the Springfield underworld, including local mob boss Frank Zito.

As Greg continued reading, his memory fully returned. The article from the *Springfield Journal Register* discussed the gangland murder of John Picco:

> The April 1932 murder of John Picco, a Springfield businessman, political operative and agent for the Italian Consular service, was a classic gangland hit, one that remains unsolved to this day. As he and his young son left the home of Picco's brother . . . two men with sawed-off shotguns climbed out of a parked car and fired three shots. Picco crumpled to the pavement, the little boy ran back to the Uncle's house saying "they killed Daddy" . . . Picco's assassination, which was in true gangland fashion, adds another name to a long list of gang victims in Springfield.

The article continued that Picco himself was no small time businessman:

> In addition to his duties as a consular officer, representing the commercial interests of Italians in this country, Picco was a business agent for a number of Italian concerns to including steamship lines, and he had interests in several Springfield businesses, including drugstores. Picco was also active in Republican politics throughout the state and had been awarded for his efforts with patronage positions, including a post as arbiter on the state industrial board. "The slain man was well known throughout the state . . . The variety of his political, business and social contacts is making it difficult for authorities to establish a motive for his assassination." John Picco was survived by his son, John Picco Jr.

Greg remembered back to when he was Fermon's Staff Officer. One evening, he and Fermon were in Springfield and went out for a few drinks. It became late so Fermon suggested they stay at his brother-in-law's house. Greg was apprehensive over their unexpected intrusion, but Fermon reassured Greg he frequently imposed like this on his brother-in-law. They arrived around midnight and Fermon's brother-in-law welcomed them into his home and introduced himself to Greg as "Jack." They opened up an expensive bottle of cognac, and played billiards and talked into the early morning hours. Greg assumed the brother-in-law's name was "Jack Picco," and based this assumption on conversations with Jack, who bragged about his family's "mob connections" and "mob history." Greg said Jack proudly displayed the same news articles that later tweaked his memory about John Picco and Frank Zito, who Jack described as his grandfather and Uncle Frank.

Jack also touted his powerful, political connections in the Republican Party. And after all, the Rhoads case was deemed too politically sensitive under a criminally convicted Republican Governor. A tainted Republican Governor who received substantial contributions from Bob Morgan who was identified as a suspect in the Rhoads murders. And Fermon and Carper had openly and repeatedly impeded the Rhoads case from being reinvestigated. Both had also been promoted to positions of great power in the state police during the George Ryan administration. Adding all this up, even as unbelievable as it sounded, it was like Nate said, "It didn't pass the smell test."

Greg shared these concerns, too, stating, "The more I thought about it, I realized that . . . [this was the] same organized crime group that had set up the Pizza Connection and . . . Joe Vitale was part of it and is a convicted felon and that he was convicted of narcotics, federal narcotics conspiracy and narcotics trafficking."

Jack also told Fermon he could help him with his ISP career, and he named others they had helped to attain power within the Illinois State Police. Throughout the evening, Greg said Jack kept emphasizing his family was not only "mob connected" but they were also "very politically powerful," and he could help Fermon's career. Jack told Fermon he needed to fax his resume to him and he would "get it to the right people."

At the time, Greg said he hadn't put much stock in Jack's claims and had even considered him somewhat of a grandiose crackpot, advising, "I told Captain Fermon I thought Jack was a good guy but he was kind of obsessed with this whole issue, maybe kind of full of it."

Greg continued that, "Captain Fermon said he was connected. And was politically connected. . . . and basically he intended to put a resume together and get it to [Jack]," who " . . . would be able to help him with his career."

When Greg confided all this to me, I was more than concerned. If it were true and Fermon's brother-in-law, as he implied, was mob connected, and had helped him in his rise to power through the ISP, maybe there was more to Fermon's impeding the investigation than I thought. It certainly brought a new light to the meaning of "too politically sensitive" and might explain Fermon's suspicious behavior. If Jack was really "connected" to organized crime, even remotely connected to the Pizza Connection case, it definitely warranted some concern. The very idea that Jack—who bragged of connections to organized crime and being politically powerful—could help someone in the Illinois State Police gain power was unbelievable to me, but faced with this and all the other concerns, this was something that couldn't be ignored anymore.

History showed that after the visit to Fermon's brother-in-law, he was in fact elevated to a newly created position in Springfield as the Statewide Investigations Officer. Fermon rose from the rank of Master Sergeant to Lieutenant to Captain in approximately one year's time, not a very common occurrence. Greg also remembered that within a week after the visit, Fermon had Ruby fax his resume to Jack. So Greg and I questioned Ruby, who remembered faxing Fermon's resume to a doctor's office that Fermon identified as his brother-in-law's.

We had one problem though; we couldn't find anyone named Jack Picco in Illinois. So I came up with the idea of having Greg call John Picco, Jr. and ask for Jack Picco. John Picco, Jr. was the nine-year-old son who had watched his father, John Picco, Sr., gunned down in the streets of Springfield. A timeline I later prepared for DII summarized the phone conversation:

> In summary, Sgt. Dixon called John Picco and asked for Dr. Picco.
> John Picco replied, "This is Mr. Picco, how did you get this number?"
> Sgt. Dixon replied, "You're in the book, and I was referred by a friend
> to Dr. Picco." Picco replied, "You mean my nephew. He's considered
> a Picco, and I can see how you figure that. His name is Leslie Jack
> Fyans. F-Y-A-N-S. He's in the book." And then Picco hung up.

With Jack identified, now all I needed was to find out how Fermon was related to Leslie Jack Picco-Fyans, as he referred to himself in newspaper articles.

I turned to private investigator Bill Clutter for a favor. I needed the marriage certificate of Fyans to make the connection to Fermon. Thanks to Clutter, we learned Leslie Jack Fyans married Paula M. Peterson. Both Greg and I knew Fermon married LeAnn Peterson—a fact we also confirmed through marriage certificates. The connection was Fermon's wife LeeAnn was the sister to Paula

Peterson, Jack Fyans' wife. Still I wanted more proof and I remembered Fermon had ordered me to give him one of my task force's cell phones. Remembering his exorbitant cell phone bills, I figured he probably made calls to his brother-in-law. Sure enough, I was right—there were hundreds of calls to Jack, both at home and at his medical office, in the phone records.

Records also indicated Dr. Leslie Jack Fyans was "a Springfield clinical and consulting psychologist." In fact, referencing his political connections, the *Springfield Journal Register,* in an article on Governor George Ryan, reported, "Fyans . . . counsels business, religious and political leaders." Who knows . . . maybe he even counseled good old George? But like George Ryan, Dr. Fyans also had his problems with the law.

In 1994, Dr. Jack Fyans was investigated by the State Police for false billing the State of Illinois Public Aid for $100,000. Obviously connections count, because the ISP case file reflected the felony charge was later reduced to a civil matter and the good doctor was placed on probation for 18 months by the Illinois Department of Professional Regulation, along with a $7,500 fine. According to the ISP Case Action Report, Jack was also forced to "reimburse the State through his company . . . $100,000.00 in overpayments and damages." A pretty sweet deal—false bill the state for a hundred grand, and if you get away with it, great! If you're caught, just pay back the hundred grand, and you're only charged 7.5% interest.

There was more. I had been to Fermon's house and seen his lifestyle. Fermon's house was located just north of Paris on 25 acres of land. The house was grandiose and Fermon also owned three Corvettes, including a mint condition classic 1959 model. I didn't know Fermon's finances other than his salary was similar to mine, but I knew I couldn't afford toys that luxurious. Still, maybe Fermon was just a wise investor, a good businessman, or in his words, "a good earner."

After gathering all this information, I went to Nate Williams. I figured with all our other suspicions, along with this new information, maybe the FBI would investigate. I didn't trust my department anymore and knew they would never do the right thing when it came to something this scandalous, especially when it came to protecting the politically anointed command. The same reason I didn't turn in Carper years earlier.

Nate still insisted I should go to DII and he promised to back up my concerns. I continued to put it off, but the writing was on the wall when he called and said he had gone to Assistant U.S. Attorney Rick Cox and informed him we had some concerns about Fermon that I was taking to DII. Now I was going to be "damned if I did and damned if I didn't." There was good reason to fear our internal investigations given their history of covering up scandalous misconduct, and once again, my department proved my fears were justified.

I wouldn't learn about the department's devious deceit and cover-up until two years later, when, in my civil trial, the second in command of the Division of Internal Investigations, Lt. Col. Richard Karpawicz, testified.

By the time Karpawicz testified, Nate Williams had already given a deposition and testified in my trial. Nate was good to his word and testified he supported my concerns. When it came to Fermon's visit to Joe's Pizza, he testified how he personally heard Fermon make the comment, acknowledging, "Yes. . . . [the] comment represented the possibility of unprofessional activity on the part of Captain Fermon." Nate continued and talked about us discussing Fermon's behavior, " . . . the nature of the conversation was did each of us hear the comment that was made, and what did we think about the comment?"

> Q: At any point in time, did you advise Mr. Callahan that you had concerns about Mr. Fermon's statements?
>
> Williams: Yes, I did. . . . I can tell you that. I told Lt. Callahan that I believed it was possibly representative of unprofessional conduct on the part of Captain Fermon.
>
> Q: And you formed that feeling based upon what?
>
> Williams: Based upon hearing Captain Fermon's comment. . . . I witnessed the comment directly. . . . I overheard the comment, and that was the basis for my opinion on unprofessional conduct.

But the cover-up by DII was obvious when Karpawicz testified that during an interview with Special Agent Williams, neither the FBI nor Nate Williams had any concerns regarding Fermon. Lt. Col. Karpawicz deceitfully claimed, "These are Lt. Callahan's concerns. There is nothing here from the FBI's concern," and he went on to testify Nate Williams said the information about Fermon's visit to the pizzeria came only "from Mike Callahan." So Karpawicz was asked again, "And do I understand your testimony here today, sir, to be that the FBI did not share Lt. Callahan's concerns?" Karpawicz again deceitfully replied, "That's correct . . . basically, yes, sir."

Karpawicz outright lied under oath and was obviously trying to cover up why DII failed to investigate Fermon's misconduct by claiming the FBI had no concerns.

Karpawicz continued with other lies when he rationalized why DII didn't deem it necessary to investigate the allegations of Fermon's inappropriate conduct:

... he [Callahan] thought it was inappropriate for Captain Fermon to have visited ... Joe's Pizza parlor when our policy ... states that officers should avoid regular and continuous conduct with criminals or felons. And the owner of Joe's Pizza isn't a criminal or a felon, and the owner is Eno Vitale and Mike should have known that through his investigation.

Karpawicz was trying to discredit me to the jury by suggesting that Joe Vitale's son, Eno Vitale, now owned Joe's Pizza and not Joe. Of course, it was well known that Joe Vitale still worked at the pizzeria—the health department license was still in his name, and the building was owned by Joe and in his name—but that didn't matter to Karpawicz. This lead to one of the most humorous cross examinations of the trial. Karpawicz was asked:

> Q: One of the things that Mike brought to your attention was this Joe's Pizza issue ... And I think you indicated that Joe's Pizza isn't owned by Joe; it's owned by Eno Vitale. ... Eno Vitale would be Joe Vitale's son?
>
> Karpawicz: That is correct. ... Yes, sir.
>
> Q: How do you know that Eno Vitale owns it?
>
> Karpawicz: He contacted me over the weekend.

After Karpawicz's stupid blunder, the courtroom fell silent, and everyone sat there stunned for a few moments. Obviously, it was apparent it wasn't just Fermon who was friendly with the folks at Joe's Pizza. Everyone was wide awake now, and after a long moment of silence, one of the jurors asked the judge to turn up Karpawicz microphone. He immediately realized how badly his comment sounded and once stoic and exuding professionalism, his eyes went straight to the floor, hanging his head between his legs like a browbeaten dog. It was an unbelievable moment and I saw the looks of disgust on the jurors' faces.

My attorney attacked Karpawicz's buffoonish admission, and he was now forced to admit, that despite Fermon's conduct being a policy violation, DII never bothered to investigate his infraction. The comical cross examination continued:

> Q: Over *what* weekend?
>
> Karpawicz: Over this past weekend.

Q: Oh, this past weekend?

Karpawicz: Yes, sir.

Q: So, you mean you just did an investigation this past weekend to learn that it's Eno who owns Joe's Pizza and not Joe?

Karpawicz: Eno contacted me over the weekend to clarify . . . who owns Joe's Pizza.

Q: Now, Eno Vitale would be Joe Vitale's son?

Karpawicz: Yes, sir.

Q: And Joe Vitale . . . still lives in the Paris area. Is that correct?

Karpawicz: I believe so. Yes, sir.

Q: And to your knowledge, he still is actively involved in . . . Joe's Pizza; is that correct?

Karpawicz: I don't know that, sir. . . . I knew that Joe was a convicted felon.

Q: And not only is Joe a convicted felon, but Joe was convicted in the largest drug conspiracy case in American history, wasn't he?

Karpawicz: That's my understanding. Yes sir [in] 1984.

Q: That was what was called the Pizza Connection. Is that correct? . . . where the Sicilian Mafia had infiltrated small towns in a number of different locations, one of them being Paris, Illinois. Is that correct? And they would use these pizza places to basically launder money, is that essentially what your understanding is?

Karpawicz: I believe that's correct. . . . To the best of my knowledge. . . . Yes, sir.

Under intense questioning Karpawicz frustratingly tried to defend why DII failed to investigate the allegations against Fermon while admitting his conduct was a serious policy violation.

Q: If I'm an ISP guy and I know these things . . . and they're being watched by the federal government . . . is it appropriate for me to go there?

Karpawicz: I don't know what Captain Fermon knew at the time he visited Joe's Pizza.

Q: I see. And you don't know that because you never bothered to interview Captain Fermon; isn't that correct?

Karpawicz: Yes, sir. That's correct.

Then Karpawicz was asked, "Whether it was true or not true, Callahan raised an allegation that, if proven to be true, would constitute a viable policy violation?" Karpawicz pathetically replied, "What's a policy violation?"

Q: . . . Mike comes to you and says: look, the FBI told us at a meeting that there was traffic going on, intercepts going on. And thereafter, Captain Fermon acknowledges that he goes to Joe's Pizza. And that, in and of itself, I think you told us would constitute a policy violation.

Karpawicz: And that violation would be?

Q: You are the number two person at DII. I don't know. You tell me. I thought you told me it would be a violation. I'm not DII. I don't know the rules and regulations. . . . If Mike Callahan had come to you and said; Steve Fermon knowingly went to a restaurant that was subject to a federal investigation that would violate policy if true.

Karpawicz: Yes, sir.

Q: . . . therefore, if what Mike said was true and it was a policy violation, that's something DII should investigate, correct?

Karpawicz: If true. Yes, sir. I am not aware of Joe Vitale's being the focus of a federal investigation.

Q: If that were true, if that allegation were true, you would agree with me that would be a policy violation?

Karpawicz: It would be poor judgment on Captain Fermon's part, yes, sir.

Q: But it would also be a policy violation?

Karpawicz: Yes, sir. I'm assuming it would be. But I don't know which one. Conduct unbecoming. . . . yes, sir. If it were true.

The number two man in charge of DII stumbled and rambled on like a buffoon, and he admitted the allegations against Fermon were a policy violation, yet DII had never bothered to investigate the allegations, so how would they know what was true or not? But in the end, this was nothing compared to the hypocrisy, deceit, lies and attempted cover-ups still to come from the mighty leadership of the Illinois State Police.

CHAPTER 17

THE DIVISION OF INTERNAL COVER-UP

---■---

The Illinois State Police Division of Internal Investigations is often referred to as "The Rat Squad." I preferred to think of them more in terms as the State Police's version of the Russian KGB because they ruled through fear. If you were just one of the rank-and-file, DII had no problem dealing with you, oftentimes unjustly or vindictively. It didn't matter if a person was guilty or innocent; if they wanted you, you were going to get done, even if it meant fabricating reports or trumping up charges. On the other hand, if you were politically protected, they would go to any lengths to cover up the misconduct, lie under oath, ignore witnesses and ignore the truth or worse. In my case, it became a deceitful web of ISP command officers at the highest levels covering up for one another, and I experienced all these deceptions first hand.

On paper, the State Police's internal investigations had policies to follow, and when allegations were made it was mandated that: "Thorough investigations *will* be conducted into allegations of misconduct to establish facts which can absolve the innocent and identify the guilty." That was DII's responsibility—investigate allegations of wrongdoing, but it was a playing field with two sets of rules.

I had heard many horror stories of how DII calculatingly destroyed careers. While some may have deserved their fate, I knew of many who didn't. That was the fear that DII held over everybody, because oftentimes their only goal was to "absolve the guilty and punish the innocent." It was well known that DII covered up for George Ryan and his cronies in the License for Bribes scandal. An editorial from the Champaign *News-Gazette* agreed:

> ... this is not the first time the Illinois State Police have been corrupted by political consideration. It's apparent now that top state police commanders squelched the initial investigation into the license-for-bribes scandal that drove Gov. Ryan from office. Federal investigators subsequently picked up the ball and have been running with it ever since in a far-reaching investigation ...

With political protection like this, the fear of DII was two-fold: knowing that, at any given time, a trumped-up case could be opened on you, and also knowing that if you spoke out against the wrong person, you risked retaliation. The fear of DII only heightened during the George Ryan administration. It was a time when the Illinois State Police placed more value on being politically correct than on being a good cop.

I was still skeptical about going forward to DII but rationalized I had too much support for the department to retaliate against me, plus the department knew I had outside advocates like Nate Williams and Mary Leahy. I also had Greg Dixon, John Strohl and Edie Casella as witnesses. A new governor who preached ethics reform and integrity in government had just been elected to office. There was also all the other DII cases that were opened on Fermon and a pending hostile work environment complaint against him. What I didn't know was that DII had already "whitewashed" all of the charges in the other cases.

The most serious issue still facing Fermon was an Equal Employment Opportunity investigation based on Ruby's allegations he had created a hostile work environment at Zone 5. When I met with the EEO investigator, I unloaded all my concerns about Fermon, and she practically ran out of the interview when I told her I had gone to Mary Leahy and the FBI. She apparently shared the information with DII, because DII Deputy Director Skip Nelson called Ruby and told her I had made some troubling allegations against Fermon. Skip was originally from this area and he and Ruby were good friends, so he told her that if I didn't want to get in trouble, I needed to come forward. With this and Nate Williams going to the U.S. Attorney's office, I was out of options. I had put off going to DII for months, and now I had no choice.

With all the external and internal pressures mounting, I reluctantly called Nelson on April 22, 2003. The conversation went better than anticipated, and after hanging up, I felt reassured. Nelson, like a true salesman, promised me DII's goal was to do the right thing in this case. I should've known better, as it was the same thing I had heard from other ISP Colonels before.

A little more than a week later, while we were in a zone meeting, Fermon got a call on his cell phone. Whatever the call was about, it shook him up. His demeanor instantly transformed, and he turned a bright crimson red—like he always did when he got upset. This was one of those rare moments where I actually saw him lose his composure, and he abruptly ended the meeting.

An hour later, Nate called and said he was just interviewed by DII Assistant Deputy Director Rick Karpawicz and, of all people, Lt. Col. Diane Carper. Nate provided a detailed account of the meeting. His supervisor, Bob Shay, and their boss, Special Agent in Charge Herb Cousins, also sat in on the interview. Nate said the two ISP Colonels questioned him about the validity of the concerns and suspicions I had reported to Skip Nelson. Nate told them he shared my same concerns, especially when Fermon mentioned going to Joe's Pizza, and told them he was concerned enough to go to Assistant U.S. Attorney Rick Cox. During the entire meeting, Nate said Carper sat there, diligently taking notes while Karpawicz asked questions. Nate explained he believed Fermon's actions were somewhat suspicious, and he didn't think Fermon passed the smell test.

His boss, Special Agent in Charge Herb Cousins, interrupted and exclaimed, "It's not somewhat suspicious. It's overtly suspicious when you put all the puzzle pieces together."

Nate admitted during the interview that he pushed me to go to DII, and I had no reason to doubt Nate, since we were professional and social friends for the last several years. I ran into Bob Shay later who told me how strongly Nate had backed me up with the two Colonels. But it wasn't too comforting to learn that Nate had to stand up for me and back me up.

"Has that piece of shit captain of yours been removed yet?" Shay asked.

When I told him no, he shook his head in disbelief.

"You know, Mike, the Bureau sometimes wonders about your command in Springfield," Shay replied.

The FBI may have wondered about the ISP command, but I just plain didn't trust them and there was more than enough reason for me to be concerned about Nate having to "back me up" to DII.

Again, I wouldn't learn why until two years later in my civil trial. Lt. Col. Carper was the first to testify about the ISP's devious attempts to cover up my allegations. Obviously the ISP's strategy was to discredit my allegations by trying to twist things around and imply Nate Williams had no concerns about Fermon. When Carper was asked if he had any concerns, she deceitfully replied, "Special Agent Williams indicated that Lieutenant Callahan was the one who brought the concerns to him . . . that Lieutenant Callahan brought the concerns to Special Agent Williams and not the other way around."

Then Carper went into one of her many memory lapses during testimony when asked if Special Agent Williams agreed or disagreed with the concerns I raised,

"I don't know that he expressed an opinion one way or the other. At this point, I can't remember. I don't know that he validated the concerns or not. I don't recall."

And her deceitfulness continued:

> Q: Am I correct that Mr. Williams said during that meeting that if in fact Mr. Fermon had gone to [Joe's Pizza] in Paris that would be problematic in the FBI's opinion?
>
> Carper: I remember that Special Agent Williams indicated that if the concerns brought to him by Lieutenant Callahan were true, it would be something that they would, they should be concerned about. . . . I don't recall if he articulated any concerns other than indicating that if what Lieutenant Callahan had told him was true, then that would be a concern.

Lt. Col. Karpawicz was not any less deceitful when he testified, "Nate Williams started by saying he talked with Lieutenant Callahan, and that Lieutenant Callahan believed that Captain Fermon was impeding his investigation, and that he was also worried about being reassigned. He also mentioned that Lieutenant Callahan was suspicious of Captain Fermon because of his family ties to organized crime . . . as well as his visit to Joe's Pizza . . ." And Karpawicz continued that, "These are Lieutenant Callahan's concerns. There is nothing here from the FBI's concerns. He is basically regurgitating what Lieutenant Callahan has told him."

Under oath, the head of DII, Deputy Director Skip Nelson, backed up Karpawicz's testimony.

> Q: So, it was your understanding based upon what Colonel Karpawicz was telling you that the FBI did not share the same concerns that Mike had expressed to you in your telephone conference with him?
>
> Nelson: Yes. That's what was conveyed to us.
>
> Q: Now, did Colonel Karpawicz tell you, did he say, the FBI has no concerns, they're fine with Fermon? I mean, was that essentially the essence of what he was saying?
>
> Nelson: Yes, sir.

Three Illinois State Police Colonels took an oath to tell the truth before God, judge and jury, but Nate Williams testimony totally contradicted the three ISP

Colonels. Nate testified about the meeting with DII and how they discussed the concerns about Fermon:

> Q: When you had those conversations with Mr. Callahan, did you yourself have those sorts of concerns?
>
> Williams: Yes, I believe I told Lt. Callahan that I had some concerns. Yes. . . . There were basically three elements. There were the comments that I overheard; there was the information that Lt. Callahan presented to me . . . And then there were [my] observations of investigative activity . . .
>
> Q: Mr. Williams, after you had these conversations with Mr. Callahan, did you forward any concerns or address any concerns or issues about Mr. Fermon with anyone . . . ?
>
> Williams: I believe I . . . discussed that with my supervisor, Bob Shay, and I also had a conversation with Rick Cox of the U.S. Attorney's Office.
>
> Q: And what did you tell Mr. Cox?
>
> Williams: I just told him that I had some concerns or that there was a possibility of concerns regarding Captain Fermon.
>
> Q: At any point in time . . . did you and Mr. Callahan discuss the possibility of Mr. Callahan taking these comments to his Division of Internal Investigation?
>
> Williams: Yes, yes. . . . this was investigator to investigator, friend to friend type of conversation. Not an official conversation between the Illinois State Police and the FBI . . . My advice was that he takes the concerns to the Internal Affairs Department of the State Police.

The three ISP colonels testified under oath that Nate Williams nor the FBI had concerns about Fermon. But Nate heard Fermon make the comment about his inappropriate visit to Joe's Pizza with his own ears. If the FBI truly had no concerns, why did Nate Williams advise me to go to DII? Why did Nate Williams go to his own supervisor and the U.S. Attorney then? Nate Williams had no reason to lie under oath. To the contrary, Carper, Nelson and Karpawicz had every reason to lie, and as time progressed, these weren't the only lies they were caught in.

Something else stood out about the meeting with the FBI. Nate said throughout that meeting, Carper diligently took notes. Yet none of her notes from this meeting were ever disclosed. Here was a meeting between the ISP and the FBI about concerns of misconduct by an ISP Captain . . . and Carper couldn't find her notes when she later testified, "I wrote down trigger words like I normally do," but when she was asked where those notes were, she testified, "I did attempt to locate them. I was not able to."

Lt Col. Karpawicz was just as negligent or maybe just as deceitful. Skip Nelson was asked if it was ISP policy and a requirement to document meetings involving allegations where complaints have been made, and Nelson replied, "Yes, sir." Yet, Nelson had an excuse ready for why DII didn't document the meeting with the FBI when he advised, " . . . Colonel Karpawicz, he keeps meticulous notes." So Nelson was asked:

Q: Alright, where are those notes?

Nelson: I have no idea.

And likewise, even though Karpawicz admitted the meeting with the FBI was "a fairly significant meeting" he also testified no report was written, " . . . because it was a meeting. I took notes." Like Carper, Karpawicz conveniently couldn't find his "meticulous" notes, either.

I was clueless to the conspiracy of deceit and cover-up by the ISP command that May of 2003. Approximately one week after the meeting with the FBI, Karpawicz called and said I needed to be at DII headquarters the next morning, May 8, 2003. He also ordered me not to discuss the meeting with anyone. I understood the confidentiality issues, and knew I could be fired for leaking information or talking about internal investigations.

Karpawicz's call created a small dilemma since I was scheduled to attend a luncheon the next day. So I called Fermon's staff officer and cancelled; I was vague and doubted Fermon would even miss or care that I wasn't there.

The drive to Springfield the next day was filled with uncertainty. This was the first time I was involved in something like this and I didn't know what to expect. When I arrived at DII headquarters, I was ushered into a meeting room. I was alone for awhile before the door opened and in walked Karpawicz accompanied by Area Commander Lance Adams—one of Fermon's best friends. My heart sank a little at the sight of Adams. Matters got worse when Lt. Col. Rich Woods from the Division of Operation also walked in the room.

So much for confidentiality. I should've smelled a "rat"—or more like rats—right then and there. Having someone from operations present during an allegedly confidential DII meeting was not the usual protocol. Even Col. Chuck Brueggemann agreed with this when he testified two years later at my civil trial, when asked, "…what you're telling me is your impression is that if there's an issue DII needs to look at, then DII needs to look at it, not Operations." And Col. Brueggemann testified:

> That's correct. That's very accurate. I am extremely careful to stay out of DII matters . . . the less I know . . . the better off that I am. . . . And that's for a few reasons. It protects the officer who's making the allegation; we want our officers to bring concerns to the attention of the department. If we can't police ourselves, we're headed down the wrong direction, so we want that information.

What a hypocrite! It was Brueggemann who had sent Lt. Col. Carper to the DII meeting with the FBI and then sent Lt. Col. Rich Woods to my DII interview. Yet Brueggemann testified he was "extremely careful to stay out of DII matters." Brueggemann continued his hypocrisy when he was asked:

> Q: . . . do you know if you had any conversations with Mr. Nelson or anyone else at DII that this was the route that they were taking?

> Brueggemann: I had discussions with him requesting a very thorough investigation be completed by their division. I wanted a thorough investigation into allegations made against Fermon, I don't care where they came from. They needed to do it, being DII.

Nelson's testimony once again proved Brueggemann was nothing more than a hypocrite. Nelson was asked, "When you met with Mr. Brueggemann, had you already made up your mind, look, DII is not going to investigate this, or was this still sort of an open question?" Nelson replied, "Based upon the information that we had from the meeting . . . we did want to talk to Colonel Brueggemann and see what he had to say about some of the concerns raised."

> Q: And . . . . Colonel Brueggemann's perspective was what?

> Nelson: That no one was trying to obstruct or impede an investigation. They just didn't feel that there was anything to pursue and that it was more suspicion than it was fact.

Much like the politician he is, Col. Brueggemann was caught talking out of both sides of his mouth when he testified he wanted "a thorough investigation," yet Nelson said Brueggemann "didn't feel that there was anything to pursue." This was the type of leadership that now controlled the Illinois State Police, leaders who had no problem lying and betraying their duty or the people's trust.

The meeting with DII lasted the better part of the afternoon, and I meticulously explained my review of the Rhoads case, Carper's impeding the investigation with all the times she deemed it too politically sensitive and the current attempts by Fermon and Carper at impeding the investigation. I provided a detailed five-page timeline outlining every infraction, policy violation, suspicion or concern of criminal misconduct I had regarding Fermon and Carper and supplied documentation supporting those concerns. The five-page timeline also identified Major Casella, Captain Strohl, Sgt. Dixon and Master Sergeant Reed as witnesses to Carper's too politically sensitive statement.

When I finished, I knew I was in trouble. Karpawicz wasn't happy with the extensive documentation, and he questioned if I had gone beyond my official duties.

"You know, Mike, you have to draw a fine line on how far you go in looking at these kind of things," he chastised. "You don't want to cross that line and get into trouble yourself."

Obviously put out, he asked, "Do you think there is anything criminal here?"

"That's not my job to determine," I replied. "That's your job to investigate and determine."

As I was excused, Karpawicz sarcastically emphasized I was not to discuss this with anyone, including FBI Agent Nate Williams. No doubt, I had definitely pissed off the brass.

Skip Nelson's secretary eventually confided to Ruby Gordon-Phillips that after I left the meeting, the three men came from the conference room laughing and arrogantly discarded the paperwork I provided in a nearby trash can. I had no idea, but my fate was already sealed that day.

ISP policy protects the confidentiality of DII interviews and disclosing the information is grounds for termination. I knew people who were fired for divulging confidential information given to DII. Yet before I cleared the city limits of Springfield, I received a call from Fermon's staff officer.

"Dude, I don't know what you're doing, but Captain Fermon just got a call from someone, and now he's on a war path and asking where you're at," he said. "He wants to know what you said you were doing today and where you're at right now." He explained that he told Fermon I was unable to make the luncheon, and Fermon didn't care at the time, but now he was on a rampage. He continued that while Fermon was on the phone, he turned crimson red and exclaimed, "He did *what*?" Then Fermon went to the back of the room, still talking and angrily pacing back and forth. When he returned to the table, Fermon immediately began grilling the staff officer and Master Sergeant Brian Henn about what they knew about my whereabouts.

Obviously my confidential meeting with DII hadn't been very confidential, but when I called Karpawicz, he denied anything was leaked. Karpawicz had lied, because a few days later Fermon wrote a memo to Carper, admitting he was leaked my allegations to DII:

> Beginning Friday, May 9, 2003, and continuing through Wednesday, May 14, 2003, I received information from several sources indicating very serious allegations about my personal and professional conduct had been reported to the Illinois State Police, Division of Internal Investigation on May 8, 2003, by Lieutenant Michale Callahan.

The memo concluded that Fermon wanted me immediately removed from Zone 5.

ISP Colonel Mike Snyders also confirmed the leak during testimony, when he remembered getting a call from Fermon on either May 8 or May 9, 2003, "I remember the phone call with Steve Fermon. I remember him calling me with the purpose of telling me that he had a very big concern that Mike Callahan was spreading allegations about him . . . . Steve told me that Mike was saying that Steve was a criminal, that he had mob connections. . . . I remember laughing or snickering and telling Steve that we . . . don't think you're connected to the mob. If we did, you wouldn't be a Captain in the Illinois State Police."

Probably true, he would've more likely been a Colonel.

In my civil trial two years later, we asked for and received Fermon's cell phone records for May 2003 to try and identify who called him the day I went to DII. But by this time the conspiracy of deceit and cover-up in the upper command had reached the highest levels, and the phone records for May 8 through May 14 were conveniently missing. When asked why, Keith Jensen, the head of the ISP legal division claimed those records were just no longer available.

It wasn't just Fermon who was leaked my allegations to DII, Carper was also told about the complaint I made against her. She was even provided a copy of the DII timeline I had prepared with the allegations against her. Carper eventually testified she was leaked all this information from DII Col. Karpawicz, who had been a Captain under her command prior to being promoted. Based on Carper's testimony, Skip Nelson was asked the following . . .

Q: Would it be appropriate for someone who was in that meeting on May 8, 2003, that Mike was present for, Woods was present for, Karpawicz was present for, and Lance Adams was present for . . . to divulge what happened in that meeting . . .

Nelson: No, sir.

Yet someone did divulge my allegations and according to Carper, it was the second in command at DII, and despite the serious policy violation—one that mandated termination—nothing was done. Of course, during testimony, Karpawicz denied ever giving Carper my timeline.

Q: Now, given the allegation against Colonel Carper, you would agree with me that it would be inappropriate for that information to be divulged to Colonel Carper?

Karpawicz: If it were true, yes, sir.

Q: Did you give her that copy?

Karpawicz: No, sir.

Of course I didn't know about all this deceit and cover-up when I went forward with the allegations against Fermon and Carper, but I soon suspected something was leaked.

Fermon became ruthless in his vindictiveness. On May 15, Greg Dixon was brought in and Fermon told him he was being taken off the federal investigation; he was advised behind closed doors "this is for your own protection."

Dixon's removal came while we were in the middle of a meth conspiracy drug case, and some of the defendants were from Paris who were associated or related to suspects in the Rhoads homicide. This had the potential to be a big break for us in gaining new information—not only in the Rhoads case but Paris in general. Once the arrests were made, there was the possibility of recruiting some informants. We had already developed two confidential informants who agreed to work for us. Things were developing at a rapid pace, but Fermon was once again impeding the case by removing Greg Dixon, and neither Carper nor the upper command seemed to care. The U.S. Attorney's Office did care, and Tim Bass questioned Greg's removal.

"What happened to, you'll get all the resources you need?" he asked.

Fermon continued doing more damage by almost single-handedly dismantling two of my narcotics task forces. These task forces were located in Decatur and Champaign, and had successfully made serious dents in the narcotic trafficking in the two cities and surrounding areas. That didn't make a difference to Fermon or Carper as they watched the task forces dismantled.

As time went on, it became obvious DII had helped to conspire and cover up my scandalous accusations. I learned the hard way, at least in this case, their mandated job wasn't that "thorough investigations will be conducted into allegations of misconduct."

The Director during this time was Larry Trent, who was a former investigator at one time in the ISP. He was asked about my allegations against Fermon: "Now it was your understanding that DII had actually opened a case on this and done an investigation?"

"That was my understanding, yes," he replied. He also said he expected a DII investigation because, " . . . It's a serious allegation," but he refused to give an opinion about my allegations, and replied, "I don't know that I had one because it was a DII investigation . . . I worked investigations long enough to know not to form any opinions until the facts come in, so I don't know."

Trent also testified that he was told DII conducted an investigation and, "It's my understanding that they were investigated, and it was unfounded." He based this on conversations with Col. Skip Nelson. DII's deception became even more obvious when Trent was asked and testified:

> Q: Now, at any point in time, did Mr. Nelson or anyone else . . . tell you that Mr. Callahan . . . in addition to making allegations against Mr. Fermon, he also made allegations against Ms. Carper?

> Trent: No.

Likewise, First Deputy Director Doug Brown also testified about DII's deception:

> Q: At any point in time were you made aware of the fact that Mike had gone to DII and raised concerns with DII about Steve Fermon, Diane Carper . . . ?

> Brown: I don't remember Diane Carper . . . but I clearly remember Colonel Nelson or somebody from DII calling me, telling me that there were allegations regarding Fermon, and that they were going to investigate those allegations. I remember him [Nelson] saying we need to take a look at this and we're going to investigate it . . . Yeah. That's my memory of that, yes.

> Q: Has anyone ever told you that Diane Carper made the statement that this case was "too politically sensitive?"

Brown: No, I don't recall that.

Q: And based upon those allegations, that's the sort of thing you would expect would be investigated?

Brown: Oh yeah. Those are pretty serious allegations.

Here were the two top commanders of the Illinois State Police testifying under oath that they considered my allegations against Fermon serious, and they expected a DII investigation. In fact they were lied to and told an investigation was conducted and completed on Fermon. Adding to DII's deceit, the two top cops admitted they were never even told about my allegations against Carper, despite both men acknowledging they were very serious allegations.

Lying is a terminable offense in the ISP unless you're a colonel, I guess.

Lt. Col. Karpawicz had already testified Fermon's visit to Joe's Pizza was a policy violation, and he admitted DII also turned their backs to my allegations against Carper. Reading from the timeline I provided to DII, Karpawicz was asked: "And that last paragraph . . . Mike's making the allegation that Diane Carper told them that the Rhoads homicide was 'too politically sensitive' to investigate. Is that what it says?" He replied, "Yes, sir."

Q: Now forgetting for one moment whether that's a true statement or not a true statement, if the allegation is made that a case is not being investigated because it's "too politically sensitive," that's a fairly serious allegation, correct?

Karpawicz: If true, yes, sir.

Q: And if true, it would certainly be a policy violation; is that correct?

Karpawicz: If true.

Q: And, if true, it would possibly be a crime, correct?

Karpawicz: If true.

Q: Now, Mike Callahan outlines three different individuals who heard that—or he maintains heard that statement also, correct?

Karpawicz: Yes, sir.

Q: It references Greg Dixon in there . . . Edie Casella . . . John Strohl, is that correct?

Karpawicz: Yes.

Q: None of those people were ever contacted and asked about that, were they?

Karpawicz: No, sir, they weren't.

Col. Karpawicz testified DII was mandated to investigate criminal allegations, and if true, Carper's actions were a criminal violation. Instead, DII had ignored this possible criminal act and instead chose to lie and cover up the crime. Karpawicz was given a chance to explain why DII didn't open a case on Carper when asked, "Why is it that you didn't investigate those allegations against [Carper]?" His lame excuse was pathetic:

> Lieutenant Callahan didn't spend very much time on the allega-
> tion that she made the comment that the investigation was "too
> politically sensitive" and that he was not to go operational and not
> look at the Rhoads . . . I've heard the term "politically sensitive"
> over the last two years on a regular basis, and it didn't ring any bells
> with me at the time.

Karpawicz's rationale was amusing, if not hypocritical, but how is any murder too politically sensitive? And after hearing Karpawicz testify, I fully understood why former governor George Ryan had used DII to investigate the politically sensitive allegations against him.

Deputy Director Harold Skip Nelson was also called to testify. As the head of DII, Nelson was also ironically designated as the "Ethics Officer" for the Illinois State Police, yet his trial testimony was 88 pages of one contradiction after another. He was so bad that, just minutes into his testimony, the federal judge allowed Nelson to be treated as an adverse witness. My uncle, a former FBI agent, sat in the stands and watched Nelson in amazement. In 30 years of law enforcement, he said he never witnessed anything so pathetic and deceitful.

"This guy's a colonel in the Illinois State Police!" he exclaimed.

Nelson testified about the allegations I brought forward on Fermon and said, "If they were proven to be true, I felt they would be very serious . . . yes, sir." But then the lying started . . .

Q: At some point in time, did you learn that Mike had made some allegations about Diane Carper?

Nelson: No, sir.

Q: Did you ever talk to Colonel Brueggemann about concerns that Mike had raised that a certain case was "too politically sensitive"?

Nelson was asked this question three times and each time he answered, "No, sir." So my attorney pointed out his blatant lie.

To point out his deceit, my attorney turned to Nelson's prior deposition: "Colonel . . . Do you recall you took a deposition in this case . . . did I ask you this question. 'Did you talk to Colonel Brueggemann about these matters?' And then did you give the answer, 'Yes, I believe that we did.'"

"Yes . . . I think I spoke to him [Brueggemann] about the allegations that Lieutenant Callahan made," Nelson admitted, and then added, "The conversation that he provided from his perspective was they had heard some of these same concerns but they didn't feel that there was a whole lot of substance to it."

But Nelson backtracked once again and the judge had enough and at this point allowed Nelson to be treated as an adverse witness. Nelson continued to dig himself deeper in a hole.

Q: . . . did you believe that the allegations against Carper were serious?

Nelson: My focus was on Captain Fermon. That was the gist of the complaint by Lt. Callahan.

Q: But you had indicated in your deposition that, "I had been told about the allegations against Colonel Carper . . . " Did you believe that those allegations were of a serious nature?

Nelson: I don't think that I had made that assessment at the time . . . not when you take the totality of the information that I received from Colonel Karpawicz . . . I figured that by talking to her boss, then he would know . . . he didn't express a great deal of concern . . . I think we wanted to continue to look into it so we went to Colonel Brueggemann, yes, sir.

Nelson continued his pathetic attempts to justify why DII did not investigate the criminal allegations against Carper.

Q: Impeding an investigation, that would be a violation of ISP policy . . . And it's DII's responsibility . . . to investigate potential violations of ISP policy. Is that correct?

Nelson: Yes, sir.

Q: So Mike had raised viable allegations against both Carper and Fermon. Is that correct?

Nelson: I don't know if you would say viable at that point . . . If proven to be true, yes, sir.

Q: You just told us that the allegations that Mike had raised . . . if they were true, would be serious policy violations. Correct?

Nelson: Yes.

Q: I want you to detail for me every single thing that DII did to investigate Mike's allegations after the meeting with Mike Callahan ended on May 8?

Nelson: We decided that we were not going to open the case and investigate the allegations.

Q: . . . ISP Policy . . . mandates a thorough investigation to absolve the innocent and identify the guilty. Isn't that correct, colonel?

Nelson: Yes, sir, it is.

Skip Nelson, like all the other ISP colonels, continued his pathetic and deceitful testimony. I watched the disgusted looks on the juror's faces and knew they saw the deceit and cover-up, too.

"We never saw so many colonels lie. They all looked so bad. We were so ashamed of all of them. They're supposed to be the top command, we expected better from the State Police," one juror told me after the trial. I couldn't argue, because so had I.

When I left DII headquarters on May 8, 2003, I had no idea that the upper command could so blatantly lie, ignore and cover up my allegations—allegations and concerns supported by the FBI and three decorated Illinois State Police officers. On June 6, 2003, Skip Nelson's memorandum to Col. Charles Brueggemann documented their deceit. The subject of the memo was "Mike Callahan" and read, in part:

During the meeting, Lieutenant Callahan provided information regarding Captain Fermon which he alleged impeded his efforts to conduct criminal investigations and questioned Captain Fermon's integrity. His concerns appeared to more specifically involve his perception of the allocation of operational resources and the prioritization of investigations and strategies. By his own admissions, he did not believe Captain Fermon had engaged in any criminal misconduct . . . Based upon our review, Lieutenant Callahan's allegations do not appear to warrant an internal investigation by our division at this time.

Despite the outright lies in his memo, Nelson was asked the following question, which only added to his deceitfulness:

Q: Now, this memorandum of June 6, 2003, it references the allegations that Lt. Callahan made against Captain Fermon. Nowhere on here does it mention the allegations he made against Colonel Carper . . . there was no other memo prepared about the allegations he made against Colonel Carper, was there?

Nelson: Not to my knowledge, no, sir.

The two top cops of the Illinois State Police had testified my allegations were "very serious" if true, they were lied to and told an investigation was conducted on Fermon. They were also lied to and told the charges against Fermon were "unfounded." They were lied to and not even told about the serious criminal allegations against Diane Carper.

The two top DII commanders testified they were mandated to investigate these types of allegations, yet no investigation was ever initiated. They ignored witnesses that were identified and they lied and misrepresented the concerns shared by FBI Special Agent Nate Williams. They were part of the leak back to Fermon and Carper and part of the deceitful cover-up.

In all, five of the top ISP commanders would testify under oath that the allegations against Fermon and Carper were very serious, if true, but how would one know if something is true or not unless you investigate it?

I didn't know it that May of 2003 but I was about to learn once again—I had wasted my time expecting any integrity or justice from the leadership of the Illinois State Police or the Division of Internal Cover-Up. I had lost my faith long ago in their leadership, and once again they gave me no reason to trust them.

They call them the Rat Squad. They exist in the sewers of the Illinois State Police, along with the upper command, filled with tangled webs of hypocrisy and deceit.

The Rules of Conduct of the Illinois State Police states, "Officers will testify truthfully when under oath."

A violation of this rule is Level 7 misconduct.

Level 7 misconduct is termination.

I often wonder to myself . . . just who is policing the police?

CHAPTER 18

ONE MAN SHACKLED, ONE MAN FREED

---◼︎---

Ruby Gordon-Phillips didn't tell me until I retired what really transpired after I went to DII. She kept the information from me for my own good, because Ruby knew the truth would only hurt and infuriate me.

Skip Nelson called Ruby and said I had "thrown some surprises" DII hadn't expected, because they only expected allegations against Fermon and not Carper, too. This obviously changed the perspective on how they were going to handle things. In fact, Nelson admitted Brueggemann was furious that I had dared to go to the FBI and then DII with allegations against two ISP command officers.

"Brueggemann wants Callahan hammered," Skip told Ruby, and Brueggemann wanted me removed from investigations as a punishment.

Skip alleged he interjected and reasoned with Brueggemann that removing only me would be grounds for a retaliation lawsuit. Nelson pointed out to Brueggemann that it was Fermon with all the baggage with his EEO complaint and other DII cases. Nelson said Brueggemann therefore made the decision to remove both of us and make it look like a workplace conflict. I had embarrassed some colonels, and since I failed to realize colonels were above the law, my head was placed on the chopping block.

Almost a month went by before I heard anything, and then Carper called me one Thursday afternoon, asking if I was available to come to her office the next day, Friday, June 13, 2003. Carper spoke with her usual businesslike demeanor, but anytime she summoned you to Springfield, it usually wasn't good.

"Am I in some sort of trouble?" I asked.

She nonchalantly assured me nothing was wrong. I told her I was scheduled off the next day since my wife was out of town, and I had no one to watch my son. I sensed she was a little flustered and Carper replied, "I'll get back with you." Within the hour, she called back and told me to be in Springfield the following Monday morning. Something was definitely up.

Captain Strohl called me later and said he was also summoned to Springfield. He didn't know why either and I spent the whole weekend speculating about Monday. I didn't think the department was brazen enough to retaliate against me for my complaints to DII; that's not something anyone should be punished for.

I knew Carper and Fermon had approached Strohl about having me fill the lieutenant's position in District 10, but that seemed unlikely since the current lieutenant wasn't retiring for almost six weeks and his replacement had already been announced. It didn't make sense to move me to patrol anyway, since I was in investigations for over 20 years. It would be like trying to teach an old dog new tricks. Instead of mentoring the people under me, I'd be the one needing mentoring. Another point to consider was that I was the only one left from the zone still involved with the federal investigation.

By Monday morning, I had convinced myself the meeting was about Fermon, and I speculated that he was being replaced by John Strohl. It made sense—and they wanted me there as support.

Strohl and Fermon were already on the second floor of the Armory Building when I arrived Monday morning. None of us had a clue as to why we were there, and a comment by Carper's secretary didn't ease the confusion.

"This isn't bad," she whispered in my ear.

Fermon was the first called to the third floor. Strohl and I were summoned about 15 minutes later. When we entered the room, Lt. Col. Diane Carper and Lt. Col. Rich Woods were sitting there on one side of the table. I sat across from them and John sat to my left. I was starting to smell a rat.

Carper was never noted for her personality or eloquence, and she didn't bother to exchange any formalities here, she just got right to the point. In a callous and emotionless voice, she coldly informed me I was being reassigned to District 10 patrol effective immediately.

I was floored and sat there dumbfounded. I realized how Edie Casella must have felt when Carper callously removed her for no reason. I felt my face flush, and it took me a while to regain my composure. My head was literally reeling, my heart was racing and I felt the sweat bead up on my forehead. I couldn't believe what I just heard. It felt like I was just stabbed in the heart.

As I regained a little composure I looked over at Lt. Col. Woods, glaring at him. *You betrayed me, you bastard.* He dropped his eyes to the table, refusing to make eye contact with me. The arrogant and vindictive smirk on Carper's face told me everything; she had obviously been told about the allegations I made against her to DII.

Everyone just sat there in silence. My senses finally returned.

"Why am I being transferred?" I asked.

"I've recently become aware of management issues and problems at Zone 5," Carper replied, adding that she perceived me as "part of the problem."

"What problems have I caused?" I asked angrily.

"You tell me," Carper arrogantly retorted.

"I don't know!" I insisted. "You tell me. I'm not aware of any problems I've caused. I've never received any reprimands, any negative counseling or any DII cases. You tell me . . . what have I done wrong?"

Carper sat there with an arrogant smirk. Words can't express how badly I wanted to wipe that gloating look off her face. Again, I demanded to know what I had done wrong and if there was any documentation, so I could defend myself. Carper just looked at me smugly, sitting there in silence.

"I've done nothing wrong!" I exclaimed. "I've only done my job!" Now the politically correct side of Carper emerged.

"This assignment is for your own good and it's for the good of the department," she patronizingly explained. "You know, I like to take people out of their comfort zone."

Of course, I was the only lieutenant during her tenure ever reassigned out of their comfort zone against their will. "This is a punishment! I'm being punished!" I snapped.

"This is not discipline," she sarcastically replied. "You're retaining your rank, the same pay and you still have a command."

What a hypocrite! If I was causing problems, why was I being put in another command. No, it was clear this transfer was a vindictive act and a strong message that I should've kept my mouth shut.

"Are you telling me you won't take the assignment?" Carper snapped. "Do you want the assignment or not?"

"I have no choice," I helplessly replied.

I looked across the table at Carper making direct eye contact and the anger welled up inside me. Here was this woman who had spent her entire career sitting behind a desk as a puppet and political hack, she wouldn't make a pimple on a real cop's ass. I had forgotten more about police work than she would ever know, and here she was flaunting her rank and power, not earned from experience but from her political astuteness. This was the insult to the injury—a "yes" person like Carper removing someone who had spent their entire career being a real cop, because of her ability to kiss ass and betray her oath, and because she was a person willing to leave innocent men in prison for the sake of the politicians who gave her that power. I despised her as she sat there coldly and arrogantly removing me as if my life, like Steidl's and Whitlock's, meant nothing to her, and under the bullshit guise I was "a problem."

The only problem I had caused was I had told the truth about her, and Carper or the ISP command didn't like the truth. I had dedicated my whole adult life to being a good conscientious cop. I thought about all the countless hours I had worked, all the cases I had worked, all the times I risked my life for the Illinois State Police . . . and this was their payback, this was their betrayal! It hit me right between the eyes: was it worth it, did any of it really matter, had it all been one big lie?

I spent over 23 years working in the trenches to earn the respect and rank I received in the Illinois State Police, and here was Carper destroying that career in a 10-minute meeting. I remember how another political hack, Director Larry Trent, arrogantly testified about how long it took the department to decide my fate that day; his callous reply, "It wasn't long. Ten minutes." Ten minutes of their time, that's what my entire career meant to them. I was guilty of simply telling the truth and trying to do the right thing, and the organization that professed "Integrity, Service & Pride" was removing me because of my integrity. Obviously, I was the one who was now too politically sensitive. Before, it was shame I felt for Carper and our leadership, now, it was the added disgust and anger. During that meeting, the little faith I had left in my department was now totally destroyed.

"What about the Rhoads case and the federal task force?" I asked Carper in a last ditch effort to get her to change her mind.

"We'll find someone. We'll address that issue later . . . at my level," she arrogantly replied. That was a good one, for three years, at her level, the bitch had not only ignored the misconduct in the Rhoads case, but she was willing to leave two innocent men in prison and helped to cover up the scandal.

"I'm sure you will," I thought, "and probably with somebody much more politically correct than I am."

That afternoon as I drove back home, I felt both betrayed and humiliated, and a rage started slowly building inside me—rage, shame and disgust for my department's leadership.

This was juicy news and word of what happened to me spread fast within the department. I didn't even have a chance to tell Lily before the calls started coming in, before I had even left the Springfield city limits. Friends from around the state wanted to confirm the rumor and offer their condolences. It wasn't about the transfer to patrol; they all knew I was being punished for something. After 23 years in the state police, 20 of those in investigations, they all knew it was a little late in the game to put me back in patrol.

The rumors were already out with the department's propaganda, and it became even more apparent when Director Larry Trent issued the standard teletype, subliminally acknowledging my punishment in all caps: "I AM PLEASED TO ANNOUNCE THE FOLLOWING PERSONNEL APPOINTMENTS WITHIN THE ILLINOIS STATE POLICE, DIVISION OF OPERATIONS, REGION III: EFFECTIVE JUNE 16, 2003." The announcement continued, advising that Captain Steven Fermon was transferred to a position in Springfield and I was being reassigned to patrol. The punishment was even more apparent when Trent announced we were both being temporarily replaced by two master sergeants. Trent ended the teletype with the usual bureaucratic bullshit: "PLEASE JOIN ME IN CONGRATULATING THESE INDIVIDUALS ON THEIR NEW ASSIGNMENTS."

I made the drive home in an emotional daze. I called Lily and remember trying to hold back the tears as I told her about the betrayal. My transfer was effective immediately, so my first stop when I got back home was at the zone. I started cleaning out my office and it was heart wrenching and humiliating—twenty years of my life sat in that office. Some of the guys came by to tell me how sorry they were about what had happened, and e-mails flooded in: "Hey Mike, hang in there, the guys in District 10 are lucky to get you," and "Keep your head up Mike, the cream always rises to the top." It was obvious that the humiliating punishment had spread throughout the department.

When I hugged Ruby goodbye that day, I couldn't hold back the tears any longer as I left my office for the last time.

Things didn't get easier.

"Twenty years in investigations! Who the hell did you piss off?" exclaimed the quartermaster when I went to get fitted for my uniforms.

I walked into restaurants wearing the uniform and people who knew me asked if I had screwed up and been put back into uniform. They knew you don't spend 20 years in investigations and then go back in uniform unless you had screwed up. They were right—I had screwed up by trying to do the right thing. It was the little things like this that started tearing away at my pride. The pride I had in my department was long gone, but now my personal pride was taking a severe beating, although I didn't recognize it at the time.

U.S. Assistant Attorneys Tim Bass and Rick Cox were beside themselves when I told them about my transfer from investigations. First, it was Greg Dixon transferred and now me.

"We feel like the Illinois State Police has kicked us in the teeth," said an angry Rick Cox. I understood how he felt, because I had just been stabbed in the back.

They asked if I had requested the transfer and I assured them it was against my will. Deep down, I hoped they could pull some weight and get me back on the investigation. They had said they felt both Dixon and I were "historically and operationally critical to the case." Also feeling betrayed, Tim Bass promised to ask the ISP command to reconsider their decision. I left their office with a small glimmer of hope.

Bass and Cox met with Carper a week later, but she wouldn't budge, and it was no surprise she offered them the standard bureaucratic bullshit. Assistant U.S. Attorney Tim Bass later explained, " . . . the purpose of the meeting was . . . to discuss Lt. Callahan's reassignment . . . to ask her on behalf of the State Police to reconsider the decision to reassign Lt. Callahan and allow him to remain in his investigative capacity . . . I was representing the United State's Attorney's Office, but was asking her that question in her capacity on behalf of the State Police." Bass continued and said Carper claimed, "She explained that the decision was, would not be reconsidered and that he was going to be reassigned . . . My recollection is that Lt. Col. Carper made some reference to this being a command decision and that it was also in the interests of Lieutenant Callahan's career."

Carper had lied once again—the transfer was definitely not in the interests of my career, and as each day went by, the anger continued to well up inside of me over her arrogant deceit. I had an overwhelming feeling of injustice thanks to the lack of integrity of hypocrites like Carper, and eventually the anger, mixed with the frustration of helplessness, slowly turned into a depression I thought I could handle.

My first days at District 10 patrol were somewhat humiliating. I didn't even have an office, e-mail or a phone. I sat at a desk in a squad room, and with the current lieutenant not leaving for another six weeks, it was obvious to everyone I wasn't even needed at the District.

But not everything that happened to me during this time was all bad news. In fact, it was somewhat ironic because the day I was removed from investigations, I received a call from an exuberant Bill Clutter. Clutter was excited over news that Federal Judge Michael McCuskey had just issued an order to the State of Illinois. The order was for the State to retry Randy Steidl or free him. Bill gave me the shortened version of Judge McCuskey's order: "acquittal for Randy Steidl was reasonably probable if the original jury had heard all of the evidence." How ironic, basically the same thing I had been telling the ISP upper command for nearly three years. Now a United States Federal Judge was saying the same thing. It wouldn't change my department's cover-ups, but it was certainly some vindication for me at a time when I really needed it.

During the conversation with Clutter, I couldn't hide my depression over what had happened to me. Bill sensed it, too, and when he asked, I told him that after 20 years in investigations, I had been reassigned to patrol. He asked if I was being punished as a result of trying to help them. Bill knew I had already gotten in trouble for the memorandum I sent to the Attorney General's Office in 2000, and I told him "yes, my transfer was meant as a punishment." Bill seemed genuinely upset, but I didn't want my problems to ruin this moment. I was happy for Randy Steidl and his legal team, they had fought a long and hard battle against a corrupt and stubborn state.

The next day, Federal Judge Michael McCuskey's order became public news and it reflected the ineffective defense counsel and attacked the credibility of the eyewitnesses used to convict Steidl and Whitlock, much the same as I had. The Champaign *News-Gazette* reported:

> A federal judge this week tossed out a 1987 murder conviction against an Edgar County man. U.S. District Judge Michael McCuskey on Tuesday vacated the conviction against Gordon "Randy" Steidl . . . McCuskey, in his 36-page ruling, granted a petition for habeas corpus. . . . McCuskey's order gives the state 120 days to release Steidl or retry him, but execution of the order is stayed pending appeal. . . . Efforts by Steidl's attorney to refute [Reinbolt's] statements had a "reasonable probability" of a different outcome in the trial, he said. . . . "A careful review of the record shows that a guilty verdict would have been unlikely based on Herrington's testimony," McCuskey's ruling said. . . . "acquittal was reasonably probable if the jury heard all of the evidence . . ."

That June of 2003, Lisa Madigan was the newly elected Illinois Attorney General and Judge McCuskey's order fell into her hands on what to do with Randy Steidl's case. During her political campaign, Madigan had referenced the State's misconduct and wrongful convictions of Rolando Cruz and others in the Jeanine Nicarico case. Madigan's campaign promise was cited by noted *Chicago Tribune* columnist Eric Zorn: "I can promise that as attorney general, I will never cover up the truth and stand in the way of justice." During her campaign, Madigan "repeatedly thundered at [her opponent] for not having done more to set right the scales of justice." In his article entitled, "Ruling to test Madigan's talk of truth, justice," Zorn continued:

> Now, U.S. District Judge Michael McCuskey has thrown a ruling at Madigan that will put her lofty campaign rhetoric to the test . . .

Zorn then pondered:

> Will she recognize overwhelming evidence of innocence when she sees it?
> Will she be encumbered by conscience as she reads the shocking record?
> Will she fulfill her promise never to act to cover up the truth?
> Or was that just cheap campaign talk?

Reading all of these news accounts was bittersweet. I was right, Judge McCuskey's ruling did nothing to change the ISP's decision to remove me, because reversing their decision would force them to admit they made a mistake, and they were already too knee deep in their deceit and cover-up in this scandal.

Shortly after moving to District 10, I received an unexpected call from Deputy Attorney General Ellen Mandeltort on June 25, 2003. She introduced herself as head of the Attorney General's Criminal Division and explained that because of Judge McCuskey's recent order, her office was reviewing the case. Mandeltort said that Herb Whitlock's attorney, Richard Kling, recommended she talk to me and Kling believed I was being punished because of the Rhoads case.

Mandeltort was a stranger to me, but at this point I didn't care much about any consequences and bluntly told her I was being punished. I explained how Carper stopped the Rhoads investigation because it was too politically sensitive. The gasp on the other end of the phone made it unmistakable that my words had obviously shocked her.

"*What?*" she exclaimed. "That's official misconduct or could even be construed as obstruction of justice!"

"Yeah, that's kind of what I thought, too, but I've been transferred to patrol as a punishment to shut me up," I replied sarcastically.

Mandeltort wanted to meet with me, but I told her I doubted my command would agree to it.

"Don't worry about that," she confidently replied. "I'll get permission for you to talk to me from Larry Trent."

Shortly thereafter, she called me back and advised that Trent agreed to the meeting and we set a date to meet at the Attorney General's Chicago offices.

Edie Casella later called and told me what a stir Mandeltort's request had caused on the second floor of the ISP Armory Building. Trent was unaware of the complaint I made to DII about Carper because Col. Brueggemann and Col. Nelson had hid those allegations from the director, and over the next few days, the upper command tried unsuccessfully to block the meeting. Obviously they were nervous because Edie was approached by Lt. Col. Mike Snyders who told her Brueggemann was worried I may talk about the too politically sensitive aspects of the Rhoads case. Snyders told Casella he felt I had misunderstood Carper's orders and he didn't put much credence on my allegations.

Edie told Snyders she also heard Carper say the Rhoads case was too politically sensitive, pulling out her Palm Pilot, she punched in the meeting date of April 4, 2001, again confirming Carper's shocking orders. Unfortunately, Col. Mike Snyders was just as deceitful and as much of the cover-up as the other ISP colonels. Two years later, during testimony, he denied the conversation he had with Edie, at least in part:

> Q: Did Edie Casella ever say she heard Diane Carper make those statements?
>
> Snyders: Not that I know of. . . . I don't remember. I remember [Casella] had concerns that Diane Carper—that she had heard through hearsay that Diane Carper had told Mike that the case was "too politically sensitive" to investigate. . . . I do remember telling [Casella] that I thought it had to be a misunderstanding. . . . I remember telling [Casella] that I think she's wrong, that I would be shocked if Diane Carper ever told anybody not to investigate any case.

Eventually Lt. Col. Rick Rokusek was assigned by Brueggemann to attend the meeting. I knew and trusted Rick Rokusek, and he assured me that while he had orders to immediately report back to Bruegemann following the meeting, he had no intention of burning me. The assurance wasn't necessary because I didn't have a problem with talking in front of Rick Rokusek or anyone else.

Ellen Mandeltort was a surprise. She didn't look anything like she sounded on the phone, nor did she look like the tough and seasoned prosecutor that was her reputation. Her language was filled with the profanities I had come to know from working with Chicago prosecutors, and I could tell she was an experienced prosecutor. Her toughness was apparent and she had no problem voicing her opinion without any concern if it was politically correct or not. I was a little taken aback when she walked into the meeting. She was a strikingly attractive woman with long dark hair and her fiery personality didn't fit her appearance.

Mandeltort said the Attorney General's Office was taking Judge McCuskey's order very seriously, and she was personally taking on the assignment. I spent the whole day going over the case and all my concerns of misconduct in the original case. When I finished, Mandeltort exclaimed, "You're more detailed about this case than I am about my own life!"

One thing was not discussed during the meeting and I asked Mandeltort why she never brought up the issue of Carper's criminal orders. Her tough demeanor suddenly turned sheepish, and she explained she made a promise to Lt. Col. Mike Snyders not to discuss that issue with me. She expressed concern that if she broke her promise, the ISP command wouldn't let her talk to me anymore.

"I will address it later, but my main focus now is the Steidl issue," she promised.

I left somewhat disappointed that the ISP had obviously gotten to Mandeltort, but the plus side was she was taking the case seriously, and I thought she would do the right thing despite any political pressures.

About a week later, Mandeltort called with more questions about the case and, with genuine sincerity, asked how I was doing.

"I'm just sitting here counting seatbelt tickets," I sarcastically replied.

"That's a shame, Mike," she sympathetically responded. "Make no doubt about it—you are being punished."

It was becoming apparent my fate was sealed. The Attorney General's Office admitted I was being punished, but obviously they were going to ignore the ISP's misconduct. The next time I talked to Mandeltort was two months later when Assistant U.S. Attorney Tim Bass asked me to contact her for help in the death investigation of Jim Stillwell—another individual with suspicious connections to some Paris businessmen.

Eventually, I inquired about the status of Steidl's case and she assured me, "We're doing DNA now Mike, and I'm turning over every stone" in what she described as a very thorough investigation. With disgust in her voice, she said she recently spent the day with former State's Attorney Mike McFatridge, and her blunt observation made me laugh.

"You were right. He is a piece of shit!" she exclaimed.

She ended our conversation agreeing with my assessment of the Rhoads case and admitted she could never prove Steidl guilty if the case went back to trial.

Mandeltort never called me again to discuss the Rhoads case or the ISP's conduct—obviously it was still too politically sensitive.

In late March 2004, Attorney General Lisa Madigan arranged a meeting with about 15 family members of Dyke and Karen to discuss her decision about Judge McCuskey's order. Andrea called to tell me about the meeting. She said she asked Mandeltort if I was going to be there since the family trusted and would listen to me. Mandeltort told Andrea she didn't know, but Mandeltort knew, because by this time I had filed a First Amendment civil rights lawsuit against the ISP, and it was the Attorney General's office defending them.

During the meeting, Andrea said Mandeltort admitted I had provided a significant amount of information they used in their investigation, and she had personally been digging through a lot of stuff in the case for over 12 months.

"If Steidl and Whitlock aren't guilty and released, then the case becomes an unsolved homicide. What are you going to do?" Andrea said she asked Mandeltort.

When Mandeltort said they were going to speak to the Illinois State Police, Andrea said family members became upset and said they didn't trust the State Police, especially since hearing about my lawsuit. Lisa Madigan intervened and told the family her office would reach out to the FBI instead.

One of the most interesting things Andrea told me was that Madigan and Mandeltort had three bodyguards there because of recent threats received from former Edgar County State's Attorney Mike McFatridge. This prompted Andrea to bring up her dislike for McFatridge and how upset the family was that he had put Dyke on trial as a dope dealer. Andrea said Lisa Madigan agreed and admitted what McFatridge did was not right and they were somewhat suspicious of him. According to Andrea, Mandeltort interceded and said she questioned McFatridge's desperation regarding this case, and it was obvious he didn't do his job as State's Attorney. She added it was obvious that McFatridge, Eckerty and Parrish had pushed Reinbolt into her confession.

Jim Dey's article in the *News-Gazette* confirmed the conflict between McFatridge and the Attorney General's Office:

> . . . Mike McFatridge, who prosecuted the original case, has expressed outrage. In a letter to media outlets, he charged that Madigan "cares more for Chicago media headlines and criminals than for the people she was sworn to protect" and characterized her decision as a "betrayal of the public trust." [McFatridge asked] "Is Ms. Madigan afraid of alienating her bleeding-heart friends by having the murder conviction restored on an appeal?"

Despite McFatridge's protests, the day after the meeting with Dyke and Karen's family, a press release announced:

> After an extensive and exhaustive investigation into the convic-
> tion of Gordon 'Randy' Steidl, Attorney General Lisa Madigan an-
> nounced that her office will no longer pursue an appeal of federal
> Judge Michael McCuskey's June 2003 decision . . . . that after care-
> ful review of evidence in the [Rhoads] case, information favoring
> the defense was never disclosed and Steidl was entitled to a new
> trial . . . . Madigan said, "This has been a very difficult decision, but
> it is the right decision based upon the evidence."

The decision to retry Steidl or free him now fell to the Illinois Appellate Prosecutor's Office. An editorial in the *News-Gazette* read, "Madigan's decision leaves
prosecutors with only two choices, dismiss the case and release Steidl from prison
or retry him with a considerably weaker legal case than they presented at his first
trial." The editorial pointed out, "The biggest hurdle facing prosecutors is the recantations of the testimony by Reinbolt and Herrington. They have both recanted
their testimony and then recanted their recantations on multiple occasions." Ed
Parkinson, of the Illinois Appellate Prosecutors office, agreed that Reinbolt's back-
and-forth statements present a big problem in a re-trial, stating, "It would be folly
for me to say that's not a concern, but the issue is how does her testimony hold up
in a re-trial."

On May 28, 2004, almost one year after Judge McCuskey's decision and after
17 years behind bars, Randy Steidl walked out of the Danville Correctional Center.
Randy Steidl was 52 years old and had adamantly maintained his innocence for
nearly two decades of incarceration. He had spent 12 of those 17 miserable years
on Death Row, but now he was a free man once again. The *Springfield Journal-
Register*'s Sarah Antonacci wrote, Steidl "was led through several doorways and
out into the prison lobby, where his friends and family were waiting with open
arms and tear streaked faces. He was given $23.93 to start his new life." After Steidl
met with reporters, the article continued, describing his life in prison:

> "Anybody who says prison isn't a frightening experience would ei-
> ther be lying or a fool," Steidl said . . . "It was quite an experience
> those first few weeks knowing when they shut that door that you're
> in a cage 23 hours a day, and when you wake up, you know the state
> wants to kill you and there's nothing you can do about it." The cage
> was an 8-by-4-foot cell that housed him and another prisoner. For
> one hour daily, they were allowed out to shower and to go to the
> yard. He'd watch television 14 or 15 hours a day or read a book.

There was no privacy. He remembers, too well, asking God not to let him wake up the next morning. "Then you get up and there's those bars again," he said.

Randy Steidl also described the perils of prison life:

> After six years at Pontiac, Steidl was moved to Menard in southern Illinois along the Mississippi River. The Flood of 1993 had swallowed the death row cell house, making the roach and rodent problem worse than ever. "There was still mud caked on my bunk. At night, here come the roaches. [I'd] Wake up at night and a roach was running across my face or the back of my neck. I slept with toilet paper shoved in my ears so I wouldn't have any [roaches] go in. After the roaches subsided somewhat, a wave of mice came in."

Once Steidl was even attacked by "gang-bangers on death row" and was "stabbed seven times. The wounds took 36 stitches to close." The article continued:

> "You just feel like someone just closed the door on your life," Steidl said. "The best way I can explain it: You're sitting there on hot coals but you can't yell out . . . " . . . It took nearly a year after McCuskey's June 2003 ruling for the doors to the prison to actually open. In that time, Steidl waited, anxiously with little sleep for months . . . "Every day feels like a week and every week feels like a month . . . After all these years, you'd think I'd be used to doing the time."

On the day of his release, "While he waited for escorts to take him out of the jail that sunny May day, the guard noted that he was in the seventh grade when Steidl went to prison." Steidl met with his attorneys and then went "into the lobby where they met his mother, brother and wife, among others." The group " . . . said a family prayer, walked out to the crowd of media, gave a few statements and left to have that long-anticipated steak and salad dinner." The news account ended: "He was no longer [inmate number] 'N72890.' Now, he was Randy Steidl."

My life was certainly a bed of roses compared to the horrible fate Randy Steidl had endured for 17 years. Still my life had become like a giant roller coaster, first going into a deep depression and then making the overwhelming decision to fight back against my department. After I met Ellen Mandeltort, I felt betrayed once again by the State of Illinois. It seemed everyone in State government was ignoring the corruption I had brought forth, and they could care less I was punished for it. As quick as I gained hope, it was just as quickly taken away. Eventually, the anger mixed with the frustration and helplessness caused me to go into a deep depression—a depression that I didn't recognize and refused to acknowledge. My life had become a haze. I was just going through the motions from day to day. My wife could explain it best because I wasn't there for her or our son.

Lily Callahan: I remember listening to Mike late at night. He thought I was long asleep—but lying next to me, he was crying with his back to me, trying to hide his tears and occasional sobs. I knew this was slowly killing him. I watched a proud man slowly dying. I knew the level of dedication and what this job meant to him. After 15 years of marriage, I knew Mike better than he knew himself. I understood the betrayal he felt—because I felt it myself. After all, I was a cop's wife. I had endured the late night phone calls . . . his long hours away from home . . . waiting up for Mike to get home . . . worried about his safety . . . this job had taken up a lot of our family time. Mike always gave 100% on his job and I was always in awe of his dedication. And that's why it hurt so much.

Mike had never been depressed in his life. He was always even-tempered, stable, patient, and loving. Once the transfer hit, that's when I noticed a major change in his personality. He became angry. He was in disbelief. He would go from anger to sadness changing moods at a moment's notice. Mike told me that he felt badly for the Rhoads family—he felt guilty. He made a promise to them that he would try and find out the truth and now he couldn't. They had moved him off the case. Mike wouldn't sleep. When he did, I'd often have to wake him up out of nightmares. He started to physically look horrible. He was bloated and glassy eyed. He just didn't look like Mike anymore.

I felt like my son and I were walking on egg shells all the time. I had no idea when the next explosive episode would occur—for no reason at all. Mike was always irritable. We were afraid to ask him a simple question for fear that he would lash out at us. One day, it came to a head. There was an argument between Mike and our 11-year-old son Tanner over something little. Mike lashed out at Tanner with a terrible anger and Tanner started crying and sobbed, "I wish I had my old dad back." I remember the hurt look on Mike's face, and I could tell that Tanner's comment hit home. I know Mike. I know how much he loves his son. When Tanner said that, I knew Tanner's words had ripped his heart apart. I watched the tears welling up in Mike's eyes. Mike didn't say a word . . . the old Mike would have called his son over and hugged him and talked with him. But Mike couldn't talk or feel in those days. He was too numb. But I knew those words had hurt him deeply.

I watched Mike turn and slowly walk upstairs to our bedroom. I let some time pass before I walked upstairs. I had been a nurse. I recognized the signs of severe depression. I was sure Mike would bite my head off, but I knew I had to do something. I knew if I didn't do something that I would lose the man I had fallen in love with. So, there was Mike—in our bedroom, curled up in a ball under the covers. I remember looking at the clock. It was a little after 3 o'clock in the afternoon. It was a bright, sunny summer day. Fearful that he might explode, I looked at him and said, "Mike, you need help." I was shocked yet filled with hope when he looked up, with tears rolling down his cheeks, he replied, "I know. I need help."

We made an appointment with our family doctor for the following Monday. Mike's blood pressure had shot up. The doctor said, "You need sleep. You look horrible." Mike had a break down right in front of the doctor. She ended up prescribing anti-depressants and sleeping pills, and she referred him to a psychologist. For a long time, my son and I didn't have Mike mentally with us anymore. I know it took a lot for him to even go to the doctor and admit he had problems. That's men in general—too proud and strong to admit a weakness.

But I knew one thing—if we didn't fight, I would never get my husband back. At least not the man I had fallen in love with and married.

During testimony, Lily was cross-examined by Carper's attorney, Michael Lied. A man who billed the taxpayers over $260,000 for his work in the two-week civil trial. During the trial, he asked my wife:

Q: What do you know of [Mike's] actual job duties once he was moved to patrol?

Lily: My husband would put on that uniform and he would walk out the door like a beaten man. He would walk like he was in shackles. He was not the same . . .

Q: Does it seem to you as though maybe your husband is obsessed a little bit about this whole situation?

Lily: I'm not going to say obsessed. I think he has been traumatized.

I had always made it clear—it was not an issue of being transferred to patrol or wearing a uniform, those were not my shackles. My shackles were the loss of faith in a department I loved and had dedicated my life to. The ideals and principles I had spent my life believing in were taken away by a department that betrayed me. Yet, Illinois State Police Director Larry Trent chose to misinterpret my wife's testimony and use it to belittle me. The state police's top cop e-mailed a memo to all ISP command which read, "Leadership," and in part, contained the following:

> The reassigned individual claimed he suffered emotional trauma at having to wear the State Police uniform that each of us wears so proudly. In fact, courtroom testimony referred to him as being "shackled" when he had to put the uniform on and required him to take anti-depressants. To hear someone describe how demeaning it was to put on the uniform each day that we hold so dear deeply disturbs me. I am proud to be an Illinois State Police Officer and proud to wear the uniform. I do not feel "shackled" and do not need medication to put it on.

I was incensed at Trent's petty and childish attempt to humiliate me, his blatant lies and vicious attack along with his obvious misrepresentation of the facts, but it was no surprise coming from the likes of him. Trent was no different than all the other politically compromised command in the ISP these days. Trent talked about the Illinois State Police uniform he was so proud to wear, but it was Trent and all the other political hacks who had disgraced and shamed the uniform of the Illinois State Police.

On March 8, 2005, Eric Zorn of the *Chicago Tribune* wrote, "Callahan . . . has already won partial vindication: A federal judge ruled in 2003 that Steidl's 'acquittal was reasonably probable if the jury had heard all of the evidence,' and Steidl was released from prison last May after Attorney General Lisa Madigan refused to attempt to retry him."

Zorn was right about the vindication, but Larry Trent just didn't understand, I wasn't the one who was shackled. The exact same evidence withheld in the Rhoads case and the exact same unbelievable eyewitnesses that convicted Randy

Steidl had also convicted Herbert Whitlock. Randy Steidl was a free man now, but Herb Whitlock remained in prison.

One man was freed, one man was still shackled.

CHAPTER 19

THE COVER-UP CONTINUES

---■---

A letter written to a local newspaper regarding my allegations against the state exclaimed, "What constitutes a cover-up? The dictionary defines it as 'something used for hiding one's real activities.' As it relates to the grisly murders of the young newlyweds [Dyke and Karen Rhoads] in July 1986, in Paris, Illinois, evidence seems to indicate the presence of a terrible cover-up. . . . I personally consider this a damnable outrage on behalf of the legal system, especially on a state level . . . "

One of the meaningless bureaucratic mission statements in the ISP is succession planning. Webster's Dictionary defines "succession" as, "a succeeding or coming after another in sequence or to an office." The Illinois State Police's definition of succession planning is "a proactive approach to ensure the right person, in the right job, at the right time, doing the right thing for the right reasons."

Of course, the State Police's version of doing the right thing for the right reasons in the Rhoads case was to cover up the scandal and preserve their image at all cost in the eyes of the public. To ensure that, you needed the "right person, in the right job, at the right time," and I obviously wasn't the right person. Image is everything to the Illinois State Police and a letter from Chuck Brueggemann illustrated this:

Dear Lieutenant Callahan,
Thank you for the recent assistance you provided in reviewing the facts surrounding the Rhoad'es [sic] homicide investi-

gation. I am certain this was a difficult task due to the horrific nature of the crime itself and the complex issues related to this case. Your investigative experience was crucial to ensuring the integrity of the case . . . *and safeguarding the reputation of the Illinois State Police.*

Yet, less than three months later, Brueggemann was instrumental in forever removing me from investigating the Rhoads case. Both Brueggemann and Carper later testified that I "wasn't focused enough." Carper, who had never conducted a criminal investigation in her life, testified, "I believe the case lacked focus. Where are we going? What's the case strategy?" So I was replaced with a man Carper said she believed had a more "global perspective of the department" and "a more global perspective in investigations."

Captain Ken Kaupas replaced me on the federal task force on July 2, 2003. And Kaupas told the group that Deputy Director Chuck Brueggemann declared this "the number one priority case in the Illinois State Police." Brueggemann, himself, had already indicated he wanted this to become an OCDETF case.

Captain Kaupas had some serious issues though, because he was suspended for inappropriately taking monies in another federal OCDETF case he was overseeing. He was also found guilty of lying in the subsequent DII investigation, but like Brueggemann hypocritically testified, "This is an issue of right people, right time, right place . . ."

The most serious obstacle for Kaupas was to overcome his "Giglio issue" of untruthfulness in his prior DII investigation. In *Giglio v. United States*, the Supreme Court held that federal prosecutors were mandated to disclose issues of credibility or unreliability whenever they used a witness who had less than a desirable history of truthfulness. Obviously, a police officer caught being untruthful in his official capacity has issues of credibility. During his testimony, Kaupas discussed his DII case. "It was just a rules of conduct violation," Kaupas sugarcoated. "I was talking with a subordinate, and I should not have done that. She had a business. We engaged in a series of conversations about going into business together. But after that had been said and done, there was a complaint filed against me." Kaupas explained, "Subsequently, I was disciplined for that—for having those conversations." When asked if there was anything else involved in his DII case, Kaupas replied, "That of a by product of the investigation, I was accused of being unfaithful—untruthful . . ."

Q: And what type of discipline did you have?

Kaupas: I received 10 days off, and I lost my command at the time, which I was the Zone 2 Commander of Investigations out of the Rockford office.

Q: So, part of your suspension was [for] being untruthful?

Kaupas: Yes.

Kaupas also discussed the problems his untruthfulness and lack of credibility created in working this number one priority case: "Well, in a federal criminal prosecutorial situation, as I understood it, there may be an issue relating to this allegation of being untruthful, as it might relate to the effectiveness of what I may or may not be able to do in that investigation." Faced with these problems, the state police reassigned Sgt. Greg Dixon to assist Kaupas in the investigation. Eventually Jeff Marlow was also assigned to the case and Brueggemann's "full court press" on the "number one priority case" in the state had only a tainted Captain and two officers assigned to it.

Kaupas also lived in northern Illinois, about a four-hour one-way commute to Champaign. For nearly two years, Kaupas drove to Champaign on a Tuesday, arriving around noon, and would leave by mid-afternoon Thursday. How dedicated and diligent . . . he was spending almost two whole days a week on "the number one priority case in the State."

Before I filed my lawsuit, Kaupas was my good buddy, reaching out in an e-mail asking for my help: "Mike do you have time to sit down with me to discuss this monster?" Kaupas encountered the same frustration I had. At first, he was promised he could hand pick seven officers of his choice. Carper quickly took back that promise and told him he could have four inexperienced agents from the next new agents' class. In the end, Kaupas was assigned only Dixon and Marlow.

In the early months of his new assignment, Kaupas spent more than a few nights drinking beer and eating pizza at my house while trying to pick my brain. As the beer took its affect, Kaupas confided he felt Fermon and Carper had impeded the investigation, and Carper had admitted to him she had given the orders the Rhoads case was too politically sensitive. Kaupas believed Carper wasn't totally to blame because she was just following orders, and he reasoned that things had come from above her and the case was too politically sensitive "because Morgan was a main contributor to *you-know-who*."

"You know Mike, when you get as high up as her level, you *have* to lose some of your integrity," he rationalized.

Maybe Carper had lost some of her integrity, but I also knew Kenny Kaupas' reputation, and it was no secret he had almost lost his job. The DII case had put a big "brick" on his career, and more than anything else, Kaupas wanted that "brick" taken off his back and to get a command back. Kenny was obsessed with getting a command back, and he admitted Carper and Brueggemann promised him a new command if he would take this assignment. This was confirmed when a captain from up north called to see how I was doing. He and I went way back—first troopers together, then working undercover in the suburbs of Chicago. He had recently went out with Kaupas and over beers Kenny gave him the impression that rather than solving the Rhoads case, Brueggemann and Carper wanted Kaupas to refute and discredit everything I had said. If Kaupas accomplished this, he would get a command again.

Kenny always had a reputation for playing both sides of the fence, and I knew he would stab me in the back if that's what it took to get rid of the brick on him. For now, Kaupas needed my help, but I followed the old adage—keep your friends close but your enemies even closer, and Kenny Kaupas sure drank a lot of my beer.

Kaupas said he fought hard to get me reassigned back to the investigation and told the upper command, "Mike had the case going strong" and "the federal agencies were all on board," but Carper wouldn't bend.

"Make no doubt about it," Kaupas told me, "you're being punished. You embarrassed some colonels and bruised some big egos." And Kaupas added, "Carper is just covering up her mistakes like she always has."

During testimony, Kaupas admitted, "I may have made that statement over pizza and beer. . . . the reason for his removal could be that he upset some people. And yeah. You know, I probably may have said, 'You're being punished.' But that's Ken Kaupas talking. . . . That's speculation."

Kaupas was asked what he based that speculation on and he candidly replied, "twenty-two years in the Illinois State Police."

Eventually, the federal task force dissolved before it even got off the ground. A master sergeant friend of mine overheard Kaupas tell Carper, "the feds either dropped the case or are doing something on their own and don't want our help." I came to believe that was what my command and Kaupas wanted all along, to distance themselves from any federal scrutiny.

During the initial months of the federal task force, Greg and I developed a couple of informants. Carper even admitted in her testimony that, "Lieutenant Callahan had developed an informant . . . And I don't recall if it was Captain Kaupas or the U.S. Attorney's folks indicated the concern that we don't want to lose this informant because now we've changed point people on the case. . . . And it was determined that Lt. Callahan could continue to be a consultant . . . " Yet, once I filed my lawsuit, Kaupas went out of his way to distance not only me, but the informants we had recruited.

During ATF's murder investigation of the two Diablo bikers in 2000, they interviewed a man named Comstock who told them he had once lived with Jerry Board. Comstock alleged that Jerry Board admitted that the night of the Rhoads murders, "his job was to burn the Rhoads house down, but it just wouldn't burn the way it was supposed to." We didn't know if this was fact or fiction. So I devised a plan to get the information "straight from the horse's mouth." The informant we recruited painstakingly took the time to become good friends with Comstock. Good enough friends that he arranged to purchase an ounce of meth from him, and Comstock bragged his meth supplier was Jerry Board. Comstock had never been to prison, and a dope deal like this could land him in federal prison for a long time. The plan was to do the meth deal, arrest Comstock and give him the option of going to prison or cooperating. If he agreed to cooperate, the final link in our plan was to have Comstock wear a wire on Jerry Board and get a conversation regarding his alleged involvement in the Rhoads murders. It wouldn't be Comstock's allegations now, but from Board himself, if it were true. A long and drawn out plan, but it had worked for me in the past, and it would be an unwitting confession to participation in a murder recorded on tape. And after all, Jerry Board's name had certainly come up as a potential suspect several times throughout the years.

If all this went as planned and we could tie Jerry Board up, maybe he would cooperate and we could well be on our way to solving the murders of Dyke and Karen. Before we could act, Fermon transferred Greg from the task force and then I was removed.

Now with Greg back on the investigation, the plan went back into action, but one day Greg called upset that Kaupas had nixed the drug deal between our informant and Comstock. We had worked long and hard to finally buy some dope and possibly make some inroads into the investigation, but Kaupas flat out refused to allow the drug transaction. I was furious and called Kaupas on his negligence, but his pathetic reason was, "The price of the dope was too high." *Too High*! This investigator who had such a more global perspective in investigations than I did didn't see the big picture here! It was the murder case we wanted to solve—to hell if we paid too much money for some dope, it would be money well spent because it was a chance to possibly solve a homicide. As time went on, I began to think Kaupas did see the big picture and had become part of the cover-up himself.

With the feds out of the way, Kaupas turned all of his attention to the Rhoads case. The decision by both the Illinois Attorney General's Office and the Appellate Prosecutor's Office not to retry Randy Steidl forced the state to comply with the federal court order and release Steidl from prison. The State of Illinois, however, doesn't like to admit mistakes and Randy Steidl walked out of prison with a big target still on his back.

Special prosecutor David Rands was assigned to continue examining the case. The *Springfield Journal-Register* quoted Rands as saying, "Our action is in no way a declaration of Steidl's innocence . . . We are continuing to investigate this case and the action taken today does not preclude charges against Steidl in the future. There is no statute of limitations on murder, and Randy Steidl remains a suspect in this case."

David Rands was another prosecutor with a penchant for putting innocent people in prison. Rands was the same prosecutor who convicted Julie Rea-Harper, another tragic case of wrongful conviction in the State of Illinois.

On the night of October 13, 1997, Julie Rea-Harper was home with her 10-year-old-son, Joel. At around 4 a.m., Julie said she was awakened by her son's screams. As she ran to his room, she was attacked by an intruder. Julie was luckier than her son; she only suffered a black eye, scratches and a cut to her arm which required several stitches, but to every mother's nightmare, her son Joel was dead from 13 stab wounds, two directly to the heart. The Illinois State Police was brought in to investigate, and despite other suspects who—as in the Rhoads case—were ignored by the investigators, Julie Rea-Harper was arrested and convicted of killing her child. Julie Rea-Harper adamantly maintained her innocence, and Bill Clutter and the Innocence Project came in and shed light on the other suspects investigators had so callously ignored. In 2004, an Illinois Appellate Court ordered Julie Rea-Harper released from prison. Despite this, Appellate Prosecutors arrested and charged Julie Rea-Harper a second time for her son's murder. The Appellate Prosecutors were familiar names to me—David Rands and Ed Parkinson.

Julie Rae-Harper was tried a second time for the murder of her 10-year-old son. This time, the jury found her not guilty, and she was freed once again. The jury, polled days after the trial, told the media they believed the prosecution and state police investigators "failed miserably" in the murder investigation. Another example of prosecutors and investigators who will do anything to get their pound of flesh—whether someone is guilty or innocent.

In 2004, David Rands and Ken Kaupas joined forces to reinvestigate the Rhoads homicide, with the specific goal of putting Randy Steidl back in prison and keeping Herb Whitlock behind bars.

The first meeting with the Appellate Prosecutor's Office and the Illinois State Police was attended by David Rands, Ed Parkinson, a third prosecutor, Captain Ken Kaupas, Sgt. Greg Dixon and Jeff Marlow. Marlow and Dixon came to the District later and told me about the meeting.

Rands started off by asking the group if anyone in the room thought the case could be retried. Every man in that room answered "no" and Rands concurred stating the lack of evidence and that the two eyewitnesses used in the state's case belonged in an insane asylum. At one point Rands interjected that it seemed "Callahan" was "right on the mark with his memo," and then he asked why all my documentation just seemed to stop. This is when my good drinking buddy, Kaupas started showing which side of the fence he was on now, and attempting to discredit me, he said he had also questioned my lack of reporting. Kaupas knew all too well why I hadn't written reports, and Greg Dixon came to my defense and explained to the group how Carper had told us the Rhoads case was too politically sensitive to reinvestigate. Greg said that after the shock on the prosecutors' faces wore off, one of them looked over at Rands and said, "You're the quarterback. What do we do now?" Greg said Rands responded, "I think we need to punt."

In a second meeting on May 11, 2004, they met with my old buddies Charlie McGrew and Jack Eckerty. Greg and Jeff said Eckerty was extremely nervous and seemed almost guilt-ridden throughout the meeting. Eckerty admitted he was never comfortable with arresting Steidl and Whitlock for the murders and he didn't think the investigation had disclosed enough to prosecute either man. He admitted Parrish was "heavy handed" at times throughout the investigation, and when it came to Reinbolt, he admitted she wasn't reliable because she changed her story "every time she talked to us."

Eckerty told the group he believed there were more people involved in the murders and admitted Bob Morgan was a suspect. Eckerty defended his actions claiming he had to follow orders, and at the point when it seemed Eckerty might break down, Greg said Charlie McGrew broke in and said, "Jack, shut up! You've said enough!" And Jack did.

Kaupas and Rands' pathetic investigative tactics soon began and it became obvious what their real goal was—and it wasn't anything to do with truth or justice. Hal Dardick of the *Chicago Tribune* illustrated some of the sleazy tactics utilized by Rands and Kaupas in an article titled, "COPS SEEK JAIL INFORMANTS IN PROBE OF '86 MURDERS":

> Illinois State Police agents are questioning dozens of former cellmates of a freed Death Row prisoner in their probe of a Downstate double murder, prosecutors have confirmed. The inmates are being asked if Gordon "Randy" Steidl or one time co-defendant Herb Whitlock ever admitted to any involvement in the 1986 Paris, Il., murders of newlyweds Karen and Dyke Rhoads. Karen Daniel, a

lawyer at Northwestern University's Center on Wrongful Convictions and one of Steidl's attorneys, called the effort to find a prison informant a "very desperate investigative tactic."

Dardick's article continued,

> Jailhouse informants, or snitches, typically trade information for leniency in their own cases. Because of that powerful incentive, they are widely viewed in the criminal justice system as among the least credible of witnesses. Richard Kling, one of Whitlock's lawyers, said he was "angry" and "saddened" that police and prosecutors were seeking out informants.

Rands defended their actions stating, "I'm well aware of the shortcomings of jailhouse snitch testimony," he said. "We are leaving no stone unturned."

How hypocritical. If they were leaving no stone unturned, why was their only focus on investigating Steidl and Whitlock.

Dardick's article continued and showed the state's desperation and more devious tactics when some of the interviews became public. A letter written to Randy Steidl from a former cellmate explained the desperation: "The inmate wrote that agents told an African-American inmate that if Steidl had not been in prison, he would have been in the Ku Klux Klan." Dardick's article referenced the obvious attempt by one of the investigators to infuriate a black inmate into "giving up Steidl" by implying he was a racist. The article continued: "Special Prosecutor Ed Parkinson . . . said last week that he was concerned about the KKK allegation. 'It's a tactic that I don't approve of, if it occurred,' he said."

Dardick's article ended with a statement from Randy Steidl: "It just seems like it's a pretty sleazy way to conduct an investigation."

The state's efforts to find a snitch were fruitless and after more than 200 inmates from over 21 different prisons were tracked down and interviewed, not one inmate said either Steidl or Whitlock ever admitted to the murders. Steidl was right, it was pretty sleazy, but Rands and Kaupas were just getting warmed up, and their tactics became even more unethical.

Even though I was removed from investigations, Carper had said I could remain in a consulting role, and Dixon and Marlow spent a lot of time consulting with me. Some of the time we spent together was to complain about the frustration they felt at the investigative tactics being utilized by Rands and Kaupas. Neither one believed they were being allowed to investigate the case objectively.

The cover-up became even more apparent from several interviews conducted throughout 2004 by Dixon and Marlow, especially when their reports divulged more proof of misconduct in the original Rhoads investigation. Yet, Rands and Kaupas did their best to cover up this information.

Since I could still be in a consulting role, Dixon and Marlow gave me their 2004 interview reports to review. Many of these interviews provided even more information that discredited Reinbolt, Herrington and their bizarre stories. For instance, through Paula Brlach, the two investigators were able to establish Reinbolt was actually at work the night of the murders when she alleged she was bar-hopping with Steidl and Whitlock.

Even more disturbing, many of the interviews disclosed how the original investigators ignored or purposefully covered up key information given to them. Some of this information shed light on some of the other suspects identified in the Rhoads homicide. These were the reports where Mike Dunlap said he told Parrish and McFatridge that it was Bob Morgan he saw just days after the Rhoads murder with Sons of Silence biker Herschel Wright and another man he believed to be Dale Peterson, doing cocaine. Yet Parrish had specifically documented in 1986 that Dunlap couldn't identify the two men with Herschel Wright. The question remained why Parrish purposefully excluded Morgan's name from his report. Then there was another interview with the frightened "neighbor woman" who identified Jerry Board leaning up against the lamp post across the street from the Rhoads house the night of the murders, yet the original investigators failed to document that information too.

As in the original Rhoads investigation, interviews in 2004 with certain people, like Stan Acklen and Carol Robinson, were also never documented, most likely because their information led to more information concerning misconduct in the original investigation. For instance, Acklen's information that Reinbolt claimed to be at the murder scene, yet seven months later she didn't even know who Whitlock was. Acklen also told Dixon and Marlow the state police had ignored his concerns back in 1987 when he came forward with this information.

There were several other reports which not only shed doubt on the two eyewitnesses, but also the state's conduct in the original investigation. But what was really disturbing to me was how Kaupas and Rands joined in the deception, and ordered Dixon and Marlow to deceptively write the 2004 interview reports to the closed Rhoads case file. They purposely never reopened the case and assigned it to a current agent and, by having the agents write the reports to the closed file, the information learned in 2004 could be hidden away.

"They told us to write the reports to the closed case file so they wouldn't have to disclose anything new in discovery to Steidl or Whitlock's attorneys," Marlow confided in me. Since much of the information was favorable to the defense, by not disclosing it, Rands and Kaupas had become part of the cover up when they purposefully hid that information away in the closed case file. Like McFatridge had told Eckerty in the original investigation, Rands and Kaupas also "wanted nothing negative that might show those guys were innocent."

I had never seen anything so deceitful like this in my entire career, but the proof sat right in front of me, reports written in 2004 with the name of long-retired Jack Eckerty still documented as the case agent. To me this was a serious infraction involving a Supreme Court ruling under *Brady* where, "The government is constitutionally required to disclose any evidence favorable to the defendant that is material to either guilt or punishment, including evidence that may impact the credibility of a witness."

The deceit and cover-up escalated when on May 29, 2005, Randy Steidl filed a federal lawsuit alleging police and prosecutors sought to frame him in a conspiracy by members of the Paris Police Department, Edgar County State's Attorney's office and Illinois State Police. The lawsuit specifically named James Parrish, Gene Ray, Mike McFatridge, Jack Ekerty, Chuck Brueggemann, Andre Parker, Diane Carper, Steve Fermon and Kenny Kaupas. The lawsuit could cost the state millions of dollars, and with so many ISP commanders named, it left little doubt that the state police would never conduct any type of truthful, unbiased or objective investigation.

At one point, it got so bad that Dixon and Marlow needed permission from Rands or the command before they could interview anyone. They had to submit in writing who they wanted to interview, the reason why they wanted to interview the person and the questions they were going to ask, and only after it was approved could they interview the person. After the interviews, they were told to turn over their notes, and their official reports were edited or watered down.

Marlow was even instructed to listen in on phone calls and record attorney-client privileged conversations between Whitlock and Steidl and their defense attorneys. In all my years in law enforcement, I never saw nor heard of a criminal investigation being conducted so unethically! Even Ellen Mandeltort later admitted to Andrea Trapp that the state police were not doing "anything by the book" in this investigation.

They were literally tying the hands of the investigators and Marlow told me how they felt the wrath of Rands and the command when they conducted an unauthorized interview of a man named Phil Sinclair, who was a close friend of Reinbolt.

During my review of the Rhoads case in 2000, I had speculated Sinclair convinced Reinbolt to become an eyewitness in order to claim the reward money offered by Bob Morgan. My suspicions were based on the contents of several letters from Sinclair to Reinbolt while she was incarcerated. Sinclair revealed shocking new information to Dixon and Marlow confirming my suspicions even more, and to validate his information, they decided to polygraph him.

The polygraph examination report read that it "was administered to investigate whether or not the subject listed above [Phillip Sinclair] has been truthful in recounting conversations he purportedly engaged in with Debbie Reinbolt concerning the murders of Dyke and Karen Rhoads." The report continued that "There was [sic] no indication of deception on the polygraph records when the subject answered the following questions:

> "Did Debbie tell you she lied about the murders of Dyke and Karen Rhoads to collect the reward money?"
>
> Answer: Yes.
>
> "Did Debbie tell you she was given information by the police about the murders and she gave it back to them?"
>
> Answer: Yes.
>
> "Did you tell any lies to the police about what Debbie told you?"
>
> Answer: No.
>
> "Did Debbie tell you she had a sexual relationship with Jim Parrish?"
>
> Answer: Yes.

The report ended with the polygraph examiner stating, "It is the opinion of the examiner, based on the polygraph records that the subject is telling the truth to the above listed questions."

This was incredible! Here was an allegation that Detective Jim Parrish—while investigating a horrible murder—was having sex with a woman who claimed to be an accomplice in the brutal crime! If this was true, this case was even more perverted than I thought! This news prompted me to recall one of Sinclair's letters to Reinbolt in prison: "To make your time easier. I will get some pictures to you. Perhaps one of J.P. in a pretty uniform. Got you excited—ha."

Sinclair also told Dixon and Marlow something else significant. Sinclair said one of his relatives was a fireman at the Rhoads house the morning of the murders. Sinclair alleged that his relative told him it was his axe that actually broke the lamp identified by Reinbolt in her testimony. That fact, if true, would have definitely discredited Reinbolt's testimony in the original trial, especially since she claimed she saw someone holding a piece of the broken lamp during the murders. McFatridge had used this information to give Reinbolt credibility before the jury that she was actually at the murder scene.

The next logical thing for Marlow and Dixon was to follow this new lead and interview the fireman, but Rands was furious when he learned that Dixon and Marlow interviewed Sinclair without his permission. They were forbidden from interviewing the fireman, and like all the other reports, the Sinclair report was hidden away in the closed Rhoads case file, from Whitlock and Steidl's attorneys. This was sounding like the original Rhoads investigation all over again, and history was repeating itself.

Eventually the state was forced to disclose the reports after Marlow revealed their attempted cover-up to me, and I in turn informed Steidl and Whitlock's attorneys of the state's deception. An article by Jim Dey of the *News-Gazette* questioned the non-disclosure of the reports by Rands:

> . . . suppose that state appellate prosecutor David Rands withheld from the defense information that Debbie Reinbolt, an alleged eyewitness to the murders of Dyke and Karen Rhoads, had told an associate that she perjured herself during her testimony, that she did so to collect reward money and that information she had about the murders was provided to her by police investigators. And suppose Philip Sinclair, the witness who made those statements, demonstrated his credibility by passing a polygraph.

Rands' arrogance revealed his disregard for the law when Jim Dey's article continued, "Prosecutor Rands said it was his opinion that he was not required to turn over the report . . . "

DNA technology was also now available and the Illinois Attorney General's Office along with Steidl and Whitlock's defense teams had tested the available evidence several times already. Each time, nothing came back linking either Steidl or Whitlock to the murders, but that wasn't good enough for the Appellate Prosecutor's Office, and the evidence was tested several more times, and each time the results were negative. Marlow confided that Rands finally admitted they were starting to look bad, because nothing was coming back on Steidl or Whitlock. Still, Rands used the DNA testing as an excuse to stall the defense attorneys, while he had secretly stopped the DNA testing. A state police forensics scientist who tested the DNA confirmed as much when she admitted to Bill Clutter that people higher up than her had stopped the DNA testing.

Kenny Kaupas always told me over beers that if I ever filed a lawsuit, he would stand up and tell the truth, but when I did, he treated me like I had the plague. Kaupas wanted that brick lifted off him at any cost, and it was no longer politically correct to be around me anymore. It was no surprise to me when Greg Dixon said Kaupas warned him, "You know, I'm not telling you to not tell the truth, but you need to stay in the eye of the storm. Remember, you still have six years left to work in this department."

But Greg Dixon isn't afraid to tell the truth, and he isn't afraid of any storm. As far as Kaupas was concerned, I sure saved a lot of money on beer after I filed my lawsuit.

During my trial, Kaupas' true character and intentions came out when Andrea Trapp and Tony Rhoads testified during my trial.

Andrea testified about when she first met me: "I met Mike in March of 2000. . . . Mike called and my brother Tony and I met with him in Champaign . . . Tony and I went into the meeting wanting him to hear concerns that we had regarding everything that had happened over those last 15 years. We felt like the original trial was not something that—justice hadn't been served. The truth hadn't been found, and we were looking for somebody to help us do that. Find the truth. [Mike] was willing to listen to us."

Her testimony continued when she explained: "We wanted somebody to look at this again. We had been looking [for] somebody to look at this again since the close of the original trial. . . . there were so many inconsistencies in the original trial, there were so many inconsistencies between Dyke and Mr. Whitlock and Mr. Steidl. . . . And we had looked for so long for somebody to help us try to sort through all of this, all of these inconsistencies, and try to make sense out of them and to find out the truth. If Herbie and Randy Steidl were guilty, fine. But we had our doubts considering so much other information that we obtained over the years and we wanted somebody to look at all of it, look at the big picture, look at everything and try and sort through it . . . "

Andrea continued on about how frustrated they had become because, "Over the years, we could never find anybody in a law enforcement capacity . . . they weren't willing to listen to anything we had to say because they had a conviction. And that was the end of it for them, and it wasn't the end for us; we knew there were other things out there that needed to be brought to light. Finally, when we contacted Mr. Callahan, he was willing to listen . . . he was just willing to listen and look into it and to see if there were, see if there was something else there, to see if two men had been wrongfully convicted, to see if there was somebody else there that might possibly be responsible for this homicide."

Then Andrea's testimony turned to Kaupas and how she first met him at a meeting in July of 2004 and, "he didn't give me a chance to voice any of my concerns. . . . He basically wanted to talk to me about Randy Steidl and Herbie Whitlock, my family's safety since Randy Steidl had been released from prison. [Kaupas] made the comment, you know, [Steidl] was guilty and we needed to make sure that they could get him back into prison and to keep Herbie Whitlock where he was."

Likewise, Tony Rhoads' testimony mirrored his sister's, and he stated, "We, neither one, were satisfied with the verdict—or what we had been handed at the first trial . . . We weren't completely satisfied that the two people who had been accused of this were the ones who had actually done it." And then his testimony turned to when he first met Captain Kenny Kaupas: "Yes. I was contacted by Ken Kaupas. . . . He wanted to get with me and to discuss this case with Steidl and Whit- lock; basically, the two guys they had in jail for right now, right at that time. . . . I told [Kaupas] I didn't want to go over it again because it's a hard thing for me to do. . . . I had talked to Mr. Callahan; [Kaupas] should have the notes from my con- versations with [Callahan]. [Kaupas] basically said that those notes meant noth- ing to him [and] not to believe anything that Michale Callahan had told me."

Then Tony broke down in tears on the stand as he explained, "He got a little bit upset with me . . . said that I was—he questioned my loyalty to my brother on whether or not I was really interested in finding out, you know, about this. He said the two guys [Steidl and Whitlock]—'We want to make sure those two scumbags . . . don't get away with this.' . . . Kaupas had questioned my loyalty to my brother, so I didn't feel like there was any reason for me and him to talk. [Kaupas] was go- ing a certain way that I wasn't certain I wanted to go . . ."

With expensive lawsuits facing the state, including Kaupas, there was no doubt the state's goal was to "make sure those two scumbags . . . don't get away with this," whether they were guilty or innocent. That factor never mattered in the least to the state.

Contradicting the testimony of Andrea and Tony, Kaupas testified, " . . . I was trying to be very broad minded and very open minded here about who or whom may have been responsible for the death of Dyke and Karen Rhoads. And not just trying to focus in on one person."

Yet, according to Andrea and Tony, they believed Kaupas was only focused on Steidl and Whitlock, and so did others. Another one of those people was Special Agent Jeff Marlow, and his frustration over the cover-up and unethical tactics was disclosed in an e-mail he wrote in 2005. This was a very powerful e-mail that was leaked to my attorney and I subsequently shared it with Hal Dardick of the *Chicago Tribune*. As a result, the front page of the *Chicago Tribune* exclaimed: "Cop: Murder Probe Thwarted Again." The e-mail, addressed to the new Zone Commander, read in part:

> . . . I no longer want to be a part of the case involving the Dyke and Karen Rhoads homicide. This case has cost me many nights of lost sleep. The amount of actual operational time spent to the case in the last two and a half years probably does not total six months. In my opinion, there has been a lack of leadership regarding the case since Captain Kaupas assumed [this] current command . . . I naively wanted to play a part in the discovery of who really killed the kids. I have maintained that my only concern is to bring justice to the families by catching the real bad guys and putting them in jail. . . . At this point, I make no attempt at hiding the fact that I feel the main two witnesses used to convict Steidl and Whitlock were created. . . . Greg and I caused a tumultuous uproar when we interviewed and polygraphed Sinclair. I have expressed concern about the fact that the Illinois Appellate Prosecutor is ramrodding [sic] this case and the perception of there being a conflict of interest. The direction of the case is now being directed by David Rands who works directly for Ed Parkinson . . . It seems they definitely have an agenda which serves to compromise further an already tragic transgression of the justice system. Obviously, the farther a true and unbiased investigation proceeds, the more one feels there was wrongdoing concerning the original prosecution. I feel that being a part of the investigation is only going to serve to supply others as a scapegoat when the finger pointing heightens. Furthermore, I do not want to be part of the attempted railroading of anyone. The frustration level is too great for such a short life. Ideally, this would be handled by an independent agency that has not been accused of wrongdoing in respect to the original investigation/prosecution. With respect, S/A Marlow.

Marlow's e-mail caused quite a commotion at the ISP Armory, and shortly after his e-mail hit the front page of the *Chicago Tribune,* I received a call from a DII sergeant who was assigned to investigate how Marlow's e-mail was leaked to the *Chicago Tribune*. I was amazed at the irony and their hypocrisy. DII wasn't concerned about the criminal accusations in Marlow's e-mail . . . their only concern was who had leaked the e-mail to the *Chicago Tribune*. How ironic! All of the leaks to Fermon and Carper about my allegations and DII was never once concerned about who leaked that confidential information. Now, their only concern was who leaked Marlow's e-mail to the public. What a bunch of hypocrites!

Marlow's criminal allegations, like mine, were never investigated. Apparently, a search for the truth was out of the question with so many ISP commanders named in Steidl's expensive lawsuit. Carper's testimony that "Captain Kaupas had, in comparison to Mike Callahan, a more global perspective of the department and a more global perspective, I believe, in investigations," was right because he had certainly gone along with the department's cover-up and deceitful intentions. And he also had that brick he wanted lifted off his back at any cost.

In the Spring of 2005, Kenny Kaupas finally got his wish and the brick was lifted off his back, and he was given a new command. The teletype went out announcing Captain Kaupas was the new Commander of District 5 in Joliet.

But the Rhoads case still remained unsolved, and the state hadn't been able to pin anything on Steidl to put him back in prison. It was obvious, Kenny Kaupas was no longer "the right person, in the right job, at the right time, doing the right thing for the right reasons."

CHAPTER 20

THE FIGHT BACK

———————■———————

Winston Churchill once said, "Never, never, never, never, in nothing great or small, large or petty, never give in except to convictions of honor and good sense."

Frustrated and with no one to turn to for help, for a while, I simply gave up. DII had obviously covered everything up and betrayed me. Then my upper command retaliated against me for speaking out against their misconduct. Despite the Illinois Attorney General's Office acknowledging my allegations were official misconduct, they too turned a blind eye. This feeling of helplessness and frustration only added to my depression. Even the antidepressants only took the edge off. I still had that empty, helpless feeling of injustice . . . and I hated it.

It was Bill Clutter who gave me an avenue to fight back when he told me about an attorney in Springfield named John Baker who could help me. Bill said Baker was one of the best attorneys he knew when it came to First Amendment protection. I looked at Bill somewhat puzzled. I was naive about civil litigation, and had no idea how the First Amendment could protect me. Bill explained a person was protected by the First Amendment if they spoke out on a matter of public concern and had been retaliated against for it. I had definitely spoken out on a matter of public concern; innocent men in prison and the state covering it up, refusing to investigate a murder and look for the truth, I think would concern everyone. Especially with the real killers still running around free. DII covering up the misconduct of the ISP command was also a concern for everyone. If they were willing to cover up something like this, what other crimes by the state would they be willing to cover up? By the time I was done talking with Bill, I was filled with hope once again.

I called the law firm of Baker, Baker and Krajewski in August 2003, and made an appointment to meet with John Baker. As the time drew closer, I started getting cold feet and felt guilty for putting my family through something like this. It was a stressful decision to fight back, and it could certainly hurt my family even more than it already had. I had a strong marriage, but stress much less than this had ruined the best of marriages. Was this worth the risk of ruining my marriage? I had also been neglecting my son for way too long, and he was getting to an age where he needed me to be more of a father. A fight like this would certainly take time away from him. Fighting a state in court would be expensive, and if I lost, could ruin my family financially. I had a lot of reasons to justify my just sitting back and doing nothing.

It was no secret about Illinois' reputation and why would anyone risk taking on such a powerful state so rich in deception and corruption. Just the thought of all this became overwhelming, and I cancelled the meeting with John Baker. I placated myself that one day I would go forward to the public, but it was better to put things off since I still had over two years left before I could retire.

"Suck it up, Mike. Think about your family," I told myself. I would soon be making a six-figure salary and there would be more raises, my retirement would be around $90,000 a year and I would have it made the rest of my life. I rationalized that I could just sit back until retirement and then maybe I'd write a book about this travesty. I had a good life . . . why mess with that? My phone wasn't going off in the middle of the night anymore. I was basically sitting behind a desk from nine to five counting seat belt tickets. It was like I had been put out to pasture. I tried to convince myself life wasn't so bad, and I wasn't the first person unfairly punished by this department.

Then the guilt started to hit, "Was I taking the easy way out, was I being a coward?" I asked myself. With all this inner turmoil, I started questioning my self-confidence and self-esteem, and couldn't get rid of the feeling I was letting a lot of people down, including my family and myself.

In the end, I couldn't get past the shame and anger I felt for those arrogant and callous assholes in Springfield. Not only for what they had done, but for what they were getting away with. It wasn't just about me anymore. No, the biggest shame and guilt were for Dyke and Karen Rhoads, their families, all the people who believed in us and came to us for help, and even though I had never met them, Randy Steidl and Herb Whitlock. I was torn between the guilt of putting my family through a fight like this and the guilt I had for giving up on my oath and myself.

Lily hit the roof when I told her I cancelled the appointment with John Baker.

"You're going!" she put her foot down. "I don't care if we end up on food stamps and living in a shack! You're going to meet with that attorney!"

My wife had become the stronger person and my biggest support, and she was steering me in the direction I knew I had to go all along.

"You're letting this eat you up inside," she insisted. "If you don't fight, it's going to slowly kill you, and I'm not going to let that happen!"

Lily was right. The anger and shame was slowly eating away at me like a cancer. If it hadn't already destroyed my soul, it would ultimately kill me, too. The next day, I rescheduled my appointment with John Baker.

The day I walked into the law firm of Baker, Baker and Krajewski, I knew I came to the right place. The law firm consisted of James Baker along with his son John and a third partner. When I met John Baker, I felt immediately at ease. He wasn't the stereotypical attorney I knew through my years in the law enforcement community. He was open, genuine and sincere; it was almost like I was talking to my brother. There was no arrogance about him, no air of intellectual superiority, and no lecturing on the finer points of the law like I expected. We went into a conference room and sat down. He sat there, listened to my story, and rarely interjected. At times, when I got emotional, he was reassuring and supportive.

The more I unfolded my story of wrongful convictions, the railroading of two innocent men into prison, the misconduct by the ISP command, the politics that interfered, the more I thought this man must think I'm some kind of lunatic. As I listened to myself, I worried he might dismiss my ramblings and write me off because who was going to believe this incredible story. Several times, my own command remarked, "This sounds like some made for TV movie."

I didn't have to worry, it was all the truth, and John Baker never doubted me or the truth. As I sat there talking in his conference room, a couple of hours passed by. I remember looking at my watch thinking, "My God, my bill is starting to get up there!" Sensing my thoughts, John Baker told me not to worry.

"Keep on talking," he said, obviously intrigued. "I'm not charging you for this."

I continued, spilling my guts and emotions to this stranger. After it was all over, I felt a great sense of relief, but John was incensed by the misconduct of the State.

"The public needs to hear this story, Mike," he said. "This is an outrage! We place our trust in our government and that it will always do the right thing." But Baker also understood the enormity of a decision like this.

"It's your decision to make," he said, "but I would like to see you stand up and fight and it won't be easy." He understood the risks, and he also said he understood if I didn't want to take that risk. There was no pressure . . . only John Baker's word that he would stand and fight beside me.

"Think about it for a few days and let me know what your decision is. It's your choice," he said.

I saw his outrage and his confidence, and I sensed John Baker wasn't afraid to take on the mighty engine of the State. I shook John's hand, and thanked him for his time. As he walked up the stairs to his office, he turned and stood looking down at me for a moment. Then he said something I'll never forget: "You know Mike, sometimes it takes just one person to stand up and make a difference."

I didn't reply to John's comment, I just nodded, but I made up my mind right then and there. As I drove home that day, for the first time in a long time, I felt good again.

That night, lying in bed next to Lily, we talked about taking on such an overwhelming fight. Did we have the strength, support and resources to take on the Illinois State Police. Always my little pillar of strength, Lily handed me a magazine article she had read that day. Underlined was a simple quote from Gandhi, "You must be the change you wish to see in the world." Gandhi was right, and I like to believe everything that happens in life is for a reason. So the next day, I called John Baker.

"I'm ready," I said, "let's fight!" And fight we did!

At the time, no one in the State Police had an inkling of what I was about to do, especially the arrogant command in Springfield, but I was about to hit them right between the eyes. On September 23, 2003, John Baker filed a federal lawsuit against Colonel Charles Brueggemann, Lieutenant Colonel Diane Carper and Captain Steven Fermon for violating my First Amendment right of Freedom of Speech. Eric Zorn of the *Chicago Tribune* reflected on my lawsuit, "The long simmering cauldron of putrid ooze that is the prosecution of Randy Steidl and Herbert Whitlock has at last boiled over . . . 24-year veteran Illinois State Police Lt. Mike Callahan . . . has issued a raft of specific and damning allegations against state police higher-ups." Zorn continued that, " . . . fellow officers confirmed under oath Callahan's accounts of meetings with balky supervisors who, they said, seemed far more interested in defending what had been done than correcting any mistakes." Zorn's column ended by acknowledging, ". . . if what Callahan and his allies say is true, it amounts to a huge and even frightening scandal that suggests a cynical dereliction of duty inside the state police hierarchy at best, a high level conspiracy to obstruct justice at worst. . . . It would be nice to say such an allegation from respected law enforcement professionals is unprecedented in the annals of Illinois justice. But it's not. Who will step in to clean it up?"

The Friday everything went public, Carper was at my district. I was in my office when two sergeants ran in and said it was all over the news about my lawsuit. Carper had obviously found out, too, because she was sitting in her squad car frantically talking on the phone to someone. She was gesturing back and forth and obviously upset, she exited her squad and began pacing back and forth as she talked. Then she began walking in circles around her car, still talking and running her hands through her hair. Yeah, the shit had hit the fan.

I could not retire until 2005, so for the next year and a half I knew I'd have to walk on eggshells. It was a stressful time, but I was also getting a lot of support throughout the rank-and-file of the state police. I received calls and e-mails of encouragement from friends, old commanders, ISP officers I had never met and retirees who were all sickened at what our department had become. They were all tired of the politics and the politically correct commanders who had ruined a once proud and honorable department's name. Their support only made me that much stronger.

During this same timeframe, U.S. Attorney Patrick Fitzgerald's office indicted former Governor George Ryan. The front page of the *Chicago Tribune* declared, "RYAN INDICTED, U.S. charges former governor with pattern of corruption." When referencing the 22 count indictment, the U.S. Attorney stated that Ryan had "repeatedly lied to Federal Agents" and noted, "What we're alleging in the indictment is that basically the State of Illinois was for sale . . ." A second *Chicago Tribune* article read:

> As a cigar-chomping governor always eager to cut a back room deal, George Ryan seemed to fit the mold of a rough and tumble Illinois politician. On Wednesday, officially under indictment on federal racketeering charges, it was taken a step further as Ryan joined the sizable and storied ranks of Illinois politicians who found themselves not only tarnished by scandal, but headed for court. Illinois has a regrettably rich history of public corruption . . . where its players weren't scared to break the rules for personal gain.

A local news article also called Ryan on his hypocrisy by reflecting that: "While his popularity plummeted in his home state, Ryan was winning widespread praise nationally and internationally as a leading critic of capital punishment. Ryan declared a moratorium on capital punishment in Illinois after it was discovered that

13 wrongfully convicted men had been sent to death row. His hypocrisy was further acknowledged when the article pointed out, "Detractors said Ryan adopted the cause to deflect bad publicity growing out of the [federal] government's Operation Safe Road investigation."

As far as I was concerned the detractors were right. This "great humanitarian" had actually commuted the sentences of people guilty of horrible crimes; yet he had turned his back on innocent men like Steidl and Whitlock, two men railroaded into prison with help from the same law enforcement agency that had protected Ryan for all those years.

My fight back became a reality in early 2004 when we started taking depositions. If the depositions were any indication of how the department was going to try and cover up my lawsuit, they were in trouble. Carper's first deposition lasted the better part of a day and contained 211 pages of testimony. For over six hours, we sat and listened to her respond with: "I do not recall," "I don't remember" and "I don't know." Even Illinois Assistant Attorney General Karen McNaught, interjected on a break, "I've never seen an ISP Colonel not know so much or not remember so much!"

As the depositions went on, the ISP's strategy became obvious. In early 2003, Ruby Gordon-Phillips had filed a hostile work environment complaint against Steve Fermon. The complaint eventually went to the ISP Equal Employment Opportunity (EEO) office. Skip Nelson's memo to the director acknowledged Ruby's complaint:

> Fermon's command and leadership of . . . Zone 5 has created a hostile work environment which includes: nepotism, bias, favoritism, intimidation, untruthfulness, racial prejudice, manipulation, and abuse of authority. . . . During the course of this investigation, DII agents encountered from several ISP employees a real concern for retaliatory action to be taken against them if they were to speak out about the work environment in Zone 5.

The head of EEO, Suzanne Yokely-Bond, personally handled the investigation, but with her political and family ties to the ISP upper command, no one expected a fair and unbiased EEO investigation. Her father was a former Deputy Director and also a supervisor and friend of Fermon's. Bond still went through the motions of an investigation by setting up interviews with a *select* group of Zone 5 employees, and interviewed a whopping 10 out of the more than 50 employees at Zone 5 during April 2003. Yet strangely, Bond never interviewed the complainant herself, Ruby Gordon-Phillips. The writing was on the wall, when Bond later lied and claimed Ruby had told Col. Nelson she didn't want to be interviewed.

Ruby testified to the opposite and claimed she never told Nelson any such thing.

"Absolutely not," she said denying any such conversation with Nelson. "I requested it," she continued, " . . . after my lawsuit was filed . . . She [Bond] tried to contact me upon one occasion. And I called her office back and never could get a hold of her. And nor did she ever try to call me again to schedule an interview."

When Bond came to Zone 5 in April 2003, she spent two days interviewing the zone personnel. Each person was informed an EEO complaint had been filed against Captain Steve Fermon, and my name was never once mentioned as part of the complaint. Bond even agreed I was not part of the complaint in her deposition, "No . . . I had allegations Captain Fermon was creating a hostile work environment."

In fact, I was one of the people interviewed by Bond, and during that interview, I gave her several examples of officers who, besides myself, had experienced Fermon's unjust wrath. Yet Bond never interviewed one of the people I referred to her, and when I told her I had gone to the FBI and Mary Leahy about my concerns with Fermon, she practically ran out of the room.

Bond never came back to the zone to continue her investigation, at least not until six months later . . . and coincidently, just two weeks after I filed my lawsuit. Even more ironic, Bond had never bothered to document one of her interviews in April . . . but again, just coincidently, she finally did document the April interviews two weeks after I filed my lawsuit. And of course now, according to Bond's assessment, I was suddenly part of the problem at Zone 5. Six months after the EEO interviews and two weeks after I filed my lawsuit, the ISP's strategy was that my removal was because Fermon and I just didn't get along and it created problems.

Sitting through the depositions and listening to Bond and Cols. Chuck Brueggemann, Diane Carper, and Mike Snyders devious lies was sickening. They testified I had created such a problem I had to be removed. Yet they couldn't identify one specific thing I did to contribute to such a horrible work environment. They couldn't attack my task forces, which were kicking ass and more productive than ever. It was amazing watching these people lower themselves and lie so badly and yet maintain such an overwhelming arrogance. Each time I attended a deposition, I lost more respect for the ISP leadership that had put themselves on such high pedestals, now relegated to becoming pathetic liars who couldn't even keep their lies straight.

Suzanne Bond couldn't even remember who she had interviewed and stated, " . . . and maybe I am wrong about this—but I thought I interviewed all the people physically assigned to the Champaign office. And then I interviewed all the master sergeants and above that were assigned to the zone. I think that's what I did." It was comical reading Bond's pathetic rendition of her April interviews. Two sergeants advised they never had a problem getting along with either Captain Fermon or Lieutenant Callahan and another said he didn't see an "us vs. them" problem. A secretary told Bond regarding Fermon, " . . . it seems like some employees are given more consideration or latitude than others, for example—Mr. Bill Kroncke and Ms. Tracy Reed." One master sergeant told Bond "he has not experienced harassment but has experienced discrimination. He stated he does not believe all people are treated equally. He stated 'clicks' [sic] are no longer a problem . . . but he wished Captain Fermon would keep him more informed." Of course, Bond never considered asking the master sergeant what discrimination he experienced or which people were not treated equally—something an EEO officer would usually want to know. Another master sergeant stated "clicks [sic] were more of a problem before . . . she said she does not think all of the people in the chain of command support Captain Fermon—for example Lt. Callahan." If Bond wanted to do me in, here was her chance, but she didn't ask the mental midget how I hadn't supported Fermon. Of course, since the master sergeant didn't report to me, she had no idea how I didn't support Fermon, and besides she was too busy at VMEG helping her agents falsify and lie on search warrants anyway.

Surprisingly, Bond actually documented information from some who believed Fermon had created a hostile work environment, but again she twisted the facts around, and at times even outright lied.

Bond wrote that one sergeant said, "his work environment is intimidating and threatening and Fermon moves people around as a way to threaten or intimidate them, not for operations. He stated Captain Fermon discriminates against both Master Sergeant Val Talley and Ms. Ruby Gordon-Phillips." Again, Bond never bothered to ask about the intimidation or discrimination he had witnessed. A third master sergeant said he believes Captain Fermon has engaged in conduct he considers intimidating and offensive. Once again, Bond never inquired about the intimidation or offensive behavior. Master Sergeant Val Talley's report gave specific examples of discrimination from Fermon and said "he does believe discrimination is a problem for both himself and Ms. Ruby Gordon-Phillips in Zone 5." Yet obviously the fix was in when Bond's final report to the director read, "None of these witnesses could point to independent sources who could verify their claims."

Ultimately, Bond and the ISP command tried to use one EEO interview to justify their fabricated reasoning that I, too, was causing a problem. Bond's deceitful version referenced an interview with Sgt. Sue Voges, who wasn't even in my chain of command. The report read that Voges said, " . . . some employees are treated more favorably than others depending on which 'team' a person is on . . . she hears of unfairness but does not have any first hand knowledge. She said it does make her uncomfortable that Lieutenant Callahan is so vocal about his dislike for Captain Fermon." Yet, during her deposition, Sgt. Voges denied making any such statements to Bonds when she testified, "No. . . . we [Callahan and I] never had a conversation about Fermon, [like] let me tell you my feelings about him or anything like that."

Sitting there in those depositions, I saw the dark side of the state police upper command. I learned about DII's betrayal, and as time went on it became obvious this had become a conspiracy of liars at the highest levels of the ISP and they would do or say anything to cover up their scandal. I listened as Carper, Brueggemann and Snyders testified they removed me based on Suzanne Bond's determination that Fermon and I were engaging in disruptive and harassing behavior in the workplace.

"My basis for believing that Lt. Callahan was engaging in behavior disruptive to the workplace was based upon Suzanne Bond's information during the course of her EEO investigation," Carper testified.

"What were these behaviors that were disruptive to the workplace that Lt. Callahan was engaging in?" John Baker asked.

"Those were not defined by Suzanne Bond," Carper comically replied.

When she was asked who I was intimidating, Carper replied, "Again, I'll reiterate. I did not dissect out from Suzanne Bond that Lt. Callahan was intimidating anyone." But Carper continued, "She [Bond] made one specific allegation that I believe that some of the individuals interviewed had believed that Captain Fermon was intimidating is what I recall."

Carper was not able to provide one specific example of anything I had ever done, either through information from Bond or anyone else where I created any type of problem, and eventually admitted her information "was probably more hearsay, impressions, observations," and, when asked if anyone complained about me, she admitted, "Boy, I can't attribute specific comments to anyone in particular."

Not surprisingly, Snyders and Brueggemann's testimony was just as inept, and when pushed on the issue, neither one was able to point to one piece of evidence, either from Bond or anyone else, of what type of problems I had created.

Lt. Col. Mike Snyders, one of our department's quintessential "yes men," testified about Bond's assessments but was no more specific than Carper: "I remember her telling us that there were clearly problems in the workplace as far as people being unhappy, people alleging workplace hostility . . . and I remember her giving some specifics. I don't remember what the specifics were." Like Carper, Snyders couldn't recall one specific thing Bond addressed concerning me, but with Fermon he remembered, "What I remember about Mr. Fermon was that he was a somewhat of a dictator type leader and that there were a lot of unhappy people in his command . . ." Snyders continued that ". . . there were concerns that he was having a relationship with a female employee [Tracy Reed] in Zone 5 that was disrupting, or leading to a lot of rumors, which should disrupt the workplace . . ."

When Snyders was asked who specifically expressed concerns about me other than Suzanne Bond, he replied, "I don't remember anyone else discussing problems with Callahan in that time frame." But Fermon was a different story when Snyders admitted several people had complained about Captain Fermon to him.

"Yes. I think a lot of people have . . . a lot of people have complained to me about Captain Fermon at Zone 5. Edie Casella. Mike Bernardini, and I don't like to bring this up, my wife Stephanie Snyders. . . . There may have been others I don't remember."

Like the other two colonels, Chuck Brueggemann had the same memory lapse.

"I probed," he claimed. "I can't recount names, but I know the probing led to her talking about a particular agent, and I believe that she referred to him as a female. . . . And that was the fact, hey, Callahan don't [sic] like Fermon and makes it clear to everybody in the office, Fermon don't [sic] like Callahan and goes around Callahan and, you know, you're afraid to talk to either one of them. . . ."

Brueggemann and Snyders got caught in even more lies when they testified they removed me based on Suzanne Bond's recommendations that May 2003, and she saw no need to conduct any further investigation into the problems at Zone 5.

"She said that she had done a number of interviews, and I even recall there being, she even bringing up, we're hearing the same thing. I don't know how much sense it makes to keep doing more interviews," Brueggemann claimed. Likewise, Col. Mike Snyders was caught in the same lie.

> Q: At that meeting on May 7th, was it discussed whether Suzanne Bond would continue her investigation into Zone 5 or did that come up?

> Snyders: It did come up. I remember her saying that she interviewed a lot of people. There clearly were two sides in Zone 5 . . . and I remember her questioning the value of continuing to do interviews; that she already interviewed a lot of people.

But, Suzanne Bond's version was totaly different than the two ISP colonels when she testified:

> At no point did I say they need to be moved ... And we had a conversation that certainly they—that being operations—could not use the EEO investigation that was still ongoing to move personnel. That you can't use that as a sole basis for moving personnel when the case is not closed and there have not been determinations and findings ...

Adding to the hypocrisy, after I filed my lawsuit, Bond suddenly decided to continue her EEO investigation by conducting a whopping four additional interviews. Of course she still excluded the complainant, Ruby Gordon-Phillips, and five others who requested an interview with Bond regarding Fermon's conduct.

Instead, one of Bond's four new interviews was with a special agent located in a satellite office in Decatur. How he would know what was going on in the Champaign office, some 60 miles away, was a mystery to me. But, of course, he happened to be one of Fermon's best friends. Such a good friend, Fermon had talked Dan Kent into giving him sergeant's pay at the rank of a special agent; despite a directive from Kent himself forbidding troopers or agents from getting sergeant's pay at the time.

The second interview in Bond's "renewed" EEO investigation was a second interview with Sgt. Voges. Of course, Bond didn't know at the time that Sgt. Voges would make a liar out of her when she testified in her deposition. The third interview was with Fermon, and Bond's report read in part:

> He stated that ... he and Lt. Callahan were no longer speaking once Lt. Callahan started leveling very serious allegations against Captain Fermon ... to DII. He stated that he submitted a [12] page memorandum to Col. Carper about Lt. Callahan's actions, which Captain Fermon describes as "insubordinate."

The memo referenced by Bond was a document Fermon prepared on May 12, 2003—just four days after I went to DII with my allegations against him. This memo read in part:

> For the past 10 months, since approximately August 2002, I have personally observed insubordinate, unprofessional, and counter productive actions and behaviors exhibited by Lieutenant Michale

Callahan . . . These actions and behaviors have resulted in the many assigned task not being completed, decreased communication and efficiency in the zone and my authority as the zone commander, to be diminished.

The 12-page memo to Carper outlined 16 policy violations I allegedly committed, and concluded that, "Lieutenant Callahan presents a daily challenge to the command and authoritative actions in Zone 5. I wish to meet with you and discuss alternatives to Lieutenant Callahan's assignment in Zone 5."

Even Carper belittled Fermon's late hour attempts to retaliate against me for my claims to DII.

"I guess my feeling was . . . if we have all these issues—someone just doesn't hand you 12 pages of issues and they just came up over night. If there are issues of that magnitude, then I would expect to see something different well before 12 pages of documentation . . ."

It was no surprise to me that Fermon's accusations were full of lies, and I had the paperwork to prove his deceit. When John Baker called him on those lies during his deposition, John experienced Fermon's arrogance first hand.

"I don't know what you're getting at here, Mr. Baker!" he angrily retorted as Baker pointed out Fermon's blatant deceit. At this point, Fermon's attorney, Assistant Attorney General Karen McNaught snipped, "He's saying they caught you in another lie!"

Fermon became so agitated that he stood up, thrust out his 300 pound frame and arrogantly bellowed, "Mr. Baker, this deposition is over, I'm leaving!" And Fermon walked out.

As John and I were leaving, I glanced into McNaught's corner office and like a scene reminiscent of the *Sopranos,* she was standing over Fermon, angrily chastising him while he sat there, with his hands folded, arrogantly smirking up at her.

The last interview in Bond's EEO investigation was with Master Sergeant Russ Perkins, who had replaced me as the interim acting lieutenant over Zone 5 narcotics. Russ was interviewed in November, five months after I was transferred to patrol. Russ and I were good friends and he had supervised one of the zone's narcotic task forces for several years.

On the Friday before his EEO interview, Russ was told Carper had submitted paperwork to promote him to the hard-rank of lieutenant. Russ also received a call from Col. Skip Nelson who confirmed his promotion and also to remind him about his pending EEO interview. Nelson subliminally gave Russ a message that the command knew he would do the right thing in his EEO interview.

The ISP command was literally dangling the carrot before the horse to get Russ to discredit me. This was obvious shortly after what happened to Russ following his EEO interview. Russ had refused to play their game, and he was too honest, later testifying, "At that meeting, I spoke positively about Callahan and negatively about the captain."

Russ paid for his integrity though, and two days after his EEO interview, Carper told him she was pulling his promotion because she no longer felt he was ready to become a lieutenant in the Illinois State Police. Obviously he wasn't ready because he had too much integrity for her.

Russ Perkins filed a lawsuit against the state police for the retaliation against him for being honest during his EEO interview. Eventually the ISP admitted the retaliation and settled with him out of court.

Despite Russ Perkins' testimony that he spoke highly of me, Bond's report was filled with more lies and twisted facts contradicting what Russ had really said in his interview. Russ' testimony reflected those lies as he picked apart Bond's deceitful report during my trial:

> . . . I did not say that others would fear retaliation if Lt. Callahan were reassigned back to the zone. I did not make that statement. And then what she omitted from this was . . . her asking this question. "Would you guys fear retaliation if Fermon or Callahan were reassigned to the office?" And I said . . . yes, I would be afraid if Fermon came back. I would have to transfer. And then she asked me about Lt. Callahan if he came back. I said no, I wouldn't fear retaliation. Nobody would . . . that's omitted from this. And I thought this was a very important point that she omitted . . .

> Q: At any point in time, did you ever have a feeling or did you think that Mike had done anything to cause a bad environment or a tense atmosphere?

> Perkins: No.

On February 10, 2004, eleven months after Ruby filed her complaint against Fermon and eight months after I was removed from investigations, and, of course, after I filed my lawsuit, Suzanne Bond sent out the following memo: "The EEO office has completed its investigation into the Zone 5 investigations hostile work environment case. The EEO office did not substantiate any EEO policy violations as a result of the investigations." Bond had ignored every claim of intimidation, nepotism and discrimination against Fermon identified by several zone personnel. On February 10, 2004, Director Larry Trent issued a follow-up memo which read, in part, "The EEO office has completed its investigation . . . While no EEO policy violations were substantiated . . . the investigation did tend to support the decision to remove Captain Steve Fermon and Lieutenant Michale Callahan from Zone 5 investigations." Of course it did . . . I had filed a lawsuit against the assholes. Suzanne Bond's shoddy, half-assed investigation couldn't come up with one specific example of one problem I had ever caused, but like everything else, the EEO investigation was nothing more than a veiled and pathetic attempt to cover up the truth and twist the facts around in order to justify the department's real reasons for retaliating against me.

It was amazing how far the department was willing to go to try and discredit me, and even more ludicrous when they tried to use Ruby and Russ Perkins. In his interrogatory, Fermon stated, "Ms. Phillips advised, Lt. Callahan is out there and that she fears for her personal safety because she said she never knew what he was going to do."

Ruby had filed a DII and EEO complaint against Fermon, and eventually a lawsuit and here he was saying she feared me. Of course Ruby denied Fermon's outlandish accusations when she testified, "I did not make those statements to Mr. Fermon. . . . Mike was the nicest person in the office. And why would you ever fear a person that was so—his disposition was so well versed. No, never . . . Never feared for my personal safety from Mike Callahan. Steve Fermon, that's a different story. But Mike Callahan? No."

Fermon also alleged Russ Perkins told him I was "nuts" or "crazy" and he, too, feared for his safety because of my behavior. Like Ruby, Russ denied under oath ever thinking or making any such ludicrous comments.

Carper's interrogatories were also filled with lies, and she alleged Ruby had told her "there was something wrong with Lieutenant Callahan." Ruby adamantly denied this, and under cross examination by the Illinois Attorney General's Office, Karen McNaught angrily tried to rip into Ruby, asking, " . . . you're calling Lt. Col. Carper a liar; is that right?"

"Oh, yes. Definitely. Yes. When it comes to saying something I didn't say, that is a lie. [I have] No problem with calling her a liar," Ruby defiantly shot back.

I had expected the arrogant ISP command to fight back, but as I sat there listening to all their outrageous lies and fabrications, I lost all respect for these pathetic men and women who called themselves our leaders. Their sleazy and fruitless attacks on my credibility only made me more determined than ever.

Keith Jensen was the head of the Illinois State Police Legal Department, and following a deposition one afternoon, he called John Baker over to the side.

"Hey John, we need to go to lunch and talk about settling this case." He looked over John's shoulder directly at me.

"You know, there's no need to drag the Illinois State Police's name through the mud," said Jensen. "And Mike, don't forget—we'll be dragging your name through the mud, too!"

I had just sat through a year of depositions and listened to the elite leadership of the ISP with all their lies and hypocrisy. Drag my name through the mud!

"Fuck you, Jensen!" I angrily replied. "Try to drag my name through the mud, go ahead and try! Give it your best shot!"

The State Police did try to give it their best shot. It wasn't long after my angry encounter with Jensen when I started receiving calls from friends—most of them my old supervisors—who said they were contacted by Jensen. I learned from them that the ISP command had analysts working graveyard shifts digging into my phone records, my computer, my old case files, all the past offices I had been assigned to trying to find dirt to muddy up my name. Obviously the department became even more desperate when some of my old supervisors called to tell me they were asked if they would be willing to testify against me—not one did. They weren't like the deceitful low-lifes we had in command now.

Still, these were the things that started to cut so deeply. It wasn't so much the ruthless attacks, the lying, the fabricated tactics by the ISP command—it was the fact that the department I had worked so hard for and believed in for all those years would stoop so low in their efforts to discredit me.

In the beginning, I remember the concern John Baker had about going to battle against the upper echelon of the Illinois State Police, the supposedly elite of the ISP—the very top command, men and women who had attained the rank of colonel. Men and women who had the power to make decisions that could affect thousands of people's lives.

"These people aren't real cops," I kept telling John. "They're political hacks who pretend to be cops."

My words were reinforced with each deposition, and afterwards I watched John Baker become more dumbfounded at what he referred to as "their arrogant stupidity." I sat there beside John Baker each time and watched as they kept digging themselves deeper and deeper into deceit.

Still, it was sad for me to sit there through those depositions. On one hand, their testimony was giving me confidence, but that happiness faded into melancholy during the drive home because I had just witnessed our elite leadership at their worst, and I couldn't help but feel ashamed of them. These were our leaders, men and women with great responsibility. They sat in positions of respect and honor. They made decisions about people's lives, even to the extent of leaving innocent men in prison. Watching them testify left me feeling empty inside, and the pride I felt for the Illinois State Police diminished after each encounter. Maybe I had believed in a lie all those years, but there was no turning back now, and I became more determined than ever to fight back. Their deceit only angered me and the betrayal of their oaths—to people like Dyke and Karen Rhoads, Randy Steidl, Herb Whitlock and to the citizens of this state—shamed me.

No, this time, they had picked on the wrong person.

CHAPTER 21

CONSPIRACY AT THE TOP

———————◼———————

It wasn't just Kaupas and Rands involved in cover-ups; DII was also back to their old tricks of sugarcoating investigations when even more accusations were made against Captain Fermon.

In March of 2003, the United States Drug Enforcement Agency (DEA) initiated an investigation on a man named Steven Snook in Danville. Assisting DEA was VMEG, and Snook was eventually arrested for being in possession of five kilos of cocaine. That was a significant amount of cocaine, and Snook was looking at some very serious federal time.

Shortly after my transfer to patrol, I received a call from defense attorney Mark Christoff, who was representing Steven Snook.

Christoff asked if I was familiar with the case, and I explained I had heard about the case but had no involvement since Fermon ran VMEG. Christoff explained he was calling because he heard I was someone who could be trusted, and his client, Snook, had some serious allegations about Captain Steve Fermon. This was probably the last thing I needed to hear since I was just hammered by the department for making allegations against Fermon, still I found it intriguing, and so I listened as Christoff described Snook's allegations. Snook was part of a large narcotics trafficking ring which operated out of Danville, and he alleged that ring was protected by Captain Steve Fermon.

This was unbelievable, but Snook claimed Fermon was close childhood friends with many of the ring members, and he tipped them off if anyone was investigating

289

them. The leader of the drug trafficking ring was identified as Michael Mascari, who was also associated with the Sons of Silence motorcycle gang. Snook alleged Fermon had called and warned Mascari to get out of state when the FBI was coming to the Danville area to arrest several of the bikers. Christoff continued his amazing story when he claimed Snook was also involved in land transactions with Fermon and other members of the drug ring, and Snook had the land deeds to back this up.

Christoff said Snook was looking to cut a deal on his prison time and was willing to take a polygraph, provide the land deeds, and even make recorded phone calls with other members of the drug ring to prove his allegations.

I was probably the last person Christoff should be telling this to, and I explained how I was just removed from investigations for turning Fermon in on other allegations of misconduct. While sympathetic to his concerns, I told him his best bet was to talk to the feds or file a complaint with DII himself. I wanted nothing more to do with those lying assholes at DII.

Mark Christoff called again several weeks later and said he had filed an official complaint with DII, but when Snook met with two DII agents they repeatedly asked him if "Mike Callahan" had put him up to filing his allegations against Fermon. Snook didn't even know my name, let alone who I was.

"I think they're after you," Christoff warned. "They didn't give a fuck about the allegations against Fermon!"

I appreciated Christoff's heads-up, but at this point in my career I didn't care anymore, and I was just counting the days to retirement. But DII couldn't hide this complaint like they did mine, and they were forced to open an investigation. Over the next year, Christoff called me occasionally to vent his anger that he believed DII was intentionally whitewashing the investigation, and that certainly didn't surprise me at all.

Christoff was right, DII was up to their old tricks and I wouldn't find out just how blatant it was until I received the discovery of their DII investigation concerning Snook's allegations. Christoff was right, DII had made me out as the bad guy, alleging I put Snook up to filing his complaint. I sat there dumbfounded at their brazenness as I read the complaint. A complaint not from Snook and Christoff, but allegedly from me:

> On July 10, 2003, the Division of Internal Investigation received information regarding allegations of official misconduct against Captain Steven Fermon . . . during an interview with District 10 Lieutenant Michale Callahan, he (Callahan) advised of a confidential source (C/S) who alleged Fermon had knowledge of organized

crime activities in the Danville area and Fermon was involved with organized crime figures and business. According to the C/S, Fermon has provided information to law enforcement activities and "protection" to these individuals.

I was amazed at the pathetic attempts DII would go to—Christoff had made the complaint to DII, not me. But their obvious ploy was to add to the department's strategy that Mike Callahan just didn't like poor Stevie Fermon.

The DII case opened on Captain Steve Fermon was based on criminal allegations of official misconduct. According to the Illinois criminal statutes, official misconduct is a Class 3 felony. DII Sgt. Freddie Outlaw read the allegations against Fermon at his DII interview:

> You are hereby advised that the following illegal or improper acts or allegations have been attributed to you. You divulged confidential law enforcement information to criminal associates in the Danville, Illinois, area. It is also alleged that you had dealings which included the transfer of real estate property of which you own to those associates.

Although Fermon was being investigated for criminal misconduct, when DII interviewed him they hypocritically acknowledged it as only an administrative matter—a much less serious infraction that DII Col. Skip Nelson characterized as "like a trooper . . . not wearing his hat."

The administrative interview of Fermon was conducted by Lt. Bill Sheridan and Sgt. Freddie Outlaw. Both Outlaw and Sheridan had little investigative experience, which made them the type of agents DII liked. Prior to their DII assignments, Outlaw ran physical training at the ISP Academy and Sheridan was the staff officer for Fermon's good buddy, former Deputy Director Dan Kent.

I was amazed at all the contradictions and oversights by the two DII investigators. Their reports reminded me of some of Eckerty's in the Rhoads investigation.

The reports acknowledged Snook was part of a drug ring that included Bradley Nicholson, Michael Mascari and Jessica Cotton. Snook, Nicholson and Cotton all had prior narcotics convictions, and Mascari was a documented member of the Sons of Silence. Fermon acknowledged this in his administrative interview when he said, "Mike was a person we would have liked to have had [as] a snitch because he . . . would have just been in the know I think . . . . at one point in time, he was a probationary member with the Sons of Silence motorcycle gang."

Snook had alleged Fermon called Mascari to warn him there was a pending bust coming down on the Sons of Silence, and told him to get out of town before the arrests came down. The FBI did conduct a large scale arrest of the Sons of Silence, and prior to those arrests, VMEG was notified for de-confliction purposes. To validate his allegations, Snook agreed to conduct a recorded phone call with Mascari, but DII agents purposefully failed to record the phone call. Instead, Outlaw listened to the call on another line, and not surprisingly, his interpretation of the conversation was much different than Snook's version.

According to Snook, Mascari admitted he was warned by Fermon about the impending arrests and that he needed to get out of town. Freddie Outlaw's version was somewhat different, and his report read, "Mascari [told Snook], if anything, Fermon might have advised him to stop engaging in certain activity because he could end up in trouble."

With DII's failure to record the conversation, it meant they were able to avoid having any actual incriminating statements on tape, thus leaving the phone call open to Outlaw's twisted interpretation.

As I continued reading the transcripts of Fermon's administrative interview, I think Christoff's suspicions were justified.

"Do you know or do you have any association with Mr. Mascari?" Outlaw asked.

"Yeah, I know him. I have no association with him. I've known Mike Mascari since some of my first memories," Fermon acknowledged.

"At any time, have you and Mr. Michael Mascari ever discussed confidential law enforcement information . . . ?" Fermon was asked this question and replied, "No. I haven't seen Mike Mascari, I mean laid eyes on him, [since] I think '96 . . ."

Fermon had just admitted that the last time he associated with Mascari was in 1996, yet one of Outlaw's own investigative reports indicated Mascari admitted receiving a phone call from Fermon since that time. So Fermon was asked, " . . . In 1998, do you remember yourself, Mascari, and Nicholson meeting at Julee's Shooting Star tavern in Westville, Illinois?"

"In 1998, meeting at Julee's Shooting Star? No. No, in 1998, I haven't seen Mascari in—as I told you earlier—seven or eight years, and that puts it back far prior to that," Fermon replied, trying to refute the information DII had overheard during the phone conversation between Snook and Mascari.

But Fermon had admitted he knew these men were felons prior to 1998, and socializing with those felons after their convictions was a serious policy violation.

The two DII studs then turned their attention to two others associated with the drug ring—Steven Snook and Bradley Nicholson. Outlaw asked Fermon,

"Uh, do you know or have you ever heard of a person by the name of Bradley Nicholson?"

"Yes . . . Yeah, I have no relationship or association with him," Fermon replied, explaining they had lived in the same neighborhood. Fermon continued, " . . . and then later, and I don't particularly know what year, but we were involved in—when I was the director of [VMEG] . . . we were involved in the arrest of some folks there in the neighborhood. And I think Bradley was one of them that we arrested at that point."

Fermon was in charge of VMEG when they arrested Nicholson in 1996, so DII brought up the real estate transactions provided by Snook between Fermon and Bradley Nicholson in 1999—three years after Fermon's unit arrested Nicholson. Fermon defended himself:

> My dad put the piece of property in my name. . . . Dad sold that piece of property to Bradley Nicholson. I didn't . . . but, dad—at one point in time—apparently Bradley Nicholson came and knocked on my dad's door and said, "Hey, I'd like to buy that lot you have and put a trailer on it," and my dad sold it to him. I wasn't involved in the transaction . . . I actually think dad sold him two lots.

But Outlaw replied:

> . . . your ownership of the property, according to Vermilion County records, it shows that . . . in September of 1999, the property was quick (sic) claimed from you to your father—and in that same day, your father sold it to Mr. Nicholson, and that transaction, that three way transaction, occurred in the same day. . . . It would seem to be that the transaction occurred in the same room, same place with all three individuals . . .

"I wasn't there, I wasn't any part of it . . . this is not my signature on the quick (sic) claim," Fermon responded. "That's my [dad who] signed my name."

Fermon's attorney broke in and interjected, "By that time, did you know that your dad was having a transaction with Bradley Nicholson?"

Fermon replied:

> . . . I knew—what dad said is he was going to sell the property to him. That's all I really knew about him, and on September 10th of '99 . . . I was in either two places. I was either in Ontario, Canada

on a fly-in fishing trip or . . . I was either there or at the state police academy taking a test. But . . . that's not my signature . . .

Fermon admitted knowing his dad was conducting a business transaction with a felon—one he had arrested three years prior, and Outlaw had acknowledged the transfer of the deeds from Steve Fermon to his father to Bradley Nicholson all took place on the same day and within an hour's time.

Maybe Steve Fermon was in Ontario, Canada, or Springfield, Illinois, that day like he said. It was something that could have been checked, but wasn't. Maybe his dad did sign his name. DII could have easily done a simple handwriting analysis to prove Fermon's story, but they didn't.

Freddie Outlaw continued the interview and told Fermon the properties had ultimately wound up in the hands of Steve Snook. According to Vermilion County records, after the land was sold to Nicholson, he quit claimed it to Steven Snook who was now in Florida serving a 20-year sentence for narcotics trafficking. Snook had alleged he acquired the land from Bradley Nicholson for nine ounces of cocaine.

Fermon was adamant and replied, " . . . that has nothing—absolutely—positively nothing to do with me. I wasn't aware of any real estate transaction between Bradley Nicholson and Steven Snook. They didn't consult me. I didn't know about it."

As the interview ended, Fermon was asked by Outlaw, "We just need to ask you . . . in your own opinion, why do you think someone would come to us with these allegations against you?" And Fermon replied:

> Why would I—well, let's just be specific, for the record. . . . Lieutenant Mike Callahan was the complainant. On June 13 of 2003, both Lieutenant Callahan and I were reassigned, based upon some of these bullshit allegations that Callahan came forward with. . . . Since that time, Lieutenant Callahan has also filed a civil rights violation suit against myself. . . . I learned that this DII case was going on when Callahan filed his suit.

With this statement, Fermon was also admitting someone had leaked Snook's DII allegations to him. By this time, I knew someone had leaked my DII allegations to Fermon, and now it had happened once again.

The Snook DII investigation was opened in July of 2003, and I wouldn't file my lawsuit until September of 2003; Fermon was not officially told he was being investigated until January 20, 2004. Yet, here he was, in his DII interview, admitting he knew about the investigation regarding Snook's claims as far back as September 2003 when I filed my lawsuit—almost four months before he was officially notified. This was the second time someone leaked confidential DII information to Steve Fermon.

Christoff had also said others were willing to corroborate Snook's allegations to DII. They offered to wear body wires and conduct recorded phone calls, but those witnesses were ignored by Freddie Outlaw. Outlaw told Christoff he was forbidden from utilizing these witnesses, or conducting any recorded overhears. Angrily, Christoff accused DII of covering up the investigation, and according to Christoff, Outlaw replied, "I have no choice. I have to follow orders."

On February 9, 2004, the case against Fermon regarding Snook's allegations was officially closed. A March 2, 2004, letter from Deputy Director Harold E. Nelson to Steve Fermon read in part:

> The above referenced personnel complaint investigation concerning an allegation of official misconduct has been completed. The investigation has determined the allegations were unfounded. The reputation of the Illinois State Police is that of a Department with high integrity. This reputation is based on the Department's commitment to resolve every allegation made against officers and to treat everyone fairly. . . .

But Colonel Skip Nelson's testimony regarding the Snook investigation certainly didn't reflect much of a department with high integrity. Nelson hypocritically testified that when allegations are made against state personnel, "I think it's laid out specifically that we shall and must investigate all allegations, and that's what we attempt to do."

So why had they ignored my allegations?

The hypocrisy continued when Nelson testified their strategy was:

> . . . to get Mr. Snook to engage Mr. Mascari in conversation where that we could discern that in fact, at some point in time, that Mascari had said what was alleged to have been said by him, that he knew Captain Fermon and that Captain Fermon had passed information on to him . . . We wanted to corroborate that.

Nelson continued that the plan was to record the conversation, "By means of an overhear," and " . . . eventually they were successful in getting in contact with Mr. Mascari and having a conversation with him."

"And was that conversation tape recorded?" John Baker asked.

"Yes, sir, I believe it was," Nelson lied.

When Baker asked where the transcriptions of the recorded call were, Nelson admitted he couldn't find them anywhere in the Snook file. There was a good reason for that, because Outlaw had only listened in on the phone conversation. John Baker continued and let Nelson dig himself deeper in deceit about Outlaw's investigative techniques.

"Are there ever times where DII does overhears and just listens in, doesn't tape record?" John asked.

"Not to my knowledge," Nelson replied, discounting Outlaw's investigative tactics.

"Now, I spoke with Mark Christoff, and Mark Christoff told me that he talked to Mr. Outlaw and Mr. Outlaw told him that this was not taped and he was not allowed to tape the overhear. Now, my question for you is, are you aware of any orders going to Mr. Outlaw telling him, don't tape this overhear?" John Baker asked. And Nelson replied, "No. . . . I've never given that order."

Maybe Nelson hadn't, but obviously someone gave Outlaw the order because no overhear was ever recorded.

Nelson was also asked what limits were put on an investigator in a DII investigation, and he testified, " . . . it's *usually open* for them to do a full and complete investigation." But it was obvious that in this investigation, that wasn't the case. And that was according to Outlaw, himself.

During the end of Nelson's testimony, he was asked, " . . . the allegations against Mr. Fermon were that he was associating with known criminals," and Nelson admitted, "Yes, sir."

So Baker asked if that was an ISP policy violation, and Nelson admitted, "Yes, it is." And then explained why, "Well, it could compromise the integrity of the department, the reputation of the department, of the officer himself."

It would also hurt the department's reputation and image if Snook's allegations were true, especially with my civil lawsuit pending against the ISP. So the last question my attorney asked Skip Nelson was more of a point than a question: "A lot of allegations over the years with Mr. Fermon being associated with felons." Col. Nelson didn't even reply; he just nodded his head up and down. Still, I couldn't help but wonder just who kept protecting Fermon . . . and why?

The current governor, Rod Blagojevich, had campaigned on a platform that he was going to clean up corruption in Illinois and bring ethics and reform back into state government. It would end up just another false political promise, but after George Ryan's administration, no one, including myself, figured anything could ever get worse.

In late 2003, John Baker received a phone call from the new governor's office requesting to meet with me, and my hopes soared. The phone call was from Thomas Londrigan, the head legal counsel for Governor Blagojevich. He told John the governor was considering clemency for Steidl and Whitlock and they would like to meet with me.

Not long after John called, Carper called confirming the meeting with Londrigan, which was arranged for that afternoon in Springfield. This was exciting, and if the Governor's Office wanted to listen to me, I was ready to talk.

It was three days before Christmas, and when I walked into the expansive but almost empty Capitol Building, a secretary said I was expected, and Mr. Londrigan would be with me shortly. Thomas Londrigan walked out after a short wait and introduced himself. He was a polished looking man exuding the aura and arrogance one would expect from a man who represents a governor, and he was all business leading me to a side room off the governor's palatial office. As I sat down across from Londrigan, I tried reading his body language, after all, my lawsuit had caused quite a stir in the state.

I thought I was there to meet on the issue of clemency for Steidl and Whitlock, but I was wrong. I handed Londrigan copies of all the Rhoads documents I brought with me.

"What's all this?" he asked. When I told him it was most of the paperwork I had accumulated over the years on the Rhoads case, he became upset: "Doug Brown told me he had given me all the paperwork! Why didn't he give me any of this? All I got from him was an old case file!"

I couldn't answer that question, but Londrigan took the paperwork.

"The Inspector General wanted to sit in on this meeting with us, but I wanted to meet with you alone," he said. It became obvious this wasn't going to be a meeting about any clemency issues.

Londrigan's focus turned to my lawsuit and the state police, and he wanted to know why I had taken so long to come forward. I understood the reason for his question and explained that George Ryan was the governor at the time and obviously the ISP command was protecting him like they had in the License for Bribes scandal. Coming forward would have been fruitless and detrimental.

"I would have gotten nowhere and who knows what would have happened to me," I explained. I rationalized that George Ryan's indictment for corruption was proof enough to back up my fears and concerns. I told Londrigan that I finally came forward because we had a new governor—his boss—who preached ethics reform and who said he wouldn't tolerate corruption. Therefore, when I went to DII, I figured they would be forced to do the right thing now, and I would be safe.

"I guess I was wrong, because look what happened to me," I sarcastically added. Tom Londrigan winced at my straightforwardness.

"Just so you know, we don't trust your DII either, and we're well aware of a lot of ethical issues at the top of the ISP command," he replied.

Londrigan said he wanted me to meet with him and the Inspector General later that week, but I was leaving on vacation the next day, so I told him the meeting would have to wait until I got back. He seemed disappointed when I refused to cancel my vacation plans, but assured me we would meet after I got back from vacation.

Londrigan continued his questioning and asked if I was talking to the U.S. Attorney or the FBI in the Northern District. I wondered why he was so concerned about me talking to the FBI or U.S. Attorney's Office, when he added, "Just so you're aware, there's a criminal case on Diane Carper and Steve Fermon."

With that, I speculated that maybe this governor was actually living up to his promise and was working with the U.S. Attorney's Office and fighting the corruption so entrenched in Illinois politics. And when I left the Governor's Office that day, a glimmer of hope had returned once again.

Unfortunately, like George Ryan's administration, this governor's was no different, and it was a good thing I didn't cancel my vacation plans because Londrigan never contacted me again. Ironically, the new governor, Rod Blagojevich, and his administration ended up being criminally investigated over the next several years by the same U.S. Attorney and FBI office that indicted and convicted George Ryan. The very same U.S. Attorney that Blagojevich's office seemed so concerned I may be talking to.

In the next few years, nothing changed in the state police and a news editorial from the Champaign *News-Gazette* reflected the political corruption that continued to influence the politically compromised ISP command and its bosses:

> This would not be a matter of great public interest if state police commanders, particularly state police director Larry Trent, inspired confidence that they are trying to do the right thing in this matter. Unfortunately, the Illinois State Police, at least under former Gov. George Ryan and current Gov. Rod Blagojevich, is operating under a huge cloud. It has been and continues to be susceptible to political influence.

It was no secret that the politically compromised ISP command had protected former governor George Ryan. And many of the ISP command, both current and past, had very powerful political ties to the politicians and the power brokers who really ran the State of Illinois behind the scenes.

John Kass of the *Chicago Tribune* referred to the power brokers as the "Combine." The Combine is defined as " . . . the corrupt, bipartisan system by which Illinois Democrats and Republicans divvy up the state at taxpayers' expense."

Springfield multi-millionaire William Cellini was one of the power brokers identified by Kass. According to his *Chicago Tribune* column, "Cellini has spent four decades as Illinois' ultimate insider, cozying up to Republicans and Democrats alike as he wielded power and influence while trying to stay out of the spotlight." John Kass's column depicted Cellini's role, "as the boss hog of the Republican half of the bipartisan Illinois Combine that runs the state . . . " His article also acknowledged that Cellini ". . . made a fortune worth at least $100 million from his political connections in gaming, real estate, asphalt pouring," and "Cellini has always been the guy behind the guy." Kass continued that, "The suits making speeches on TV aren't real politics. They're just the suits making the speeches. It is the men on the inside who matter, flying below the radar to swoop down to the public trough and feed without much notice. Men like Bill Cellini."

Former U.S. Senator Peter Fitzgerald reflected on Cellini's power, "His clout cannot be understood. He is a behind-the-scenes figure who always ends up cultivating whoever the governor is. . . . Governors come and go, but Cellini has always been there raking in the dough."

William Cellini's name was already familiar to me and everyone else in the ISP, and we all knew about his clout with the state police command. He had made a fortune renting buildings and office space to a lot of state agencies, including the state police. When it came to the state police, Cellini's influence went deeper, and it was no secret that several of his family members and associates, current and past, were placed in powerful positions within the state police, including the current Director of the Illinois State Police.

One of Cellini's many enterprises was Argosy Gaming Company, which started the first riverboat gambling casino in Illinois and continued to grow into four other states. Illinois State Police Director Larry Trent was the former vice president of security and risk management for Cellini's gambling casinos. Trent also brought along with him Keith Jensen and appointed him as the head of the ISP Legal Division. One of Jensen's law firm partners was also a major stockholder in Cellini's casinos. And now with Trent as the ISP director, under Governor Rod Blagojevich, the state police conveniently took over control of the riverboat casinos from the Illinois Department of Revenue.

There were several others in the ISP related to Cellini, and all sat in influential positions. One was even the former deputy director, who Fermon's brother-in-law, Jack Picco-Fyans, said used *their* connections, both political and otherwise, to attain his rise to power in the state police.

I knew master sergeants who claimed they had seen Fermon hobnobbing and having breakfast with William Cellini in Springfield, and there was information from the feds given to me that Cellini, himself, had gone to Governor Blagojevich to protect Steve Fermon against my allegations. So was Cellini Fermon's clout?

No one ever understood Fermon's meteoric rise in power within the ISP, nor how he could skate on so many DII and EEO allegations, but he had, and it seemed the ISP command was going out of their way to protect him.

I could only speculate if it was political influence like this that was protecting Fermon. And I didn't know it at the time, but five years later, in 2008, the *Chicago Tribune* front page would declare, STATE'S ULTIMATE INSIDER INDICTED: " . . . the spotlight found Bill Cellini on Thursday when a federal grand jury indicted the millionaire Springfield businessman and pulled him into the center of the ongoing probe of corruption in the administration of Gov. Rod Blagojevich."

The indictment against Cellini alleged that, along with Stuart Levine, Antoin "Tony" Rezko, Chris Kelly and Governor Rod Blagojevich, he was involved in a conspiracy and extortion scheme to generate "millions of dollars in kickbacks and campaign donations from firms seeking state business."

Ironically, former Governor Jim Thompson's law firm would defend William Cellini; the same law firm who defended convicted and former Governor George Ryan, and Governor Rod Blagojevich on his civil and criminal problems. Shortly after the indictment, Cellini's attorney issued a statement that their client "is completely innocent of these charges, and he will fight this case because he has done absolutely nothing wrong."

One of the associates, Antoin "Tony" Rezko, a Chicago millionaire whose wealth was fueled in large part by "the pizza pie," and a close Blagojevich advisor and fund-raiser, was eventually convicted federally on 16 of 24 counts for fraud. Stuart Levine, another associate also caught in the pay-to-play politics of Illinois government, would cooperate with the federal government and agreed to become a key witness against Rezko and others to come. Now the feds had their sights set on power broker William Cellini and Governor Rod "the unreformer" Blagojevich, a governor who was by now showing his true colors to the people of Illinois. As *Chicago Magazine*'s David Bernstein pointed out in his article "Mr. Un-Popularity," "Blagojevich is more unpopular than the widely unpopular Republican President, George W. Bush" and "arguably the most unpopular governor in the country."

Bill Cellini's guilt or innocence was still yet to be determined, but I couldn't help but reflect back to something Eric Zorn wrote in his column when Randy Steidl was finally freed, "Some say justice delayed is justice denied. But this week, it simply looks like justice."

CHAPTER 22

TRIAL BY JURY

———————◼———————

Presiding over my civil rights trial was Federal District Judge Harold Baker. The Illinois Attorney General's Office represented the ISP commanders named in my lawsuit. Approximately one month before trial, Lisa Madigan's office filed a motion to dismiss my lawsuit. Madigan's office claimed my speech was not constitutionally protected because it didn't touch on a matter of public concern, and an EEO investigation compelled "Callahan's reassignment."

Judge Baker rejected their motion in a very thorough and detailed 12-page response, stating that, "Callahan spoke out on two distinct but related issues." The first issue addressed my allegations that the ISP command impeded the reinvestigation of the Rhoads case because it was too politically sensitive, and Judge Baker wrote, "The wrongful conviction of two men is certainly a matter of public concern—especially when the real murderer might escape prosecution."

The second issue raised was my DII complaint about Fermon, and the judge addressed this, too: "Callahan, Dixon and the FBI agent believed that Fermon was compromising a federal investigation. Fermon admitted patronizing a restaurant central to the investigation, after which valuable sources of information 'dried up.'" Judge Baker also acknowledged that, "The FBI agent encouraged Callahan to take the matter to DII. Callahan's report of conduct undermining a federal criminal investigation is undoubtedly a matter of public concern."

Judge Baker concluded, "Callahan spoke out on a matter of public concern."

Two innocent men were in prison and that wasn't a matter of public concern to the State of Illinois? Actually this case had been just the opposite—the Rhoads case was a matter of concern to cover up by the state.

Judge Baker also rejected the feeble attempt to rationalize my re-assignment as a workplace problem when he pointed out that when Bond conducted her interviews in April she didn't even interview the complainant Ruby, and when she met with ISP command, she told them "the Zone 5 investigation . . . had not revealed anything urgent . . . and . . . cautioned them that they could not move any individuals based solely on her information because her report was incomplete."

Judge Baker rationalized that Bond didn't document her interviews until after I filed my lawsuit, and "several individuals who have seen her written accounts of their interviews describe them as inaccurate and incomplete."

The judge finished his assessment that, "Written as it was, six months after the interviews and four months after Fermon and Callahan were transferred, a jury might put little faith in the scant negative information about Callahan contained in Bond's written report. In fact, a reasonable jury might view the report as an after-the-fact attempt to cast a legitimate cloak over a retaliatory reassignment."

Judge Baker concluded that my transfer to patrol wasn't the way things are usually handled at ISP by stating, "Callahan was a seasoned officer whose investigative skills were highly regarded," and that I was transferred to patrol before the old lieutenant even retired, and another lieutenant had already been named as my replacement. Judge Baker also acknowledged that, "Carper had asked Strohl if Callahan might be interested in a patrol position and Strohl informed her that Callahan would not be."

The judge also pointed out the DII leak to Fermon was "another departure from the usual procedure that such reports be kept confidential." So Judge Baker concluded, "The suspicious circumstances surrounding Callahan's transfer, the peculiar disclosure of Callahan's DII complaint to people in Fermon's chain of command, and the timing of the events could lead a reasonable jury to conclude that Callahan's speech was a substantial or motivating factor for the reassignment." Judge Baker denied the State's motion in its entirety.

As the trial neared, the media attention grew, and Eric Zorn of the *Chicago Tribune* noted, "It would be nice to say an allegation from respected law enforcement professionals is unprecedented in the annals of Illinois justice. But it's not. Make no mistake. State Police officials are the subject of very serious allegations of misconduct, and the Attorney General's Office is representing the state police against the man leveling those allegations."

With one month before trial, the State attempted another stall tactic, and Lisa Madigan suddenly wanted an investigation by the Illinois Inspector General regarding my claims the Rhoads investigation was deliberately sandbagged because it was too politically sensitive. How ironic. Now the Attorney General, two years later, was finally calling for an investigation on the ISP, and even more ironic, despite Madigan's official request, the Inspector General never bothered to initiate an investigation. This stall tactic gave Madigan the excuse to hire high profile and expensive attorneys from prestigious Chicago law firms to represent the ISP defendants. Judge Baker saw through Madigan's hypocrisy and ruled that it was a little late in the game for Madigan to just now be concerned about misconduct I had reported to her office two years earlier in 2003.

On March 18, 2005, after 25 years in the Illinois State Police, I retired. No teletypes went out acknowledging my retirement, no goodbye send-offs. I just went to the district and quietly turned in my equipment. I shook hands with the guys who were in post that day and simply said goodbye. That was it. That was how my 25 years of dedicated service to the State of Illinois ended, but I was ready to go. I had lost all respect for my job and for the leadership of the Illinois State Police. I was ashamed of what the ISP leadership bragged we were and what we had really become, and I couldn't live with those lies anymore. The political hacks had burned a lot of us out; and I had heard several others agree that, "This sure isn't the same department I signed up with."

The state police command was more devious than I thought, and three days before the start of the trial a distraught Edie Casella called me. Edie was in tears. She is a sensitive person and has a tremendous amount of pride, and for the last few years, her pride took a pounding from the department. She wasn't politically correct enough for them, and now she was on the phone in tears after taking another beating.

Edie said ISP legal counsel Keith Jensen ordered her to a meeting earlier that afternoon, where she was confronted by Jensen, Director Larry Trent and one of the newly appointed defense attorneys, Michael Lied. Edie said Lied, supported by Trent and Jensen, threatened to drag her name through the mud by bringing up her one and only DII case.

Jensen told Edie that if she testified that Carper said the Rhoads case was too politically sensitive, then she should have come forward with the misconduct earlier, and Jensen threatened Edie with another DII case for failure to report Carper's criminal conduct. What a bunch of hypocrites.

I had told the department about Carper's misconduct two years earlier in 2003, and they ignored it. I also identified Casella, Strohl and Dixon as witnesses, and not one of them was ever interviewed. Now, suddenly two years later and just days before my trial, it was deemed serious misconduct that Casella did not report it, or was this just plain intimidation of a witness? I talked with Edie a long time that night and eventually she calmed down, but I worried if they had gotten to her.

The first day of the trial was imposing, but there was no looking back now. I had a lot riding at stake—my family's welfare, my reputation and the truth that needed to be told. I felt reassured as I walked through security and got words of encouragement from the U.S. Marshals, some of them retired ISP. It was up to a jury now, and during jury selection, my confidence grew as one of the potential jurors said he had read about my case and couldn't be objective. He was excused by the judge, and as he was leaving the courtroom, exclaimed, "I'm all for you Callahan! Go get 'em!"

I was sitting there in the vast courtroom and there was the mighty State and all its $200-an-hour attorneys seated in the center of the courtroom. Like four pristine peacocks they sat there, and behind them in the gallery sat two of Madigan's Assistant Attorney Generals. The state also had several paralegals at their disposal, and there was Keith Jensen and an ISP intelligence analyst sitting there with their laptops. Sitting directly behind the pristine peacocks were Colonel Charles Brueggemann, looking like the fake politician he was, the arrogant Captain Steve Fermon and what appeared to be a heavily medicated Lt. Col. Diane Carper.

The four high-priced legal beagles for the State were Joseph Gagliardo and Lawrence Weiner, representing Captain Fermon, Michael Lied, the man who had tried to bully Edie, representing Carper, and Iain Johnston, representing Brueggemann. Why Fermon got two attorneys was beyond me.

Then there was my legal team—John Baker and me—sitting off at a side table.

John's plan was to call John Strohl to the stand first, and then Edie Casella. They were both sitting in a private room waiting to testify when Keith Jensen, still up to his sleazy attempts to intimidate witnesses, came in and once again threatened DII charges against them if they testified that Carper had said the Rhoads case was too politically sensitive. His sleazy attempts didn't work.

John Strohl was the first to testify, and despite nothing to gain but future ostracism from the ISP command, and despite the threat of trumped up DII charges against him, Strohl took the stand and told the truth. He told the jury how shocked he was when Diane Carper, in May of 2000, issued the orders we could not touch the Rhoads case because it was too politically sensitive. Jim Dey of the Champaign *News-Gazette* depicted Strohl's testimony in his column:

"Well, they were in prison and maybe they were wrongfully convicted. I mean, that's not something we're supposed to be doing in this country," Illinois State Police Capt. John Strohl, explaining . . . why he supported reopening an investigation into the convictions of Randy Steidl and Herbert Whitlock for the 1986 Edgar County murders of Dyke and Karen Rhoads. Capt. Strohl, a commander of [the] local state police district, got it right. But if allegations in a lawsuit filed at the U.S. Courthouse in Urbana are correct, people at the highest echelons of the Illinois State Police didn't share that view and worked actively to block a reinvestigation of the Rhoads murders out of concern for political fallout.

Major Edie Casella was the second witness called to the stand. Edie told me later how nervous she was, and how Jensen intercepted her just outside the courtroom. She said as he opened the courtroom door for her, he leaned over and whispered in her ear that she was a "broken woman," and they knew she was paying for my legal fees. Then he asked her why she was doing this "to poor Chuck." Jensen's sleazy innuendos backfired, and Edie said she became so infuriated she forgot all about her nervousness. Edie Casella testified for almost two days, and she too testified about the shock of Carper repeatedly shutting us down in the two separate attempts to reinvestigate the Rhoads case. It was when Edie read the last line of the Rhoads Homicide Assessment that she got the biggest reaction from the jury: "It is safe to assume if the events occurred in the exact manner as prescribed by all the witnesses and at the approximate times, it would have been almost impossible for Steidl and Whitlock to have committed these murders."

I saw the question cross their faces: if this were true, why had the ISP command refused to reinvestigate the case and leave two innocent men in prison?

Greg Dixon was equally as strong on the stand as he told the courtroom how Carper deemed the Rhoads case too politically sensitive and "she said it a couple of times that it came from above her." Greg also testified that Fermon didn't support reinvestigating the Rhoads case and, " . . . indicated he wasn't behind that and we didn't have the resources," Dixon recalled.

Hal Dardick's *Chicago Tribune* article also summarized Greg's testimony about the concerns about Fermon's inappropriate conduct:

An Illinois State Police captain ate two years ago at a pizza parlor owned by a convicted felon with alleged mob ties, according to court testimony Wednesday. Within months of that meal, an investigation by more than a dozen state and federal agencies into central Illinois . . . collapsed, Sgt. Greg Dixon testified. "Law enforcement officers are not supposed to patronize a business owned by a known felon," Dixon said. " . . . I thought DII should at least look at it, to at least clear Capt. Fermon," Dixon said. "It looked pretty bad from my point of view."

In the years to come, these three officers who stood up and told the truth in my civil trial were ostracized by the upper command of the Illinois State Police. You would think that a department that proclaimed "Integrity, Service and Pride" would have acknowledged them as heroes for speaking the truth and protecting the good name of the Illinois State Police. John Baker poignantly pointed this out to the jury:

> It's your job to access the credibility of witnesses in this case. . . . The people we called to testify, did any of them look like they were happy to be here? . . . These people have to work for the Illinois State Police. They don't want to be here. This is the last place in the world they want to be. . . . Did you see Greg Dixon's face as he answered his last question? He didn't look happy. He wasn't happy about the things—the problems, concerns, that he had. He has to work with these people. These people are still his bosses. He has absolutely nothing to gain from this lawsuit. Nothing. Other than the fact that he has to face these people every day. Same with Edie Casella. What is Edie Casella doing? What does she get out of this? Nothing. She doesn't get anything. Not one thing. She has to work in Springfield on the same floor with these people.

John Baker changed direction in the trial, and it was the mighty command of the ISP that was called up, one by one. Abraham Lincoln once said, "Tis better to be silent and be thought a fool, than to speak and remove all doubt." The defense attorneys should have heeded Honest Abe's advice when it came to the testimony of the ISP's elite command.

Eight colonels, two captains, a retired master sergeant and Suzanne Bond were called to testify on the State's behalf, and the jury watched as, one by one, each of those high ranking colonels lied or got caught contradicting their deposition testimony. Some just made plain fools of themselves. When the trial was over, many of the jurors told us how ashamed they were of all the ISP colonels. They had lied, they said, and they expected much better from the leadership of the state police.

Director Larry Trent, the self-proclaimed top cop in Illinois, was one of the first to testify. John Baker questioned Trent about my removal from investigations and he impeached his testimony almost immediately.

When I was removed from investigations, Trent said he had only talked with Brueggemann about my removal. Now here in the trial, Trent was obviously trying to deflect any guilt from Brueggemann so he testified that he had also talked with Col. Nelson who had conducted an investigation in the zone. Trent was caught in two lies.

Baker turned to Trent's prior deposition to catch him in the first lie. Reading from the deposition, John asked, " . . . it's my understanding that your basis for approving the move was strictly based upon the conversation that you had with Mr. Brueggemann. Correct? Now would you agree that that was the question that I asked you?" Trent replied, "Yes, I would," and he was forced to admit he had only talked to Brueggemann.

Baker turned back to Trent's trial testimony.

"But you indicated a second ago that you spoke to Mr. Nelson about that issue?" asked Baker. Trent replied, "I believe I did."

So Baker once again turned to Trent's deposition: "The next question I asked: 'Did you speak to Skip Nelson about it?' Is that the question I asked . . . And what was your answer?" And Trent answered, "No." The attorneys for the State tried to interject, "Objection, Your Honor. This is not proper impeachment." But the judge overruled, and it was too late. The damage was done. The self-proclaimed top cop of the State of Illinois was impeached under oath.

My attorney then turned Trent's attention to his second lie. Trent testified that Nelson had conducted an investigation in the zone. So Baker brought up the allegations I made to DII and asked, "The allegations that Mr. Nelson gave to you . . . they were fairly significant or serious violations. Is that correct?" And Trent replied, "Allegations, yes," but he admitted DII was mandated to conduct an investigation and he had expected the allegations to be fully investigated. Trent was then forced to testify DII told him an investigation was conducted and completed, and he acknowledged DII had lied and never opened an investigation like he was told. In fact, Trent admitted he was never even told about my criminal allegations against Diane Carper. In a scathing editorial by Gary Henry of the *Paris Beacon-News*, Trent's hypocrisy was discussed:

> Instead of adopting a defiant attitude of "we're right and they're wrong," Trent should have called onto the carpet ISP Deputy Director Harold "Skip" Nelson because internal investigations dismissed

Callahan's allegations without doing the required investigation. Instead of circling the wagons, Trent should recognize that his ultimate bosses, the citizens of Illinois via the jury, have delivered a directive to dismantle the bureaucratic machinations of a command structure that apparently valued political damage control more than a need to look at a flawed investigation. . . . Trent's apparent refusal to learn from the Callahan suit calls into question his ability to reform the Illinois State Police.

This was only the beginning, and the other high and mighty of the ISP were also lining up to testify, and if anything, their testimony was worse.

First Deputy Director Doug Brown testified he agreed my allegations to DII were serious, and he was also lied to that a DII investigation was conducted and completed on Fermon. Like Trent, he admitted he was never even made aware I had made criminal allegations against Carper. It was becoming obvious to the jury that DII had obviously lied and been a part of covering up Carper and Fermon's misconduct.

Lt. Col. Michael Snyders appeared before the jury resplendent in his ISP uniform, and after being sworn in, turned to the jury, stood at attention, thrust his chest out with his hands firmly fixed by his side and proclaimed to judge, jury and audience how proud he was to wear the uniform of the Illinois State Police. After watching his testimony, someone should have told him it's not the uniform that makes the cop but the integrity of the person wearing it, and like others, Snyders had trouble with contradicting his prior deposition testimony.

The array of colonels continued. DII Deputy Director Skip Nelson's testimony was filled with so many lies, contradictions, attempted cover-ups and hypocrisy, it was outrageous. Nelson was so bad that the judge interrupted Baker and told him he could treat Nelson as an adverse witness. Nelson was forced to admit to the jury that DII was mandated to investigate all allegations made against ISP officers, and he agreed my allegations were very serious if true. Then moments later, Nelson told the jury my allegations didn't warrant an investigation, admitting the mandated investigation never occurred.

The most buffoonish testimony went to Lt. Col. Rick Karpawicz. In the beginning, Karpawicz strutted into the courtroom looking very professional, and his appearance was both stoic and confident as he seated himself in the witness stand. When he left that day, he was anything but stoic or confident as he practically ran from the courtroom, looking like a whipped dog with his tail between his legs. Gary Henry from the *Paris Beacon-News* agreed:

Karpawicz started as a fairly strong defense witness. . . . According to Karpawicz, Williams and the other FBI officials insisted that Callahan was alone in his concerns and the concerns were little more than suspicious . . . That differs from the testimony of Williams . . . He told the court that he shared Callahan's concerns about Fermon . . .

Under cross examination, Karpawicz stumbled in his testimony, getting caught in one contradiction after another. Shaken, Karpawicz didn't address the court as he once did, and started mumbling, his head hanging down with his eyes focused on the floor directly between his legs. With each new lie, I watched one juror or another roll their eyes or wave their arms in disgust at Karpawicz's shameful testimony. The *Paris Beacon-News* article continued:

A witness and an attorney engaged in a circular dialogue Thursday that always returned to the same unresolved point. Attorney John Baker was attempting to elicit from ISP Lt. Col. Richard Karpawicz why internal investigations did not investigate allegations by now retired ISP Lt. Michale Callahan. . . . Karpawicz was called as a defense witness and he offered a succinct explanation during direct examination about why [DII] did not pursue the Callahan allegations. "There weren't any policy violation," said Karpawicz. Baker latched onto that statement. He wanted to know how DII could decide there were no policy violations when the division did not conduct an investigation.

The *Paris Beacon-News* continued with Fermon's visit to Joe's Pizza:

"I don't know what Captain Fermon knew," said Karpawicz. "Because you didn't interview Captain Fermon?" Baker replied, and Karpawicz replied that was correct. After some prodding, Karpawicz did acknowledge it would violate ISP policy for an officer to visit an establishment knowing it [was] the subject of an investigation. Karpawicz became so flustered at this point, the contradictions began spewing out of his mouth: Baker again raised the issue of Fermon going to a restaurant while knowing it was under surveillance. "There were no policy violations," said Karpawicz. "Didn't you just say if it were true, it would be a policy violation?" retorted Baker. Karpawicz tried to avoid a direct answer by saying he was not aware that Vitale was under a federal investigation. Baker produced the documents Callahan provided to DII outlining how Callahan learned of the investigation and also stating Fermon was apprised of the investigation by a different federal agency. "Is it a policy violation?" asked Baker. "If true, it is poor judgment on Captain Fermon's part," said Karpawicz. "Is it a policy violation?" Baker asked again. "Yes, if it were true," Karpawicz rejoined.

John Baker also asked Karpawicz why DII never investigated the allegations against Carper, and his rationale was just as ludicrous.

"Lt. Callahan didn't spend very much time on the allegation that she had made the comment that the investigation was too politically sensitive and that he was not to look at the Rhoads case," he said.

Yet Karpawicz admitted that Carper's conduct, if true, was both a policy violation and a crime. A potential crime that DII ignored, refused to investigate, and instead lied to cover up. Karpawicz's testimony was so bad that, after the trial, one of the jurors was discussing the deceitfulness of the ISP colonels, and he exclaimed, "And, oh, my God . . . that Col. K!"

John Baker changed tactics when he called Fermon to the stand by limiting his questions only to the discovery documents that related to Fermon's manipulation of the Rhoads case. John's strategy was to wait until the defense called Fermon and then engage the captain in a vigorous cross-examination. His plan backfired, because the defense never put Fermon on the stand.

After the trial, Baker asked Keith Jensen why Fermon didn't testify.

"John, you can take a turd and you can polish that turd all you want, but the problem is, when you get done polishing that turd, you still have a turd," Jensen replied.

I was sure glad Keith Jensen wasn't on my side!

Suzanne Bond was also called to testify, but she was so pathetic, a juror later told us, "She was a joke! We all knew EEO was there to cover up for the bigwigs."

Judge Baker agreed with the jury's assessment stating, "The court's function is not to second-guess what the jury might have thought of the EEO report issued so many months later. It is enough to note that there was evidence to support a good dose of juror skepticism. . . . The jury apparently viewed the EEO report with skepticism . . . In fact, the hostile environment were related to allegations against Fermon, not Callahan. The jury may have concluded that the EEO investigation was commandeered as a way to justify the transfer."

Up to this point, I didn't think the ISP upper command could look any worse. Their testimonies were a mixture of arrogance and pompousness filled with hypocrisy, deceit and untruthfulness. Even my anger started to subside, replaced with a sadness and shame for what they were doing to the name of the Illinois State Police. The worst came when Lt. Col. Carper took the stand.

I can't prove it, but Carper appeared to be on some heavy medication. I watched her sit through the trial with a blank, unknowing look on her face. During others' testimony, I looked at Carper sitting next to Brueggemann, and she wasn't even paying attention, instead, she sat there listlessly doodling on a notepad. If this woman wasn't tranquilized, then I wasn't a very good drug cop. When Brueggemann saw me staring at Carper, he reached over and slapped her notepad and barked, "Cut it out!" Carper sat back in her chair, but 30 seconds later, she picked up her notebook and started doodling again.

And I certainly didn't expect what happened when Carper took the stand. After identifying herself for the court record, she turned to the jury, her eyes wide with a vacant stare, wearing a forced ear-to-ear grin, with her teeth tightly gritted together.

"I absolutely did not say that the Rhoads case was too politically sensitive," Carper said through her clenched teeth, and then she repeated it.

Everyone in the courtroom sat there stunned for a moment, and I don't think anyone in the courtroom had any doubts that Carper was heavily medicated.

John Baker returned a wide-eyed stare at Carper, and then calmly stated, "All right. There has already been a lot of testimony about it. I suppose I should ask you first where you're presently employed."

During testimony, Baker and Carper discussed the allegations I made against her to DII, and after John referenced the timeline document I provided to DII, Carper admitted DII had leaked both my allegations and the timeline to her.

"And in that document, your handwritten notes right underneath the words 'too politically sensitive,' you write, 'Lie.' Correct?" John asked her.

"That is absolutely correct," Carper replied.

Baker questioned if I was lying why didn't she turn me in to DII for the serious policy violation, and Carper only replied, "this was a personal note to myself."

Yet in cross examination, Carper's attorney, Michael Lied, unwittingly assisted in catching his client in a lie about the timeline I provided to DII on May 8, 2003. Lied asked Carper when she first learned I made a complaint against her to DII, and she replied, "Within the last four weeks."

Baker immediately latched onto Carper's lie during cross-examination and asked her, "Colonel, you also indicated that the first time you were ever aware that Callahan had gone to DII [was] the last four weeks," and Carper testified, "That is correct."

Earlier in her testimony Carper had admitted she received the DII timeline where she had written "lie" on it from DII Col. Karpawicz sometime between May 10 through May 19, 2003, or when DII wrote a memo on June 6, 2003, indicating they were not going to open a case on my allegations. Therefore Carper had admitted in her prior testimony she received my allegations against her two years earlier in 2003, but now here she was testifying she just became aware of my DII allegations against her four weeks prior to the trial in 2005.

During her testimony, Diane Carper also continually denied she said the words "too politically sensitive," advising the court, "It upset me that I am being characterized as saying 'too politically sensitive' when I absolutely did not. Those are his recollections. That's his thoughts. And I don't know whether he has convinced himself that I said that or he believes that, but I can't change his mind if those are his thoughts."

"They are also the thoughts of three other people who testified here," Baker responded.

"Well, I did not say 'too politically sensitive,'" Carper retorted.

However Carper did admit to the court, "During May of 2000, there were parameters that were provided to Captain Strohl and Lt. Callahan which originated from Col. Parker," and she testified, "Colonel Parker described it as 'politically sensitive.' I have described it as 'politically sensitive.'"

So Carper was asked what the difference was between a case being too politically sensitive to reinvestigate and a case that was politically sensitive and couldn't be reinvestigated, and she replied, "'Too politically sensitive' implies based around what is being said, that it's too politically sensitive to touch [the] Rhoads/Steidl case. That's not correct. Is it politically sensitive? Why? Because my boss said so."

That was Carper's only rationale, but then she admitted her bosses also wouldn't allow us to reopen the Rhoads case due to the "ground rules" established by Andre Parker.

"Will you tell us to your best recollection what the ground rules were?" Baker asked her.

"My best recollection is that we were not going to immediately reopen the Steidl or the Rhoads case. . . . "

And "immediately" to Carper meant for more than three years.

The local press reported on Carper's testimony:

> "I absolutely did not use the term 'too politically sensitive,'" Lt. Col. Diane Carper . . . said Thursday in U.S. District Court in Urbana. Carper testified . . . that higher command officers felt that the Rhoads

murder case had been decided by juries and appeals court rulings. She said definite ground rules prohibited Callahan and other state police investigators from immediately reopening the Rhoads murder investigation. . . . Carper said she told Callahan, "We will do the right thing."

Another news account described Carper's outlandish testimony:

> Three witnesses in addition to Callahan testified that Col. Carper said the proposed investigation was "too politically sensitive" to pursue. In her defense, Carper said she described it as "politically sensitive" but denied trying to thwart the probe. It's clear, however, that Callahan's probe was derailed. As for Carper's description, what should politics, however it is described, ever have to do with a murder investigation, particularly when two men may be serving life sentences for murders they did not commit? This case reveals every citizen's worst nightmare, an ethically compromised police organization looking the other way instead of doing its duty. Unfortunately, this is not the first time the Illinois State Police have been corrupted by political consideration.

When Chuck Brueggemann took the stand, he displayed the arrogant and pompous demeanor that was his reputation. He looked more like the insincere George W. Bush than he did a colonel in the ISP. After being sworn in, he arrogantly corrected my attorney before the court, by advising his name was pronounced with a short "i" instead of a long "u." His demeanor was immediately checked when the judge also apologized for mispronouncing the colonel's name.

Realizing he misplayed his hand, the politician in Brueggemann immediately surfaced and he flashed a wide fake smile.

"I am referred to many ways, sir," said Brueggemann. "You can call me Chuck. I would prefer that."

"No. I will call you colonel," replied John Baker.

Most of Brueggemann's testimony was an attempt to distance himself from the Rhoads case and deflect any involvement with DII. He added he was careful to stay out of DII matters and not get involved with investigations they conducted. His testimony might have been more convincing if he had not sent Carper to the meeting with the FBI, and Lt. Col. Woods to my DII interview.

Despite telling the jury he stayed out of DII matters, Baker caught Brueggemann in a big lie when he asked, "At some point in time, you somehow learned Mike told DII that Col. Carper had made the statement that the Rhoads homicide was 'too politically sensitive.'"

Brueggemann was caught when he replied, "That is not correct . . . What I learned was the term 'politically sensitive' was attributed to Lt. Col. Carper."

"That wasn't the allegation," Baker retorted. "The allegation was 'too politically sensitive.' You would agree with me, if that were true, it's a fairly serious allegation?"

"It would depend on what the context of the discussion was . . . If, what you're referring is that an investigation would not occur because of somehow it was politically involved, that would be extremely inappropriate. I would agree with what you are saying, yes," Brueggemann responded.

But Brueggemann had told the court he never heard the words "too politically sensitive" attributed to Carper, and he acknowledged it would be "extremely inappropriate" if she had. To catch Brueggemann in his lie, Baker went to Brueggemann's prior deposition testimony and asked, " . . . you responded to me, 'It would only have been in the context of discussing this particular Rhoads case, Mike's concern, and, quite frankly, I didn't give it a whole lot of thought because I would never believe that Colonel Carper would ever say that. Having been involved in this agency for 20 years, I don't believe I have ever known of a case that was too politically sensitive. In particular, a murder, I mean, there is just no way.'"

"So, you had heard the words . . . and not a whole lot of thought was given to it?" Baker questioned Brueggemann's deceitful testimony.

Brueggemann had no choice but to acknowledge his prior deposition testimony under oath.

After the trial was over, John Baker was discussing Brueggemann, Carper and Fermon with one of the Illinois Attorney Generals, Karen McNaught, and she interjected, "Brueggemann was the biggest snake of all of them."

The whole trial was a good cop vs. bad cop scenario, but we didn't have to point that out to the jury. Right before the defense was ready to put on their case, the court recessed. We were sitting in our chambers off the courtroom when Lawrence Weiner knocked on the door and entered. Weiner provided a list of the witnesses the defense planned to call. John immediately noticed that both Fermon and Carper's names were excluded and asked why they were not being called to defend themselves.

"Yeah, after Carper's stellar performance? What? We're going to put her on again," Weiner sarcastically replied.

"What? The State doesn't have enough Prozac?" John asked.

"You got it," Weiner acknowledged with a smirk.

The defense did not call one person from Zone 5 to back up the ISP allegations that I caused problems at the zone. John Baker had already called Russ Perkins and utilized Sue Voges deposition testimony to expose the deceitful EEO investigation. John Baker had skillfully refuted the defense at every phase of the trial.

During closing arguments John's heartfelt closing addressed the court:

> When I stood before you two weeks ago, I told you that this was a case about the search for truth and about the search for justice. Mike Callahan's search for truth and the search for justice on behalf of Dyke and Karen Rhoads. All Mike wanted to do, since . . . April of 2000 is answer some questions. . . . That's it. But at every turn, Mike was not allowed to get those answers. . . . Mike is an investigator. . . . We had everybody from the ISP, from the director down, top brass down. Not one could find anything negative about Michale Callahan. I can tell you, it wasn't for the lack of looking. . . . No one criticized or complained of Mike's job as an investigator. . . . The only people who gained in this are the powers that be because they have sent very clear messages. "If you don't do what we want, if you step out of line, this is what we are going to do to you. This is the power that we have. This is how we are going to control you." They are the only ones who win in that situation. . . . Everyone is a loser. People of the State of Illinois are losers. The only winner in this scenario are the powers that be who can send a message to Mike Callahan and everyone else, "If you go and you make statements that we don't like, this is what is going to happen to you."

His closing continued:

> You have a voice in this case, you have a loud voice. Whatever you do, your voice will carry. It will be heard throughout the State of Illinois. You will send a message to the Illinois State Police and to every other police officer in the State of Illinois. . . . how many times do we hear, have we read in the newspapers about people who are wrongfully convicted being released? How many have been let off in Illinois from death row? . . . And when those mistakes happen, we should want police officers like Michale Callahan who are there, who are willing to stand up and to fight

for those people who have been denied their rights. That's all Michale Callahan was trying to do.

The defense attorneys for Fermon and Brueggemann each took a turn in closing arguments, but their only defense was the fabricated theory this was just a case of "Callahan not liking Fermon." But if that was the case, why had I filed allegations against Carper, too?

It was Carper's attorney who gave the most dumbfounding closing argument. Michael Lied addressed the jury: "The whole issue is about the word 'too.' She was perfectly prepared to say, 'I did say the situation was politically sensitive.' She told you why . . . There is no way around it. It was a politically sensitive situation." Lied continued, addressing the "too politically sensitive" statement:

> Now, I admit there are some other people that do say she did, including Mr. Callahan . . . It may be they misheard and read into this something that they didn't expect and some people heard the word "too." Let's say you think Diane Carper did say "too politically sensitive." Remember, what else? She said this directive came from above her. The directive that the Rhoads case was too politically sensitive came from above her and it came specifically from Colonel Andre Parker . . . Colonel Carper, she is the messenger. It's fundamentally unfair to hold her liable for merely passing an order from her boss.

Then Lied turned his attack on me, "He [Callahan] told his doctor he was counting the days to retirement. He didn't suck it up. He quit. He filed a lawsuit. He wasn't a good soldier."

"Good soldier?" I almost jumped out of my seat and knew exactly how Steidl must have felt when he slugged McFatridge. For twenty-five years I had dedicated myself to being a good cop, and I wasn't the one willing to leave innocent men in prison. That was being a bad soldier?

John Baker vehemently defended my honor, replying to Lied's sleazy attempt at attacking my credibility:

> Mr. Lied came up here and he said to you Michale Callahan wasn't a good soldier. He just didn't accept his transfer from Colonel Carper. He wasn't a good soldier. They don't get it. It's the same thing from the very beginning. How dare he [Callahan], how dare he question them, how dare he question a supervising officer. That's what he did when he went to DII. He questioned supervising officers and they

couldn't stand it, and that's why they moved him. How dare he. He wasn't a good soldier. You want to know what? The Illinois State Police defines what constitutes a good soldier. . . . It's the oath.

And after reading the State Police oath, he passionately exclaimed:

> That is what constitutes a good soldier . . . you determine who was a good soldier. Michale Callahan was a good soldier. He stood up for himself and he stood up for others. He stood up for what was right. He sought out justice. That's what cops are supposed to do and that is what Michale Callahan did!

Michael Lied had also said in his closing remarks, "the directive the Rhoads case was 'too politically sensitive' came from above Carper and it came specifically from Colonel Andre Parker."

John Baker addressed this, too:

> And where is Andre Parker? Andre Parker works for the Illinois State Police. You didn't see him coming in here and testifying wearing his uniform and testifying here before you as to what these parameters were and what his instructions were. Why not? If he gave these instructions to Colonel Carper, why wouldn't he be here? He wasn't here.

There was a reason for that, as over the years, Andre Parker denied to several people he ever prohibited the re-opening of the Rhoads case. In 2007, after Captain John Strohl retired, he gave me an e-mail from Carper after a meeting where Parker denied he prohibited the Rhoads case from being re-opened. It was dated just days after my trial ended, and the e-mail from Carper simply read, "I guess Parker gets the last laugh."

But no matter who issued those terrible orders, if it was your loved one brutally murdered in the middle of the night, were these the actions of a "good soldier"?

When the jury left to deliberate, I was pretty confident they had seen through the State's feeble attempts to cover up the truth. Nearly six hours later we were summoned back to the courtroom for the verdict. As I stood there waiting for the judge to read the verdict, I looked over at my wife, my son and my mother. No matter what the verdict was, standing there looking at my family who had always stood by my side, I knew this whole ordeal had been worth it.

The front page of the *Chicago Tribune* exclaimed: "JURY AGREES TROOPER WAS PUNISHED FOR INVESTIGATION" and the story reflected how the jury of five men and four women who heard nine days of testimony awarded me nearly $700,000 in damages. The jury agreed Captain Steven Fermon and Lt. Col. Diane Carper had violated my First Amendment rights. Brueggemann had skated, but we still won!

I was back in the news again when Hal Dardick's *Chicago Tribune* article headlined, "JUDGE BACKS COP IN MURDER PROBE": "A federal judge Tuesday upheld a jury's finding that a former Illinois State Police lieutenant suffered a retaliatory job transfer for accusing superiors of thwarting a politically sensitive double-murder probe."

Judge Baker's seven-page determination read, in part, "It seems indisputable to the court that Callahan's speech was protected by the First Amendment. The plaintiff offered significant, highly persuasive evidence in his favor. . . . The jury was in the best position to determine the credibility of the witnesses and obviously found the plaintiff's evidence more persuasive."

When Brueggemann's attorney, Iain Johnston, attempted to bill me for his client's deposition, Judge Baker interjected, "A defendant in a civil rights suit can obtain an award of fees only if the suit is adjudged frivolous. Callahan proved a prima facie case against Brueggemann."

Apparently the jury thought so, too. An *Illinois Times* article depicted the polling of the juror's real feelings about Brueggeman after my trial:

> One juror contacted by the *Illinois Times* says that much of the deliberation time was spent trying to find evidence to include Brueggemann, the deputy director, in their verdict. "There was no doubt in our mind that Brueggemann was also guilty. We just didn't have the proof," she says. "He's obviously a diplomat who knows how to cover his ass."

CHAPTER 23

A BLATANT MISCARRIAGE OF JUSTICE

———————————————■———————————————

In a true David vs. Goliath battle, we literally kicked their ass.

After the trial, I went through a feeling of jubilation followed by an incredible sense of relief, but it was also a bittersweet feeling. I didn't want it to be perceived that I was badmouthing the Illinois State Police or the countless men and women who had dedicated their lives to that proud organization. My issues were with those few who had defamed our once proud name. The morale of the department was hitting new lows, first under the George Ryan administration and even more so under the new Rod Blagojevich administration. The men and women of the Illinois State Police were sick and tired of the corruption and the political hacks that were ruining the ISP's reputation. In the days following my trial, there was a lot of media attention.

News columnist Terry Bibo of the *Peoria Journal Star* articulated the concerns of the men and women of the Illinois State Police in an article entitled, "Police Brass Setting Bad Standard," when she wrote:

> From Cairo to Chicago, the higher-ups of the one time first class investigators are leaving a trail that demands an investigation of its own. More than a dozen people, including troopers, contacted me after I wrote a recent column urging Governor Rod Blagojevich to investigate the state police brass. Almost all agreed, then added their own questions for good measure. "I spent 28

plus years with ISP," says a trooper who has retired but still fears retaliation.

The anonymous officer continued, "The current director and governor seem to have taken our reputation down as low as its probably ever been. I'm ashamed of what has been done to all of us, and the organization. The sad part . . . no heads ever seem to roll."

Illinois State Police Director Larry Trent also had no problem being vocal after the trial and attacked the jury's decision as "a blatant miscarriage of justice." Trent told the press, "While the verdict is a disappointment to the Illinois State Police, I am confident that these officers did nothing wrong . . ."

Spoken like the seasoned investigator Trent claimed to be, and so much for his testimony in not "forming any opinions until the facts come in." Because how could Trent know if they did anything wrong or not if the allegations were never investigated in the first place?

An editorial from the *News-Gazette* detailed Trent's hypocrisy:

> Afterwards, Illinois State Police Director Larry Trent said he was "Sick to my stomach" about the jury's finding that two top state officials, Col. Diane Carper and Captain Steve Fermon, had retaliated against Lt. Michale Callahan. All citizens should be sick to their stomach about the jury's verdict, but not for the reasons that disturb Trent. The State Police Director was sickened because he disagreed with the verdict. But what is sickening is what the trial revealed—top officials in a powerful law enforcement agency who are willing to let political considerations dictate whether they investigate a horrible crime.

The day after the jury found Carper and Fermon guilty, Trent also issued a scathing memo to all the ISP command entitled "Leadership." The purpose of the memo was obviously meant to twist the facts of the trial testimony and to discredit me:

> As many of you know, three of our command officers were recently sued for allegedly stopping an investigation because it was politically sensitive, causing the reassignment of an individual from investigations to patrol. According to the plaintiff, the assignment was in retaliation for speaking out about the subject of the investigation. The Illinois State Police, its command and employees, do

A BLATANT MISCARRIAGE OF JUSTICE

not retaliate against individuals for exercising their First Amendment Rights. No retaliation occurred in this case.

What a hypocrite! I was reminded of Kevin Eack's bureaucratic e-mail: "Ensure that at no time . . . the transfer be characterized as disciplinary in nature . . . Rather, it should be . . . characterized as . . . 'operational needs' and the 'best interests of the Department.'" Then Trent's attacks turned on me, skewing the facts regarding testimony:

> The reassigned individual claims he suffered emotional trauma at having to wear the state police uniform that each of us wears so proudly. He believes that investigations are far more "prestigious" than patrol. In fact, courtroom testimony referred to him as being "shackled" when he had to put the uniform on and required him to take anti-depressants. . . . I must share with you my high regard for the Illinois State Police uniform and all that it represents. To hear someone describe how demeaning it was to put on the uniform each day that we hold so dear, deeply disturbs me. I am proud to be an Illinois State Police officer and proud to wear the uniform. I do not feel "shackled" and do not need medication to put it on.

Trent didn't just misinterpret my testimony, he outright lied. During my testimony, I never demeaned the uniform of the Illinois State Police. My case had nothing to do with wearing an Illinois State Police uniform, but it had everything to do with the shame people like Trent were placing on the name of the Illinois State Police. My case was about their betrayal, deceit and arrogant attempts at covering up a terrible scandal. My wife had testified that my being "shackled" was an illustration of my depression at the unfair retaliation I received from the department.

No matter what the reassignment was—patrol, investigations, or whatever—it was never about the assignment, it was about being punished for standing up to the corruption the department was trying to cover up. Larry Trent just didn't get it. My shackles were the politically compromised leaders like him that sullied the ISP uniform. I was livid when I read Trent's propaganda. The last time I read a memo like this was from another Director of the ISP on the Rhoads case: "Please be ensured, the foremost interest in the Illinois State Police in this and any case is to seek the truth and ensure justice is served." As I read Trent's e-mail, I thought the same thing I did about that letter—it wasn't worth the piece of paper it was written on.

322

Trent's propaganda had repercussions when his memo was given to the media. The Associated Press recounted reactions from the governor and other state politicians:

> State Police Director Larry Trent was wrong to send a memo denouncing a jury verdict against his agency and denigrating the whistleblower who sued, Governor Rod Blagejovich said Wednesday. "I don't like it. I think it's inappropriate," Blagojevich said outside the capital. Blagojevich said he had talked to Trent . . . A house committee chairwoman also lectured Trent Wednesday on respect for the legal system and reproached him during an appropriations hearing for getting "pretty personal" in the memo. Trent declined comment after the hearing . . .

The news article continued with Trent getting maligned for his malicious attacks on my character:

> [House] Representative Lovana "Lou" Jones, D/Chicago, Chairwoman of the House Public Safety Appropriations Committee, took Trent to task for that comment. "That was pretty personal, and if you look into it further, it had really nothing to do with the man not wanting to wear a uniform," Jones said after Trent testified on the police agency's proposed budget. "When someone works on the job and they feel like their rights have been violated—you can call them a whistleblower or whatever—they have a right to go to a jury or to a judge."

Trent's memo also attacked the jury's decision in my trial:

> Sadly, the jury misinterpreted the evidence and found in favor of the plaintiff and against two of the three defendants, Captain Steve Fermon and Lt. Col. Diane Carper. ISP personnel and command have not and will never stop or impede an investigation no matter how politically sensitive. . . . I believe the verdict to be a blatant miscarriage of justice that will be overturned upon appeal. . . . Let me make it perfectly clear that I fully support Captain Fermon and Lt. Col. Carper. The Illinois State Police will never abandon those who have been falsely accused.

I was amazed at Trent's hypocrisy. "ISP personnel and command have not and will never stop or impede an investigation no matter how politically sensitive?" What, did Larry Trent miss Carper's testimony? Carper herself testified that both she and Andre Parker deemed the Rhoads case politically sensitive and that certain ground rules prohibited us from immediately re-opening the Rhoads investigation, and there was testimony from five different ISP officers that she prohibited re-opening that investigation for over three years.

Then the Director continued his assessment, "I believe the verdict to be a blatant miscarriage of justice." How ironic. When I was pushing to reopen the Rhoads case and to review the convictions of Randy Steidl and Herb Whitlock, I was repeatedly told, time and time again, by the ISP command that a jury had spoken and found them guilty. It didn't matter that the original juries in the Rhoads murders hadn't heard the truth. It didn't matter that there was misconduct in the original investigation. It didn't matter that evidence favorable to the defendants was withheld in the original trial. All I ever heard from ISP Command was—Steidl and Whitlock were convicted by a jury. Yet here was Larry Trent claiming the jury's decision in my civil trial was "a blatant miscarriage of justice."

Gary Henry of the *Paris Beacon-News* also attacked Trent's hypocrisy in an article entitled, "How ironic! ISP Director's allegations of unfair trial sound familiar":

> It's ironic how events sometimes play out. When a jury found that Illinois State Police Captain Steven Fermon and Lt. Col. Diane Carper violated the First Amendment rights of Lt. Michale Callahan, ISP Dierector Larry Trent insisted that a different verdict would have resulted if jurors heard "suppressed evidence." How ironic! Trent's allegations about suppressed evidence resulting in an unfair trial are exactly what supporters of Gordon "Randy" Steidl and Herbert Whitlock have continually argued since the 1987 trials that convicted the two men of brutally murdering Paris residents Dyke and Karen Rhoads—a case which the Callahan matter was built.

Henry then attacked Trent's "miscarriage of justice":

> The jury believed that Callahan's transfer from investigations to patrol was punishment for wanting to reopen a case that superior officers deemed "too politically sensitive." . . . During the Callahan trial . . . defense attorneys emphasized several times how two different juries weighed the evidence in reaching the guilty verdict

against Steidl and Whitlock and how Callahan should have been satisfied with the work of the original juries and not tried to re-open the case. The attorneys claimed the appellate courts, not an ISP investigation, was the proper forum to review the homicides. Again, how ironic that despite the arguments of lawyers hired by the state to defend Fermon and Carper, Trent blasts the jury's decision as "a blatant miscarriage of justice."

Being the seasoned investigator he claimed, I would think that Trent would have recognized the need to at least now investigate the allegations against Fermon and Carper, but the ISP still refused to look into the matter. Professor Larry Golden of the University of Illinois at Springfield wrote:

This brings up the actions of ISP Director Larry Trent. Given the court decision [in Callahan's case], Illinois citizens would hope that the director would express some concern that an injustice was done to Callahan and that disciplinary action would be taken against any officers under his command to engage in such behavior. Instead, Trent chose to condemn the verdict and attack Callahan . . . Illinois has enough evidence and knowledge with innocence cases to know that something must be done to hold these prosecutors and law enforcement officials accountable.

Trent's callous disregard continued to get political backlash. Cindi Canary, Director of the Illinois Campaign for Political Reform, criticized Trent's position in an Associated Press story. She questioned if the Director of the Illinois State Police understood the importance of encouraging whistleblowers to point out wrongdoing. "You have to create room for people to speak up when they see injustices or wrongdoing. And you can't punish the messenger," said Canary.

The Chicago *Sun-Times* reported on another lawmaker who questioned Trent's character: "One lawmaker scolded Trent's memo, saying even if he disagreed with the verdict, he should respect the jury process. 'I happen to think jury trials and jury decisions are kind of sacred,' said Ron Stephens." Added Stephens, "I would hope the department would say there must have been a problem here and take another look at it, rather than just criticize the jury and the lieutenant."

Lisa Madigan, the Illinois Attorney General, had already publicly requested the Illinois Inspector General to investigate my allegations. With the political backlash that my civil suit caused, Governor Rod Blagojevich also requested an investigation into my allegations suggesting political interests stalled exploration into a double murder case. Blagojevich also requested both the Illinois Inspector General and the U.S. Attorney's Office to investigate the matter.

"The lieutenant's allegations concern us," spokeswoman for Blagojevich Abby Ottendorf told the press. "We're eager to work with outside investigators to see if there was an effort to obstruct justice by the previous administration."

Despite the governor and Attorney General publicly calling for an investigation, the Inspector General never conducted any investigation. After all, this is Illinois.

Other ironies abounded—Captain Fermon became Commander over Medicaid Fraud, the same unit that made a case against his brother-in-law for bilking the State Public Aid system out of $100,000. Carper also continued as the Lieutenant Colonel over Zone 5 and the renewed Rhoads investigation. It boggled my mind that someone who had just been found guilty of impeding the case could still be assigned as the commander overseeing the allegedly renewed investigation. Randy Steidl had also filed a lawsuit naming Carper along with five other ISP command officers as defendants. Did anyone actually think the ISP would do the right thing in the renewed investigation and search for any truth with this lawsuit pending? Despite denying it later in federal affidavits, several of the ISP criminal investigators involved in the renewed Rhoads investigation would openly communicate about the criminal investigation with Iain Johnston, the civil attorney for the ISP command. Why would investigators conducting a criminal investigation in a murder case communicate with the civil attorney on a multi-million dollar civil suit? That alone was against ISP policy.

In 2004, Jeff Marlow and Greg Dixon had already complained to me on many occasions they believed they were not being allowed to conduct a thorough, truthful and unbiased investigation. Marlow's lengthy e-mail had shown that.

The State only dug in deeper with Steidl's lawsuit and even more so when their attempts to have his lawsuit dismissed failed, when Judge Harold Baker denied their motion. The state attempted to have Steidl's lawsuit dismissed against Carper and the other ISP command because they were not part of the original investigation. Baker dismissed this in his ruling by stating, " . . . the ISP defendants argue they were not personally involved in Steidl's investigation or prosecution . . . This argument is not persuasive. Defendant Eckerty, a former ISP officer, was involved in the investigation, and allegedly assisted in fabricating the evidence used to convict Steidl. When Callahan reviewed the Rhoads case and uncovered evidence of serious wrongdoing involving an ISP officer, it was incumbent upon the ISP to investigate and rectify the situation."

Judge Baker continued with his assessment that, "Eckerty's past involvement placed the responsibility upon the then-current ISP chain of command to discover the truth and make it known to others instead of turning a blind eye to the situation. It rings hollow to argue that the ISP defendants had no duty to do anything because Steidl was already presumed guilty."

The ISP's civil attorneys tried to argue that my review of the Rhoads case in 2000 was simply the opinion of a subordinate officer—an opinion they had a right to ignore. Judge Baker didn't agree and responded:

> The complaint alleges considerably more than the "opinion of a subordinate" officer—it alleges numerous specific facts inconsistent with Steidl's guilt. At the very least, those facts should provide a reasonable law enforcement official to believe that one of its subordinate officers had, years earlier, been involved with a knowingly inadequate and/or wrongful investigation of a double murder for which two innocent men were convicted. No reasonable person would believe that the ISP defendants efforts to perpetuate a cover-up did not violate Steidl's right to present evidence of his innocence.

But the biggest blatant miscarriage of justice was that even though Randy Steidl was freed, Herbert Whitlock still remained in prison. Despite the same evidence and same unbelievable eyewitnesses that convicted both men, one was free and the other was still in prison.

Defense attorneys Richard Kling and Susana Ortiz were seeking a new trial for Herb Whitlock in Edgar County, but the Appellate Prosecutor's Office—specifically David Rands and Ed Parkinson—were fighting to deny Whitlock a new trial. Marlow's e-mail had "accused Rands' office of 'ramrodding' this case," but Rands denied Marlow's allegations, stating that, " . . . his office is not focused solely on Whitlock and Steidl." Rands told the *Tribune*, "My intent in the investigation has always been to identify, if possible, and prosecute, if possible, any persons responsible for these homicides."

Susana Ortiz disagreed with Rands and voiced her opinion regarding Marlow's e-mail: "It shows a culture of corruption at the Illinois State Police . . . I think you do need an independent, outside investigation."

Because of Marlow's e-mail, Kling and Ortiz asked Madigan's office to declare error in Whitlock's case, but the Attorney General's office declined to take any action, and they conceded to Richard Kling behind closed doors that the

ISP was stonewalling and throwing up roadblocks. The Attorney General's office stepped aside despite knowing about my criminal allegations against the ISP and their own assessment that "there were fatal flaws" in the original investigation and prosecution of Whitlock and Steidl.

Richard Kling told the press, "He was surprised and disappointed that Attorney General Madigan 'ducked the issue' but characterized it as a setback not a defeat."

Whitlock and his defense team had no choice but to go to battle against the Appellate Prosecutors in Edgar County before Judge H. Dean Andrews.

In 2004, the Illinois Appellate Prosecutor's Office had chosen not to retry Randy Steidl when they faced these same facts. But the Illinois Appellate Prosecutor's Office refused to take that same stance when it came to Whitlock. Prosecutor Ed Parkinson argued, "It appears that what the petitioner [Whitlock] really wants is the same treatment as Randy Steidl." And why wouldn't he? Parkinson himself had publicly questioned the credibility of the two eyewitnesses in the investigation. Larry Golden, political and legal studies professor, rationalized the logic behind the Appellate Prosecutors' stubborn stance detailing what he referred to as, "The Prosecution Complex: . . . When . . . prosecutors continue to pursue individuals despite such new evidence, it can result in what author Thomas Frisbie calls the "Prosecution complex," which he describes as "a mind-set that spurs some prosecutors, police officers and judges across the country to pursue convictions at all costs in high-profile cases. . . . "

Golden reasoned, "It is this mindset that leads prosecutors to continue to resist efforts to release Herb Whitlock . . . "

When the courtroom fight to gain Whitlock a new trial began, Kling asserted his client deserved a new trial due to outrageous misconduct on the part of the original prosecution, and started by discrediting the State's lack of evidence.

Kling attacked the credibility of the Reinbolt knife and introduced a videotape of Reinbolt telling the Attorney General's office in 2004 she could not identify the knife if a new trial was staged. In the taped interview, Reinbolt said, "I can't, I mean, in the room that night, the night, you know, at the time of the murders, you know, I don't know, things went fast. I don't know what it was. I can't possibly say, 'yes, I saw the knife.'" Reinbolt continued, stating, " . . . I thought there was a knife used . . . whether it was that one or not, I don't know." Yet, Reinbolt testified in the original trial it was her husband's knife she gave to Whitlock!

Then Kling turned his attention toward the broken lamp/vase found in the Rhoads bedroom. The state alleged Reinbolt's credibility because she was able to identify the broken lamp inside the Rhoads' bedroom. During the recorded interview with the Attorney General's Office though, Reinbolt said a vase was broken but she was told by Mike McFatridge, Detective Jim Parrish and Jack Eckerty that it had to be a lamp.

According to Reinbolt, " . . . they had several intense discussions about the vase/lamp during mock trials at the Edgar County Courthouse as they prepared her for testimony." Reinbolt told the AG's Office, "It didn't much matter to me what it was . . . I got tired of arguing with them."

Kling and Ortiz also called a series of witnesses who testified about Parrish and Eckerty's intimidation tactics, which included kicking chairs, slamming fist into tables and physically backing people into corners while striking their fists in front of the witness. There were also several witnesses who said they provided information that disputed Reinbolt and Herrington's story, but the same intimidating tactics were used to convince the witnesses they were wrong.

Kling also called Whitlock's trial attorney, Ron Tulin, to testify. In addition, Tulin had prepared an affidavit admitting he erred in defending Whitlock in his original trial. Tulin admitted he should've raised more questions about the Reinbolt knife and failed to call in experts to refute that piece of evidence. Tulin also stated that he erred when he did not address the issue of the lamp/vase which perjured Reinbolt's testimony.

"It would have been scientific evidence that what she said was not true. . . . It has bothered me all these years. . . . I just came over and told the truth today." Tulin testified.

The most interesting witness called by Whitlock's defense team was retired Illinois State Police Sergeant Jack Eckerty. The *Chicago Tribune's* Hal Dardick recounted Eckerty's testimony:

> Retired Illinois State Police Sgt. Jack Eckerty took the stand Friday, but he had trouble remembering details about the double-homicide investigation he led nearly 18 years ago. "I don't recall," he said more than a dozen times when asked about investigation details allegedly never disclosed to the defense in Whitlock's 1987 trial. Eckerty couldn't remember if he took a key witness [Herrington] for a polygraph test, who requested a $2,500 family relocation payment for the other main witness [Reinbolt], whether he sat in on mock trials or even whether he signed an affidavit related to the case.

Eckerty looked even more buffoonish when Kling showed him the affidavits Eckerty had personally signed. Eckerty did not remember when and where the first interview with Herrington took place. He did not remember if he ever plied Herrington with alcohol—which was against ISP policy—and he did not recall why there were no reports written in reference to the electronically recorded overhears between Herrington and Whitlock.

Eckerty did remember that Bob Morgan who employed Karen Rhoads had shown up at the Rhoads home the morning they were slain. He also remembered Karen Rhoads once told a friend that she saw a machine gun and cash at a facility owned by Morgan. When Kling asked Eckerty if he told me, during one of our phone conversations, that Bob Morgan was a suspect in the Rhoads case, Eckerty didn't recall the conversation. Kling asked Eckerty if he remembered telling private investigator Bill Clutter that Morgan was a suspect, and Eckerty's memory was refreshed, admitting "since Morgan was Karen Rhoads' employer, he was looked at as a suspect."

Kling also referenced the other phone conversations between Eckerty and me and he admitted—on one occasion—he phoned me because, "He was concerned about word on the street that he was tied to the mob, and he was a dirty cop."

The ISP polygraph examiner, Mark Murphy, was called in to reference Herrington's deceitful polygraph results and disclose Herrington's first undocumented interview where he claimed "Jim and Ed" committed the Rhoads murders.

Both Clutter and I were also called to testify on Whitlock's behalf. As I pulled up to the Edgar County courthouse, I wondered how many of the Paris residents viewed me as either a friend or foe. There were tons of reporters with cameras roaming around the corridors of the old courthouse, but not too many people in Paris knew what I looked like, so I was able to walk through the corridors without being questioned, and I was led into a chamber off the courtroom.

When it was my turn to testify, Rands tried to attack my credibility as a homicide investigator. I remember looking at Rands and how disgusted I was. I knew he and Kaupas had ramrodded the Rhoads investigation, not giving the investigators the freedom to interview who they wanted or to follow the leads they had developed, not being allowed to document certain interviews, having them write reports to a closed case file to hide any new information, ordering the investigators to listen and record attorney-client privileged conversations and how he had lied and secretly stopped the DNA testing. He disgusted me. What a hypocrite.

Despite Rands' cover-ups and ramrodding, I was pretty confident Whitlock would get his new trial. There was no way this judge could turn his back on all this: even an Edgar County judge.

On June 23, 2005, Judge H. Dean Andrews issued his 72-page opinion on Whitlock's request for a new trial. For eighteen years Whitlock had steadfastly maintained his innocence. Randy Steidl was freed after a federal judge and the Illinois Attorney General's office refuted the evidence used to convict both men, determined that evidence favorable to the defense was withheld in the original prosecution and cited the lack of credibility of the eyewitnesses used against the two men.

Edgar County Judge H. Dean Andrews saw things differently and concluded Whitlock did not deserve a new trial. Richard Kling made no effort to hide his disgust and exclaimed, "This judge was sitting in a different courtroom, the opinion does not appear to be based on the law or the facts that were introduced . . . I don't understand how the judge, given the inconvertible, un-rebutted evidence and his decision, can sleep at night."

A lot of people believed Judge Andrews' decision was ludicrous, and a *News-Gazette* scathing editorial entitled, "Rhoads murder case continues to confound" pointed out that while "some people might consider Kling's reaction" to be that of any attorney who just lost a hearing, Kling's " . . . expectations of victory weren't unrealistic because the last time a judge reviewed a conviction stemming from the Rhoads case, the defendant went free."

The *News-Gazette* editorial was referring to Federal Judge Michael McCuskey's 2003 order for the State to retry or free Steidl. Despite reviewing the same evidence, Andrews didn't see the case the same way McCuskey did, but Judge McCuskey also didn't attend a fundraiser for George Ryan in Paris back on June 23, 1998, like Andrews did when his wife donated one thousand dollars to Ryan. There were others there that night, too, that sparked my interest, including Stuart Levine, who was later indicted and then cooperated with the federal government, playing a big part in the convictions of people like Tony Rezko and others in the continuing criminal investigations into Governor Rod Blagojevich and the state's politically corrupt pay-to-play politics. One of the biggest contributors also present that night in Paris was Robert Morgan, who gave good old George $10,000.

Despite Morgan being acknowledged as a suspect in Whitlock's hearing, Judge Andrews still sat on the bench and listened to all the concerns and all the lies and then denied Herb Whitlock a new trial. The *News-Gazette* editorial summarized that " . . . Andrews relies heavily on Reinbolt's trial testimony that linked Steidl and Whitlock to the murders, a surprising stance given the back-and-forth nature of her subsequent statements. She has made so many conflicting statements since the trial that no jury could reasonably rely now on her conflicting testimony, but Andrews has accepted her trial testimony." Therefore, " . . . Andrews rejected defense claims, suggesting that questions about the credibility of the two alleged witnesses to the killings were of little significance . . ."

I had to keep reminding myself . . . this was Edgar County . . . this judge was from Edgar County . . . and what do you expect? Just like my dad had warned me years ago about this lawless community.

A few days after the ruling, an angry citizen summarized Judge Andrews' decision in a letter to the *Terre Haute Tribune Star*: "I think it is very wrong, but I guess it's not what you know, but who you know. Justice goes to who can afford it, and the crooks in Paris still walk. I think Whitlock's attorney presented evidence that showed he didn't do what he was accused of doing. Boss Hogg is alive and well."

Boss Hogg may be alive and well, but for Herbert Whitlock, this was definitely "a blatant miscarriage of justice."

CHAPTER 24

THE MIGHTY ENGINE OF THE STATE

---■---

As Bob Dylan sang in "Hurricane," " . . . Couldn't help but make me feel ashamed to live in a land where justice is a game." Oftentimes, following my civil rights trial, I sat back and marveled at the arrogant, in-your-face disregard for the law and blatant corruption by the State of Illinois. I kept reflecting back to Eric Zorn's column: "another frightening example of how the engine of the State, once in motion, can roll right over the innocent as well as the guilty."

But not all of the state's politicians were above the law, at least federal law, and on April 17, 2006, former Governor George Ryan was convicted on all counts of the racketeering conspiracy he was intimately involved in, and he became the third Illinois Governor to be indicted and criminally convicted in a court of law.

By Ryan overseeing the corruption in his offices of Secretary of State and then Governor, he was indirectly responsible for the deaths of six children. Jim Dey of the *News-Gazette* reflected on Ryan's guilt:

> Civil War Gen. William Sherman used to say that "war is hell." But what really did he know? He was never a crooked Illinois governor who was subjected to an intense federal investigation. Now, that's hell. . . . Ryan, a classic backstabbing, deal-making, unprincipled, amoral hack who made it to the top of the state's political dung heap, is in deep trouble. . . . Ryan's discomfort is not about to end. [Defense attorney Dan] Webb calls it "hell," but that's overdoing it.

333

Jim Dey attacked George Ryan's "hell":

> Here's what hell is. The whole Ryan corruption investigation began in 1994 when a piece of a semitrailer fell off a truck and struck a minivan driven by Scott and Jannis Willis, causing fire and a crash that killed six of their children. Losing six children to an accident caused by a semitrailer driver by Ricardo Guzman, who bribed secretary of state employees to get his commercial license illegally so the payoff money could go into Ryan's campaign fund—now that is hell.

George Ryan and his crony Lawrence Warner were the 74th and 75th defendants convicted by the feds since November 1998, and not one person charged was acquitted.

On September 7, 2006, George Ryan was sentenced to six and a half years in federal prison, but just how saddened was George Ryan? In his article, "Ryan's light sentence isn't the only joke," the *Chicago Tribune*'s John Kass reflected on not only the judge's light sentence but Ryan's character: "Judge Pallmeyer must believe in the potential goodness of all people. But she didn't hear Ryan laughing in the washroom after she imposed her light sentence. Ryan was joking with his buddy Big Jim." The "Big Jim" to whom Kass referred was former Governor Jim Thompson. Former Gov. Thompson was now part of the prestigious law firm that was defending Ryan pro bono. The article continued with Kass' account of Ryan and Big Jim in the restroom:

> "Wonder what [defense lawyer Dan] Webb is going to say to the media," Ryan said, chuckling, spry enough in his allegedly weakened and infirm state that he bent quickly, like a portly gymnast in hard shoes, to see if anyone was hiding under the stalls. A young reporter who was dressed in a nice suit—and so didn't look like a young reporter but more like an attorney—wanted to use the facilities. "Got a ticket?" wisecracked Ryan, smiling, hearty, apparently crushed by the tough sentence he might not ever serve. A few minutes earlier, though, he was seeking mercy, speechifying, oozing contrition without ever offering a real apology, just like a politician. He even used his deep George Ryan political voice. The people of Illinois, Ryan said, "expected better and I let them down and for that, I apologize. My failures will never leave my mind as long as I live . . . I should have been more vigilant."

Kass' article sarcastically reacted to Ryan's insincere apology and lack of genuine remorse:

> He meant he should have been more careful. But there was no apology to the Willis family, sitting nearby, for his order to cut off the investigation of the license-for-bribes scheme that helped lead to the crash that killed their six children. . . . "Do I think we accomplished something in this investigation?" federal prosecutor Patrick Collins said. "Yes I do. Are there still problems with public corruption? Absolutely. Deterring corruption in Illinois is a difficult job. It is a mutating virus."

Assistant U.S. Attorney Patrick Collins was right. There is a mutating virus of corruption in Illinois, and it doesn't matter which party—Democrat or Republican. The public can thank former U.S. Senator Peter Fitzgerald for attacking that virus when he appointed Patrick Fitzgerald (no relation) as the U.S. Attorney in the Northern District of Illinois. In an article by John Kass, Senator Peter Fitzgerald was quoted, "I intended to appoint someone who is not a political hack but independent of both political parties. . . . And I said they're going to be screaming like a stuck pig when I do this," Kass reported. "They squealed back then. And others have more squealing to do."

By 2007, most of Illinois' citizens were hopeful that a federal investigation on Governor Rod Blagojevich would also have him squealing. When George Ryan was found guilty, Governor Rod Blagojevich hypocritically told the press, "Today's verdict proves that no one is above the law. And just as important, it proves that government is supposed to exist for the good of the people, not the other way around, and certainly not for the personal enrichment of those who hold public office."

But Rod Blagojevich is also the consummate politician, and a local news editorial described his true character:

> Politicians—you've just got to love 'em. They can say or do anything, no matter how implausible or hypocritical, without batting an eye. The latest example of that . . . comes from Illinois Governor Rod Blagojevich. . . . This is a governor who's so uninvolved and uninterested in the issues that even his Democratic allies wonder why he wanted to be governor. Well, the answer is that Blagojevich, like many other candidates, is far less interested in doing something than he is in being something.

The scandal of political corruption with "unreformer" Governor Rod Blagojevich continued George Ryan's legacy, and U.S. Attorney Patrick Fitzgerald's office and the FBI continued to target Blagojevich and his cronies for the same pay-to-play politics that convicted George Ryan. The *Chicago Tribune,* in May of 2007, reported, "Blagojevich has steadfastly refused to answer questions about the federal investigation, including specifics of why his campaign has paid the prominent law firm Winston & Strawn nearly $1 million since 2003." The article also pointed out that, "Blagojevich has not been accused of any wrongdoing" however the governor " . . . has repeatedly deflected specific questions by saying 'we do things right.'"

As in the George Ryan investigation, the feds indicted, convicted and plucked away at the friends and cronies of the esteemed Blagojevich, and they would also step up their investigation on him. A *News-Gazette* article articulated the continuing federal investigation, "Political corruption in Illinois has been deemed so extensive that the FBI has sent an extra official corruption squad into the state." And U.S. Attorney Patrick Fitzgerald told the press, "If morals don't get them, I hope the fear of going to jail does."

In the beginning of his administration, Gov. Blagojevich introduced Executive Order Number 4, which bans retaliation against whistleblowers. Executive Order Number 4 reads, in part:

> Any officer, employee or appointee of any agency is banned from
> retaliating against, attempting to retaliate against, or in any man-
> ner interfering with a whistleblower . . . as described in the whistle-
> blower protection act. Any officer, employee or appointee of any
> agency who knowingly violates the provisions . . . shall be subject
> to disciplinary action, including but not limited to discharge.

Despite this executive order and state statutes that mandated termination, Fermon and Carper remained on the job making their six-figure salaries. Obviously in the State of Illinois, whistleblower acts are meaningless for those who are politically connected.

Terry Bibo of the *Peoria Journal Star* depicted the ISP and governor's failure to act in her article, "State Police Starting to Smell":

> At one time, the Illinois State Police represented a gold standard
> of investigations. If they did something, you believed it. I did, any-
> way. Not so much these days. Now there are so many questions
> about the state police that it may be time for somebody to inves-

tigate the investigators. Somebody, maybe, like the governor. So far, it isn't happening. . . . But this is just the latest worm in a can somebody ought to clean out. Maybe the governor doesn't want to open it because a couple of things that have crawled out involved Blagojevich himself.

By this time the vast majority of the citizens in the State of Illinois were hoping Blagojevich would end up getting indicted and imprisoned like his predecessor, and a statewide poll showed the citizens of Illinois believed "Blagojevich's administration is either just as corrupt as or more corrupt than George Ryan's crew." His approval rating would continue to drop even lower than George Ryan's had, and, if possible, even lower than George W. Bush's.

As expected, the state police and its small army of $200-an-hour attorneys appealed my case.

"You kicked our ass," Lawrence Weiner joked to John Baker following the trial. "Those state police upper command officers were a bunch of fucking morons."

But Weiner then greedily rubbed his thumb and fingers together and bragged to John how much money he had made. And Weiner had made a lot of money—along with all the other defense attorneys. In Dusty Rhodes' *Illinois Times* article entitled, "The good, the bad and the expensive: You won't believe how much you paid to defend a couple of ISP officers," she wrote, "There are many good cops working for the Illinois State Police. Keep repeating that phrase to yourself as you read on; otherwise, you might think ISP is awash in scofflaws. There are many good cops, many good ones." Rhodes continued:

> I hear from a few—some active, some retired and working for ISP on contract, some (without juice) just plain retired—by phone and e-mail and forwarded messages. In blunt and bitter missives, they bewail what they perceive as the tarnishing of their agency's sterling reputation. . . . So, I'm bracing myself for more e-mails and phone calls when the guys hear how much the four private attorneys appointed to represent Carper, Fermon and a third official (no finding of guilt against him) have billed us taxpayers.

"Are you sitting down?" Dusty asked, "It's $685,059.13, just through May 31."

Weiner was right, they had made a lot of money, and just for the two-week trial; they planned on making more through appeals. The problem as I saw it was the money was at the taxpayer's expense. Of course, it was the politicians, not the tax payers, who chose to spend the money on the high-priced attorneys who acknowledged they had "fucking morons" for clients. The unanswered question in my mind was how much money their law firms contributed back to the Illinois politicians?

During this timeframe, the George W. Bush administration was pushing the United States Supreme Court to limit government employee's freedom of speech in a California case, *Garcetti v. Ceballos*. With Bush able to appoint two new cronies to the Supreme Court, it looked like the Supreme Court was set to strip away the First Amendment rights of government employees to speak out, even on corruption.

The State of Illinois appealed my case based on that ruling, a state rich in corruption relying on the United States Supreme Court to take away the freedom of speech and muzzle government employees from speaking out about its misconduct.

As far as the Rhoads case, the so-called renewed investigative efforts by the state police continued focusing on putting Randy Steidl back in prison, and soon I learned some of the investigators were resorting to the same devious and desperate tactics as in the original investigation.

As expected, the civil attorneys for the state police appealed Federal Judge Harold Baker's motion to dismiss Steidl's lawsuit, and the appeal went to the United States 7th Circuit Court of Appeals. Iain Johnston, one of the attorneys in my civil trial was retained to defend the Illinois State Police command at the taxpayer's expense.

The state's argument contended that the current ISP command officers who impeded my reinvestigation should not be held responsible for the misconduct in the original case and had no constitutional obligation to take any action. It was obvious the ISP upper command believed they had no ethical or moral obligations, like George W. Bush, they also wanted to use the Constitution of the United States to protect their misconduct.

But the United States 7th Circuit Court of Appeals rationalized that, "We are persuaded that the ISP Officials . . . had ample notice that the knowing suppression of exculpatory material that was in the files at the time of the trial violated the defendant's constitutional rights . . ." and " . . . some of the available evidence would have shredded the State's case." Then scathingly, the court added:

> We have found no case that is directly analogous to the alleged misconduct of the police here. (This is essentially good news: we sincerely hope this type of behavior is rare.) We therefore must de-

cide whether the alleged actions were 'so egregious' that no reasonable person could have believed that they were permissible . . .

The 7th Circuit Court of Appeals determined, "We therefore conclude that the
district court correctly denied the ISP officials' motion for dismissal . . ."

The state police doesn't give up easily, and it was becoming obvious that they
were willing to resort to almost anything when Marlow's e-mail hit the front page
of the *Chicago Tribune* and revealed he did not want to be a part of the "ramrodding" or "railroading of anyone" in the Rhoads investigation. A DII investigation
was initiated, but the investigation wasn't concerned about Marlow's allegations
of misconduct but rather who had leaked the e-mail to the *Chicago Tribune*.

While DII never found the leak, there was speculation DII eventually got to
Special Agent Jeff Marlow. Earlier in his career, Marlow was fired from the ISP for
allegations of drunk driving. He was eventually exonerated and fought successfully to get his job back. From talking to Jeff, I knew the five years he fought to get
his job back took a toll on him and his family. He laid wood floors and worked at
McDonald's to make ends meet and still have enough money to take on the powerful state. He said his daughters and wife often had to go without Christmas and
birthday presents. With the changes in direction I began to see in Marlow after his
e-mail hit the front page, I began speculating that he been called onto the carpet
by DII. I questioned not only his demeanor, but the radical change in direction
he began taking in the Rhoads investigation. Had the ISP called Marlow on the
carpet for his e-mail, and threatened to fire him once again, telling him he could
spend another five years fighting to get his job back? If this was true, it was an
intimidating and very powerful threat, but intimidation by our department was
definitely not something new.

Jeff and I had stayed in contact after I retired, but now he began suddenly
distancing himself from me. It wasn't long after this that I started getting a lot
of phone calls from people in Paris who said that now Jeff Marlow was trying to
discredit me, and unlike before, he was suddenly convinced that Randy Steidl and
Herb Whitlock were guilty of the murders of Dyke and Karen Rhoads.

I don't know if Marlow was intimidated or not: it was only rumor and
speculation. I do know that on January 27, 2007, I interviewed 71-year-old Bud
Cunningham. At one time, Bud Cunningham owned the Barn Tavern in Paris,
and had occasionally employed Randy Steidl before he was convicted of the
Rhoads murders. When I spoke to Bud Cunningham, his story was as disheart-
ening as when I reviewed the original Rhoads case. Bud prefaced his story by
telling me that not long after being diagnosed with cancer he turned to cocaine

and became addicted—an addiction that eventually led to an arrest and conviction. Not a menace to society, he was placed on probation, and Bud told me for the last two and a half years, he was clean and stayed away from cocaine.

On December 27, 2006, an old girlfriend unexpectedly appeared at his door, and Bud invited her inside. He said she quickly produced two small corner baggies containing cocaine residue, and offered to sell Bud and his son the two baggies.

"There wasn't enough in the baggies to even give you a good hit," said Bud. "It was just a lot of residue."

Undaunted, the ex-girlfriend took the baggies and tapped the remaining residue into a pipe and lit it up; Bud admitted he was weak and took a hit off the pipe.

Not long after her departure, Bud said "a small army of police officers" stormed into his house, stating they were conducting an unannounced probation visit.

"There were an awful lot of police from all over the place," Bud said. "It seemed like there had to be eight or more."

Bud said the small army of police was led by Sheriff's Deputy Roger Hopper, who, coincidentally, is also Jeff Marlow's cousin. From my experiences, a seventy-one-year-old non-violent man on probation didn't normally warrant a small army of police for an unannounced probation visit. From my experience, very rarely does a probation officer even ask for police assistance when making a home visit, especially on an old man with no history of violence.

The reports I obtained later verified Bud Cunningham's story. Eight men, five police officers—one of them the Chief of Police—and three probation officers, stormed into Bud Cunningham's home that day. Once inside Bud's home, he said they immediately found the two baggies of cocaine residue the ex-girlfriend left behind. Bud took the responsibility for the cocaine, and the police report reflected this: "Bud was asked about the corner bags found on his floor and under his bed and he advised that it was his house so he was responsible for the baggies . . ."

Bud found out later that his ex-girlfriend was arrested for writing a bad check, and had missed her court date, and as a result, received a visit from the police. Not long after that visit from police, she, not surprisingly, showed up at Bud Cunningham's door with the cocaine. It sure sounded like Bud Cunningham was set up to me.

Bud was taken into custody for possession of a controlled substance and was told that they were also going to file a petition to revoke his probation. With this hanging over his head, it wasn't long before he received a visit from two Illinois State Police officers—Special Agents Jeff Marlow and Matt McCormick. Bud said the two agents got right to the point, and Bud said Marlow told him his case would disappear if he could tell them Randy Steidl admitted he was involved in the Rhoads homicide.

Bud told the agents he never spoke to Randy about the Rhoads murders and said he didn't believe Randy Steidl could kill anyone. Marlow became irate and accused him of knowing something, calling him a liar. Bud stood his ground and said he told the agents, "On my mother's grave, I don't know anything. I won't lie for you."

The agents continued hammering away at him, but Bud repeatedly told them he would not lie for them. When the agents finally started to leave, he said Marlow told him to think things over and his case would go away, or he threatened that Bud would be charged and could spend the rest of his life in prison and die there!

Marlow and McCormick made a second visit to Bud Cunningham two days later. Bud said, once again, the agents started hammering away at him, telling him they knew he had information that Steidl was somehow involved in the Rhoads murders. The agents made the same threats as before, but Bud continued to vehemently deny knowing anything about the Rhoads murders, once again claiming on his mother's grave that he knew nothing.

The angry verbal attacks and intimidation continued with the threats Bud was going to die in prison if he didn't talk. The agents became angrier, he said, repeatedly calling him a liar, and Bud said he told them this whole thing is about Randy's lawsuit against the state and they were trying to railroad Steidl back into prison so the state wouldn't have to pay him. But Bud reaffirmed that he wasn't going to lie for them. When the agents continued threatening him with going to prison, Bud said he told them his cancer medicine cost $3,500 a shot, which he took three times a year, so to go ahead and put him in prison and the state could pay for his shots. Finally frustrated, he said the two agents left, cruelly telling him he was going to die in prison. Bud Cunningham was charged with possession of the baggies of cocaine residue in Edgar County.

Twenty-one years earlier, members of the Illinois State Police, Paris Police and Edgar County State's Attorney office used Darrell Herrington, the town drunk, and Debbie Reinbolt, a self-admitted alcoholic and drug addict, to railroad Steidl and Whitlock into prison. In Jeff Marlow's 2005 e-mail, he stated, "At this point, I make no attempt at hiding the fact that I feel the main two witnesses used to convict Steidl and Whitlock were created."

But history has a funny way of repeating itself. Because now, here in 2007, Jeff Marlow was attempting to coerce Bud Cunningham—a man with a cocaine problem—into lying and becoming a witness against Randy Steidl. More than twenty years later investigators were resorting to the same desperate tactics once again, but this time, Randy Steidl was more fortunate, because Bud Cunningham had a lot more integrity than Darrell Herrington or Debbie Reinbolt.

That certainly wouldn't keep the state in the years to come from continuing to look for more Herringtons and Reinbolts. As for Bud Cunningham, the harmless old man was sent to prison on October 16, 2007, for possessing cocaine residue, but at least he still had his integrity, and that's a lot more than I can say for the cops who put him there.

That same year, in 2007, Andrea Trapp received an anonymous letter that was as equally disturbing:

> Ms. Trapp:
> This correspondence is to advise you of certain aspects of the Rhoads murder case which you [may] not be aware of.
> During Herb Whitlock's trial appeal of two years ago. An informant contacted the Illinois Attorney General's Office for the purpose of providing information confirming the innocence of Whitlock, as well as directing the prosecutors toward the true perpetrator!
> The informant provided direct contact information, however he was never contacted, interviewed or questioned by the Illinois Attorney General's Office. This despite the allegations made by the informant that his attempts to provide same information to the Illinois State Police Investigators resulted with the ISP Investigator placing his weapon to the ribs of the informant with the threat of death if he revealed the information to anyone.
> By withholding this information, the Illinois Attorney General's Office has intentionally and willing[ly] prolonged the wrongful incarceration of an innocent man, while allowing the true perpetrator to remain free.
> It should be apparent that the State of Illinois, for whatever reason, is not committed to solving this case.
> Perhaps it is time to ask for intervention by the Federal Prosecutor's Office.
> Best Wishes and Good Luck!!!

What did this letter mean? I knew that Ellen Mandletort had frustratingly admitted, "It's not about justice anymore, it's all about image, money and politics now," and I knew she had told Andrea that the state police was not playing by the book in this case. Of course they weren't, they were being sued and their image was being tarnished, but what about the State of Illinois in general? Then another disturbing letter came to Andrea Trapp on May 22, 2008, written from the same anonymous source. In part the letter read:

> If you are to get to the heart of this conspiracy I strongly recommend an interview of the Illinois Attorney General's Office former Chief of Investigations William Walsh. Inquire as to the following:
>
> 1. Why were you dispatched to Paris, Illinois, to monitor the last appeals trial of Whitlock?
>
> 2. Who sent you?
>
> 3. Were you, or were you not, in possession of crucial evidence that could have incriminated Bill Morgan while exonerating Whitlock and Steidl?
>
> 4. What was the reason for your discharge from the Illinois Attorney General's Office?

William Walsh was at one time the Chief of Investigations for the Attorney General's Office, but when Clutter interviewed him, he denied knowing anything about the Rhoads case. He was the Chief of Investigations for Illinois Attorney General Lisa Madigan and he didn't know anything about the Rhoads case? Yeah right! And there's no corruption in the State of Illinois' government, either. Maybe it wasn't about justice anymore . . . maybe it was all just about image, money and politics.

CHAPTER 25

FREEDOM OF SPEECH?

———————————◼———————————

There's a saying that, "All that is needed for evil to flourish is for good people to remain silent." Oftentimes I've been asked if speaking out against such a corrupt state as Illinois was worth it, and was I worried about the safety of my family? I have only one way to answer that: like an old adage says, none of us can ever be afraid to speak out, because if we are, then evil will surely win.

After my civil trial, we went through several settlement hearings and in the beginning, I couldn't deal with the state. My case was never about money and that wasn't the reason I went forward. The state wanted me to sign a gag order, and they should've realized by this time, they didn't have enough money to silence me. So the State of Illinois relied on the George W. Bush administration and the United States Supreme Court to silence people like me.

By this time, former Governor George Ryan was imprisoned and our current governor, Rod Blagojevich, was hopefully not far behind him in the midst of a federal criminal investigation. So, it wasn't just the politically compromised ISP command looking bad, Illinois' citizens had more than enough reasons to distrust their state government.

At the same time, Americans nationwide began questioning the George W. Bush administration filled with all its deceit, deception and blatant disregard for our civil rights. Clarence Darrow once said, "When I was a boy, I was told that anybody could become president; I'm beginning to believe it." Darrow's witticism could sarcastically apply to George W. Bush, and for eight years Americans endured his administration, filled with its liars and lies. The Bush administration's hypocritical, deceitful and elitist attitude alienated and deteriorated the respect for the United States worldwide. By the end of his term, there was no doubt that the majority of Americans, along with the rest of mankind, considered Bush and his administration the worst in American history. The middle class and poor became nothing more than cattle to the Bush administration, butchered in a war America was deceitfully led into. Under his majesty King George's reign, the Constitution of the United States also became a meaningless piece of paper thanks to the cronies he appointed to the United States Supreme Court. The protections once guaranteed to the American people were picked apart by his new appointees and the other conservative justices on the court.

One of the men Bush appointed was Chief Justice John Roberts. He was just the type of person George W. Bush wanted on the Supreme Court, and as the joke goes, one day his majesty, King Bush, met with the Chief Justice.

"Chief Justice Roberts," Bush said. "I need your help. The President of Iraq is telling me his country needs a Constitution like ours—something to protect his people."

"John, do you think you could help me out with this?" Bush asked.

"Sure, Mr. President," Chief Justice Roberts quickly replied. "Just give them ours, we're not using it!"

Unfortunately, under the new "Bush" Supreme Court, the joke became a reality, and during his administration, George W. Bush appointed a second justice named Samuel Alito. These are powerful positions and the justices take an oath to "support and defend" the Constitution of the United States and our Bill of Rights for the American people against government misconduct and abuse.

One of our most cherished protections is the First Amendment, which gives United States citizens Freedom of Speech, that "Congress shall make no law respecting an establishment of religion, or prohibiting the free exercise thereof; or abridging the freedom of speech, or of the press; or the right of the people peaceably to assemble, and to petition the government for a redress of grievances."

Yet with the two new Bush appointees in place, the political makeup of the Supreme Court drastically changed, and the Bush administration encouraged the Supreme Court to take away the First Amendment protections from those citizens working as government employees while "on the job." In 2006, the Supreme Court looked at a 9th Circuit Court of Appeals case, *Garcetti vs. Ceballos,* which involved:

[Prosecutor Richard] Ceballos reported to his supervisors that he believed that a police officer had falsified an affidavit used to obtain a search warrant in a criminal matter under the prosecutor's supervision. His superiors retaliated by taking several adverse actions against him. His supervisors, the District Attorney, Los Angeles County, and the U.S. Department of Justice . . . urge[d] the Supreme Court to rule that public employee speech should automatically [be] excluded from First Amendment protection if it is communicated as part of the employee's job duties—regardless of whether the speech addresses a matter of public concern . . .

The *New York Times* depicted the ramifications of *Garcetti vs. Ceballos*:

. . . a First Amendment case, *Garcetti vs. Ceballos* . . . is crucial not only to government workers across the country, but to all Americans concerned about free speech and national security. . . . government employees owe their ultimate allegiance not to their supervisor or president but to America; it's Constitution, laws and citizens. . . . As a result, those workers we depend on for our safety have often faced a terrible conundrum: either remain quiet and allow fraud and wrongdoing to occur, or speak out and risk retaliation.

The article concluded:

Supported by the Bush administration, lawyers for Mr. Garcetti and the California Counties Association are rehashing arguments that government managers have always used against granting these protections to employees—namely that providing these rights might lead to management paralysis and a deluge of litigation. But the Supreme Court in the past has dismissed these unfounded predictions, realizing that our court system is equipped to weed out frivolous lawsuits. . . . America should be encouraging those civil servants who step forward to make our country stronger. Cutting off protection is a recipe for disasters of mass proportions.

Still, indications were the Bush administration might get its way, and just one week before the Supreme Court looked at *Garcetti vs. Ceballos*, an Associated Press article reported:

The Bush administration pressed the Supreme Court on Wednesday for a ruling that would make it harder for government whistleblowers to win lawsuits claiming retaliation.... Bush administration lawyer Dan Himmelfarb said . . . that government employees are not entitled to free-speech coverage for things they say in the scope of their job . . .

First Amendment advocates retorted against the Bush administration:

Stephen M. Kohn, a leader with the National Whistleblower Center, said that a victory for the government would mean "whistleblowers who expose waste, fraud, and corruption will have less constitutional protection than Ku Klux Klan members who burn crosses on their front lawns."

On May 30, 2006, the protections previously guaranteed by the First Amendment were shredded thanks to five conservative Supreme Court Justices, Anthony Kennedy, Antonin Scalia, Clarence Thomas and Bush's two new appointees, John Roberts and Samuel Alito. In a five to four decision, the high court reversed the 9th Circuit's decision in *Garcetti vs. Ceballos*. Despite the other four Supreme Court Justices vehemently dissenting, the five Bush administration advocates held, in part, *"When public employees make statements pursuant to their official duties, they are not speaking as citizens for First Amendment purposes, and the Constitution does not insulate their communications from employer discipline . . . "*

The *Rock River Times* commented on the court's shameful decision in their article, "High Court Ruling Gags Government Whistleblowers":

Joanne Royce, general counsel for the Government Accountability Project (GAP) said: "The Supreme Court's ruling strikes a shameful blow against free speech rights and a vigorous democracy—public employees' ability to serve as guardians of good government are severely restricted by this opinion. . . . A deeply divided, but majority court . . . upheld the values of 'employer control' over the traditional American values of freedom and protection of public discourse and professional dissent. This ruling will have a serious chilling effect on the willingness of public employees to risk their livelihood to expose government fraud and waste. Our democratic traditions and the American taxpayer are sacrificed to the alter of 'employer control.'" The ramifications of the court's decision are devastating to public employees who try to speak out in the interest of the American people, GAP said. . . . by restricting the speech of whistleblowers, the Supreme Court has made government more open to fraud and corruption. GAP said public employee truth-tellers . . . uncover corruption, fraud and national security shortcomings. Muzzling those contributions to the nation's well-being can have very grave consequences. Without whistleblowers, government is under no compunction to act in an accountable and ethical manner.

The *Rock River Times* continued, quoting the GAP's head legal director, Tom Devine: "This decision is outrageous. Canceling the doctrine of 'duty speech' means that government employees only have an on-the-job right to be 'yes people' parroting false information and enabling illegality."

This was dumbfounding; this meant while I was off-duty, I was a citizen, but when I was at work protecting our citizens, I didn't have the same rights as a citizen. The bigger question was did this ruling actually take away my right to speak out on government corruption while I was at work? This didn't make sense, because who would be in a better position to see corruption than an employee exposed to it. How would any corruption ever be uncovered then? What type of democratic government wants to muzzle its employees and silence them in the first place? And what type of a government wants to protect government misconduct by allowing it to be covered up?

If I wasn't speaking as a citizen, what the hell was I speaking as then? When I took the oath to become an Illinois State Police Officer, I certainly considered myself a citizen and apparently, so did the State of Illinois, because the oath states, "I solemnly vow to the people of the State of Illinois, upon my honor as an *officer* and *citizen,* to discharge the duties of an officer of the Illinois State Police to the best of my ability . . . " Yet now, according to these warped scholars, I didn't have the same rights as a citizen while I was doing my job? How ludicrous is that?

Justice Kennedy wrote for the majority, continuing, "*Thus, a government entity has broader discretion to restrict speech when it acts in its employer role, but the restrictions must be directed at speech that has potential to affect its operations.*"

Government *operations* like keeping innocent men in prison and covering up police misconduct would certainly be affected if an honest cop spoke out on that type of misconduct. So was the Supreme Court restricting freedom of speech in order to protect government *operations* like this?

Was this Supreme Court ruling giving governments and its officials the right to commit crimes, ignore its criminal acts or cover them up, if they chose to, like DII and the ISP command did in my case? Who will police the police if they refuse to police themselves? Who will hold government officials accountable for their actions if they can silence the employees who would turn them in for their wrongdoing?

Hypothetically, how are the circumstances of my case any different than if I had watched one of the state police commanders commit a murder and I reported their crime to DII. But DII refused to investigate the murder and instead deceitfully helped to cover up the crime. Isn't this Supreme Court ruling giving the government the ability to ignore or even cover up their criminal acts by silencing the employees who would speak out? We hear about police misconduct daily. I watched the State Police Command ignore the VMEG officers who were violating the Fourth and Fifth Ammendments of the Constitution. They were committing Brady violations. But DII and the State Police Command wrote it off as "just a management issue." Is violating someone's Constitutional protections "just a management issue?"

Now according to the wisdom of the Supreme Court majority, I wasn't protected by the First Amendment if I spoke out on crimes like this, and the government was free to silence me, and to retaliate against me for speaking out. What is even worse, by silencing a police officer, they put him in the unenviable position of being damned if he does and damned if he doesn't. For to remain silent in a crime, the officer is forced to become part of the crime, but now to speak out could cost him his job with no protection. That was certainly not going to encourage many government employees to come forward if they observed any corruption.

And what does this mean for American citizens if our police can commit crimes and the agency has the right to ignore them or cover them up with no one internally, free to speak up? Where is the accountability?

Justice Kennedy addressed this, continuing with the majority's asinine rationale: *"Exposing governmental inefficiency and misconduct is a matter of considerable significance, and various measures have been adopted to protect employees and provide checks on supervisors who would order unlawful or otherwise inappropriate actions."* The majority illogically rationalized, *"The dictates of sound judgment are reinforced by the powerful network of legislative enactments—such as whistleblower protection laws and labor codes—available to those who seek to expose wrongdoing."*

In Illinois there were no "whistleblower" laws or protections on the books when I went forward, and even now, the laws are useless, especially in a state as corrupt as Illinois who ignores them. In my case, the governor ignored his own executive order to protect whistleblowers. His office did nothing. Even more hypocritically, the governor and Attorney General publicly requested the Illinois Inspector General's office to investigate the state police's misconduct, but there was never any investigation. So what happens when governments refuse to investigate their own misconduct or hold anyone accountable? What happens when governments ignore their whistleblower laws and refuse to look into misconduct? What protection is available for a government employee now if he or she reports misconduct? How many government employees, in their right mind, will risk losing their job to report corruption with no real protections? And in corrupt states like Illinois, whether it's on paper or not, whistleblower laws are useless. Even the Illinois Speaker of the House Michael Madigan and Senate President James J. Cullerton acknowledged this during the Blagojevich administration in a letter to the public. The letter read in part; "We . . . have the chance to strengthen Illinois laws concerning the operation of state ethics commissions . . . whistleblower protections . . . all reforms . . . blocked by Blagojevich."

Along with the roadblocks from Governor Blagojevich, ISP director Larry Trent also had a hand in stopping whistleblowers. Trent had imposed a gag rule which forbid state police personnel from talking to the media or any other outside sources. Lt. Governor Pat Quinn criticized Trent publicly and "told the state police director that the edict would have detrimental effects on good faith whistleblowers," and Quinn suggested, "that the state police directive is an attempt to discourage troopers from telling the truth about wrongdoing . . . The tone of the letter I think was one that would sort of say to a lot of employees of state police, keep your mouth shut and look the other way."

But the majority's logic continued by reasoning: *Our holding likewise is supported by the emphasis of our precedents on affording government employers sufficient discretion to manage their operations. Employers have heightened interest in controlling speech made by an employee in his or her professional capacity. Supervisors must ensure that their employee's official communications are accurate, demonstrate sound judgment and promote the employer's mission.*

The politically compromised state police definitely had "heightened interests" in controlling my speech because they certainly wanted to cover up the Rhoads scandal, not expose its misconduct. Doing the right thing could tarnish the ISP's image and also result in expensive lawsuits. By affording *government employers sufficient discretion to manage their operations* the high court was also allowing the ISP officials the discretion to ignore innocent men in prison and ignore the misconduct by their personnel.

Kennedy continued, "*Supervisors must ensure that their employee's official communications are accurate, demonstrate sound judgment and promote the employer's mission.*"

Certainly I had not *promoted the employer's mission,* which was to cover up the innocent men sitting in prison or expose my command's misconduct, so is this type of "mission" the court wants to protect?

Did DII, the Director of the State Police, the governor, the Attorney General or anyone in Illinois government ever *ensure my official communications were accurate and demonstrated sound judgment?* A jury eventually did, a federal judge did, but no one in state government ever ensured anything, they just tried to deceitfully cover everything up.

DII didn't do their mandated job and investigate my criminal allegations, and in fact, they helped in the cover-up by lying. The Director and First Deputy Director acknowledged under oath they were lied to by the two DII colonels and that DII had failed to *ensure my communications were accurate.* The two DII colonels' were even caught lying under oath when they said FBI special agent Nate William's had no concerns.

The Governor, Attorney General and Inspector General also failed to ensure the accuracy of my communications when they turned a blind eye and failed to investigate my allegations. Who could I turn to then for protection, when all of Illinois government was ignoring my communications? My First Amendment protection was my only recourse and now the United States Supreme Court was taking that away.

The American people are the only ones who lose if government employees are silenced, because only a corrupt government gains from that, and the five Justices who took an oath to protect the Constitution of the United States for the citizens of the country were the ones who were now violating their oath. Because the Constitution of the United States was not created to protect government or government misconduct.

Was the Supreme Court majority actually giving government agencies carte blanche to commit criminal acts, cover them up, or give them the right to refuse to investigate their own misconduct or crimes? Is that the type of "employer's mission" the high courts wanted to protect?

The Court rationalized an employee is protected if they go outside their department and report misconduct as a regular citizen would. Of course, with strict policies in place prohibiting ISP employees from going outside the department, like Trent's gag rules, what employee is going to risk getting fired and lose their livelihood by going public and then trusting judges like those in our Supreme Court to protect them?

Four of the nine Supreme Court Justices vehemently opposed the fascist ruling made by the majority. A *Washington Times* article discussed the dissenting justices opinions, stating, "The four reliable Supreme Court liberals—David H.

Souter, John Paul Stevens, Ruth Bader Ginsberg and Stephen Breyer—dissented in three separate opinions." The article concluded, sarcastically bemusing the majority's ruling, "Kudos to the two new justices, as well as the erstwhile conservative Mr. Kennedy, for reminding government employees that the liberties they are afforded as citizens are not the same ones they are afforded at the office."

In his dissenting opinion, Justice Stevens pointed this out, " . . . public employees are still citizens while they are in office. The notion that there is a categorical difference between speaking as a citizen and speaking in the course of one's employment is quite wrong." Justice Stevens continued, "Moreover, it seems perverse to fashion a rule that provides employees with the incentive to voice their concerns publicly before talking frankly to their superiors."

In a separate dissent, Justice Souter wrote, " . . . private and public interests in addressing official wrongdoing and threats to health and safety can outweigh the government's stake in the efficient implementation of policy . . . " And Justice Ginsberg joined in dissent: "Still, the First Amendment safeguard rests on something more, being the value to the public of receiving the opinions and information that a public employee may disclose. Government employees are often in the best position to know what ails the agencies for which they work. . . ."

The dissenting justices reasoned that government employees in their official capacity should be protected by the First Amendment, especially those "whose specific public job responsibilities bring them face-to-face with wrongdoing and incompetence in government, who refuse to avert their eyes and shut their mouth." The justices continued, "And it has to account for the need actually to disrupt government if its officials are corrupt or dangerously incompetent."

In the years to come, the effect of the Garcetti ruling on the First Amendment wasn't just in the State of Illinois—it's happening all over America. The *ABA Journal*'s January 2008 article, "The *Garcetti* Effect," noted:

> When he dismissed their federal claims last March, U.S. District Judge W. Allen Pepper Jr. was nevertheless pained at the fate of three Mississippi prison officials who claimed retaliation after they reported that a fellow officer had beaten an inmate. The judge knew where to direct his misgivings: at the U.S. Supreme Court's 2006 decision in *Garcetti v. Ceballos* . . . which denied public employees First Amendment protection for speech pursuant to their official job duties. "This court is gravely troubled by the effect of Garcetti upon a factual scenario such as that before the bar," Pepper wrote. "It allows no federal constitutional recourse for an employee in the

state of Mississippi who is fired for reporting fellow government employee's misconduct."

The Illinois State Police appealed my case based on this United States Supreme Court ruling, as if taking away my freedom of speech would change things. They were too pathetic to realize it didn't change any of the facts of their deceit or misconduct. They were already exposed, and a jury saw their deceit and even the Supreme Court's egregious ruling couldn't change that. They were exposed to the media and to the people. They were exposed for what they did to Dyke and Karen and their families, and to Randy Steidl, Herb Whitlock and their families and they couldn't change any of that. Their only consolation was that the Supreme Court's ruling would protect them from someone else speaking out on any future misconduct. A message to all employees: government will protect government's self-interests at any costs, even by covering up corruption and allowing retaliation against those speaking out about the truth.

Governments are run by politicians, and politicians appoint judges, and obviously they both are going to protect government's own selfish interest at any costs, even if it means covering up the misconduct of corrupt government officials and their criminal acts.

Whose freedom of speech will the Supreme Court limit next, what type of "job" or "employee" will lose its First Amendment protections next? Will it be the newspaper reporter, the talk show hosts who make fun of government inefficiency, the television networks, or will it be the Hollywood producers who make movies depicting stories of government scandal, corruption and inefficiency?

It all comes down to one question: what type of a government wants to muzzle its citizens and employees from being able to speak out freely?

In May of 2008, the United States 7th Circuit Court of Appeals reversed my First Amendment civil rights case. Jim Dey's editorial explained the shock from those within the media and the community, "THE LAW EXCUSES, BUT THE FACTS CONDEMN":

> In a perverse legal ruling, Illinois State Police commanders have been spared from taking responsibility for their egregious misconduct. The good guys don't always win. There's no other way to explain last week's federal appeals court decision overturning a jury verdict in favor of former Illinois State Police lieutenant Michale Callahan. . . .

Dey's article continued about the State's misconduct and cover-up:

Callahan's case, however, is almost as troubling because it involves his charge that top state police commanders decided not to complete a reinvestigation of the Rhoads murder case because it was, in the words of one superior, "too politically sensitive." Since when do police officials, whose duty it is to follow the evidence wherever it leads, turn a blind eye to criminal conduct because of politics—in a murder case, no less. Well, this is Illinois, so the answer is more often than one might think. It's obvious now that the Illinois State Police top command, kowtowing to its political masters, turned a blind eye to corruption in the administration of former Illinois Governor George Ryan . . . . Sadly; it looks as if the state police were equally reluctant for the same reason to authorize a second look at the Rhoads case.

Dey's article articulated how, despite a jury decision, the appellate court ruled, "In light of Garcetti, we hold that the First Amendment does not insulate Mr. Callahan's statements from employer discipline." The article ended:

So, even if what Callahan said was true, which the jury found, he has no recourse. Larry Trent, who heads the state police, denounced the jury's verdict immediately after it was rendered. So there's no doubt that he and his underlings celebrated its reversal. But they have escaped public censure on the most narrow of legal grounds, and the basic facts of this case remain undisturbed. Leaders of this politically compromised and ethically challenged agency should be hanging their heads in shame over their failure to do their sworn duty.

When I first got the call about the 7th Circuit's decision, I felt that same helpless feeling of injustice the day Carper had so callously removed me from investigations. My faith in my department was destroyed that day and now my faith in all government was destroyed. I tried to keep reminding myself that judges are appointed by politicians, and because of politics, like my command, these judges obviously wanted to protect government and its interests at any cost.

I remembered how the ISP command said it took all of 10 minutes of their time to make the decision to remove me. After all those years of dedication, that's all I had meant to the ISP and that's how I felt now. I was teaching at a middle school when I received the call from an outraged Chief of Police friend of mine.

Trying to hold back the tears, I called my wife, and went home to read the judge's pathetically written decision, an opinion the *Illinois Law Bulletin* proclaimed as the most "egregious" post-Garcetti ruling to date.

Ironically, like the 10 minutes it took my command, Judge Kenneth Francis Ripple's opinion was ten pages of watered down and inaccurate accounts of the facts. Totally disregarding what a jury saw in my two week trial, Ripple wrote, "the hostility between Mr. Callahan and Cpt. Fermon made Zone 5 a difficult work place," and "the EEOO reported to ISP's upper command that the hostility . . . was sufficiently serious to warrant action." Obviously the judge hadn't bothered to read where the head of EEO testified she told the ISP upper command they couldn't remove me based on her incomplete investigation. So much for judicial review and the fact a jury also saw through the EEO sham and decided accordingly.

But I continued reading, amazed at the totally inaccurate information written by the judge: "Although Mr. Callahan requested that the court grant him injunctive relief that would restore him to his position in Zone V, the district court did not grant such relief and Mr. Callahan has not brought the matter to this court by a cross appeal." What was Ripple talking about? He either hadn't taken the time or didn't realize the reason I never asked for my position in Zone 5 back was because I was retired before we even went to trial. What, I was going to come out of retirement so I could work for the people I just exposed?

It didn't matter what a jury had seen or decided, Ripple even hypocritically acknowledged the State's claim that I conducted a surreptitious investigation beyond my official duties, and then I took that information to the FBI before going to DII. So how could I be doing my official duties if they determined I did a surreptitious investigation beyond my official duties?

The court didn't care that DII failed to "ensure the accuracy" of my allegations and had refused to do their job and conduct an investigation.

The court didn't care that DII and the other state police commanders had lied and deceitfully participated in covering up my criminal allegations. The court didn't address the questions of whether I was a citizen or employee doing my official duties when I was at home off-duty with my wife the night the Deputy Governor called and my department wouldn't let me talk to him. No, the appellate court's job was to continue the cover-up and protect the government's misconduct at all costs, exactly what good old King George and his cronies wanted. So the 7th Circuit ruled, "Mr. Callahan spoke not as a citizen but as a public employee, and that speech is not entitled to protection by the First Amendment."

How ludicrous, I always thought I was a citizen when I spoke up, and I certainly didn't realize that once I put my gun and badge on, I stopped being a citizen!

Shamefully, the State Police and the State of Illinois could only rely on having my First Amendment rights, my freedom of speech, taken from me to win their appeal, something I'm sure a state so rich in political corruption is very proud of, but Jim Dey was right . . . the decision doesn't change the facts of this tragic story.

The jury saw it, too, and many of them called my attorney after the appellate court's ruling to acknowledge how "absolutely wrong" they believed the court was, and how incensed and angered they were because they saw the misconduct, lying and cover up themselves.

As time passed, I put things in perspective and the injustice of the Court's actions pales in comparison to the injustice done to Randy Steidl and Herb Whitlock. Or even more so, the injustices done to Dyke and Karen Rhoads and their families. I also realize how lucky I am, because my son is alive, not killed in a war that we as a people were deceptively led into by a government which hypocritically claims we are a nation of freedom and democracy. No, all the government took from me was my Freedom of Speech.

There are still days that the injustices anger me, not so much because of what happened to me personally, but because of all the hypocrisy, deceit and cover up, and for destroying my faith once again in something I used to believe in.

Woody Guthrie was right, "Some will rob you with a six-gun and some with a fountain pen."

CHAPTER 26

OF THE PEOPLE, BY THE PEOPLE AND FOR THE PEOPLE

■

In this story, there are no heroes, only victims, and there are still so many unanswered questions. Some of the questions may eventually get answered, while others will remain unanswered forever. This is a story about a search for the truth, but as it unfolded, it became a conspiracy of lies, deceit, misconduct and cover-ups by a powerful and corrupted state.

The jurors in my trial said this was a story that needed to be told. They were as sickened by the arrogance, hypocrisy and deceit as I was. Sadly, this story does nothing to solve the mystery of who killed Dyke and Karen Rhoads, but it is still a story that needs to be told in order to hold a corrupted government and its officials accountable for their actions.

When I decided to write this book, I told myself it was for the Rhoads family—for people like Andrea Trapp and Tony Rhoads, to try in some small way to fulfill the promise I made to them years ago when they came to us for help. All they wanted was the truth and some justice. I saw their pain and their frustration, and I, too, experienced the same frustration. So did my family and friends. As a lieutenant in the Illinois State Police, I had the opportunity to help them . . . and that's all I ever wanted to do. I never got that opportunity. Oftentimes, I reflect on that fateful day in May 2000 when Lt. Col. Diane Carper first spoke the words "too politically sensitive." Although I wasn't the one speaking them, I still feel the shame of those three words.

In hindsight, maybe I could have done things differently. Maybe I should have come forward sooner, but I knew that was a fruitless endeavor, and the state proved my fears were justified. Instead, I stood by, continuing as best I could, hoping one day I would get the opportunity to reinvestigate the murders of Dyke and Karen. For three years, myself and others tried in vain to get the arrogant ISP command to listen to reason, and instead they turned a blind eye to the injustices. When confronted by the power of the politically compromised ISP command, for way too long I was helpless to do anything, and that guilt and shame will always be with me, a guilt for not being able to fulfill my promise and the shame for the people in my department who dishonored the words Integrity, Service & Pride.

As this tragic story unfolded, it became a conspiracy of lies and liars at the top of the ISP hierarchy, and revealed the politics that controlled them, a frightening example of what government is capable of becoming and doing if it's allowed to go unchecked and be held unaccountable. I saw firsthand that the mighty state is not only powerful, but as equally deceitful and devious—and would disregard the truth all for the sake of image, money and politics. I saw firsthand that the mighty state was willing to wrongfully imprison two innocent men and then keep them imprisoned to cover up a scandal. I saw the mighty state ignore and make a mockery of the murder of a young couple.

When I finally decided to fight back, I had no idea what my family and I were going to go through, but with the strength of my beautiful wife at my side, I went forward. She was the rock that stands by me to this day. Our life became a giant roller coaster filled with a myriad of highs and lows. Many marriages would not have survived the stressful and vicious attacks, the vain attempts to discredit not only me, but also my wife. Together the state and Bob Morgan's public relations man pathetically planned strategies to try and bait me into a lawsuit, conduct surreptitious tape recordings of me, hired private investigators to discredit me and spread false and vicious rumors that my wife and I frequented "sex clubs," were swingers, and that I had a sexual affair with Andrea Trapp. These were new lows, even by Illinois' corrupt standards, and showed just how vindictive, pathetic and desperate they were to try and discredit the person who had exposed their misconduct. Their devious and sleazy attempts didn't work and only made us stronger.

After the 7th Circuit Court of Appeals reversed the jury's decision in my case, the state vindictively sought to recover thousands of dollars in court costs, but they were again stymied when Judge Harold Baker's order denied it, stating, "The court agrees with Callahan that he should not be obligated to incur the significant costs sought by the defendants. Callahan prevailed on summary judgment, on the defendants' pretrial appeal, and at trial. The Seventh Circuit reversed the judgment only 'in light of Garcetti.' The reversal of Callahan's otherwise *remarkably successful case* (italics added) is due to a change in the case law."

With the state's warped strategies and futile attempts to discredit me, they somehow think it will change the facts of this story or twist the truth around enough to minimize their misconduct. The state forgets I am in pretty good company, and it's not just me who saw through their deceit. A jury did, the media had, and more powerful entities like Federal Judges Michael McCuskey and Harold Baker, the Illinois Attorney General and the State 4th District Appellate Court all saw and ruled on the misconduct that occurred both in the past and in the years after.

For more than eight years I experienced firsthand what a corrupt government filled with arrogance, deceit and hypocrisy is capable of doing, but in the end, their own worst enemy is their own incompetence and lies.

It was mind boggling to see people who I had worked with and for, who had taken the same oath I had, lie and cover up the truth and shame the name of the Illinois State Police. I saw politicians, governors and prosecutors turn a blind eye to the deception and misconduct. I saw laws ignored and the corruption continue unabated with absolutely no accountability and with no one in government willing to address the misconduct. My faith was destroyed by a government which does not serve the people, but is only self-serving to itself.

Still, it's a fight I took on . . . and a fight I won. A decision I would never change.

At the time, it was my First Amendment right to speak out, it was this protection that enabled me to fight back, to take on a corrupted state and win. Now the government has taken that freedom away, too, not just from me or other government employees, but from every American citizen. The words freedom of speech are as meaningless as Integrity, Service and Pride.

There were many brave people who stood up or stood by me and fought alongside me. John Baker certainly believed in my fight and fought diligently by my side. There were others, including Bill Clutter, Michael Metnick, Karen Daniels, Larry Marshall, Richard Kling, Susana Ortiz and Dave Protess, who stood up to the state long before I did. It was the TV series *48 Hours* and news columnists, including Eric Zorn, Hal Dardick, John Kass, Terry Bibo, Dusty Rhodes, Gary Henry, John O'Connor and Jim Dey who, long before I, questioned the state's version of the truth. When it came to my personal fight, there were those within my own department who also courageously stood by me, men and woman who risked being ostracized by a state police command that, despite a decision by a jury and judge, arrogantly refused to admit it was wrong.

Edie Casella, John Strohl, and Greg Dixon were career men and women and decorated officers who were faced with the daunting task of testifying against their very command. They had nothing to gain by testifying against the people who controlled their futures. They owed me no allegiance, and despite threats and intimidation, they still had the courage to stand up and tell the truth.

Over coffee, John Strohl solemnly told me how coldly the upper command was treating him. Although he was the senior captain in the region, now he was bypassed for a much younger and more inexperienced "yes" man.

"Springfield doesn't want commanders like me because I tell it like it is," John sadly rationalized.

John Strohl was right—we had become an organization of "yes" men and woman, afraid to speak out, just what the government wants. John quietly retired in 2007 just like I had. No goodbye parties or recognition for his many years of service. Springfield didn't want commanders like John Strohl anymore, they wanted puppets whose strings they could pull any time they wanted.

Likewise, Major Edie Casella was treated coldly and shunned by the ISP upper command who, at one time, were her peers. It was worse for Edie because her office was on the same second floor as Brueggemann, Snyders and Carper. For the remainder of her career, she was silently ostracized until she also quietly retired in 2006.

There were no acknowledgments from Director Larry Trent announcing these commanders had retired after all those years of personal sacrifice and dedication.

Greg Dixon also suffered ostracism, but he wasn't in a position to retire. Randy Steidl filed a civil lawsuit against the ISP upper command, and not long after that, Greg was again taken off the Rhoads investigation. Greg was told he "needed a break" from the case. Since 2000, he was assigned to and then taken off the Rhoads case four times, and now with a lawsuit pending, the last thing the state police command wanted was an unbending man of integrity like Greg Dixon searching for the truth. Greg's fate was sealed when he refused to cooperate with Iain Johnston, the ISP brass' civil attorney, but Greg was right—why should a criminal investigator involved in an allegedly unbiased and truthful investigation get involved with a civil attorney if you want to maintain the integrity of the criminal investigation. Without Greg Dixon in the way, Iain Johnston had an open line of communication with the investigations personnel in the Rhoads case. Greg told me how a lieutenant boldly told him he had "an anchor" around his neck because of the Rhoads case, and for the rest of his career he faced a department that tried to falsely accuse and retaliate against him.

There were others in the state police who testified on my behalf who were also retaliated against, including Russ Perkins. After standing up and telling the truth to EEO, Russ had his promotion taken away, but he fought and filed a successful lawsuit.

Ruby Gordon-Phillips didn't fare as well. She went through more than just ostracism; there was so much harassment and internal pressure from the ISP command that Ruby developed health problems and was forced to retire early.

Then there were people like Dave McLearin who also stood up for me. Dave was long retired and had no reason to help fight my battles, but he was a man of honor and known throughout the state for his integrity and reputation as a good cop. Dave took four bullets for this state, yet they tried to denigrate his reputation on the stand over unfounded, petty allegations. There were no depths to how low the ISP went to try and discredit the good people who stepped up and just told the truth in this case.

"These were the type of police officers we expected to see from the Illinois State Police," one juror later told me.

The juror was right—these were the type of cops you would expect to see stand up and represent a police organization that claimed so much Integrity, Service and Pride.

In her column, "State Police Starting to Smell," Terry Bibo acknowledged, "There are all kinds of questions; they're all over the map. Something's rotten here. And it needs to be cut out before it spreads to what's left of the good guys. Somebody investigate." But no one in the State of Illinois ever stepped up to investigate.

Why would a state so rich with political corruption ever police itself or investigate its own misconduct? In Illinois, that just doesn't happen. Disgraced and former Governor George Ryan had already gone from the State Capitol to a federal prison. Governor Rod "the Unreformer" Blagojevich continued to be investigated by the federal government with the vast majority of Illinois citizens hoping he would end up in a prison cell next to his predecessor.

Despite getting caught in all the deception and hypocrisy, nothing much changed in the state police leadership.

Larry Trent continued on as Director and the morale in the ISP continued to plummet in the years to come. Doug Brown continued on as the First Deputy Director until he retired in 2008 with a six-figure retirement for the rest of his life. Col. Charles Brueggemann stayed on as the Deputy Director of Operations until Brown retired and then he became the First Deputy Director. Lt. Col. Mike Snyders also became a Deputy Director. Col. Harold "Skip" Nelson remained as the Deputy Director of DII and as the ISP Ethics Officer until 2008, and then he took Brueggemann's spot as the Deputy Director of Operations. Lt. Col. Rick Karpawicz retired in 2006, also with a six-figure retirement for the rest of his life.

As for Lt. Col. Carper, in 2005 she was promoted to Assistant Deputy Director over the Division of Administration. My good friend, Col. Jim Fay, was her boss. Over a few drinks, Jim confided she was having a hard time with being the scapegoat for the brass, admitting she had covered up for the likes of Dan Kent, Chuck Brueggemann and Andre Parker. Still, Carper continued being the "good soldier," and retired with a six-figure income in 2008.

Captain Fermon was hidden away somewhere by the department and no one ever seemed to know what he did or where he was at. He no longer had a command, but he continued making his six-figure salary on the taxpayer's dime. And the state police kept on replacing "yes" men and women with other "yes" men and women.

Then there are the real victims in this story. In our justice system, an individual is innocent unless they are proven guilty beyond a reasonable doubt, and I would defy anyone to prove Randy Steidl or Herb Whitlock were proven guilty of murdering Dyke and Karen Rhoads beyond a reasonable doubt.

For 17 years, Gordon "Randy" Steidl was caged in a cell, his freedom taken from him. No amount of money can give those missing years back to him. Could you imagine sitting in prison for 12 years, each day waiting for the state to kill you while knowing you're innocent? Wondering when the state is going to strap you to that gurney. Had Randy Steidl been put to death, the state's misconduct would've been covered up forever, the perfect murder committed by the State of Illinois.

For years, Steidl's defense team relentlessly fought a state that refused to admit its mistakes. Instead, the state chose to ignore its misconduct and cover up the scandal. If not for the dedication, diligence and honesty of Federal Judge Michael McCuskey, the State of Illinois would have—with all probability—gotten away with it, continuing to cover up the transgressions against Steidl.

The mighty engine of the state continued to roll on with their $200-an-hour private attorneys and private investigators to defend the state police employees who are accused. According to a Freedom of Information request I filed, to date the taxpayers of Illinois have paid the private attorneys over two million dollars to protect the people who long forgot the oaths they took to protect those taxpayers.

But why do the taxpayers of Illinois continue to pay for expensive private attorneys to represent the state police employees? It is Illinois Attorney General Lisa Madigan's job to defend all state employees, not private attorneys. There was never any investigation by the Illinois Inspector General that Madigan publicly called for. That was only smoke and mirrors which allowed an open faucet of money to flow into the private attorneys pockets. Sometimes billing the state taxpayers as much as $72,000 a month.

It continued to amaze me just how devious the state would get, and in 2008, I was given reports from the private investigators hired by the state's civil attorneys. There were months of interview reports conducted by the private investigators, and despite refusing to turn them over in discovery, claiming they were confidential and privileged, they were caught sharing those same reports with Bob Morgan's public relations man. Why would the state share their privileged and confidential reports with a man their own clients admitted was a suspect in the Rhoads murders? Even worse, I also received documentation where the state police criminal investigators were sharing reports with Bob Morgan, and there were e-mails of correspondence between Morgan's public relations guru and my old State of Illinois attorney buddies, Ed Parkinson of the Illinois Appellate Prosecutor's Office and Keith Jensen, Head Legal for the Illinois State Police. Was this all one big conspiracy?

In 2004, Randy Steidl was freed, but Herb Whitlock remained in prison fighting for a new trial. The Illinois Appellate Prosecutor's Office and Illinois State Police fought diligently to keep Whitlock from getting a new trial, and Judge H. Dean Andrews had denied Whitlock a new trial based on the absurdity that Herrington and Reinbolt were credible witnesses.

When reviewing Steidl's case, even Jorge Montes, chairman of the Illinois Prisoner Review Board, said Darrell Herrington and Debbie Reinbolt "by our estimation had lost all credibility." Yet Judge Andrews believed differently.

Richard Kling and Susana Ortiz appealed to the State of Illinois' 4th District Appellate Court, and on September 7, 2007, Herb Whitlock finally caught a break. In a 53-page decision from the 4th District Appellate Court, Herb Whitlock was granted a new trial. The three appellate judges unanimously concurred, "We hold that because of the State's suppression of evidence favorable to the defense . . . We find a reasonable probability that but for these errors, considered cumulatively, the verdict would have been different."

Regarding Judge H. Dean Andrews' absurd decision, the Appellate court ruled, "The trial court's decision to the contrary is *manifestly erroneous*. Therefore, we reverse the judgment and conviction and remand this case for a new trial on the charge of the first-degree murder of Karen Rhoads."

Finally someone in the State of Illinois stepped up and did the right thing, and it looked like Herb Whitlock might be on his way to freedom.

The decision then fell to the Attorney General's Office to either appeal the Appellate Court's decision or send the case back to Edgar County. Eric Zorn's *Chicago Tribune* article depicted Lisa Madigan's October 7, 2007, decision, " . . . the Attorney General's office will not appeal an Appellate Court decision to overturn the 1987 conviction of Herbert Whitlock for the murder of Karen Rhoads. The case now returns to the Edgar County Circuit Court, where the Office of the State Appellate Prosecutor must decide whether to retry Whitlock . . ."

Herb Whitlock was one step closer to freedom, or was he? The Appellate Prosecutor's Office had already proven to be stubborn and hypocritical throughout Whitlock's 21 years in prison. Neither Ed Parkinson nor David Rands wanted anything more to do with the Rhoads case, so Whitlock sat in prison while the Appellate Prosecutor's Office assigned a new prosecutor to review the case. For three more months, Herb Whitlock sat in prison while his case was once again reviewed.

But after spending over two decades in prison, on January 8, 2008, Herb Whitlock listened as Judge James R. Glenn announced to a packed Edgar County courtroom, "Mr. Whitlock can be released." Twenty-one years of deceit and cover up by the State of Illinois was over for Herb Whitlock and he was once again a free man.

"It's a long time coming," said defense attorney Richard Kling. "It took 21 years too long."

I sat in the packed courtroom that day and watched Whitlock become a free man. I couldn't help but feel a little vindicated, and finally there was some justice for him. Later, I stood in the rain outside the Edgar County Jail when Whitlock took his first steps in 21 years as a free man. Hal Dardick of the *Chicago Tribune* reported:

> Whitlock said he was looking forward to meeting his 7-year-old grandson later Tuesday, but he fretted about his ability to relate to children after so long behind bars. He will need to adjust to the contemporary world. He has never used a cell phone, automatic teller machine or the Internet. He never saw a razor with more than one blade until he was moved to a new prison in 2005.

Yet in another moment of sleaze, the State of Illinois once again showed its true colors, depicted in Eric Zorn's column, "Prosecutors add shame as Paris case ends":

> Herb Whitlock's parting gift from the state of Illinois was a shot of slime. Prosecutors moved Tuesday to drop murder charges and set Whitlock free after nearly 21 years behind bars. But instead of just letting him go gracefully, they grumped and groused and accused him again of participating in the grisly 1986 killings of newlyweds Dyke and Karen Rhoads in Paris, Illinois. Assistant appellate prosecutor Michael Vujovich told reporters that, "we've always believed

[Whitlock and his former co-defendant Randy Steidl] were responsible for the killings" and noted that the murder charges "could be reinstated at any time." "Previously unknown information has come to light which requires additional investigation," said the peevish motion that granted Whitlock, 61, his freedom. But, the motion said, the Illinois State Police simply don't have time to "complete their investigation and re-evaluation" of this "previously unknown" information before the Feb. 22 speedy trial deadline.

The state police had *allegedly* been reinvestigating this case since 2003—right after Federal Judge Michael McCuskey issued his order to retry or release Randy Steidl. It was five years later now, and they still didn't have anything to prosecute Steidl or Whitlock and I knew it. They had tried intimidating and manipulating people like Bud Cunningham, and that didn't work, but the state police kept searching for other Debbie Reinbolts or Darrell Herringtons.

I knew about their alleged "previously unknown information" from the discovery documents provided by Vujovich to Kling, and the "information" was actually learned by the state police nine months earlier.

The information referenced an interview with yet another "Debbie Reinbolt" type of witness, a self-admitted dope dealer whose ever-changing story to investigators was chock full of holes. The multiple reports started out with Whitlock showing up on her doorstep with another man between 3:00 a.m. and 4:00 a.m. on the night of the murders, and she said Whitlock's t-shirt had dried blood on it, which he explained was from butchering some rabbits. She also remembered Whitlock and the other man smelled like smoke. It was disturbing as I read Jeff Marlow's reports, and in his second interview, the woman suddenly remembered and changed her story that now Whitlock was covered in blood when he came over. Eventually the woman also conveniently changed the time all this occurred to around 1:30 a.m.

This was the best the State could do? A self-admitted drug dealer who 21 years later suddenly remembered all this information, and her story went from "some dried blood" to Whitlock's t-shirt being "covered in blood." Was Jeff Marlow taking report writing lessons from Eckerty and Parrish? Like Eckerty and Parrish's reports, there were big holes in Marlow's reports, too. If Whitlock had blood on him and smelled like smoke at the times the woman said, the investigators had forgotten one key point: since the Rhoads fire didn't start until 4:30 a.m., to infer Whitlock was involved in the murders because he smelled like smoke at 1:30 a.m. or 3:00 a.m. meant it couldn't be from smoke from the Rhoads fire because it happened much later.

There were other contradictions in her story so the state police reports indicated they gave her a polygraph, a polygraph she couldn't pass because it came back inconclusive. Jeff Marlow was persistent though and a different polygraph examiner was called in, and the woman conveniently managed to pass the second polygraph, or so the state says.

The state's new Debbie Reinbolt later admitted to Bill Clutter to the same types of intimidation and manipulation that occurred with the original Reinbolt. She told Clutter that Marlow had tracked her down and accused her of being a drug dealer.

"Did you think you were in trouble?" Clutter asked her.

"Well, yeah. I'm still in trouble. Everything feels unsettled," she replied.

The woman also told Clutter she was interviewed in the original homicide investigation by Deputy Ted Todd, another interview never documented in the original investigation, and she had disclosed this information to Marlow.

"They couldn't find a record of me talking to him," she said Marlow claimed.

And Marlow's investigative report also conveniently left out the information that she had talked to Ted Todd 21 years earlier.

Between all the state's sleaze and the excitement of his new-found freedom, Herb Whitlock still took time that day to express his compassion for Dyke and Karen Rhoads.

"They lost their lives," Whitlock said. "At least I have my life."

But the biggest victims in this tragic story were Dyke and Karen Rhoads and their families. Jim Dey's article summarized the Rhoads family's feelings when Whitlock was released that day stating, "While Herb Whitlock and Randy Steidl today have the freedom they have sought for so long, Dyke and Karen still do not have the justice they deserve," according to a Rhoads family statement. The Rhoads family said they find it "impossible to believe that the Illinois State Police have any interest in performing their job duties in a manner that promotes justice for Dyke and Karen."

Certainly there were no greater victims than Dyke and Karen Rhoads, their lives brutally taken from them that hot, July night in 1986. Murdered in the sanctity of their bed, they lay six feet under the ground in a cold grave. They never got the opportunities at life most of us take for granted. They never got the chance to raise a family or grow old together.

The search for truth and justice for them was a mockery. The state's unproven motive defamed Dyke's name, and 21 years later the state police investigators are pathetically clinging to this same motive, trying to intimidate and manipulate people like Bud Cunningham or coerce Dyke's friends and family members into still making Dyke out as a drug dealer. For the Rhoads and Spessard families, there is no closure, because there has never been any real search for the truth, and there never will be. Especially now with the state police facing expensive lawsuits from both Steidl and Whitlock.

Andrea Trapp once told the press that Dyke and Karen "ended their lives and started a nightmare for the rest of us for the rest of our lives. . . . I want [authorities] to find the evidence needed to go to trial, instead of the wishy-washy case Mike McFatridge had 18 years ago."

Karen's mother, Marge Spessard, also questioned the state, "I just find it interesting because there have always been questions that we've never understood. . . . We're still waiting for the end." For them, that end may never come.

Certainly nothing the state does from this point on will ever be believable; their credibility, like Herrington's and Reinbolt's, at least in this tragedy, forever tainted by their conduct. With all the deception, botched information and tainted evidence, it would be almost impossible for anyone to solve and prosecute the murders of Dyke and Karen Rhoads. John Adams was right, "Facts are stubborn things," and the state cannot alter those facts as hard as they might try.

In his "Twelve Steps to Reopening an Old Murder," retired homicide Sergeant David Rivers refers to one of the most important steps as: "Try to determine who has benefited the most, financially, from the death of the victim."

Darrell Herrington benefited from Dyke and Karen's death. He went from the town drunk peddling his bicycle around town to a pretty affluent man. Any secrets Darrell Herrington had died with him in early 2007, but there were others who had gained even more wealth.

One of those was suspect Bob Morgan, who eventually took a state police polygraph and passed, clearing him as a suspect in their eyes. In 2008, one of his long-time employees also defended him to Andrea Trapp one drunken night. Andrea said the man had consumed quite a bit of alcohol and admitted to her that Dyke and Karen were not killed over a bag of cannabis or anything involving Dyke.

He said Karen had stumbled onto something at work and it wasn't the machine gun incident, claiming Karen had walked up on something that was being put into the "bumper of a car." Admitting they were doing a lot of things back in those days they shouldn't have, he told Andrea she was barking up the wrong tree by accusing Bob Morgan, the car was being loaded that night for someone else, another Paris businessman.

There were several other suspects identified in the Rhoads murders, including Special Agent Jeff Marlow's relatives, Duke and Jerry Board. Their names had come up during the original investigation, but were never documented, and then came up again years later in the ATF investigation of the Diablo murder investigation. Despite that, neither one has ever been interviewed by anyone in the ISP about the murders of Dyke and Karen.

Phil Stark's name had also surfaced as a suspect, but the ISP has never investigated why Jack Eckerty hid Stark's reports in a bogus ISP case file.

Other suspects, including Herschel Wright and Dale Peterson, are long dead. Later Clutter learned that Randy Wright, Herschel's brother, gave a man information about Whitlock's innocence. That man was, in turn, the one who gave the information to the Attorney General's investigators referenced in the letters to Andrea Trapp. The man also told the Attorney General's Office that Jack Eckerty had allegedly put a gun to Wright's rib cage and threatened him after Herrington drunkenly admitted to Wright he had testified untruthfully and was going to burn in hell for it. According to the source, Wright was told by Eckerty to forget everything he had heard from Herrington. This information was also ignored by the Illinois Attorney General's Office who wrote the man off. Randy Wright was still alive and could easily have refuted or confirmed the information, but that was never done, there were two lawsuits filed by this time, and besides it wasn't about justice anymore, it was all about image, money and politics now. This story has a lot of questions, and when I asked questions, the state didn't want me looking for the answers and they still don't want the answers.

I can't say who committed those terrible murders in 1986. Like everyone else, I have my own suspects and suspicions, but I could never prove in a court of law who killed Dyke and Karen, not that a court of law means that much to me anymore anyway.

Five times I went forward to the state police upper command to try and reinvestigate this case, each time with more questions and more suspicions of misconduct that needed to be answered, and each time I was told it was "too politically sensitive."

Eventually, when I wouldn't quit trying, and turned in my command, the ISP hierarchy got rid of me, they transferred me and tried to intimidate and silence me. They thought I'd be silent, I'd quit trying and just accept their deceitful cover-ups. They were wrong, and they underestimated me, and they underestimated a lot of other people.

That is what this book is about, a powerful state failing to do its duty, to search for the truth, no matter what it is, ignoring and covering up a terrible crime. A state willing to railroad and then leave two innocent men in prison, all for the sake of image and politics. This book serves as a warning to everyone of what government, at its worst, is capable of becoming, and this book is a warning that the voice of the people is being muzzled in order to cover up government misconduct like this.

As for me, it takes more than a court ruling to defeat me. I fought because I cared, and I exposed the misconduct, hypocrisy and deceit at the highest levels of state government. The courts can never change that, only keep others like me in the future from being able to come forward and speak out.

For me personally, no matter what happens in the future, I won. I showed that a person can stand up to a powerful and corrupted government and be heard, but I didn't realize how much I had won until later. A victory bigger than any man, woman, husband, wife, father or mother could ever wish for.

One day Lily went through my then 12-year-old son's backpack and found an essay written by Tanner. As I started to read, I wiped back the tears as I realized I had made an important difference, and everything I had fought for was worth it. The tears continued to blur my vision as I read my young son's innocent words:

> In my life so far, there have been very few people who have influenced me or made a great impact on me. There is one person though, and I will probably never totally know the full impact he's made on my life just by being my father. He's changed and shaped me to stand up for myself and do what's right over the many years, while he's been fighting to do the right thing and stand up for himself . . . Ever since I was a child my dad has been like many other fathers have been, caring and responsible for me. He was in the State Police for about 20 years as a Lieutenant and loved his job. Then there was a situation at work where his right to speak out about the truth was taken away from him. His goal was to try and save two men who were wrongfully convicted and put in prison and were railroaded into death row. My dad got more and more stressed out about work and rarely had time for me. At this point, I was too young to understand what was happening, and I got the wrong idea from the problem. I couldn't believe that my dad who had once played with me and did everything with me was now too busy . . . to even notice me. I might have been selfish, but I was too naive to know what was happening with my father and the real stress he was under from his work. My father had all the evidence to support his case and had friends

from work who backed him up 100 percent, but he still got demoted from his job for using his right to speak out. Over the years, my dad became depressed and fell into a hole with no way out. Things got worse between me and my father. We got in fights more frequently and he got mad at me more often due to stress and hard work he was going through to prove everyone wrong. My dad became more strict and stern about things and at one point, I broke down in the middle of one of our fights telling him how I wanted my old dad back. This made him realize he was being too hard on me and he became more understanding . . . and we became closer and spent more time. Soon my dad finally had enough . . . he stood up for himself, and showed everyone . . . he could stand up and do something about it. A couple of years later, I found myself nervous and shaking in the seat of a court room, waiting for the judge's final decision. Reporters were everywhere, jotting down notes while my mom was sitting next to me tensely waiting. The verdict came, and we had won the case. I had never felt any better knowing after years of struggle it was finally over. We were all happy that it was over and even more proud of my dad for what he went through for us. In the end, I grew up to respect my dad more than anyone else. He's shown me what it takes to do the right thing even under the hardest circumstances, and he helped me grow into a better person. I will always remember what he has done for me and will never forget how he has molded me to be who I am today.

I learned that day what really matters in life, and no man, no father can ever ask for anything greater than this.

I often reflect back to the day I stood at the bottom of the stairs at John Baker's law firm, looking up at John as he spoke.

"Mike," he said, "it's your decision to make. But remember, sometimes it takes just one person to step up and make a difference."

John Baker was wrong. I don't think one person can make a difference. But maybe—just maybe—if one person speaks out and the people listen, then it *can* make a difference. Then maybe, one day, we will truly become a nation of the people, by the people and for the people.

Epilogue

———————■———————

On November 4, 2008, fed up with the George W. Bush administration and all its hypocrisy, lies and liars, the American people showed their distrust in our government when millions turned out to voice their opinion and the world watched as a nation voted for change and new hope.

On November 26, 2008, John Baker filed a Petition for Writ of Certiorari to the United States Supreme Court. Is the Supreme Court's intention to continue to muzzle government employees to protect corrupt governments like the state of Illinois? Governments that are willing to ignore its crimes or even help to cover them up, while taking away the freedom of speech of the men and women willing to speak out against the corruption?

On December 9, 2008, Illinois Governor Rod Blagojevich and his Chief of Staff were arrested by the Federal Bureau of Investigation after U.S. Attorney Patrick Fitzgerald's office issued a scathing 78-page complaint and affidavit detailing a plethora of political corruption and criminal conduct by his administration. Rod Blagojevich became the second governor in a row in Illinois to face federal charges.

Robert Grant, special agent in charge of the FBI's Chicago office, declared of Illinois, "If it isn't the most corrupt state in the United States, it's certainly one hell of a competitor."

On January 9, 2009, the Illinois House of Representatives voted 114-1 to impeach Governor Rod Blagojevich.

"It's our duty to clean up the mess and stop the freak show that's become Illinois government," said Representative Jack D. Franks.

On January 30, 2009, the Illinois Senate voted 59-0 to remove Governor Rod Blagojevich from political office forever.

On March 20, 2009, Illinois State Police Director Larry Trent announced his resignation, effective immediately. "Six years is a long time to spend in a difficult, demanding and volatile political environment," Larry Trent stated. He was replaced two days later.

On April 2, 2009, former Governor Rod Blagojevich, powerbroker William Cellini, Robert Blagojevich, Christopher Kelly, Alonzo "Lon" Monk and John Harris were indicted by U.S. Attorney Patrick Fitzgerald's office in a 19 count federal indictment alledging conspiracy, extortion, wire fraud and more in what federal prosecutors dubbed the "Blagojevich Enterprise."

It's uncertain if the United States Supreme Court will hear my case or not. Irregardless, we as a people remain vulnerable to falling prey to corrupt government misconduct when our freedom to speak out is taken away. Who will hold government accountable for their actions? I have fought and continue to fight a long and hard battle, and it's obviously not over, but I will never be defeated, and the words from one of the greatest men in history give me strength:

> People are often surprised to learn that I am an optimist. They know how often I have been jailed, how frequently the days and nights have been filled with frustration and sorrow, how bitter and dangerous are my adversaries. They expect these experiences to harden me into a grim and desperate man. They fail, however, to perceive the sense of affirmation generated by the challenge of embracing struggle and surmounting obstacles. They have no comprehension of the strength that comes from faith in God and man ... The past is strewn with the ruins of the empires of tyranny, and each is a monument not merely to man's blunders but to his capacity to overcome them ...
>
> *Martin Luther King, Jr.*

There is still no closure for Dyke and Karen Rhoads or their families.

Integrity, Service and Pride?

INDEX